THE NEGRO
IN
DEPRESSION
AND WAR

THE NEGRO
IN
DEPRESSION
AND WAR

Prelude to Revolution
1930–1945

EDITED WITH COMMENTARY BY

BERNARD STERNSHER

CHICAGO

Quadrangle Books

To Little David

SECOND PRINTING

Library of Congress Catalog Card Number: 76–84111

PREFACE
A PERSONAL NOTE

Having been born and raised in Massachusetts, having earned my B.A. at the University of Alabama, having lived for five years in Rochester, New York, where I was a county committeeman in a predominantly black ward which later was the scene of a major riot, and having resided for seven of the last eight years in Union, New Jersey, a community five miles from Newark that has been ordered by the United States Office of Education—as this is written—to take steps to alter the racial composition, now 98 per cent black, of one of its elementary schools, I can claim more than scholarly, armchair acquaintance with race relations in various situations. The range of my experience, such as it is, brings to mind a classroom assignment I carried out almost twenty years ago for Professor Arthur A. Ekirch in his course on the Civil War and Reconstruction. I refer to a term paper entitled "Methodological Criticism of J. G. Randall." It criticized Randall's use of analogies in his famous text (since thoroughly revised by David Donald).

I shall present only three of the analogies to which I took exception:

While the manner of living of the slaves was on a low scale, they were no more wretched than millions of European peasants.

. . . slavery still persists in nineteen countries and that institution still holds in its grasp a population of approximately five million people.

If as a result [of its unbalanced economy] the South had missed somewhat of financial and industrial leadership, it had also escaped the cost of such leadership in terms of human suffering and the destruction of culture types.

After expounding on the difficulties involved in the use of analogies in history, I concluded that Randall's analogies shifted the reader's attention from undesirable developments in one place to those in another. I conceded some validity in the implications of such methodology for historical causation: the multiple occurrence of situations in which a significant portion of the population suffers degradation tells us something about the possibilities, and perhaps the probabilities, of human behavior, whether in China, Ethiopia, Kenya, Tanganyika, or Liberia (all of which Randall mentions in connection with the second analogy cited above), or in Tuscaloosa or Rochester. But I noted that such use of analogies can blur the line between causal and moral justification.

That there are now serious problems in race relations in every part of the nation does not mean that no one is to blame. It means that everyone is to blame. Recognition of this fact requires no endless exercise in self-condemnation, and I do not mean by this to drain our subject of moral content. On the contrary, the taking for granted of the moral dimension of race relations is the basis of remedial efforts. Historians can surely make a contribution to our understanding of the difficult task we face, but if any of my academic colleagues equates scholarship with concern and compassion, he should read John Sekora's historical study, "Murder Relentless and Impassive: The American Academic Community and the Negro College" (*Soundings*, Fall 1968).

It is easy to say that all Americans should get on with the job of keeping the United States one nation by closing the gap between our profession and our practice. This exhortation is made so often that it tends to become routine. Yet the ominous nature of its implications reflects a real condition. In 1968 the National Advisory Commission on Civil Disorders declared, "Our nation is moving toward two societies, one black, one white—separate and unequal." In 1969 a report, "One Year Later," issued by the Urban Coalition and Urban America, Inc., found the nation still moving in the same direction. The urgency of the need for remedial efforts can perhaps best be felt by considering the highly probable, if not absolutely certain, result of the failure to make them.

CONTENTS

THE NEGRO
IN
DEPRESSION
AND WAR

I

Introduction

There are two main reasons for this collection of readings—one historical, the other historiographical. The "Negro Revolution" is often dated from 1954 (the Supreme Court decision on segregation in public schools) or 1955 (the bus boycott in Montgomery). Every student of history knows that when a series of events is called a "revolution," the revolution has a long background. The era immediately preceding the Negro Revolution would, of course, have had great historical significance even if there had been no blacks in the United States at the time—the Great Depression and World War II affected virtually every American in some way. Though these historical developments had an impact on both whites and blacks, what the Negroes encountered differed from the experiences of whites at that time (which could be said of the Negroes' lot at any other time in American history) and from the Negroes' previous experience. In short, considerable continuity, in the form of segregation and discrimination, as well as change, characterized Negro life in the years 1930–1945.

Louis Ruchames says, "It takes two races to make segregation work."[1] Although the context of this assertion is the contrast between new black militancy and previous black subservience, it also says something about the doctrines and deeds of those Negroes who now advocate black separatism. It is in accordance with Ruchames' dictum that the second and third sections of this anthology are entitled "White Action" and "Black Reaction." The heading "White Action and Inaction" might have been used in-

1. Louis Ruchames, "Segregation and Discrimination in the Twentieth Century," in Howard H. Quint, *et al.*, eds., *Main Problems in American History* (Homewood, Ill.: Dorsey, 1968, rev. ed.), II, p. 413.

stead, but even a cursory inquiry into race relations indicates that white inaction, whether arising from a specific, conscious decision not to act or from general or unconscious indifference, is, at least in a certain sense, a form of action. Action by whites or blacks can obviously be physical (including the threatened as well as the actual use of force) or nonphysical (legal, social, and so on), and both action and inaction by whites and blacks can, broadly speaking, affect Negroes favorably or adversely.

Usually "inaction," when applied to whites, denotes indifference to or calculated neglect of Negroes' interests, but white inaction can also be beneficial to Negroes. Consider the case of President Franklin D. Roosevelt, who in the 1960's has been charged by some historians with ignoring the cause of civil rights.[2] Many scholars, to be sure, identify solid gains by Negroes in the Roosevelt era (the "Black Cabinet" of Negro advisers on Negro affairs in various agencies; the giving to Negroes of direct federal aid, admittedly vitiated by discrimination in the giving; the words and works of Eleanor Roosevelt and a number of administrators), but they often write as if the President had nothing to do with these advances. If in an immediate sense New Deal policies toward Negroes depended on the various department and agency heads, to the extent that Roosevelt did not shackle administrators like Will Alexander, Hallie Flanagan, Clark Foreman, Harold Ickes, W. Frank Persons, and Aubrey Williams, he followed a course with respect to blacks of beneficent inaction. Moreover, as Elmo Roper observes, "If one may judge a President by the caliber of appointments he made to essential positions . . . then Roosevelt must be put very high indeed as a picker of men."[3] When discussing the activities of Will Alexander,[4] Ickes, and others, one should remember how they got their positions in the first place.

Roosevelt also followed a course of inaction in other ways. The reader ultimately must judge the President's explanation of his failure publicly to support an anti-lynching bill:

> I did not choose the tools with which I must work. Had I been permitted to choose them I would have selected quite different ones. But

2. Barton J. Bernstein, "The New Deal: The Conservative Achievements of Liberal Reform," in Bernstein, ed., *Towards a New Past: Dissenting Essays in American History* (New York: Pantheon, 1968), pp. 278–279.

3. Elmo Roper, *You and Your Leaders: Their Actions and Your Reactions, 1936–1956* (New York: Morrow, 1958), p. 69.

4. Wilma Dykeman and James Stokely, *Seeds of Southern Change: The Life of Will Alexander* (Chicago: University of Chicago Press, 1962).

I've got to get legislation passed by Congress to save America. The Southerners by reason of the seniority rule in Congress are chairmen or occupy strategic places on most of the Senate and House committees. If I come out for the anti-lynching bill now, they will block every bill I ask Congress to pass to keep America from collapsing. I just can't take that risk.[5]

This brief discussion of "action" and "inaction" is presented not as an exercise in verbal gymnastics, but rather one more reminder that race relations in the United States are, in all their ramifications, an extremely complicated subject.

Negro gains during the New Deal, 1933–1938, may appear slight from the standpoint of the 1960's, but they are more impressive when judged against the Negroes' situation in the 1920's. Thus, evaluations of the New Deal's effect on blacks usually record both pluses and minuses with varying degrees of relative emphasis. Frames of reference differ, and what is a plus to a Negro can be a minus to another man—to Frank Boykin, Alabama Congressman, for example, who, pressured by his constituents, complained bitterly to President Roosevelt about the employment of Negroes in federal agencies.[6]

In some ways changes in Negro life were greater during the war than during the New Deal. As a student of the Roosevelt era, I think this development represents a particular illustration of a somewhat neglected general point. In the evolution-or-revolution debate which has occupied a number of New Deal historians, the redistribution of income and new departures in fiscal policy are frequently adduced by the exponents of the "revolution" estimate of the New Deal. In fact, redistribution of income was conspicuously greater during the war than under the New Deal,[7] and it has become a commonplace that the function of fiscal policy as a countercyclical instrument was demonstrated far more strikingly during the war than in the 1930's.[8] In general, John Brooks finds the change in American society from 1939 to 1965 greater than the change from 1933 to 1939.[9] This is not to depreciate the sig-

5. Quoted in Walter F. White, *A Man Called White* (New York: Viking, 1948), p. 170.
6. Richard Polenberg, ed., *America at War: The Home Front, 1941–1945* (Englewood Cliffs, N.J.: Prentice-Hall, 1968), pp. 114–115.
7. Douglass C. North, *Growth and Welfare in the American Past: A New Economic History* (Englewood Cliffs, N.J.: Prentice-Hall, 1966), pp. 174–180.
8. Robert L. Heilbroner, *The Making of Economic Society* (Englewood Cliffs, N.J.: Prentice-Hall, 1962), pp. 163–168.
9. John Brooks, *The Great Leap: The Past Twenty-five Years in America* (New York: Harper and Row, 1966).

nificance of the New Deal for Negro American history, or to impose qualifications on Erwin D. Hoffman's designation in his article "The Genesis of the Modern Movement for Equal Rights in South Carolina" of the 1930's as a "germinal decade" in the development of the civil rights movement. Nor must one be a disciple of Werner Sombart, who identified war as the single most important causal agent in modern history, to note that in assessing the impact of the New Deal on American life in general and Negro life in particular, one should not overlook the consequences of the war or mistakenly ascribe them to the New Deal. A student of the relative status of Negroes in the years 1940–1960, remarking that "an era of faster change in non-white status was inaugurated by the entry of the United States into World War II,"[10] describes gains in status with respect to occupation, employment, income, and education. As important as these advances may have been, it now appears that the most important development in race relations during the war was the rise of mass black militancy.

If the era immediately preceding the Negro Revolution demands attention, so does the period just before that. This collection could have worked its way in time back to 1619 or earlier, and in space across the Atlantic to Africa, as some others have done. The question of coverage suggests the historiographical reason for the book. Louis Harlan writes: "There is little historical writing as yet on Negroes in the Depression and World War II . . ."[11] I hope this volume is at least a small contribution toward filling this gap.

10. Norval D. Glenn, "Some Changes in the Relative Status of American Nonwhites, 1940 to 1960," *Phylon* (Second Quarter 1963). Glenn points out that for all practical purposes "nonwhites" means blacks (p. 109n).
11. Louis Harlan, *The Negro in American History* (Washington, D.C.: American Historical Association, Service Center for Teachers of History, Publication No. 61, 1965), p. 25.

THE NEGRO IN
THE NEW DEAL ERA

LESLIE H. FISHEL, JR.

*Leslie H. Fishel, Jr., offers a comprehensive, balanced survey of
the Negro under the New Deal and at the time of the New Deal—
there was, after all, more to the 1930's than the New Deal. He also
summarizes developments in race relations in the 1940's and the
early 1950's.*

❊

The rhythm and the tone of the New Deal was set by the man in
the White House, since Franklin D. Roosevelt was the spokesman
and the master of his administration. His first public statement,
the inaugural address of March 4, 1933, pierced the depression-
fostered gloom and stabbed deftly and surely at the nation's physical and psychological ills. In stark contrast to his predecessor,
Roosevelt recognized the prevailing despair, "the dark realities of
the moment," and committed himself and his administration to a
brighter future. He lashed out in Biblical terms against the prof-
iteers and the selfish among the monied classes and laid down an
emphasis which would characterize his administration more than
he then realized: "The measure of the restoration lies in the extent to which we apply social values more noble than mere monetary profit." Identifying himself with the unemployed and underprivileged—"our greatest primary task is to put people to work"—

Reprinted by permission of Scott, Foresman and Company from *Wisconsin Magazine of History*, XLVIII (Winter 1964), 111–126. (Reprinted in
abridged form in *The Negro American: A Documentary History* by Leslie
H. Fishel, Jr., and Benjamin Quarles, copyright © 1967 by Scott, Foresman
and Company.)

he compared the depression to a war emergency and he warned that he was prepared to mobilize the resources of the federal government to fight it.[1]

Like so many of FDR's speeches, including his informal radio fireside chats, the written version of this one paled on paper. His voice exuded warmth and a personal inflection which brought him close to his listeners. His own physical affliction and the way he bore it earned him deserved admiration and gave encouragement to those who had afflictions of their own, even a darker skin. John Gunther testified to Roosevelt's attraction for people as "concrete and intimate. . . . He set up goals in human terms that the average man could grasp for."[2] The general public responded to his magnetism; one of his secretaries selected a list of salutations which were used on letters addressed to him, and they ran the gamut from "Dear humanitarian friend of the people" to "My Pal!" and "Dear Buddy."[3] Almost all of his callers remarked on his personal charm and persuasiveness.

These characteristics of FDR the man, taken with his consummate ability to personalize his understanding of human exploitation and underprivilege, made him the most attractive President, for Negro citizens, since the Civil War. Robert Vann, publisher of the Negro weekly Pittsburgh *Courier*, who was brought into the 1932 campaign by some of Roosevelt's lieutenants, advised his race to "go home and turn Lincoln's picture to the wall. The debt has been paid in full."[4] Yet, like Lincoln, Roosevelt's actual commitments to the American Negro were slim. He was more a symbol than an activist in his own right. His compassion, though real, was tempered by his own background, by the enormity of the decisions which came up to him, and by political considerations. An enthusiastic politician, he used political weights and measures on a political scale to judge the evidence, and the Negro was often found wanting. When Walter White, the executive secretary of the NAACP, obtained an audience through the good graces of Mrs. Eleanor Roosevelt to plead for the President's public support of the anti-lynching bill, FDR demurred because he needed Southern votes in Congress on other matters.

Nevertheless, the FDR image eventually became a favorable one; his picture hung in living rooms and infant sons carried his name. At first, though, Negroes waited to be shown. Their publications granted him the benefit of doubt when he spoke about justice and equality, in the hope that he was talking, too, to Negroes. He called lynching murder, remarked W. E. B. Du Bois, and "these things give us hope."[5] His acknowledgment, through his Secretary of Labor, of the National Urban League's survey of economic conditions among Negroes was, in the words of an *Opportunity* editorial, "an evidence of his deep interest in the Negroes' welfare."[6] By midway through his first term, FDR had captured the admiration and affection of the Negro people and, with that, their votes. During the campaign of 1936, Negroes were outspoken in their support of the Democratic national ticket. Sixteen thousand Harlem residents traveled to Madison Square Garden in September of that year to attend a political rally, and sixty other cities held similar and simultaneous rallies. The New Yorkers mixed a rich fare of music and entertainment with leading New Dealers talking politics, but it was an African Methodist Episcopal Bishop, the Reverend C. Ransome, who symbolized the affair and its meaning by reading a "New Emancipation Proclamation." The vote in November was anticlimactic; the second Roosevelt had weaned the Negro away from the Republican party.

Roosevelt did not publicly associate himself with Negro projects or Negro leaders before 1935, but his programs and some of his associates were more aggressive. Early in 1933, he approved of a suggestion that someone in his administration assume the responsibility for fair treatment of the Negroes, and he asked Harold Ickes to make the appointment. A young white Georgian, Clark Foreman, came to Washington at Ickes' request to handle the task, and brought in as his assistant an even younger Negro of great promise, Robert C. Weaver. Foreman successfully made his way through the burgeoning maze of new agencies which were springing up and did a respectable job of calling to the attention of agency heads and their assistants an awareness of the special problems of Negroes. Along with Ickes, Daniel Roper, the Secretary of Commerce; Harry Hopkins, FDR's relief administrator; and Aubrey Williams, a Hopkins deputy, were sympathetic to committing the New Deal to work more generously with and for Negroes.

From the first, the various New Deal agencies carried the major burden of this emphasis, since they translated words into bread and butter, shelter and schooling. For the Negro, the most significant were the Federal Employment Relief Administration (FERA), the National Recovery Administration (NRA), the Works Progress Administration, later called the Work Projects Administration (WPA), the Agricultural Adjustment Administration (AAA), the Tennessee Valley Authority (TVA), the National

Youth Administration (NYA), the Civilian Conservation Corps (CCC), and the public housing efforts of several agencies. There were others in the alphabetical jungle which assisted Negroes, as whites, in more specialized ways, such as the Federal Writers' Project and the Office of Education studies. The very number of agencies added credence to the emergent fact that, for the first time, the federal government had engaged and was grappling with some of the fundamental barriers to race progress.

It was one thing to engage and grapple with a problem at the federal level, and another thing to implement it at lower levels. Most of the New Deal agency programs ran afoul of local laws and customs and most of them capitulated on very practical grounds. As a consequence, Negroes vigorously attacked the inequities, even while they appreciated the limited benefits. FERA, the first New Deal agency to work directly to alleviate the plight of the destitute, tried by locally administered dole and work-projects to pump more money into circulation. Until the end of 1935, when it was abolished, it administered most of the direct relief and work relief programs which the New Dealers initiated, distributing about four billion dollars. Its progress was dogged by racial discrimination, since the design of projects and allocation of funds remained in local hands. Jacksonville, Florida, Negro families on relief outnumbered white families three to one, but the money was divided according to proportions of the total city population. Thus 15,000 Negro families received 45 per cent of the funds and 5,000 white families got 55 per cent. Along the Mississippi River, from Natchez to New Orleans, Negroes were passed over for skilled jobs and frequently received less than the stipulated minimum wage. When the state of Georgia squeezed out of the FERA administrator the right to fix hourly wages for Negroes below thirty cents an hour, *Opportunity* mournfully questioned, "Does this presage the end of that heralded concern for the Forgotten Man?"[7]

If the relief program raised questions of discrimination, the NRA brought howls of indignation. In the words of a Negro labor specialist, the NRA administrator, General Hugh A. Johnson, was "a complete failure" for not properly recognizing the Negro.[8] The industrial codes established under NRA deferred to geographic wage and employment consideration so that the Negro worker generally earned less money for equal time and was frozen out of skilled jobs. A young Negro lawyer, John P. Davis, organized the Joint Committee on National Recovery in the fall of 1933 to persuade federal authorities to rectify these policies. "It has filed briefs, made appearances at public hearings," he wrote, and "buttonholed administrative officers relative to the elimination of unfair clauses in the codes," but to little avail.[9] In self-defense, NRA officials explained the difficulty in bucking local customs, pointing out also that the NRA was responsible only for industrial workers. Agricultural laborers, domestic servants, and the service trades were not included, and most of the unskilled workers were exempted by statute from wage and hour minimums. "It is not fair," wrote an NRA administrator in a Negro journal, "to blame the NRA for not curing all these ills, if such they be, within a year."[10] Until the Supreme Court decreed its demise in the spring of 1935, the NRA was a favored whipping boy for Negroes, as well as for others. "The Blue Eagle," a Virginia newspaper observed, "may be [for Negroes] a predatory bird instead of a feathered messenger of happiness."[11]

The TVA and the AAA came under fire in the early years of the New Deal for similar reasons. Negro critics raged at the all-white model towns, such as Norris, Tennessee, which were established in conjunction with TVA. Homes for white workers on the project were substantial, while Negro workers lived in substandard temporary barracks. Skilled jobs went first to whites and most labor crews were segregated. TVA, it appeared to two observers in 1934, "aims to maintain the *status quo*."[12] A year later, the situation seemed little better. In one sample two-week period, Negroes were 11 per cent of the working force, receiving only 9.5 per cent of the payroll. Under AAA, Negro tenant farmers and sharecroppers, as the most dispensable laborers, suffered first from the crop reduction policy and found themselves without employment. Concerned about the evolving discriminatory pattern, the NAACP in 1934 devoted a major share of its energy to trying to prevent white landlords from illegally depriving their Negro tenants of crop-reduction bonuses.

Two New Deal programs for young people operated with a minimum of discrimination: the CCC and the NYA. The CCC established segregated camps in the South and in some parts of the North; the great bulk of the integrated camps were in New England. By 1935, its peak year, CCC had over a half million boys in camp. In general, Negroes stayed in CCC camps longer than whites, were not moved up to administrative posts in camps as readily as whites, and were restricted to less than 10 per cent of the total enrollment. Since the proportion of young Negro men in need was substantially higher than this, the quota system was actually inequitable. The NYA, which Mary McLeod Bethune served as administrator of Negro affairs, was shaped to help young men and women in school and with schooling. It grew out of the university and college student relief program established under FERA, and by the end of its first six months, in late 1935, had distributed more than forty million dollars. Conforming to existing state and regional patterns, the NYA still managed to help a critical age group among Negroes.

The debit side of the New Deal's efforts to assist Negroes fell far short of its material and psychological credits. Never before had Negro leaders participated in government affairs as freely and as frequently. The Department of Commerce had E. K. Jones, on leave from the National Urban League; the NYA had Mrs. Bethune; Interior had William H. Hastie and Weaver; the Social Security Board had Ira DeA. Reid; Labor had Lawrence W. Oxley; the Office of Education had Ambrose Caliver, to mention a few. Never before had there been so great a stress on improving the education of Negroes. Many relief programs included elementary education and training classes as part of the regimen. Negro colleges and universities received funds for buildings. The Office of Education, along with other agencies, began an important study of the status of Negro education.

Professional opportunities opened up in government, although not at the rate at which Negroes were graduating from college. For the first time, Negroes were employed as architects, lawyers, engineers, economists, statisticians, interviewers, office managers, case aids, and librarians. Nonprofessional white-collar jobs, which had rarely been within reach of the race, now became available to trained stenographers, clerks, and secretaries. While many of these jobs centered around programs for Negroes within the government, such as Negro slum clearance projects, Negro NYA offices, and the like, they broke the dam which had hitherto kept Negroes out of these kinds of positions.

Harold Ickes, a former president of the Chicago chapter of the NAACP, was the first New Dealer to be recognized as a tried friend. He quickly ended discrimination in his department and set the example by placing professionally-trained Negroes in responsible positions. He first drew FDR's attention to Hastie as a candidate for the federal judge vacancy in the Virgin Islands, and Roosevelt made the appointment in 1937. Ickes appeared at predominantly Negro functions and in 1936, on the occasion of an address at Howard University, even went so far as to wear a University of Alabama hood with his cap and gown because "it seemed to have the best color effect . . . ."[13] While Ickes could not breach established segregation patterns in housing, one-eighth of the federal housing projects planned before the end of 1935 were in mixed neighborhoods. Approximately one-half of them were in Negro slum areas and, thanks to the negotiating skill of Ickes' assistant, Robert C. Weaver, the contracts for a substantial portion of these called for the employment of both skilled and unskilled Negro workers.

Eleanor Roosevelt, the New Deal's conscience, made it her business to reaffirm by word and deed her faith in the equality of opportunity for all. She included Negro and mixed organizations on her itineraries, welcomed mixed groups of adults and children to the White House, and spoke up for the race at critical times. In 1936, as part of a long memo on political strategy in the presidential campaign, she urged party leaders to ask respected Negroes like Mrs. Bethune to participate among Negro groups. The penalty for her unflagging advocacy of the Negro's cause was abuse or occasionally embarrassing questions. As the European war spread after 1939, she confronted questions about the Negro's loyalty. "Rarely," she told a group of New Jersey college women in 1940, "do you come across a case where a Negro has failed to measure up to the standard of loyalty and devotion to his country."[14]

Eleanor Roosevelt was more than a symbol of the New Deal's conscience; she was a vehicle for approaching and influencing the President. She performed this service for Walter White when the anti-lynching bill was before Congress. When the DAR refused to allow Marian Anderson to sing in Constitution Hall, Mrs. Roosevelt was the intermediary who secured permission to use the Lincoln Memorial for the concert. It was useful for the President to have his wife serve in these varying capacities, absorbing some of the criticism, supplying him with information he could get from no other source, and sparking his conscience, when that was needed. This relieved the President from having to punctuate his speeches and press conferences with references to the Negro. Before 1935, these were almost nonexistent; after 1935, they increased in frequence and directness, but Roosevelt did not directly commit himself, as his wife did, until his famous Executive Order 8802 of June, 1941, established a Fair Employment Practice Committee to supervise all defense-contract industries.

In many ways, 1935 seemed to be a pivotal year for the President's public statements to and about the Negro. His annual message to Congress in January asserted that "in spite of our efforts and in spite of our talk, we have not weeded out the overprivileged and we have not effectively lifted up the underprivileged." Uplift and underprivilege were two words which Negroes understood, two words which footnoted their history; yet Roosevelt did not mention the Negro specifically. Shortly after that, he told WPA state administrators that "we cannot discriminate in any of the work we are conducting either because of race or religion or politics," and although he went on to speak of political pressures, the word "race" was there for Negroes to see. In two other public statements later in the year, FDR paid lip service to the accomplishments of the race and by 1936, an election year, he proclaimed his policy that "among American citizens there should be no forgotten men and no forgotten races."[15] The transformation was more one of degree than of conviction; Roosevelt was beginning to speak to the Negro, however rarely, rather than to lump him without identification into massive generalizations. But his eye was ever on the balance of political forces and he never voluntarily came out foursquare for the Negro.

In perspective, Roosevelt's circumspection on some domestic issues was less significant than his New Deal legislative program. Labor unions received substantial encouragement from Section 7a of NRA and from the Wagner Act, although the White House maintained an equivocal position toward both labor and management. The jump in union memberships and the rise of the Committee on Industrial Organization, first within the AF of L and later as the independent Congress of Industrial Organizations (CIO), gained impetus from the newly established right to strike and the newly created federal board to mediate labor disputes. A strengthened labor movement confronted, as one of its problems, the question of Negro members. Older unions such as the United Mine Workers and the International Ladies Garment Workers welcomed Negroes without distinction. When the CIO broke from the AF of L, its nucleus of unions including the new and somewhat fragile organizations in the automobile, rubber, and steel industries accepted Negroes on an equal basis, except in those localities where race friction was high. The United Textile Workers attempted to do the same, but the existence of textile plants in southern states made this task more onerous. It was not enough for a union to resolve, as the CIO did, to accept members without regard to race, creed, or color, or even, as the UAW and the organizing committees of the steelworkers did, to offer Negro workers a chance to join up. Negroes still hung back, alternately tempted and frightened by management's offers and threats. The wave of the future was with the industrial unions, and *Opportunity*'s declaration to Negro steelworkers that it would be "the apotheosis of stupidity" for them to stay out of the union battling for recognizance in 1937, was prophetic.[16] The success of the Brotherhood of Sleeping Car Porters, under the leadership of A. Philip Randolph, in gaining recognition as the bargaining agent with the Pullman Company after a twelve-year struggle, marked the beginning of the race's influence in national labor circles and on national labor policy. After his union was recognized, Randolph prodded the AF of L to grant it an international charter, making it an equal with other member unions, and he never eased up his fight to liberalize the AF of L's racial policies. Even though he was not persuasive enough to break down these craft and railway-union prejudices, Randolph emerged before World War II as a dominant voice in Negro circles and a power to be reckoned with in American unionism.

Of the many voices which spoke out for and against the race, none was more deceptive than that of the Communists. Before 1935, their ideology committed their followers to support a separate state for Negroes, the so-called Black Republic, and insisted that they work independent of all other groups toward this end. When the NAACP unsuccessfully defended the Scottsboro boys— nine young Negroes accused of rape on an Alabama freight train in 1931—the Communists abusively blamed the NAACP for the failure. With shrill bravado, they muscled the NAACP out of the picture and took over the defense. They were unsuccessful in court, but they publicized the case all over the world as an example of capitalistic exploitation and milked the American public for uncounted (and unaccountable) thousands of dollars. In 1935, the Communist ideology swung over to a united-front tactic, and they abandoned their attacks on existing non-Communist organizations and held out the carrot of co-operation. Their purpose was to mix with these organizations and either subvert them directly or gain control behind the scenes. The National Urban League and the NAACP quickly recognized the move for what it was and co-operated at a chilly distance. The League had to dissolve some of its worker's Councils, established in northern cities, because the Communists took them over. The NAACP agreed to work with Communist support on the Scottsboro case, but continued to warn against close co-operation.

Failing to engage the two dominant Negro organizations, the Communists jumped at the chance to work with these and other Negro groups through the newly formed National Negro Congress. The brainchild of New Deal critic John P. Davis, it was organized under the co-sponsorship of almost forty Negro organizations and met in Chicago in 1936 with close to 900 delegates. The Communists stayed in the background—Davis was sympathetic —and the resolutions were non-Stalinist, but Davis was elected executive secretary and maintained close touch with Communist leaders. The 1937 Congress met in Philadelphia with even larger crowds. But soon after that the more conservative organizations and individuals withdrew their sponsorship and the Congress, handicapped by lack of funds, began to crumble. Some local councils established by the Congress were active in Western cities, but after 1937 the Congress as a national group dwindled into impotence and in 1940 became an openly controlled Communist organization. This take-over followed the Stalin-Hitler pact and signalized the 180-degree pivot which American Communists were forced to execute, exploding the united front movement. Organizations like the NAACP which had worked with Communists at a distance suddenly found themselves subject to vituperative and irrational attack, but the vast majority of Negroes merely continued to ignore Communism as a method of achieving their goals.

With the exception of the church, the major Negro organizations felt the sting of mass apathy. "We recognize our lack of skill at mass appeal," NAACP's Roy Wilkins admitted in 1941.[17] The national office of NAACP attracted men and women of an intellectual bent whose convictions on race matters had not changed with the seasons, since the organization was still dedicated to the abolition of segregation and discrimination. But the spark which had sent John Shillady, Walter White, and James Weldon Johnson into race-hatred areas, North and South, burned low. On the national level, the NAACP fought its battles in court, in Congress, and in the press, but not in communities where racism flourished. At local levels, it depended upon its branches, many of which were woefully weak in finances and leadership, to seek out and rectify racial problems of every description. Its base was too narrow for its superstructure, and its bones creaked from inaction at the community level; yet it thrived because it learned to speak the language of influence in political circles and because it chose wisely the cases of discrimination and segregation which it pursued through the courts. Indeed, the road to the 1954 desegregation decisions was charted, bulldozed, paved, and landscaped by the NAACP.

The National Urban League was tested during the depression and not found wanting. Its leadership was similar to that of the NAACP, except that to the extent that its goals were more specific, framed in terms of employment, family welfare, health, and education, it was accused of being more timid, dominated by white liberals, and hostile to trade unionism. Its chief executive, E. K. Jones, replied to these criticisms in a private memo in 1941. The League, he said, was not a Negro but "truly an interracial movement. . . . Any movement of this character which advocates understanding through conference and discussion must necessarily refrain from advocating mass action of one race calculated to force the other group to make concessions." Gunnar Myrdal, the Swedish sociologist whose monumental study of the Negro in America was published during World War II, found that the League worked actively with unions and held "the lead as a pro-union force among the Negro people."[18] Urban League branches were beginning to receive local support from Community Funds, which gave them greater strength and a source for independent leadership. Taken together, these two Negro organizations, in spite of their lack of popular support, moved together in harmony along parallel paths to the great good of the race.

The Negro's church maintained its grip on the masses during these years as it had for centuries, but its hold was loosening. Strong in numbers and appeal, the church had inherent weaknesses which gradually reduced its potency in modern America. It was not one church but many, from the strong African Methodist Episcopal (AME) and African Methodist Episcopal Zion (AMEZ) to the independent colored branches of the Baptist denomination. To these were added smaller denominations and sects and store-front evangelical churches which dissipated the religious energies of the race. The differences were more personal than ideological; in fact, except for the split between the liberal and the fundamentalist churches—a split matched in white denominations—there was no basic theological difference. The churches' hierarchies stood in the way of closer co-operation. The Negro church was all-Negro and proudly so, a self-perpetuating, segregated institution which made no effort to reach across race barriers, individually or institutionally. In the North, this would have been troublesome for white churches, whose precepts were in advance of practice. Negro preachers generally stayed in Negro pulpits. In the South this would have been almost impossible. The Northern Negro church bred isolation; the Southern Negro church fostered accommodation. Fettered by a strain of fundamentalism and emotionalism, and weakened by the diffusion of denominations, the Negro church had little appeal for the younger generation. In the 1930's and 1940's it struggled without success to find a vehicle for its latent power, but its leadership had lost touch with the material and moral issues of the day. It failed to see its obligation as a participant in the fight for equal rights. "We are the policemen of the Negroes," a Southern colored preacher observed in 1941. "If we did not keep down their ambitions and divert them into religion, there would be upheaval in the South."[19] For the second third of the twentieth century, this message was anachronistic.

It would be simplistic to suggest as have some recent novelists, such as James Baldwin in *Go Tell It on the Mountain*, that the church's withdrawal for fear of upheaval led directly to upheaval, but there is a trace of truth in it. When Harlem rioted in 1935, *The Crisis* explained that only the patience of the Negro had delayed it that long. Patience was not enough to encounter the "sneers, impertinence, and personal opinions of smart-aleck investigators, supervisors and personnel directors."[20] Unemployment, rent gouging, and the belief that Harlem had not received its share of relief money snapped the uneasy calm; the riot erupted with a frenzied attack on whites and the purposeful looting of food and clothing stores. The prompt on-the-scene appearance of New York City's popular mayor, Fiorello H. La Guardia, helped restore rationality. When the United States entered World War II, Harlem still seethed from overcrowding, white insolence, and price gouging, and again rioting broke out, followed by riots in other cities, most notably Detroit. The hands of the clock had swung half circle and the Negro had learned from the white how to use violence and lawlessness when order and law were not sufficient.

Toward the end of the 1930's the federal government turned more and more of its attention to the European conflict, the economy flourished as the industrial bastion of the embattled Allies, and the Negro had committed himself to the New Deal and to President Roosevelt. Polls in 1940 showed that Negro voters overwhelmingly supported Roosevelt for a third term, and the polls

were right. The reason for this support was not difficult to sur-
mise. Outside of what the Democratic Administration had tried
to do directly and indirectly, the decade itself was marked with
identifiable milestones of progress. In athletics, Jesse Owen was
an Olympic champion, and Negro football players starred on
many of the major college teams. Professional baseball still re-
sisted, but its time was not far off. In interracial activities, conferences on a variety of subjects began to meet with overbearing
regularity and, though self-consciously interracial, the pattern developed almost irrevocably. College students and adults met to
talk about education, religion, economic matters, and, of course,
civil rights. Even in the South, the indomitable Mrs. Bethune organized an interracial conference at the college she founded, and
the white University of Florida tentatively sent delegates. In the
deep South, interracial conferences were held on a segregated
basis; Eleanor Roosevelt told of attending one in Birmingham and
inadvertently sitting in the colored section. "At once the police appeared to remind us of the rules and regulations on segregation.
. . . Rather than give in I asked that chairs be placed for us with
the speakers facing the whole group."[21] White Southerners began
to speak up for the Negro. They were still a small minority, but the
mere fact that a white state supervisor of schools in Georgia would
admit to the inequalities of segregated schools, or a white North
Carolina legislator would question a decreased appropriation for a
Negro college, was a sign of change. The rise of Huey Long in Louisiana brought a different attitude, one of ignoring race differences without changing race relationships. The all-white Mississippi Education Association established a committee in 1938 to
recommend ways in which students might study Negro life, and
several Northern newspapers in 1940 editorially acknowledged
the importance of Negro History Week. The tide had turned, and
Negroes credited the turning to the New Deal.

The sudden shock of the surprise attack which drew the United
States into World War II served more to expose sore spots than to
blanket them in loyalty. In the First World War, the protests
against unequal treatment were slow to develop and not widely
heard, but the Second World War was different. Even before Pearl
Harbor, clamors arose from the South warning that the Negro was
not going to "come out of this war on top of the heap as he did in
the last one."[22] However distorted the comparison, the attitude
was clear, and it influenced the government's decision to extend
pre-Pearl Harbor patterns into the war period.

The Negro soldier remained separate in the armed services, and not always welcome. Judge William L. Hastie resigned as civilian aide to the Secretary of War in protest against the dissembling tactics of the Army Air Corps to keep the Negro on the ground. *The Crisis*, returning to a World War I cry, criticized the appointment of Southern white officers for Negro troops and the explanation that they could handle them better. When FDR queried Walter White about the carelessness of the Negro press and the consistency of its attack on the war effort, White replied that better treatment for Negroes in the armed services and the invitation of Negro editors to presidential press conferences and top briefings would clear up the problem.

White became an important man in the war effort and was finally sent overseas as a war correspondent in early 1944. He toured every major front in Europe and the Pacific and his reports did not make soothing reading. Wherever he went, he later wrote, "there was a minority of bigots who were more determined to force their bigotry on others than they were to win the war." This was particularly true of officers, both Northern and Southern. Separation, he found, bred this spirit, especially when key officers were "prejudiced or weak, or both." When Negroes and whites actually fought together, as they did during the Battle of the Bulge in December of 1944, attitudes changed, according to polls among white officers and men. "After the first day," a white South Carolinian admitted, "when we saw how they fought, I changed my mind."[23] The top combat brass, such as General Dwight Eisenhower and Admiral Chester Nimitz, were willing to co-operate, but they were hemmed in by Washington orders and junior officer reluctance.

At home, the intense feelings bared by war boiled up with wearying constancy. In the spring of 1941, A. Philip Randolph organized the March on Washington movement which threatened to march if the White House did not declare for fair employment practices in defense industries. President Roosevelt issued his famous Executive Order 8802 in June, establishing the FEPC and the principle of government concern with employment discrimination. Randolph continued the movement during the war, but it lapsed as the older organizations themselves became more militant.

The prosperity of war industry and the proscriptive Southern mores once again attracted thousands of Negroes to Northern cities. The consequent overcrowding and war tension heated racism to the boiling point, as the riots in New York, Detroit, and Los Angeles demonstrated. For the Negro, racism was the same wherever it appeared. In Roy Wilkins' words, "it sounds pretty foolish to be *against* park benches marked 'Jude' in Berlin, but to be *for* park benches marked 'Colored' in Tallahassee, Florida."[24] Negroes could not understand why whites drew distinctions between the Nazi ideology of Aryan supremacy and the American ideology of white supremacy. Even back in 1933, *The Crisis* expressed its "unholy glee" at Hitler's attack on the Jews: "Now that the damned include the owner of the [New York] *Times*, moral indignation is perking up."[25] The paradox which Wilkins illustrated could only be resolved by a change of face on the part of white America.

The war itself, by drawing thousands of men and women into a collaborative effort with whites, made such a change possible. Negroes served in the armed forces in all ratings and at all ranks, though segregated. War industries hired skilled Negro men and women at supervisory and managerial levels. Government used colored workers in great numbers and in more sensitive positions than ever before. The Negro's political power was organized in an unprecedented manner during the wartime presidential election. The younger generation of Negro men and women who had grown up in prosperity and matured in depression were awakened to the infinite possibilities of an assimilated society, and from them came the trained leadership to plan the campaign.

The death of Roosevelt and the end of the war in 1945 terminated an era. The office of the Presidency now symbolized a concern for justice and equality for all Americans, including Negroes. The White House had taken a stand in favor of the principle of equal rights, although the practice had lagged. The new President, Harry S. Truman, a man of lesser parts, was to take the next practical step and declare in specifics his belief in the equality of men of whatever race under the law. Where Roosevelt concealed the particular in the general principle, Truman spoke out without check. Where Roosevelt used the excuse of war to delay integration, Truman used the excuse of peace to accelerate it. Where Roosevelt used the federal government to increase economic opportunities for all, Truman used the federal government to increase economic opportunities for Negroes. While the Truman Fair Deal never approximated the energy and the excitement of the Roosevelt New Deal, it was the former which capitalized on the Negro's readiness to take an equal place in American democracy.

Three major strands marked the period between the end of the war and the Supreme Court's 1954 desegregation decision. One related to the improving economic condition of the Negro, a second to the reports of three presidential committees, and the third to the increasingly significant role of the United States Supreme Court in racial matters. The Negro's improving economic condition stemmed from a variety of causes. In microcosm, the successful introduction of Jackie Robinson into baseball's National League in 1947 is exemplary, since his break-through eventually opened the gates in almost every professional sport. In like manner, the appointment of Ira DeA. Reid to the faculty of New York University was a break-through in higher education of lesser quantity but equal quality. Other major universities and colleges eventually followed suit. The forceful policy of the CIO, led by the United Auto Workers, brought the AF of L into line. The Negro, Walter Reuther warned in late 1945, "should not allow his painful experiences with many of the old craft unions of the American Federation of Labor to embitter him against all labor unions." Both the Negro and the AF of L took the hint.[26] Some craft unions still held out, generally by subterfuge, but the weight of the major unions and their two national federations swung unequivocally to the side of equal opportunity without regard to race.

Dark spots in the improving picture still plagued the nation. Housing was a special need and a particular irritant, since the restrictive convenant, even after the Supreme Court ruled in 1948 that it had no legal standing, was sufficient to block integrated neighborhoods, North and South. The Negro young people were restive under segregated conditions and their still limited economic opportunities. When Thurgood Marshall warned them in 1946 against a widespread disobedience movement on the grounds that it "would result in wholesale slaughter with no good achieved" and alienate public sympathy of "the cautious and the timid," his counsel only helped to delay student nonviolent protests for a decade.[27] In those federal programs where local agencies exercised jurisdiction, the Negro was frequently abused, and President Harry S. Truman, early in 1947, asked his Civil Rights Committee to add this to its already full agenda.

In establishing the President's Committee on Civil Rights in December, 1946, Truman had already spoken in general terms about the preservation of civil liberties. It was, he stated, "a duty of every Government—state, Federal and local." But he pointed out that when state or local governments failed in their responsibilities, the obligation fell back on to the federal establishment. The committee was instructed to review what Truman called "these weak and inadequate statutes" and recommend new legislative or other methods to protect the civil rights of American citizens.[28] The committee, a group of representative men and women under the chairmanship of industrialist Charles E. Wilson, published its *Report* the following year, the first intensive study of its kind by a government-appointed committee. It was a sweeping endorsement of federal activity in the civil rights area and a severe indictment of the many discriminatory practices found in state and local governments.

The *Report* had immediate and far-reaching repercussions. The President's Executive Order 9980 established a fair employment procedure within the government structure. Executive Order 9981 was even more significant since it, in effect, abolished discrimination in the armed services. The committee established by this order to study the situation and make recommendations published its report, *Freedom to Serve*, in 1950, by which time all three of the service branches had abolished the quota system of enlistment and segregation in any form, including separate units and limited opportunities. The Navy was first in its implementation, having started even before the President's order, and although the Army dragged its feet, the committee was satisfied that the order and its execution were effective. A year later, a third Executive Order, 10308, established a President's Committee to insure compliance by government contractors with contractual regulations prohibiting discrimination because of race, creed, color, or national origin. The committee's report was filed early in 1953.

The political reverberations to these dramatic steps by President Truman echoed in the halls of Congress and almost split the Democratic party asunder. In 1948, the Dixiecrats walked out of the Democratic convention in protest to the strong civil rights plank which the young junior Senator from Minnesota, Hubert Humphrey, had pushed through. Truman's election victory that year, in the face of the walkout and the left-wing Progressive Party, was convincing evidence that civil rights had attracted voter support. In Congress, this message from the electorate went unheeded; Southern Democrats and conservative Republicans, whose constituencies sent different messages to them, blocked all efforts to write civil rights into statute.

Outside of politics, the nation moved slowly but certainly away from segregated positions. Professional associations in southern states began, somewhat tentatively, to invite Negroes to membership—lawyers, social workers, nurses, and librarians. The state medical association in Florida stood alone in admitting colored doctors, while other dentists and teachers in the South remained aloof. The American Friends Service Committee began a four-year program in 1951 to eliminate segregation in Washington, D.C.; and in Dallas, Texas, a year earlier, the theological seminary of Southern Methodist University opened its doors to Negro students. In the North, several states adopted open-occupancy laws for public housing, and in key cities like New York, Philadelphia, Detroit, and Washington, Negroes moved into upper- and middle-class neighborhoods without difficulty.

These were straws in the wind rather than set patterns. A full quota of segregation in education and housing, employment, and places of public accommodation still existed. But as the walls began to develop cracks, the role of the Supreme Court emerged as the most significant factor in the equation. Before the milestone decision of 1954, the Supreme Court had charted a course which led, almost inevitably, to that end.

Before World War II, the Supreme Court rendered decisions in three areas involving Negro rights. One was an outgrowth of a group effort by Negroes in Washington, D.C., to persuade a store which catered to Negroes to hire them. The Court determined that this was a labor dispute within the meaning of the Norris-La Guardia Act and that the New Negro Alliance was entitled to picket and pass out literature to accomplish its aim (New Negro Alliance v. Sanitary Grocery Co., 1938). Southern efforts to exclude Negroes from jury service were undermined by the Court's decision in Smith v. Texas (1940) which, in the words of Justice Hugo Black, himself a Southerner, asserted that "for racial discrimination to result in the exclusion from jury service of otherwise qualified groups . . . violates our Constitution and the laws enacted under it. . . ."[29] And in the field of education, where the NAACP had begun to place its major legal redress emphasis, the Court found for the petitioner, Lloyd Gaines, in Missouri ex rel. Gaines v. Canada (1938). Gaines had been refused admission to the University of Missouri Law School because he was a Negro. "The basic consideration," the Court said, "is not as to what sort of opportunities other States provide, or whether they are as good as those in Missouri, but as to what opportunities Missouri itself furnishes to white students and denies to negroes solely upon the ground of color."[30]

The Court did not go beyond the limits of "separate but equal" facilities, but insisted, at the least, that equal facilities exist. Missouri hastened to appropriate a half million dollars for a Negro law school and invited Lloyd Gaines to use a two-room basement establishment in the interim. Before the NAACP could contest this dubious implementation by the state of Missouri, Gaines disappeared and the case was abandoned.

During and after the war, the Court continued to chip away at the encrustations of law which prevented Negroes from full participation as citizens. Its decisions in a series of cases involving the railroad brotherhoods, jury selection, the white primary, and the restrictive covenant generally favored the Negro. In 1948 and again in 1953, the Court made it patently clear that restrictive covenants were not enforceable, in any way, in any court of the land, federal or state. The states of Texas, Mississippi, and Georgia were instructed by the Court in separate decisions between 1947 and 1954 that "the Constitution requires only a fair jury selected without regard to race," and that the various devices used by these states and some of their local subdivisions denied minority groups the equal protection of the laws.[31] In 1944, the Court overruled a 1935 decision and insisted that primaries were sufficiently related to official state actions, even if they were declared to be private, to be regulated by the Fifteenth Amendment. Nine years later, the Court asserted that a private county association of long standing which served as a pre-primary selector of nominees was subject to the same constitutional provision.

Negroes in general and the NAACP in particular could take some satisfaction in knowing that the court was slowly opening basic rights, but in the area of education the progress was even more marked. The NAACP invested heavily of its time and funds in widening educational opportunities by court action. The University of Maryland in 1935 had capitulated at the graduate-school level without taking the case to the Supreme Court. Three years later Missouri was instructed to educate a Negro law student, but its subterfuge worked so well that it tried it again in 1942 by establishing a two-room graduate school in journalism for one qualified Negro graduate student. The University of Oklahoma followed suit when the Supreme Court allowed Missouri's effort to stand, but the end was in sight. In 1950 Texas was told by the Court that its Negro law school had to be equal to that of the white University of Texas Law School, and the doors of the latter were duly opened to Negroes. In a parallel case, Oklahoma was rebuked for permitting a Negro student to be segregated within its state university, and the practice ceased. With a Supreme Court which read the Constitution as a document protecting the rights of all citizens and with the opening of universities at the graduate level, the time was ripe for an all-inclusive appeal for educational opportunities.

The twenty years between the inauguration of Franklin D. Roosevelt and the eve of the Supreme Court desegregation decision were the most revolutionary two decades in the history of the American Negro up to that time. In part, the elemental movements had little to do with race matters; depression, war, prosperity—these were not issues of black and white. Yet they determined a basic posture change: that whites and Negroes would work closely together on matters of national and international importance which had nothing to do with race. Perhaps the most startling development to emerge from these decades was that prominent Negroes began to assume responsibilities in government, business, labor, athletics, education, and the social services which had no connection with race. Negroes, finally, were working in critical jobs because they were needed, and not simply because they were Negroes. Ralph Bunche of the United Nations, Jackie Robinson of the Brooklyn Dodgers, Ira DeA. Reid of Haverford College, to name just a sampling, were men who were doing their jobs—and who happened to be Negroes.

While this was the wedge, slowly to be driven into the grain of American society, pressures which mounted throughout these two decades supplied the hammer to drive it home. Some of these pressures were cumulative, like the development of substantial numbers of highly skilled and highly educated Negroes, and the steady flow of Negroes from farm to city, from South to North. Other pressures were selective, like the magnetism of FDR and the dogged determination of Harry S. Truman. There were economic forces, like the dawning awareness by retailers of the Negro market and the sudden realization by most unions that integration meant greater strength. Then, too, there were such forces as the quiet efforts of Southern liberals to make integration in higher education successful.

The Negro himself was a pressure on the wedge. Still smarting as a second-class citizen, more ready than ever to step up to equal citizenship, he used every resource available. Some were peaceful and passive, like the continuing desire for education and the calculated use of votes. Some were peaceful and active, like the push to break down labor union and employment barriers and the play to get more national publicity. Some were outside the law and violent. These efforts were not concerted and not always effective, but the total impact was pervasive. American society could no longer sit back, consoled by the thought that the Negro was not yet prepared. By the end of these two decades, he was ready, and in the decade to come, the young men and women of his race would make this clear.

NOTES

1. Franklin D. Roosevelt (ed.), *The Public Papers of Franklin D. Roosevelt* (New York, 1938), II: 11, 12, 13.
2. John Gunther, *Roosevelt in Retrospect: A Profile in History* (New York, 1950), 37.
3. Lela Stiles to FDR, April 25, 1940, in Elliott Roosevelt (ed.), *FDR: His Personal Letters* (New York, 1950), II: 1018–1019.
4. Quoted in Arthur M. Schlesinger, Jr., *The Politics of Upheaval: The Age of Roosevelt* (Boston, 1960), III: 430.
5. *The Crisis*, XLI: 20 (January, 1934).
6. *Opportunity*, XI: 167 (June, 1933).
7. *Ibid.*, XII: 360 (December, 1934).
8. T. Arnold Hill in the *New York Times*, June 25, 1937, p. 7.
9. John P. Davis, "What Price National Recovery?," in *The Crisis*, XL: 272 (December, 1933).
10. Gustav Peck, "The Negro Worker and the NRA," in *ibid.*, XLI: 262 (September, 1934).
11. Quoted in the *New York Times*, August 19, 1933, p. 10.
12. Charles H. Houston and John P. Davis, "TVA: Lily-White Construction," in *The Crisis*, XLI: 291 (October, 1934).
13. Harold L. Ickes, *The First Thousand Days, 1933–1936: The Secret Diary of Harold L. Ickes* (New York, 1953), I: 541.
14. *New York Times*, December 29, 1940, p. 12.
15. Roosevelt, *Public Papers*, IV: 16, 262; V: 538.
16. *Opportunity*, XV: 133 (May, 1937).
17. Quoted in Gunnar Myrdal, *An American Dilemma* (New York, 1944), II: 836n.
18. *Ibid.*, II: 840, 841.
19. *Ibid.*, II: 876n.
20. *The Crisis*, XLII: 145 (May, 1935).
21. Eleanor Roosevelt, *This I Believe* (New York, 1949), 173–174.
22. *Washington Post*, February 26, 1941, quoted by Rayford Logan (ed.), *What the Negro Wants* (New York, 1944), 8.
23. Walter White, *A Man Called White* (New York, 1948), 246, 248, 250.
24. Roy Wilkins, "The Negro Wants Full Equality," in Logan, *What the Negro Wants*, 130.

25. *The Crisis*, XL: 197 (September, 1933).
26. Walter P. Reuther, "The Negro Worker's Future," in *Opportunity*, XXIII: 203 (Fall, 1945).
27. *New York Times*, November 23, 1946, p. 17.
28. *To Secure These Rights, The Report of the President's Committee on Civil Rights* (New York, 1947), vii.
29. 311 U.S. 130 (1940).
30. 305 U.S. 349 (1938).
31. The quotation is from the majority opinion of Justice Stanley Reed in Cassell *v*. Texas, 339 U.S. 286 (1950).

RACE RELATIONS IN THE
UNITED STATES, 1917–1947

W. E. B. DU BOIS

W. E. Burghardt Du Bois, the first Negro to earn the Ph.D at Harvard, was the outstanding black intellectual of the first half of the twentieth century. In 1905 he organized the Niagara Movement, a group of Negro intellectuals and professionals who mounted the first effective protest against Booker T. Washington's program of conciliation and black submission. He was one of the founders, in 1910, of the NAACP and for many years edited Crisis, *its magazine. Du Bois expressed his discontent with the Negro's plight in his column, "As the Crow Flies." He taught sociology at Atlanta University, where he directed a series of studies of Negroes while he wrote prolifically himself. Among his books are* Black Folks Then and Now, Black Reconstruction, *and* The Souls of Black Folk. *Du Bois often clashed with conservative Negroes in the NAACP and at Atlanta University. He died in 1963 at the age of ninety-five. (See Francis L. Broderick,* W. E. B. Du Bois: Negro Leader in a Time of Crisis *[Stanford: Stanford University Press, 1959], and Elliott M. Rudwick,* W. E. B. Du Bois: A Study in Minority Group Leadership *[Philadelphia: University of Pennsylvania Press, 1960].) In this selection Du Bois surveys race relations over three decades, discerning some significant gains while seeing vast room for improvement and formidable obstacles to be overcome both domestically and internationally.*

＊

There can be no question but that the relations between American Negroes and the balance of the population in the United States have improved during the last generation.

Reprinted by permission from *Phylon*, IX (Third Quarter 1948), 234–247.

One of the causes of this change of attitude has been the increasing willingness and, indeed, compulsion among observers of social phenomena to depend upon some kind of social measurement for their judgments rather than upon individual observation. Consequently, today we have some increase in measurements for social phenomena; they are not many and scientists have not yet quite made up their minds that it is possible to measure the acts of men. It is undoubtedly difficult and calls for much more careful methods than we have put in practice; but the time is coming when we are going to measure human action and more and more depend upon such measurements for our social judgments.

There are certain general facts and figures upon which we can base valid scientific judgment. The Negro population of the United States between 1920 and 1940 increased by about two million persons; doubtless between 1917 and 1947 the increase was more than three millions. The Negro in the South between 1920 and 1940 had an increase of less than a million, while the Negro population of the North and West doubled. So too, while the rural Negro population is today decreasing, the urban population has doubled.

The chief characteristic of the last 30 years has been the organized systematic attack upon race discrimination by careful and widespread program. The NAACP, established in 1910, and brought actively to work by the First World War, began the first organized effort to center the thought of the country upon the enormity of lynching; then it started a systematic fight for political and civil rights. Its accomplishment has been one of the most important and successful efforts of this sort in the history of modern civilization. It has received very little financial support from white sources or from rich people, but has been financed up to 90 per cent of its revenues by Negro laborers. Its efforts have been along the lines of education, agitation, lectures, organization, literature, and court cases. Its chief workers have been Negroes.

It is interesting to remember that in 1900, Judge Emory Speer of Georgia told a white audience frankly that some day Negroes would gather funds and hire first-class white lawyers to go before the courts and attack discriminatory legislation in the South, and that they had a chance in that way to overturn it. It did not occur to this Southern white judge that the Negroes might not only hire white lawyers like Moorfield Storey and Clarence Darrow, but would also have colored lawyers, like Charles Houston and Thurgood Marshall, who would go before the highest courts and obtain favorable decisions.

Organized efforts toward bettering race relations have been widespread in the United States. In 1919 the Commission on Interracial Cooperation was formed in the South. It had national offices in Atlanta, Georgia, and several branch offices. It published pamphlets and held conferences. The Southern Regional Council formed in 1944 has taken over the work of the Commission. The Commission on Race Relations of the Federal Council of Churches of Christ in America was organized in 1921. It held national interracial conferences, instituted "Race Relations Sunday," distributed the Harmon Awards, and carried on various other activities. The interracial work of the National Council of the Young Men's Christian Associations has been a part of the YMCA work beginning with the first association among colored men in 1853. In the YWCA, interracial activity has taken place in the National Student Council where there is an interracial committee, in the National Interracial Committee and in the Sub-Committee on Christian World Education.

A Committee on Race Relations of The Society of Friends was formed after the First World War, and there is a Race Relations Section of the Friends Service Committee.

The American Civil Liberties Union, formed in 1917, and reorganized in 1920, has done considerable work in extending the rights of Negro Americans. The Urban League has acted as an interracial agent to a wide extent in industrial fields. The International Labor Defense was formed in 1925. It gave attention to the struggles of labor and capital and the interracial aspects of such trouble.

Rachel Davis Du Bois started a movement for interracial education which was later known as Intercultural Education. A Bureau for Intercultural Education was started in 1939. Local interracial movements are illustrated by the Springfield Plan, started in 1939, with a committee to teach democratic citizenship by the practice of democracy on all levels of school and community life. Starting in Springfield, Massachusetts, this movement has spread through New Jersey, Pennsylvania, Ohio, and all the way to the West Coast. Great foundations like the Carnegie Corporation, the General Education Board, the Phelps-Stokes Fund, the Rockefeller Foundation, have all worked in certain aspects of race rela-

tions. The Julius Rosenwald Fund has been especially notable in
its scholarship, school, and health activities.

The Race Relations Division of the American Missionary Association started in 1942 and has studied especially centers of
race tension in various parts of the country. The Southern Conference for Human Welfare was started in 1939 and it has become a strong organization for civil rights, political action, and
equalization of educational opportunity. It has issued various
publications and held large conferences. The American Council
on Race Relations formed in 1944 has sought to federate many of
the race relations activities in the nation.

There are no overall figures which can show the result of these
efforts, but they have without doubt had considerable effect. They
represent a prolongation, with more careful and scientific attention, of the old interracial movement, which while it was based on
sentiment with considerable propaganda, nevertheless did make
numbers of people conscious of the problems of other groups of
folk.

Probably the greatest and most effective effort toward interracial understanding among the working masses has come about
through the trade unions. The organization of the CIO in 1935
was an attempt to bring the mass of workers into the union movement as contrasted with the AFL effort to unionize only the skilled
workers of industry. As a result, numbers of men like those in the
steel and automotive industries have been thrown together, black
and white, as fellow workers striving for the same objects. There
has been on this account an astonishing spread of interracial tolerance and understanding. Probably no movement in the last 30
years has been so successful in softening race prejudice among
the masses.

Turning now to results of these movements let us note the im-
provements of the last 30 years. We can begin with the most striking and outrageous evidence of racial friction, namely—lynching.
The figures are impressive. Between 1900 and 1916, 1,183 Negroes were lynched; and 419 between 1917 and 1926. In the next
decade the number lynched was reduced to 136, and in the decade
which ended in 1947, the lynchings were reduced to 43. This was
a tremendous improvement. If we compare specifically the year
1917 with 1947, thirty-five were lynched 30 years ago, and one
last year.

But this, again, is only a rough measurement. Just what consti-
tutes a lynching is hard to put down in words. It is a specie of mob

violence which results in the death of a man whose guilt has not been judicially ascertained; but in addition to that, there are the judicial lynchings—the rapid, unfair trial and railroading of men to prison or to the gallows. There is violence of various sorts, and especially the astonishing fact that no member of a lynching mob has ever been adequately punished for his crime.

During the period 1900 to 1946 there were nearly 3,000 lynchings, and in this period 135 persons were convicted of being members of lynching mobs. Of these, the conviction of seven was reversed later, while 17 others escaped with fines. Others were convicted as follows: 10 received prison terms of less than 1 year; 16 got one to two years; 21 received terms of three to five years; 47 were sentenced to serve 10 or more years; the sentences of 11 were indeterminate, and in the case of six the term was unknown.

One curious change is worth noting. From 1889 to 1918 it was commonly believed that lynching was caused by rape and that most Southern white women lived in perpetual fear of "Big Black Brutes." Then the NAACP proved by figures that most Negroes lynched were not even accused of rape, and in recent years the charge has been forgotten. The amount of mob violence against Negroes in the United States, and particularly in the South, has greatly decreased. Race riots are now rare.

Negroes have been excluded from jury duty in the South, and in many cases in the North, but the courts have consistently declared this unconstitutional and the appearance of Negroes on juries is more common today, although still not usual.

The protection of rights of American Negroes in courts and jails has received attention especially in cases of extraordinary and known injustice. The Scottsboro cases brought widespread effort on the part of the NAACP and other organizations and was partially successful. Other cases have been defended with more or less success down to the extraordinary outrage recently perpetrated in Georgia, in the case of half-grown sons defending their mother. Further cases come before the courts in the matter of extradition of alleged criminals who have escaped from the South into northern states. This has led to a number of investigations and refusals to extradite.

It is, of course, well known that during and since Reconstruction times, the courts in the South have been used largely as instruments for enforcing caste rather than securing justice. This is still a widely-followed procedure. It makes more criminals than it cures, black and white. There is no reliable index of the extent of crime among Negroes. Their reported proportion of all offenses punished was 22 per cent in 1910 and 23 per cent in 1940. It is probably true that anti-social offenses among Negroes has increased in the last generation and is increasing.

One small indication of change in the social structure is the number of Negro policemen. The presence of Negro police means that arrests are no longer purely a matter of race. To consider the South alone, in 1917 there was not a single Negro acting as a policeman so far as I can ascertain. In 1947, at least 12 states employed Negro policemen in more than 50 cities. Of course, even in these cases Negroes in theory, if not in actual law, exercise no power of arrest over whites.

The change in the political situation of Negroes is large. As late as 1928, 34 outstanding Negro leaders wrote:

We are asking, in this appeal, for a public repudiation of this campaign of racial hatred. Silence and whispering in this case are worse than in matters of personal character and religion. Will white America make no protest? Will the candidates continue to remain silent? Will the church say nothing? Is there any truth, any issue in the campaign, either religious tolerance, liquor, water power, tariff or farm relief, that touches in weight the transcendent and fundamental question of the open, loyal and unchallenged recognition of the essential humanity of twelve million Americans who happen to be dark-skinned?

This was an exceptional campaign with race and religious hate, but it contrasts with today.

Negroes are voting today more widely than ever before. In the North, they vote with no racial handicap, but with all the handicaps of the poor and inexperienced. In the border States, Negroes vote generally; in the southern South, somewhere between a fourth to a third of the Negro populations is beginning to vote. The number disfranchised is still large but it has notably decreased.

Here the fight has been tremendous and exhausting. For a long time the outrageous "Grandfather Clause" which gave poor whites in the South a hereditary right to vote, was allowed to stand by the Supreme Court. It was not declared unconstitutional until 1915. By that time primary elections restricted to whites became a universal method of disfranchising Negroes. The NAACP began a fight to enter the white primaries.

In 1927 the Supreme Court ruled that the state of Texas could not exclude Negroes from the primary by state law. Thereupon,

Texas put the power of exclusion in the hands of the executive committee of the Democratic Party. The Supreme Court then decided that this procedure was unlawful. Thereupon the Democratic Party in convention passed a resolution excluding Negroes. This case was carried to the Supreme Court in 1935 and the Court curiously enough decided that this method of excluding Negroes did not violate the Federal Constitution.

However, the Supreme Court, in 1941, contradicted itself in a case concerning white voters when the Court declared that the primary election was an integral part of the regular election. Thereupon this matter was taken again to the Court, and in 1944, by an eight to one decision, the Court said that Negroes could not be excluded from primaries on account of race and color. States like South Carolina, Mississippi, and Alabama have tried to evade this decision; but so far it has stood and Negroes have begun to vote in the primary elections of Southern States.

A further method of estimating the change in race relations would refer to the number of Negroes holding office, especially elective offices. In some cases the number has not increased. There were in 1947 6 members of city councils throughout the United States as compared with 10 in 1917—a decrease. On the other hand, there were only two Negro members of state legislatures in 1917 but 33 in 1947, including at least two senators. In the Federal Congress, there are two Negro members today as compared with none in 1917. Some 13 judges and magistrates of Negro descent are presiding over courts as compared with none in 1917 and one American Negro is governor of a territory. In both New York and Cleveland, Negroes have for years been prominent members of the City Civil Service Commissions. There are several internal revenue collectors.

The whole matter of civil rights for Negroes has been focused and emphasized by the report of the President's Committee on Civil Rights and by the appeal of the NAACP to the United Nations. Civil rights cover a large variety of subjects, many of which like that of intermarriage have not been brought before the courts lately. But phases covering education and travel have come up repeatedly.

Negroes for a long time have been decreasing in illiteracy. Nine-tenths of them were illiterate at the time of emancipation. We have had a series of figures which reduced the illiterate population to 10 per cent according to the census of 1940; but the experience of the draft shows that this report is inaccurate and that today probably a fourth of the adult Negro population is by any thorough standard, illiterate.

Figures show us that in 1910, 45 per cent of Negroes from six to 25 years of age were in school, and in 1940 64 per cent, or in round numbers, 1,600,000 in 1910 and 4,188,000 in 1940. Notwithstanding this, the school situation among Negroes is bad, especially in regard to the elementary public schools in the South. While much has been said and large sums given for Negro education, the amount and facilities furnished were at no time equal to the need and to the demand. If we had done for Negroes half as much as Russia has done for her peasants, there would be no Negro illiteracy today.

On the other hand, the more fortunate class of Negroes has been pushing into schools during the last generation. In 1917, 475 Negroes received the Bachelor's degree from college courses. In 1947, 6,000 received such degrees. The Negro enrollment in higher institutions, white and black, was perhaps 5,000 in 1910, certainly 25,000 in 1930, and 70,000 in 1947.

Let us remember that as late as 1900 Charles Dudley Warner, speaking undoubtedly for the most cultivated section of the American people, gravely declared:

> On almost all the southern plantations, the Negro was taught to work, to be an agriculturist, a mechanic, a material producer of something useful. He was taught this fundamental thing. Our higher education applied to him in his present development operates in exactly the opposite direction. This is a serious assertion. Its truth or falsehood cannot be established by statistics; but it is an opinion gradually formed by experience and the observation of men competent to judge, who have studied the problem close at hand.

Mr. Warner strongly commended the leadership of Booker Washington. This illustrates the sort of public opinion we were confronting when at the opening of the century we fought for higher education for Negroes.

Discrimination in education has been several times attacked in the courts but lately the first success came in the matter of discrimination in teachers' salaries. It was long notorious that teachers with the same training worked under a different salary scale because of race. Indeed, the training of southern Negro teachers was in many cases better than that of the white teachers —because, excluded from graduate work in southern universities, they attended and graduated in many cases from the best northern institutions. By 1947, 32 cases concerning educational inequalities had been brought to court; 23 were won, 17 by dissent, and six by court decision. Four cases were lost, one dropped, and four were pending.

Next, the fight was made on the universities. The custom of establishing state universities for whites, with either no facilities or poor ones for Negroes, was general in the South. Four states gave Negroes scholarships to study outside the state. The Murray case was brought and won against the University of Maryland in 1935. A Negro thereupon entered the Law School of the University of Maryland and was graduated. Others have entered since.

In the celebrated Gaines case, the Supreme Court held in 1938 that the State of Missouri could not bar a person from the University of Missouri on grounds of color or race, but must provide equal educational facilities within the boundaries of the state. This decision was strengthened in an Oklahoma case in 1948. Most southern states are now trying to establish graduate study in Negro state colleges. Eight have done nothing yet to comply with the mandate of the Court. The South has, however, tried to get Congress to establish the right of states to organize regional graduate schools for Negroes. The question of race discrimination by Federal law in such schools has arisen and no step has yet been taken.

In the Sweatt case, a Texas Negro sued to enter the Law School of the University of Texas. The state set up a separate Negro law school but Negroes then went to court and declared that separating by race in schools was in itself an evidence of inequality. The case is still pending. All leading universities of the north now admit Negroes, Vassar and Princeton being among the last to yield.

College-bred Negroes show increasing instances of unusual ability. There is no Negro institution that has a chapter of the Phi Beta Kappa honorary fraternity, and recognition of Negro ability is not always certain in white institutions. Yet we find that between 1910 and 1917, 15 Negro students were elected to Phi Beta Kappa, while between 1937 and 1947, 40 were so elected. Between 1910 and 1917, 6 Negroes received the Degree of Doctor of Philosophy while between 1937 and 1947, 279 received such degrees. And in addition to that there were 35 other Negroes awarded doctorates in education, science, and law.

The health of Negroes has been so neglected because of low income, living in slums, and lack of physicians and hospitals that a theory of natural and inborn racial health inferiority has been widespread and only in the last decade successfully questioned.

Today this Negro population has better health than it had a generation ago, although naturally it still lags behind the white. Between 1920 and 1947 the life expectancy of Negro males increased from 40.5 to 57.5 years. The crude birth rate in the United States for 1945 was 23.3 per thousand for Negroes and 19.2 for whites. The corresponding death rates were 12.0 and 10.0 per thousand.

It is still a wide-spread custom to refuse Negroes hospitalization even in serious cases. Some ten years ago, one of the most prominent Negro social workers was allowed to die in a little Georgia town because she was refused admission to the white hospital. Other cases nearly as bad as this continue to take place. There are not nearly enough physicians and dentists to care for the colored population, even if their work were confined to this group. Medical schools discriminate against the admission of Negroes and medical societies still hinder their work. Still, the American College of Surgeons has granted them admission.

The economic situation of Negroes is of fundamental importance, and while the data are not easy to collect, nevertheless significant changes are clear. If we confine ourselves to 1920 and 1940, during these 20 years there was a vast shift from the tenant farms of the South, making a proportional increase in domestic and personal service, a small decrease in manufacturing and transportation, and a very considerable increase in trade and professional services.

During these 20 years the number of ministers has greatly decreased, but with the result of weeding out the casual and untrained and replacing them with men with larger professional training. The physicians and surgeons have increased a little; the dentists proportionately more than the physicians. The number of nurses has doubled. The lawyers have increased considerably and the teachers have greatly increased.

If comparison could be made between 1917 and 1947, the change would be even more startling and significant, showing that the American Negro is escaping from the slavery of southern agriculture and getting into trade and professional service.

The economic status of Negroes has improved because of the migration from South to North during the World Wars. Some jobs thus gained were lost after the war, but in many cases the Negroes retained their jobs. President Roosevelt's FEPC had wide effect and there is strong demand for its enactment into Federal law. In five states, laws forbidding discrimination in employment have been passed and fairly well enforced. At any rate, the fundamental question of the right of Negroes to work and to receive decent wages has been forced upon the attention of the nation.

The result of this mass up-grading and migration to cities is felt in the demand for housing. For many years the Negroes have been segregated by custom in the oldest part of cities, in ghettos where the accommodations were the worst. These areas were neglected by the city government and became centers of crime and anti-social activities. Most of the structures in these slums were owned by white landlords, the rents were high, and repairs were seldom made.

In the South, race segregation was not a matter of law but of custom, and varied from complete separation in living quarters to large mingling of races in certain cities and sections but with certain class distinctions. When the Negro came North and when those in the North tried to move out of the alleys onto the main streets and were able to pay for property, mob violence often ensued and a series of segregation ordinances and state laws was passed. These were taken to court and declared unconstitutional in 1917, 1927 and 1930. They were followed during the last 25 years by a series of covenants, skillfully and carefully drawn, and in 1926 the Supreme Court of the United States dismissed a covenant forbidding sale of property on appeal from a court order enforcing a covenant forbidding sale of property to Negroes of the state.

The covenants began to increase in number until it was estimated in 1947 that five square miles of St. Louis and 10 square miles of Chicago were restricted to settlement by white people. When the Second World War brought numbers of colored people to Los Angeles, in that city alone from 1943 to 1947 more than 20 covenants affecting 100 Negro families were added. The courts continued for the most part to declare that the covenants were legal and enforceable. The break came in 1945, when the Superior Court of Los Angeles dismissed suits against some 30 property owners, Negro and Japanese, in a covenanted area.

The Supreme Court of the United States decided against Negro complaints in 1944 and refused to review a decision of a lower court in 1945. Nevertheless, in 1948 came the epoch-making and clear-cut decision outlawing the enforcement of such contracts by state or Federal law. It must be remembered that, in order to consider this case, one third of the court had to declare itself ineligible to sit on the trial, presumably because these three men themselves lived in covenanted areas. There is probably no other civilized country where such national hypocrisy could be so clearly confessed.

Probably no phase of discrimination has irked the American Negro more than the so-called "Jim Crow" cars for travel, because of its publicly insulting character. These have been attacked recently in the matter of interstate travel and dining car service. The Supreme Court has decided that railroads must provide accommodations for Negroes equal to those for whites and in several cases damages have been paid to colored people for being refused service in diners or on Pullman trains. In one case, it was decided that segregation in interstate travel according to state law was permissible, but in 1946 the United States Supreme Court decided that the Virginia law segregating passengers in buses in interstate travel was unconstitutional. In 1941, the Supreme Court decided in the case of Congressman Mitchell that railroads must provide accommodations for Negroes equal to those provided for whites.

The question of the admission of Negroes to theaters has long been agitated; in the case of movies in most northern states, discrimination has been broken down so that they enter freely; theaters are more generally open. But this is not true in the capital city of Washington, nor in the Southern states. The Daughters of the American Revolution made themselves notorious by refusing the rental of their hall in Washington to Negro artists. The Baltimore Public Library tried to refuse to train colored librarians but lost their case before the Supreme Court.

Wide effort has long been made to separate Negroes from whites, so that they would have no real knowledge and understanding of each other, and be prevented from that natural human intercourse that makes for friendship and common striving. Most white Americans have no Negro friends and no ordinary opportunity of making them. For years, social contact was restricted to service and employment where it was often close and human. In recent years there has been increase in normal social intermingling between Negroes and whites, and today it is much more common to meet Negroes in social gatherings, at dinners and celebrations than it used to be. There is some increase in intermarriage but no change in the intermarriage laws, which are clearly unconstitutional and certainly silly.

In religion, the advance, while important, has not been great.

The churches still form the most segregated part of our social organization. The efforts of the Methodists to bring all Methodism together has been so far as the Negroes are concerned, only partly successful. There were three Negro Catholic priests in the United States in 1917; now there are 22. In 1917, it was difficult for a Negro to enter a Catholic theological seminary in the United States or any of the colleges or parochial schools except a few segregated schools. This has changed, and lately many seminaries, colleges and parochial schools have opened their doors. There are more Negro Catholics, but Negro membership in white Protestant churches has not greatly increased. Protestant seminaries have seldom barred Negro students. There are several interracial churches.

In science there is a larger willingness to consider the scientific achievements of Negroes as has been instanced in the universal acclaim of George Washington Carver and the election of E. Franklin Frazier as President of the American Sociological Society. And what is more fundamental, the admission to a larger extent of Negroes to fellowships as laboratory assistants and teaching positions in several universities and many northern public schools. The freedom of Negroes in fields of art and literature has grown decidedly and now depends upon opportunity and ability more largely than ever before.

In the field of sports, which must loom large because of public liking for such recreation, there has been some letting down of bars, especially in track competition and in baseball. A small beginning has been made in tennis. But the bars still are high in golf, bowling, and as jockeys in horse racing.

In many national organizations there has been notable cooperation between white and colored groups and a strong tendency of general organizations to pay attention to the Negro part of our community. It is striking to see today colored Boy and Girl Scouts, photographed along with their fellows, and to have appeals for summer outings for children emphasize and include colored children. This was not the case 30 years ago.

In the larger efforts of social uplift, throughout the North, the color line has been pretty successfully attacked. In the South, this, of course, is not so, although even here there is certainly greater awareness of the necessity for some action. It is indicative of the new attitude that a great many national organizations refuse to meet in parts of the country where hotel and other accommodations cannot be furnished to their Negro members. We have a right then to acclaim substantial advance in race relations in the years between the founding of the Rosenwald Fund in 1917 and today—30 long years of internal and world strife.

First of all and fundamental, an improvement in general attitude and hopefulness. Science and the general public have attacked the concept of ineradicable race differences with devastating success. A great many of the old clichés have either disappeared or are less emphasized. The eternal and ineradicable differences between races are no longer mentioned, or at least not as often. The changing of human nature in the matter of prejudices does not seem today as impossible as it once did. We no longer maintain that laws do not help in social evolution or that the amalgamation of races in the United States and elsewhere is impossible.

All this gives us hope and courage. Yet we know quite well that the race problem in the United States is not settled and it is perhaps too much to say that it is even well on the way to settlement.

The American Negro still forms the most poverty-stricken part of our nation. He is still subjected to caste restrictions and discriminations to an extent untrue in the case of any other group of Americans.

But that is not the most serious aspect of our present condition. This aspect is that the American Negro is part of a world situation. Negroes are in a quasi-colonial status. They belong to the lower classes of the world. These classes are, have been, and are going to be for a long time exploited by the more powerful groups and nations in the world for the benefit of those groups. The real problem before the United States is whether we are really beginning to reason about this world-wide feeling of class dominance with its resultant wars: wars of rivalry for the sharing of the spoils of exploitation, and wars against exploitation. The result of world-wide class strife has been to lead modern civilization in America and Western Europe toward a leveling of culture pattern—toward conformity to certain standards which became predominant in the 19th century. We have refused continually to admit the right of difference. The type of education, the standards and ideals in literature and art, the methods of government must be brought very largely to one single white European standard.

If this is going to continue to be the attitude of the modern world, then we face a serious difficulty in so-called race problems. They will become less and less matters of race, so far as we regard race as biological difference. But what is even more important, they will even become less and less matters of conflicting cultures. The populations of the world will tend to solve all of their problems of living according to one standard and, if that standard is wrong or inadequate, it means the dissolution of modern civilization or its revolutionary change. This, of course, is exactly what we are facing today.

The cultural standards of Western Europe dominate the world. The race and cultural problems are the ways in which group methods of solving human problems come in conflict with this predominant European method and the question before us is: Are we going to allow deviation from the one assumed standard, or, if we cannot help permitting it, what kind of problems of conflict in culture corresponding to those in race do we face tomorrow?

In other words, can we have in this world groups who in divergent and different ways are facing the problems of life? And the question as to whether we can or not is, of course, a question of cultural democracy. We have been talking about political democracy, and we have meant by that the possibility of governing by allowing all elements in the community to express their ideas and seek their realization. Insofar as the idea which is adopted is by the sympathy and tolerance of the community allowed to hold sway until public opinion wishes it changed, in just so far is political democracy successful. Democracy, therefore, in politics means tolerance and sacrifice even more than it means power.

But the whole political life is dependent upon the cultural standards round about. So long as these cultural standards are in agreement with practically little opposition we can have the kind of democracy prevalent in England in the 19th century among the middle class Britishers. But when we get beyond that and when we get ideas of life and action which are widely divergent, then the tolerance must also be broader and the intelligence which carries on the community must be greater. That, I take it, is the problem which faces the world today. There is a determination in America and Great Britain, shared to a less extent by Western Europe, that only *one type* of cultural organization can be allowed because it is the only true and successful type.

There is, on the other hand, on the part of the overwhelming majority of people in the world, a feeling that the Anglo-Saxon type of cultural organization has failed and that new cultural patterns should be tried, and that for the trial of these new cultural patterns there is demand for cultural democracy and intercultural tolerance. That without this, civilization in its present form is doomed.

On the other hand, what we can look forward to, and what the racial strife in the United States ought to teach us to look forward to is that it is possible to have in this world a variety of cultural patterns; that men can live and work together in tolerance and mutual appreciation; that by vast and spiritual natural selection out of those different cultures may arise in the future a more and more unified culture, but never completely unified, which would express and carry out the cultural possibilities of the mass of men.

II

White Action

Contemporary criticism of Roosevelt as the sponsor of the New Deal attacked him for going too far, but, Thomas C. Cochran writes, "almost all historians remain in agreement that the reform legislation was necessary."[1] Perhaps the best known of the dissenting minority of historians is Edgar Eugene Robinson, who condemns the New Deal from a conservative-constitutionalist position.[2] Cochran also notes that "when he [Roosevelt] is criticized now it is usually for not going far enough."[3] This is particularly true of the New Left historians, though their basic position on this question has two parts: the New Deal, they hold, did not go far enough—indeed, barely moved at all—in the direction of substantial change, but it went far enough to undermine demands for, and thereby prevent adoption of, measures that would have produced really fundamental change.[4] In this sense, according to a critic of the New Left historians, "reform becomes destructive—more destructive, paradoxically, than failure to reform."[5] Presumably, from the standpoint of the New Left his-

1. Thomas C. Cochran, *The Great Depression and World War II, 1919–1945* (Glenview, Ill.: Scott, Foresman, 1968), p. 35.
2. Edgar Eugene Robinson, *The Roosevelt Leadership 1933–1945* (Philadelphia: Lippincott, 1955).
3. Cochran, *Great Depression and World War II*, p. 35.
4. Barton J. Bernstein, "The New Deal: The Conservative Achievements of Liberal Reform," in Bernstein, ed., *Towards a New Past: Dissenting Essays in American History* (New York: Pantheon, 1968); Jacob Cohen, "Schlesinger and the New Deal," *Dissent* (Autumn 1961); Lloyd C. Gardner, *Economic Aspects of New Deal Diplomacy* (Madison: University of Wisconsin Press, 1964); Howard Zinn, ed., *New Deal Thought* (Indianapolis: Bobbs-Merrill, 1966), Introduction, pp. xv–xxxvi; Zinn, "The Grateful Society," *Columbia University Forum* (Spring 1967).
5. Jerold S. Auerbach, "New Deal, Old Deal, or Raw Deal: Some

torians, the desirable alternative to the direct application of drastic reform would have been the indirect achievement of radical reconstruction by refraining from reform and permitting chaos and desperation to prevail.

It is possible to agree with the New Left historians not only as to what the New Deal *was*—a patch-up stopgap which saved the capitalist system—but also as to what the New Deal *should have been*—the bringer of well-being in all ways to all Americans—without being a New Left historian. For the New Left historians, who are also social critics, do not deal adequately, in some instances hardly at all, with the question of what the New Deal *could have been*. In the 1930's American institutions were what they were, the American people were what they were, and Roosevelt—who was like the people in many ways[6]—was what he was. FDR, to be sure, was unlike the people in some ways, possessing qualities that enabled him to reach the top of what Disraeli called the "greasy pole."

Historians' comments on Progressive leaders who preceded FDR shed light on the question of why political leaders, Roosevelt included, are what they are. The individualism of Progressive leaders has been cited as contributing to the decline of their movement.[7] Herbert F. Margulies comments:

Implied in such analysis is the notion that the leaders of the Progressive movement might have been of a different character, and had they been something other than what they were, the ultimate fate of progressivism might have been different.[8]

Margulies cites George E. Mowry's demonstration that it was statistically highly probable that a given Progressive leader would be highly individualistic.[9] If the Progressive movement was in the end weakened by the individualism of its leaders, this trait may have had much to do with their becoming leaders of the movement in the first place. True, the axiom that it takes one set of

Thoughts on New Left Historiography," *Journal of Southern History* (February 1969), p. 23.

6. Paul K. Conkin, *The New Deal* (New York: Crowell, 1967), p. 10, calls Roosevelt's beliefs "simplistic and conventional."

7. Robert S. Maxwell, *La Follette and the Rise of the Progressives in Wisconsin* (Madison: State Historical Society of Wisconsin, 1956), pp. 173–194, cited in Herbert F. Margulies, "Recent Opinion on the Decline of the Progressive Movement," *Mid-America* (October 1963), p. 264.

8. *Ibid.*

9. *Ibid.*, pp. 264–265; Margulies cites George E. Mowry, *The California Progressives* (Berkeley: University of California Press, 1951), pp. 291–292.

qualities to attain a position of leadership and another set to be effective in that position is, abstractly considered, valid; but, as life goes, a political leader carries all his qualities with him to the top of the pole.

James MacGregor Burns refers to Roosevelt's "staccato" intellectual habits, and Paul K. Conkin deplores the President's inability to grasp systems of thought with their analytical and remedial efficacy.[10] Howard Zinn implies that Roosevelt should have been a thinker of the caliber of John Dewey or Reinhold Niebuhr, among others.[11] Dewey and Niebuhr, of course, lacked political "availability" and could not become presidential candidates with a chance of winning the election. Moreover, if they had been politically effective, according to Conkin's logic they would have lost their intellectual force and energy.[12] The realistic alternatives to FDR as Democratic nominee in 1932—a good year for Democrats—were men like Al Smith, Newton D. Baker, and John Garner. It is conceivable that Roosevelt, having won the nomination and the election, could have used Dewey's and Niebuhr's ideas in a systematic way, but to do so he would have had to be a different man. To say that he should have been something other than what he was is like saying that if Charlemagne had been more imaginative he would have discovered America in 792. (There is a difference, it is true, between limitations on action stemming from Roosevelt's nature and those arising from conditions in general.)

There is also the question whether the American people would have accepted the systematic implementation of Dewey's and Niebuhr's ideas. To raise this question is to suggest that the times as well as the man, or "That Man in the White House," make history. Although one may wonder what kind of a President Baker or Garner or Smith would have been,[13] one cannot explain the history of the period 1933–1945 solely in terms of the personality of the squire from Hyde Park.[14] Admittedly there was an area of

10. James MacGregor Burns, *Roosevelt: The Lion and the Fox* (New York: Harcourt, Brace, 1956), p. 334; Conkin, *New Deal*, pp. 7–15, especially 10 and 14.

11. Zinn, *New Deal Thought*, p. xvii.

12. Auerbach, "New Deal, Old Deal, or Raw Deal," pp. 25–26, commenting on Conkin, *New Deal*, p. 105.

13. Frank Freidel, review of *Roosevelt: The Lion and the Fox* by James MacGregor Burns, in *American Historical Review* (January 1957), p. 421.

14. Dexter Perkins, *The New Age of Franklin Roosevelt, 1932–45* (Chicago: University of Chicago Press, 1957), pp. 70–74, is excellent on this point.

discretion within which Roosevelt considered his alternatives of action, and his policy decisions within this area can be accepted or rejected or debated. The choices FDR might have made, however, fell within a range that was narrower than the New Left historians recognize.

Historians who agree that the times as well as the man make history often inquire whether Roosevelt was ahead of or behind his times, whether he was bold or timid. Frequently they consider a corollary of this question: did FDR move in advance of or did he follow public opinion? As one might expect, the answers vary. The "revisionists" insist that the President was bold enough to expose the fleet at Pearl Harbor in 1941, while other historians conclude that in formulating and implementing an anti-Axis policy, FDR was "reluctant" and a party to appeasement.[15] Dexter Perkins qualifies the alleged boldness of some of Roosevelt's actions in the field of foreign policy, such as the destroyers-for-bases deal of 1940 with Britain, by pointing out that public opinion concerning these measures was decidedly favorable.[16] In domestic affairs, in the view of some historians, FDR sponsored a revolution,[17] which implies considerable boldness, while other scholars stress the evolutionary character of the New Deal.[18] The President's hesitancy with respect to the enactment of the Wagner Labor Relations Act is often cited as illustrating the way he followed public opinion and his cautious approach to new departures. Less attention is paid to a presidential attitude that

15. Robert A. Divine, *The Reluctant Belligerent: American Entry into World War II* (New York: Wiley, 1965); Arnold A. Offner, *American Appeasement: United States Foreign Policy and Germany, 1933–38* (Cambridge, Mass.: Harvard University Press, 1969).

16. Dexter Perkins, "Was Roosevelt Wrong?," *Virginia Quarterly Review* (Summer 1954), reprinted in Gerald N. Grob and George Athan Billias, eds., *Interpretations of American History* (New York: Free Press, 1967), II, 414–418; William L. Langer and S. Everett Gleason continually question FDR's boldness, in terms similar to Perkins' view, in *The Challenge to Isolation, 1937–1940* (New York: Harper, 1952). Ernest R. May summarizes public opinion research and concepts in "An American Tradition in Foreign Policy: The Role of Public Opinion," in William H. Nelson, ed., *Theory and Practice in American Politics* (Chicago: University of Chicago Press, Phoenix Books, 1964), pp. 100–121.

17. Carl N. Degler, *Out of Our Past: The Forces That Shaped Modern America* (New York: Harper, 1959), Chapter 13, "The Third American Revolution," pp. 379–416.

18. Richard S. Kirkendall, "The Great Depression: Another Watershed in American History?," in John Braeman, *et al.*, eds., *Change and Continuity in Twentieth-Century America* (Columbus: Ohio State University Press, 1964), pp. 146–189, and Kirkendall, "The New Deal as Watershed: The Recent Literature," *Journal of American History* (March 1968).

perhaps more strikingly makes the same point—Roosevelt's reluctant acceptance of the less controversial act establishing deposit insurance.[19] Some historians judge the reforms of 1935 as the result of FDR's belligerent response to "thunder on the right," a response merely accelerated by "thunder on the left."[20] Others consider these reforms the product of the President's belated reaction to "a public clamor . . . for much more to be done."[21]

Virtually every student of Roosevelt and the New Deal looks upon him as a political animal and assigns great weight to this trait as a determinant of his conduct, but, again, estimates vary. Rexford Tugwell sees FDR as exhibiting the "ambivalence of a political reformer seeking to bring about changes while maintaining his own sources of strength"[22] because he had to "gain his people's victories against odds, often, and always against potentially powerful opposition."[23] In 1956 James MacGregor Burns held that the President, in his unwillingness to "risk endangering the integration of his followers in trying to improve their position . . . failed to exercise creative leadership."[24] In 1960 Burns took a quite different view, stressing the limitations on executive leadership."[25] Similarly, in 1948 Richard Hofstadter called Roosevelt an "opportunist,"[26] but in 1960 he confessed, "My opinion of F.D.R. has gone up as my understanding of what can and cannot be done in the political processes has increased."[27]

Politics does not provide the whole explanation of the decisions Roosevelt made within the area of discretion noted above. Burns, whose indictment of FDR's politically derived caution has just been cited, also asserts that "the main reason for the President's

19. John A. Woods, *Roosevelt and Modern America* (London: English Universities Press, 1959), p. 40.

20. Basil Rauch, *The History of the New Deal, 1933–1938* (New York: Creative Age Press, 1944), pp. 138, 159; Burns, *Roosevelt: The Lion and the Fox*, pp. 224–225.

21. Clarke A. Chambers, ed., *The New Deal at Home and Abroad, 1919–1945* (New York: Free Press, 1965), p. 11.

22. Rexford G. Tugwell, *The Democratic Roosevelt* (Garden City, N.Y.: Doubleday, 1957), p. 370.

23. Rexford G. Tugwell, "The Compromising Roosevelt," *Western Political Quarterly* (June 1953), p. 341.

24. Burns, *Roosevelt: The Lion and the Fox*, p. 487n.

25. James MacGregor Burns, "Two-Party Stalemate: The Crisis in Our Politics," *Atlantic* (February 1960), p. 40.

26. Richard Hofstadter, *The American Political Tradition and the Men Who Made It* (New York: Knopf, 1948), Chapter 12, "Franklin D. Roosevelt: The Patrician as Opportunist," pp. 311–347.

27. Quoted in David Hawke, "Interview: Richard Hofstadter," *History 3* (New York: Meridian Books, 1960), p. 139.

failure in the economic sphere . . . lay neither in the political situation nor his divided advisers. . . . His main trouble was intellectual."[28] Certainly the best politics is the adoption of policies that deal effectively with the most pressing problems of the times. If FDR "was likely to be on the scene for some time," Tugwell writes, "his policies would have to meet the administrative tests."[29]

Roosevelt's first tasks were to combat the depression, then to win the war. Accordingly, race relations had little of the urgency they have acquired in recent years.[30] The determination of priorities by a political leader often involves giving greater weight to one moral consideration than to another, which means, as Henry Taylor observed in 1836, that

> The rules of political morality seem to be less ascertained and agreed upon in general opinion than any other branch of philosophy that applies itself to the life of man; and this is owing perhaps to their being in their nature less determinate; for though the *first* principles of this, as of all other morality, are plain and definite, the derivative principles and their application in practice are not so.[31]

Nor does the decision that emerges from a calculation of priorities necessarily reflect the decision-maker's personal attitudes, as in the case of Lincoln's emancipation policy as he explained it in his famous letter to Horace Greeley: "I have stated here my purpose according to my view of official duty; and I intend no modification of my oft-expressed personal wish that all men everywhere could be free." Finally, if the calculation that one consideration must be subordinate to another is, let us say for purposes of discussion, in error, then the calculator may not be timid but simply wrong (he could, it is true, be both timid and wrong). In "The Secret Papers of FDR," Allan Morrison writes that Roosevelt's "failure to fight for civil rights can be ascribed to his conviction, *mistaken or not*, that such action would have split his party down the middle and torpedoed the entire edifice of social legislation for which he strove" (italics added). Even Morrison, who thinks FDR is over-rated as a benefactor of blacks, does not pronounce judgment on the strategic validity of the President's determination of priorities.

Running through the selections in this section are the dual

28. Burns, *Roosevelt: The Lion and the Fox*, p. 334.
29. Tugwell, *The Democratic Roosevelt*, pp. 370–371.
30. Auerbach, "New Deal, Old Deal, or Raw Deal," pp. 21–22.
31. Henry Taylor, *The Statesman* (New York: New American Library, 1958), p. 80.

themes of (1) limited white action—by the President, by a New Deal agency, by the Supreme Court, by Protestant denominations, and by labor unions—in behalf of the Negro, in the face of (2) determined white opposition to action beneficial to blacks (white Communists, some of whose activities in behalf of blacks are described by John Williams in "Struggles of the Thirties in the South," comprised only a small percentage of the white population). Let us say, again for purposes of discussion, that Roosevelt should not have limited at least his own action with respect to race relations as much as he did, that he was timid in this field because he was a timid man, or in the sense that even if his basic political calculations were wrong, he still could have helped black citizens more than he did. Implications to the contrary notwithstanding, I am prepared to accept the designation of FDR's policies toward the Negro as timid[32] in terms of the second alternative just noted. The question remains whether greater presidential boldness would have produced significant substantial results. In all probability, Roosevelt could more easily have accomplished more for Negroes in the executive sphere than through legislation (although in his article, John Salmond, while deploring the President's acquiescence in the CCC's discriminatory policies, emphasizes "a strong section of prevailing white opinion" as a causal agent).[33] President Truman defied the Southern wing of the Democratic party, for example, but the first civil rights act since 1875 was not passed until 1957, ten years after the President's Committee on Civil Rights issued its report, "To Secure These Rights."

In any event, let us suppose that in the area of civil rights all

32. Commenting on John A. Salmond's article, "The Civilian Conservation Corps and the Negro," reprinted in this anthology, Dwight W. Hoover, ed., *Understanding Negro History* (Chicago: Quadrangle Books, 1968), p. 311, writes that FDR "did much for Negro rights. . . . It is unfair to cast Roosevelt as a contemporary civil libertarian, but the memories of his opponents as well as his friends have distorted the record. In retrospect his policy seems timid."

33. Perkins, *The New Age of Franklin Roosevelt*, p. 74, asserts that FDR's "actual domination of the legislative process has been much exaggerated. His role was highly important at the outset; but by the beginning of his second term he had certainly ceased to control Congress." The necessity of operating the Resettlement Administration under an executive order of 1935 and the demise of its successor, the Farm Security Administration, at the hands of Congress in 1946, indicate the difficulty in the Roosevelt era of aiding underprivileged farmers, many of them black, through legislation. See Sidney Baldwin, *Poverty and Politics: The Rise and Decline of the Farm Security Administration* (Chapel Hill: University of North Carolina Press, 1968).

the executive orders issued since 1941 and all the bills passed
since 1957 had been issued and passed in the Roosevelt era—as
far as legislation is concerned, before June 1938, when the passage of the wages-and-hours bill marked the end of the New Deal
proper. Would problems in race relations now be minimal, or, if
that is a loaded question, how much better would they be? In
attempting to answer this question one confronts an historical
phenomenon more significant than Roosevelt's timidity (or political prudence). FDR has been dead nearly a quarter of a century, and the bills have been passed. Yet we are moving in the
direction of "two societies, one black, one white—separate and
unequal."[34]

34. Compare the white attitudes toward Negroes as of 1942, cited by
Richard Dalfiume in his article "The Forgotten Years of the Negro Revolu-
tion," with white attitudes as of 1963 in "How Whites Feel About Negroes,"
Newsweek (October 21, 1963), p. 50. "The Negro in America," *Newsweek*
(July 29, 1963), p. 16, reports that two in five Negroes think the white man
wants to keep blacks down, and one in five is "deeply alienated."

MY SECRET TALKS WITH FDR

MARY MCLEOD BETHUNE

Mrs. Bethune, a leading figure in Negro women's organizations and president of Bethune-Cookman College, became director of the Office of Minority Group Affairs in the National Youth Administration in 1934. (See Rackham Holt, Mary McLeod Bethune: A Biography [Garden City: Doubleday, 1964], and Catherine Owens Peare, Mary McLeod Bethune [New York: Vanguard, 1961].) FDR frequently called her to the White House for consultation, and in this selection she recalls some of their private conversations. She had deep personal affection for the President and firmly believed in his genuine humanitarianism and his determination to improve the lot of black citizens. "There are those," she writes, "who criticize FDR's slowness to move against basic evils in our midst and his obvious dislike of extreme methods of achieving his objectives. But it is important to understand that his methods were those of a man of great experience and insight."

❋

It will be four years this month since Franklin D. Roosevelt died. In those four years his enemies and detractors have worked incessantly to turn the minds of the people against what he stood for and did, have sought generally to tear down the great edifice of social legislation and true democratic practice which FDR built up in his lifetime.

By and large, though, the stature of Franklin D. Roosevelt has grown immensely in the four years since his death. Today he ranks second only to Lincoln as an outstanding figure of genius and achievement in our national history. Four years after he breathed his last in Warm Springs, he still dominates our national

Reprinted by permission from *Ebony*, IV (April 1949), 42–51.

political life, the one personality who charged this nation with a new energy and gave common people hope and dignity during some of the most critical years through which the country has passed.

I knew Franklin D. Roosevelt as a friend and as a political leader. I talked with him personally on scores of occasions, heard him laugh at a particularly funny story, or ruminate in silence over a grave piece of news. I have seen FDR when he was seriously ill, and when his voice was hoarse and full of suffering. I have looked into his face, gaunt and ashen from the frightful burdens of state and the exertions of an arduous schedule, and my heart has been filled with pity and sorrow for a great man who was working himself to death. I have chatted with FDR in the bright summer sunshine on the lawn of his Hyde Park family home and been filled with joy by his bright humor and strong optimism. I knew FDR over the years when he was fighting reaction in Albany and Washington, when he struck out at poverty through the New Deal and made enemies of the "economic royalists."

I heard his great eloquence denounce greed and intolerance from one end of the land to the other, and I discussed with him the problems of my people in many an off-the-record private talk held in the President's study in the White House. I loved that voice and was thrilled by it on innumerable occasions. To me it represented the voice of sanity and progress and humanism, and when it was stilled forever on April 12, 1945, I felt that the peoples of the world had lost one of their finest spokesmen and that the earth itself was a poorer place thereby.

America needs his kind of idealism today when war and depression face us as imminent possibilities. The world has need of his kind of leadership with all of its courage and clarity.

There are those who criticize FDR's slowness to move against basic evils in our midst and his obvious dislike of extreme methods of achieving his objectives. But it is important to understand that his methods were those of a man of great experience and insight. He was a man of great depth of mind and seldom made rash moves. I had many opportunities to study the man at work and in the midst of a crisis, and I was struck by the calm, exact, almost mathematical way in which he thought and moved.

I often expressed to him my impatience with the slowness of the democratic process. I remember going to see him one evening in 1943. I was feeling particularly distressed that day over reports

I had received on flagrant bias shown against Negroes seeking to enter the National Youth Administration in certain parts of the South. I called him direct that afternoon, and must have sounded awfully agitated.

"Anything wrong?" he asked in that fine strong voice.

"Yes," I answered, "quite a lot."

"Come over after dinner, Mrs. Bethune," he said, "I'll be glad to see you."

I entered the White House in a grim mood, and was escorted upstairs by an attendant who took me up in the President's private elevator.

"He's waiting for you now," the attendant said with a smile. I walked down the hallway to the President's private study and found him waiting for me with a pleasant smile on his face. Sitting in his chair near the door, he waved a greeting with his hand which held his famous cigarette holder.

"Come in, Mrs. Bethune," he called out. "I'm always glad to see you. And do you know why?" I said I didn't.

"Because you always come for others and never for yourself," he said.

His face relaxed and his eyes, though still bright, were searching my features. "How are you," he asked gently. "What can I do for you?"

I told him about the situation in NYA in the South, about the lack of training facilities for Negroes in certain Southern states and of the refusal of state governments to allocate funds for Negro NYA activities. Negroes could not enter the technical training schools established under NYA.

I was visibly disturbed and made the President aware of how I felt. I caught his arm and clung to him. "The Negro people need all of the strength that you can give, Mr. President, in opening up opportunities for them," I told him.

He looked at me seriously for a few seconds, and then said, "Mrs. Bethune, I shall not fail you. I'll see Aubrey Williams tomorrow, and everything that can be done to open up these sections of the South to NYA training for Negroes will be done. Your people and all minorities shall have their chance."

Altogether, I suppose, we talked for 40 minutes, touching on such subjects as anti-Negro discrimination, and the progress our forces were making in the war abroad. As I left, I shook his hand warmly and told him:

"Mr. President, the common people feel they have someone in the White House who cares." The President smiled gratefully and waved a goodbye.

That was not the last time that I felt impelled to speak out strongly to the President on conditions confronting Negroes in the South. More than once I proposed pretty drastic steps to end the hideous discriminations and second-class citizenship which make the South a blot upon our democracy. But FDR usually demurred, pointing out that a new Reconstruction in the South would have to keep pace with democratic progress on a national scale. He strove to bring the whole country into a unified understanding of freedom. He tried to hold the whole country together so that the whole might be one.

But President Roosevelt did not complete his work. Had he lived I am convinced that he would have launched new, bold offensives against bigotry and Jim Crow everywhere. But it would have been according to *his* plan.

Frequently I would ask him with some impatience why this couldn't be done at once or that done immediately. He would think awhile, and then say very carefully and patiently, "Mrs. Bethune, if we do that now, we'll hurt our program over there. We must do this thing stride by stride, but leaving no stone unturned."

FDR taught me much about practical politics and how important it is that we understand their meaning if we are to make progress in the political arena. My contact with him was one of the great experiences of my life.

He would say things that would remain with you for the rest of your life. Thus, one day, I think it was at a reception in 1940, he beckoned to me and opened up a conversation I shall always remember. "You know, Mrs. Bethune," he said, looking out of the window and yet speaking directly to me, "people like you and me are fighting, and must continue to fight, for the day when a man will be regarded as a man regardless of his race or faith or country. That day will come, but we must pass through perilous times before we realize it, and that's why it's so difficult today because that new idea is being born and many of us flinch from the thought of it. Justice must and will prevail."

That is why I believed so deeply in Franklin D. Roosevelt.

My friendship with FDR was based on more than personal regard for a great man. It flowed, to a large extent, from a long-standing acquaintanceship with the Roosevelt family, especially his mother, the late Mrs. James Roosevelt, one of the most gracious and genuine persons I have been privileged to know.

I first met that grand old lady at a luncheon Eleanor Roosevelt gave for representative women's leaders at the old Roosevelt family house in New York in 1924. I had just returned from a European tour and attended the luncheon as president of the National Association of Colored Women. Mrs. James Roosevelt, Sr., was present at the luncheon and it was there that I first met her.

I can still see the twinkle in Mrs. James Roosevelt's eyes as she noted the apprehensive glances cast my way by the Southern women who had come to the affair. Then she did a remarkable thing. Very deliberately, she took my arm and seated me to the right of Eleanor Roosevelt, in the seat of honor! I can remember, too, how the faces of the Negro servants lit up with pride when they saw me seated at the center of that imposing gathering of women leaders from all over the United States. From that moment my heart went out to Mrs. James Roosevelt. I visited her at her home many times subsequently, and our friendship became one of the most treasured relationships of my life. As a result of my affection for her mother-in-law, my friendship with Eleanor Roosevelt soon ripened into a close and understanding mutual feeling. She is today one of the dearest friends I have. Our lives have become deeply intertwined.

Strange as it may seem I did not meet FDR until 1934 when, as Negro Affairs Director, I attended a meeting of the Advisory Committee of the National Youth Administration held at the White House. I had been invited to become a member of the Advisory Committee upon its formation early that year.

I got to know FDR well during these Advisory Committee meetings which frequently were pretty intense affairs. The first meeting was unforgettable. FDR often referred to it in later conversations with me. The meeting had been called to review and report upon the first year's achievements of the National Youth Administration. I was asked to deliver a report on minority group activities. Speaking directly to the President, I told him what the NYA meant to minority groups. I told him that in many parts of the South the $15 and $20 monthly checks meant real salvation for thousands of Negro young people. I explained how we were working with the WPA authorities in providing adult education facilities for the parents of these young people.

"We are bringing life and spirit to these many thousands who for so long have been in darkness," I said. "I speak, Mr. President, not as Mrs. Bethune, but as the voice of 14,000,000 Americans who seek to achieve full citizenship. We want to continue to open doors for these millions."

When I had finished, I saw that tears were coursing down President Roosevelt's cheeks. He leaned across the table and grasped my hands in both of his.

"Mrs. Bethune," he said, "I am glad I am able to contribute something to help make a better life for your people. I want to assure you that I will continue to do my best for them in every way." He choked a little. Tears flowed from his eyes. There was a stillness in the room for a moment and then the meeting dispersed. As I left the room, Aubrey Williams who was National Youth Administrator, placed his hand on my shoulder, and said:

"Mrs. Bethune, thanks to you, a marvelous impression has been made tonight for the cause we all represent."

Two weeks later I received a letter from the White House, informing me that the President wished to see me. I went to Washington and hurried to the office of Aubrey Williams. Aubrey was smiling broadly.

"I have wonderful news for you," he said. He told me that President Roosevelt had decided to set up an Office of Minority Affairs of NYA and that I was to be its administrator. I pleaded with Aubrey that I could not accept the appointment because of the great pressure of my work at the college.

"You'll just have to find someone else for the job," I told him.

Aubrey's face was grave. "I'm afraid you'll have to do it. Don't you realize this is the first such post created for a Negro woman in the U.S.?" I was silent, realizing that here indeed was a heavy responsibility.

"You will have to do it," Aubrey repeated emphatically. It was not an easy decision to make. I thought of the splendid job Frances Perkins was doing in the Department of Labor, and Mary Anderson in the Children's Bureau of the same department, and I felt that if these talented white women were working at such responsible jobs at a time of national crisis I could do the same thing. I visualized dozens of Negro women coming after me, filling positions of high trust and strategic importance. God, I knew, would give me the requisite strength, wisdom and administrative ability to do the job. I told Aubrey I would accept.

Later that day we went over to see the President. Aubrey told him of my decision. The President turned to me, beaming, "I have thought over very carefully the message you brought to me some weeks ago," he said, "and we have decided to open a department that Aubrey here has chosen to call, the Office of Minority Group Affairs. We have appointed you to administer this office. I want you to know that I do not believe anybody can do this work more acceptably than you can."

I said, "Thank you, Mr. President, for your thoughtfulness and deep concern for my people and all minorities that need help. You have been most gracious in permitting me to share so deeply in such a great cause. In accepting this appointment, I assure you that I shall give it the best that I have and shall follow very closely the guiding hand of our great Administrator, Aubrey Williams, who is giving so fully of himself for this cause that is so dear to your heart."

FDR was visibly impressed. "Aubrey," he said, after a pause and looking in my direction, "Mrs. Bethune is a great woman. I believe in her because she has her feet on the ground; not only on the ground, but deep down in the ploughed soil." I shall never forget that compliment.

It was always pleasant and stimulating to work with Aubrey Williams. Aubrey is one of my favorite people whose faith in the liberal way has grown stronger with the years. He is, I am convinced, one of America's foremost fighting liberals who has made a very real contribution to the Negro's cause.

The office of Minority Affairs functioned for 10 years and brought many tangible benefits to Negro young people throughout the country. It worked vigorously to erase race differentials operating in the NYA and to extend training and educational opportunities for Negroes. On higher education alone, our office distributed some $100,000 yearly, mainly to the graduate schools of such institutions as Howard, Fisk, Atlanta Universities and many of the Northern universities where Negroes were studying. No government agency did more to stimulate higher education among Negroes than did the Office of Minority Group Affairs of the NYA.

President Roosevelt maintained a consistent interest in this phase of the NYA program and was once instrumental in actually saving it from total destruction by Congress. A Congressional Committee had earmarked our $100,000 special higher education fund for elimination in a new sweeping economy program affecting such agencies as NYA and the WPA. There were long faces at the NYA headquarters in Washington. One morning Aubrey Williams told me of the real danger facing our program and suggested that I speak to FDR about it. I got his secretary, Matthew Connelly, on the phone at once and arranged an appointment for that very day.

I found the President in his office, looking a little worried, but still managing to greet me with a charming smile. I began by referring to the attempt to wipe out the $100,000 fund for graduate training for Negroes and told him what a disaster that would be for the potential leaders of the Negro people who were seeking training in various fields. As I urged him to stop Congress from making the projected cuts in the NYA appropriations, I became so excited that I shook my finger in the President's face.

"Think what a terrible tragedy it would be for America," I cried, "if by this action by a committee of Congress, Negroes would be deprived of the leadership of skilled and trained members of their race!" Suddenly I realized what I was doing, and stopped, staring embarrassedly at my finger now pointing at the President's nose. I apologized for being so demonstrative.

"Oh Mr. President," I said, "I did not mean to become so emotional."

FDR smiled quietly, "I understand thoroughly, Mrs. Bethune," he said. "My heart is with you." After hearing him promise to "see what I can do," I left.

That week Congress voted to continue the full appropriation grant to our National Youth Administration program.

Once at a meeting of NYA administrative heads held with the President at Hyde Park in 1937, I had the pleasure of lunching with the Chief Executive and telling him more about the Negro's problems. As we talked, the President told me how important he considered youth to the future of the nation. "We must continue to work to guarantee life and strength to American youth, Mrs. Bethune," he said. "We must equip them in body and mind with the necessary proportions to combat the problems of life."

The conversation turned to the South, and I told FDR how Negro youth were gradually being integrated into NYA programs there. He was very pleased. "I know something about the difficulties of work in the South," he said, "and I know you have the tact, common sense and courage to work these problems out. You know, it takes these qualities to handle these problems, and I think you have got them in abundance. I want you to know that you have meant more to our program than I can express in words. Aubrey thinks of you as his right hand. I want you to stand by us in the difficult times that are ahead of us."

As my work brought me more and more into contact with the President I became much better acquainted with his wife, whom I regard as one of the most distinguished Americans of our time and one of the great women of all time. My association with Eleanor Roosevelt has been one of the most enriching of my entire life. Our friendship has combined a deep, abiding understanding with a warm kinship that has been strengthened over the years.

We have traveled together all over this country, and have addressed all kinds of meetings from a hundred and one platforms from coast to coast. We have worked together to establish a co-operative interracialism on various college campuses, and have sponsored conferences on race relations in the heart of the South. My admiration for her liberal outlook and fighting courage has increased with the development of our friendship.

Eleanor Roosevelt has done more to better race relations and to give the "human touch" to the affairs of state and the democratic struggle than any other woman I have known.

She and I have been closely associated in many things almost continuously since I arrived in Washington early in 1934 to assume my duties as head of the Office of Minority Affairs of the NYA. In the intervening years we have not hesitated to draw on each other's experience and counsel. We have had frequent consultations, either at my home on Vermont Avenue or at the White House or in New York at her Washington Square apartment, on such matters as Negro affairs, the political situation, women's problems, the South, my school, the National Council of Negro Women, and the international picture.

During FDR's years as President Mrs. Roosevelt held a series of meetings at the White House for the benefit of Bethune-Cookman College, at which I was introduced to selected groups of her friends and visiting dignitaries.

One afternoon in 1944 I received a telephone call from Mrs. Roosevelt, saying she wished to have a talk with me. I asked her whether I should meet her at the White House.

"Are you busy?" she asked.

"Well, just a little," I replied. "But I'll come over if you want me to."

"Stay where you are," she said, "I'll be over in a few minutes."

Twenty minutes later I happened to look out the window, and saw Mrs. Roosevelt striding briskly along Vermont Avenue. I gasped. She had walked over from the White House.

One of the most stirring events in which Mrs. Roosevelt figured was a huge meeting held at Bethune-Cookman College in 1941. Mrs. Roosevelt was the main speaker, and over 20,000 persons had come from all over southern Florida to hear her. The sight of these many thousands of Southerners, white and black, mingling freely and democratically on the campus of a Negro college in Florida, was an unforgettable experience. Aubrey Williams, who was present, was terribly moved by the scene. So were the score of public officials and representatives of every college in Florida who had come to pay their respects to the First Lady of the land.

On another occasion we were both scheduled to address a mass meeting in 1943 at the Golden Gate Ballroom in Harlem, held in aid of Bethune-Cookman College. I was the first speaker, and as I reached the climax of my appeal for support of the college, my voice cracked and I began to cough badly. The audience became a little uneasy. Mrs. Roosevelt, who was sitting at the far end of the platform, got up at once, walked over to the table placed in the center and poured me a glass water. She handed it to me, smiling graciously, and said, "Drink this. It will help."

It was a very dramatic gesture, full of simplicity and kindness.

A little over a year ago, Helen Gahagan Douglas, that fine liberal Congresswoman from California, gave a garden party at her Hollywood home for Eleanor Roosevelt and myself. Among the guests were many famous names in the film colony. Actors, writers, directors, producers. Toward the end of the afternoon, Mrs. Roosevelt brought Walter Wanger, the famous producer, over and introduced him to me.

"You know, Mr. Wanger," she said with a smile, "you ought to think seriously about making a film of Mrs. Bethune. Her career is one of the great romances of our time." I was flattered, but Mr. Wanger quickly caught the idea and said he would seriously look into the picture possibilities of such a theme.

Who wouldn't be proud to know such a woman. Who wouldn't feel thrilled, as I did on the night of March 3, 1948, when at a testimonial dinner given for me at the Hotel Commodore in New York, Eleanor Roosevelt told the audience: "I am happy to be counted among the people who can call Mrs. Bethune friend, and I hope that my friendship with her will be lasting and grow warmer and warmer as the years go by." I would like to add that this is also my most fervent hope.

As the world crisis sharpened between the years 1938 and 1941 and the shadow of a new, terrible world war lengthened across the globe, FDR became increasingly preoccupied with America's role in the international drama; the necessity to devote more and more time to holding the line at home against the attacks of his domestic enemies made him literally one of the busiest men on earth. Yet I was able to see him practically any time I requested an audience. He always seemed to be able to find time to see people who, in his words, were "doing things." I was privileged to be considered a member of this circle. From 1933 to 1945 I saw FDR six or seven times each year. He never refused to see me, and I, realizing the tremendous burden he was carrying, never asked to see him unless on a matter of importance. He knew that and hence always granted my requests for conferences.

Sometimes he asked to see me. There were a number of these times when he wanted to discuss with me problems that were weighing on his mind, usually issues of direct concern to the Negro people. In such instances he would have either Marvin McIntyre or General Edwin M. Watson, his secretaries, call me.

"Mrs. Bethune," they would say, "the President would like to see you today. Can you come over this afternoon about 3?" I can't remember a single occasion when I was too busy to see the Chief Executive. One just couldn't turn down an urgent call from President Roosevelt to come over to the White House.

Our White House conferences almost always took place in the East Wing and were generally held in his office. Evenings we would talk in his study or sometimes in one of the reception rooms. The physical pattern of our conversations had a certain similarity about them. He would wave to me gaily with his widely-publicized cigarette holder. Sometimes I would enter as he was in the act of inserting a cigarette into the holder. He would look up, smile, and say, "Come in, Mrs. Bethune. I'm so glad to see you. Have a cigarette?"

He would thrust an open cigarette box toward me, nodding his head gently. "Do have a cigarette."

"Mr. President," I'd say, "I haven't learned to smoke yet." His brow would wrinkle a little, and he would search his mind quickly for his last impression of me.

"You haven't," he would say. "Well, I have a duty to perform yet, haven't I? I must teach you how to smoke." We would both laugh at that.

At the height of World War II Franklin D. Roosevelt was frequently made aware of the widespread discontent among the Negro people arising from their restricted role in the war effort and repeated violence against Negro servicemen throughout the South. I had occasion to speak to him personally about these things. Several times in 1943 and 1944 I, together with Walter White, the executive secretary of the NAACP, and Dr. Channing Tobias, director of the Phelps-Stokes Fund, conferred with the President on the mounting grievances of Negro servicemen.

"I'll press every button I can press to see that these conditions are cleaned up, that colored Americans in uniform are given equal protection of the law and that the unfortunate problems you speak of are overcome," he told us one day. Some changes did result from our protests and proposals. Certainly the projected Jim Crow rest and rehabilitation centers for returning combat veterans never materialized. That was one victory for which FDR must be given large credit. As soon as it was reported that the Army was planning to establish "separate" hotels in New York and Chicago to accommodate Negro overseas veterans, White, Tobias and I saw the President and urged him to use all of his authority to stop it. FDR instructed General George C. Marshall, then Chief of Staff, that there was to be no segregation in the Army's rehabilitation program, and there was none.

Later, at the request of General Marshall, I visited one of the Army's rehabilitation centers in Atlantic City and saw white and Negro GI's billeted together at the same hotels, and getting along wonderfully. I asked one Negro GI how he was getting along. "Everything's just wonderful," he told me.

"You can thank your President," I whispered.

When President Roosevelt died suddenly in the little white cottage at the top of Pine Mountain at Warm Springs on the afternoon of April 12, I was in Dallas, Texas. I had gone there to make a speech at Samuel Houston College. Because of the poor state of my health, Dr. James Lowell Hall, my physician, accompanied me on the trip.

It had been a trying day, and I was sitting in the living room of the home of a Dallas friend. Suddenly Dr. Hall burst into the room, his face full of grief. He was visibly agitated.

"I don't want you to excite yourself," he said, "but I have very bad news for you . . . the worst possible news."

"What is it?" I asked fearfully.

"It has just come over the radio that President Roosevelt has died."

I sat, stunned, for ten minutes, saying nothing to anybody. It was hard to realize that he was gone. When the awful reality of the tragedy came home to me, I collected myself and sent a wire to Mrs. Roosevelt at the White House. I told her how I felt at the terrible news and that I was coming to Washington.

I had some difficulty getting a plane back to Washington. All of the planes were booked to capacity. Finally, following the personal intervention of the State Democratic Chairman we were able to get two plane reservations for Dr. Hall and myself. It was a long, sad flight. We arrived in Washington at 9 the following morning. I was immediately informed that arrangements had been made for me to participate in a national radio broadcast consisting of messages from leaders and spokesmen of all walks of life. I was asked to speak for the Negro people.

After the broadcast, I got in touch with the White House and learned that the body of the President was arriving the following day. With a heavy heart I went over to Constitution Avenue early the next day and saw my favorite President return from his last trip. I attended the funeral services held in the East Room of the White House on April 14th and found it impossible to restrain my feelings. I wept openly like a little child. I looked at the flag-draped bier and my mind went back to the time when we first met, and I had moved him to tears by my impassioned plea for my people's rights. I recalled holding his hands and looking into his fine, strong face, and telling him how much the common people depended on him. I remembered all this and many other wonderful little things that he had done for me and for my people.

As I left the East Room I was conscious only of a vast sense of loss that pervaded the democratic world. On that day I felt that something big and fine and brave had dropped out of the world, that we had lost our greatest leader. There were sobs and tears in the East Room that day and all over the world. I felt like I had lost a dear, close relative. And indeed, I had.

THE SECRET PAPERS OF FDR

ALLAN MORRISON

In this selection Allan Morrison, a member of the staff of the Ne-gro Digest, weighs Roosevelt's record after examining cor-respondence in the Franklin D. Roosevelt Library at Hyde Park. Morrison, as noted above in the introduction to this section, does not pronounce judgment on FDR's basic political calcula-tions, but he conveys the distinct impression that he is much less sympathetic than Mrs. Bethune toward the President's perform-ance regarding race relations. He denies that Roosevelt was the Negro's "20th-Century Emancipator."

❀

That Franklin Delano Roosevelt was a great President, humani-tarian and a master politician is an indisputable fact, but that he was the Negro's "Great White Father," his 20th Century Emanci-pator and his God, is becoming a subject of growing debate, even among Negro Democrats.

Like Lincoln, but much sooner after death, FDR's motives and behind-the-White House deals and compromises are being brought to light and re-evaluated today without the hysteria of war or the desperation of a depression. The flood of books and ar-ticles that are being published on the life of FDR bid fair to over-taking the voluminous and ever-increasing Lincolniana.

A mountain of material among the private papers of FDR which have recently been made available to the public will release another literary avalanche. To get a better portrait of FDR and his beliefs as well as actions on the Negro I recently spent several days searching through his correspondence in the Hyde Park li-brary. I found that Mr. Roosevelt did not do as much for the Negro

Reprinted by permission from *Negro Digest*, IX (January 1951), 3–13.

as is believed and was never as liberal as he seemed. His thinking on the Negro was fuzzy and he always had to be pressed for remedial action which seldom came.

Consummate politician that he was, FDR never acted on an idealistic impulse, but weighed each move in terms of its tactical importance. The struggle to realize his political program was to him a constant search for realistic strategy, a sort of running chess game. He felt he knew the strength of his opposition, both in Congress and throughout the country, and fashioned his strategy to win the support of the vital majority. "First things first," was an axiom of FDR's.

Tragically, the gnawing problem of the Negro people's marginal existence in the world's strongest democracy did not seem to have a very high priority on his list of things to be done. He regarded the Negro as an integral part of the nation, entitled to but often denied equal citizenship rights. But he did not apparently consider the Negro's cause vital enough to jeopardize the bulk of his legislative program to which he was committed and for which he needed the votes of anti-Negro Southern congressmen and senators.

This overriding respect for the Southern bloc was a dominating factor in FDR's total strategy. He was convinced that to alienate the Southern Democrats in Congress would have been fatal to the New Deal. The record shows that throughout his years at the White House FDR leaned over backwards to keep from offending Southern legislators and thus losing votes he believed to be crucially important. His failure to vigorously champion civil rights legislation can only be explained by his desperate resolve to maintain the unholy alliance he had formed with the Southerners in his party.

There was another reason why he frequently failed to take a forthright position regarding the Negro. Included in his immediate circle of advisers and secretaries were several Southerners, flinty veterans of the Washington scene like Steve Early, Marvin McIntyre and Jonathan Daniels. These gentlemen read the President's mail, often drafted most of the replies to letters which went out over FDR's signature. FDR's secretarial staff constituted themselves the watchdogs of his political interests. He leaned strongly on them for advice on touchy issues like the persistent protest by Negroes against the whole framework of segregation.

One of the functions of FDR's advisers was to think up politely-worded brush-offs to Negro organizations and individuals who wanted the President to do something about embarrassing things like discrimination in government-run cafeterias in Washington, Southern poll taxes and the Army's racial policy. Part of their job was to keep the President from antagonizing either of the disputants in the nation's race question and avoid making commitments that might split the party.

The ubiquitous Eleanor Roosevelt was a source of constant irritation to certain of FDR's advisers who felt her activities with and for Negroes were damaging to the President's relations with the white South. "My husband had had advisers and people who worked with him who were from the South," Mrs. Roosevelt told me recently. "They felt that some of the things I did were inadvisable, but they never prevented me from doing them."

FDR never tried to discourage his wife from voicing her belief in human equality or engaging in the multitude of activities across the country that brought her into close contact with Negroes. In her autobiography, *This I Remember*, Mrs. Roosevelt comments as follows on how her work in race relations was viewed by certain members of the President's staff: ". . . other people were frequently less happy about my actions. I knew, for instance that many of my racial beliefs and activities in the field of social work caused Steve Early and Marvin McIntyre grave concern. They were afraid I would hurt my husband politically and socially."

A proposal made by FDR in the Spring of 1941 before the march on Washington movement grew to threatening proportions shows that he was not averse to using the racial quota system as a means of creating more jobs for Negroes and thus warding off the multiplying attacks on America's treatment of its largest minority at a time when the non-fascist world regarded this country as the "arsenal of democracy."

FDR's Negro critics claimed he had no plan for the alleviation of the Negro's plight, that his gestures on racial relations were not spontaneous but dictated by the searing exigencies of politics. There is evidence that on May 26, 1941, he wrote a memorandum to William S. Knudsen, the director-general of the Office of Production Management, which contained a rather naive plan for dealing with the problem. The cryptic memo dictated to a secretary read: "Knudsen-Hillman O.P.M. To order taking Negroes up to a certain % in factory order work. Judge them on *quality*. The 1st class Negroes are being turned down for 3rd class white boys. ?? FDR"

Knudsen, whose role in the FEPC battle left a sour taste with Negro leaders spearheading the fight, promptly replied to the President's memorandum with a weak alternative which he credited to Sidney Hillman, his then associate director-general of the O.P.M. "I have talked with Mr. Hillman," Knudsen wrote FDR, "and he will quietly get manufacturers to increase the number of Negroes in defense work."

Knudsen, who was against federal action of the FEPC type, cautioned FDR against his percentage plan of integration. "If we set a percentage," he said, "it will immediately be open to dispute. Quiet work with the contractors and the unions will bring better results." Three days after FDR dictated his "percentage plan" memorandum, A. Philip Randolph threw his Sunday punch at him in a letter formally notifying him that a National Negro March On Washington Committee had been set up to accomplish precisely what the government had failed to do. Knudsen's "quiet" methods proved utterly unavailing.

Though FDR had been asked more than once to end racial discrimination in government employment, he had not done so, and it was not until the FEPC fight had been successfully waged that he was prevailed upon to issue a similar charge to the heads of all government departments. His letter to department heads was sent on Sept. 3, 1941, and was actually suggested by Mark Ethridge, the Louisville newspaper man whom he had appointed FEPC chairman. The behind-the-scene discussions on this matter make interesting reading now.

Ethridge wrote Steve Early on Aug. 20, discussing the functions of the new FEPC and referring sneeringly to Negro mass pressure which had brought it about: "As you know the Negroes wanted the executive order as a sort of second Emancipation Proclamation. They wanted the setup entirely outside of the Office of Production Management with LaGuardia as chairman and, I suppose, somebody like Winston Churchill would have satisfied them as executive secretary. I think the agitators had got themselves into such a position with a threatened march that they wanted to make the abandonment of the march appear to come as the result of a great victory." Ethridge referred to a letter which had been prepared for FDR's signature which explained that since the President had ordered no discrimination in private industry obviously there could be no discrimination in government agencies.

FDR envisioned the New Deal as a great, all-embracing plan

for the rehabilitation of America's depression-ridden population, and refused to consider Negroes separately even though they suffered in a different, sharper way than the rest of the people. Beset by a series of emergencies in the early critical days of his first administration, he found no time for minority problems. His 1933 inaugural address said nothing about the Negro's position. The President's Negro critics seized on this in an effort to prove that the government was unfriendly to the Negroes' cause. His failure to mention the Negro in his inaugural address was commented on by Negro nationalists and Communists alike.

Lionel A. Francis, President-General of the Universal Negro Improvement Association, wrote FDR pointing out the "need for immediate and determined action towards the alleviation of the underprivileged position of our people, economically, socially, and politically, and that discrimination should not continue to render inoperative, in the case of our people, measures intended for the relief of the nation as a whole." This reasoned, wisely phrased warning was ignored by the President on the advice of one of his aides who read the communication and passed it on to the President with a brief penciled comment, "This does not reflect opinion of the thinking people."

FDR, who wanted to voice the aspirations of the "forgotten man," was often reminded during his first year of office that the Negro people were the "most forgotten of forgotten men." Roosevelt's earnest efforts to speak for "forgotten people" brought him hundreds of letters from Negroes all over the country, most of which reiterated the theme that the Negroes stood lowest among America's forgotten people, and that definite, special action was needed in their behalf. Typical of these was a moving letter, simply written, from a Negro in Scranton, Pa., who criticized Republican inaction in the past, and told the President: "I think you have a chance to make the Democratic Party progressive enough that it will stand out for the people and the country, to be remembered even longer than Lincoln or Washington." It was signed, "One of the many forgotten men."

As if in answer to the many countless appeals from Negroes to be included in the New Deal, FDR, in an address at Howard University Oct. 26, 1936, declared: "Among American citizens, there should be no forgotten man and no forgotten race."

Negroes had already started their historic switch from the party of Lincoln to the party of Roosevelt, and were fast becoming the pivotal factor in national politics. During the first two years of the New Deal, FDR was deluged with letters, statements, resolutions, memorandums, petitions and proposals for the improvement of the Negroes' position. These dealt with the Negroes' various ills and grievances, lynching, disfranchisement, peonage, and the maladministration of justice typified by the Scottsboro case. FDR was bombarded from all sides with appeals for special legislation to correct these racial abuses. Most of this correspondence was handled by either the late Louis Howe or Marvin McIntyre, using a form letter which said, "Your letter of . . . . . with accompanying copy of petition has been received and will be brought to the President's attention."

Roosevelt did break with tradition by appointing a number of Negro advisers, most of whom had rendered yeoman political service to the Democratic Party. Some of the members of this "black cabinet," as it was called, possessed high talent and training. Few of these appointments came from FDR. A good many of them were the result of insistent suggestions by Mrs. Roosevelt, Harold L. Ickes, and Dr. Will W. Alexander, former head of the Farm Security Administration. These appointments led to others, and the whole race relations picture in Washington changed drastically as job barriers to Negroes in the federal government were broken down.

The Negro's new aggressiveness in politics paid substantial dividends even though resistance to change was strong at all levels of New Deal officialdom. Negro federal employees increased from 50,000 in 1933 to over 200,000 in 1946. Segregation was wiped out in a number of government agencies, and Negroes were eventually allowed to eat in most department cafeterias in Washington. These changes, however, could not be credited to FDR personally, or his so-called "black cabineteers," but to the Negroes' rising militancy and political strength.

Apart from his personal servants, Roosevelt saw few Negroes regularly. One of his best political friends was Dr. William T. Thompkins of Kansas City, whom he appointed Recorder of Deeds for the District of Columbia. He knew a number of Negroes in the Democratic Party fairly well, such as Robert L. Vann; Julian Raincy, Boston, and F. B. Ransome, Indianapolis; and the dynamic Mrs. Mary McLeod Bethune. FDR probably saw Mrs. Bethune and Dr. Thompkins as often as any other Negro leaders, certainly he seemed to derive more enjoyment from talking to these two staunch Democratic workers than with most of the others. Mrs. Bethune, who first met FDR in 1934 and had numer-

ous meetings with him after that, has described his unwillingness
to support the kind of action that would lose southern support:

"More than once I proposed pretty drastic steps to end the hideous discriminations and second-class citizenship which make the
South a blot upon our democracy. But FDR usually demurred,
pointing out that a new Reconstruction in the South would have
to keep pace with democratic progress on a national scale. He
strove to bring the whole country into a unified understanding of
freedom. He tried to hold the whole country together so that the
whole might be one.

"But President Roosevelt did not complete his work. Had he
lived, I am convinced that he would have launched new, bold offensives against bigotry and Jim Crow everywhere. But it would
have been according to *his* plan."

On another occasion, FDR told Mrs. Bethune, "People like you
and me are fighting and must continue to fight for the day when a
man will be regarded as a man regardless of his race or faith or
country. That day will come, but we must pass through perilous
times before we realize it, and that is why it is so difficult today, because that new idea is being born and many of us flinch from the
thought of it. Justice must and will prevail." A glance at the Roosevelt papers, now open to the public, reveals little about the work-
ings of FDR's complicated mind, but they clearly prove that Roosevelt had no plan or policy to guide him in dealing with the ever
present race problem.

"FDR was an improviser as well as a compromiser," says Walter
White, who knew him well and who found frequent occasion to
criticize him most vigorously. "My main criticism of him over and
over again was that he did not go as far as he had power to go. I
don't think that he had any sense of prejudice, however."

FDR was often asked to make statements against lynchings and
in favor of anti-lynching legislation. One such appeal from the
Chicago NAACP was intercepted by Steve Early who bluntly replied to the Association's request: "The President is unable to
comment individually on any bills pending before Congress."
That same year, FDR did denounce the lynching evil in an address
delivered to the Federal Council of Churches of Christ in America.

His failure to declare himself on Negro issues became increasingly obvious four years after his election, so much so that in
1936, George W. Lawrence, President of the National Bar Association, told Steve Early in a letter, "So far as I have been able to
ascertain, President Roosevelt has made no statement, either in

his address or in his messages to Congress, as to proposals submitted to the Democratic National Convention concerning the
attainment of full citizenship rights of Negroes."

Lawrence warned that FDR's attitude on Negro voting freedom,
civil rights, and anti-lynching legislation "will determine in a
large measure whether he will receive the support of the millions
of colored American citizens." The 1936 vote proved, however,
that Negroes approved of the Roosevelt record, not because they
had received any special racial benefits, but because of the progressive features of the New Deal's relief and recovery measures.
Republican efforts to win back the Negro vote were fruitless.

As the international situation became more critical, Roosevelt
felt increasingly dependent upon Southern reactionaries to support his foreign and domestic policy. Civil rights bills died in Congress without determined administration backing. FDR had never
supported the many proposals for the repeal of poll taxes by federal enactment. He was loathe to start an open fight with the
Southern reactionaries on what he considered "secondary" issues.
FDR was determined to stay clear of the sensitive questions of
race for as long as possible, and by so doing, prevent a revolt by the
Southern wing of his party. In following this policy, he was almost
brutal in rejecting the many impassioned appeals for White House
leadership in the fight against bigotry, disfranchisement, and Jim
Crow.

On June 26, 1936, Walter White wired FDR expressing the
grave disappointment of "politically independent Negro Americans" over failure of the Democratic convention in Philadelphia
that month to include in its platform any reference to lynching,
disfranchisement, and economic injustice of which Negroes were
the chief victims. He urged the President to correct this omission
in his acceptance speech. FDR did no such thing, but preserved
party unity and insured Southern support of his ticket.

Mrs. Eleanor Roosevelt, who was far more informed on Negro
life than her famous husband, has defended FDR's policy of holding the Southern group in line at the expense of vital domestic
changes. "It's quite obvious," she stated recently to me, "that in his
relationship with Congress he had to hold the Southern vote. . . .
He had to have the Southern vote, for instance, on such things as
re-armament for Pearl Harbor."

Mrs. Roosevelt also clears up a subject which students of the
Roosevelt era have frequently found perplexing, namely her reported differences with FDR on strategy involving measures to aid

the Negro people. Some Washington observers claimed that FDR and his wife did not see eye to eye, for instance, on the necessity for FEPC. To this Mrs. Roosevelt replies: "I do not remember our differing on the principles underlying the FEPC. There may have been some question in his mind as to the timing because of doing things at the proper time, and not jeopardizing issues which he felt of primary importance."

The Negro's "fight to fight" in World War II probably caused FDR more worry and presented him with more difficult dilemmas than any other campaign with which he had ever been confronted. The War Department was especially vulnerable because of its stubborn stand against liberal use of Negro manpower in combat units.

When a delegation of Negro leaders called upon the President, demanding that something be done about the pitiful representation of Negroes in the services and the subordinate role assigned them almost everywhere, he told them flatly that Negro units would be organized throughout the Army, both combat and service types. He added that the government had not yet developed plans for training Negro officers or medical commissioned personnel or Negroes in the Air Corps.

Knox was even more blunt. He said the racial integration problem in the Navy was beyond immediate solution. "Men have to live together on ships," he explained, adding that it was impossible to have "Southern" and "Northern" ships.

There is a widespread belief still current that FDR did not approve of Army Jim Crow. However, on Oct. 9, 1940, he OK'd and he initialled a decisive statement outlining "War Department policy in regard to Negroes." It said that Negro units would be activated in each major branch of the service and that the number of Negroes in the Army would be proportionate to the Negro population of the nation.

The White House soon learned that FDR's approval of the War Department's segregation policy had been received with bitterness by Negroes throughout the nation. Negro Democrats were particularly chagrined over this basic concession to the South made by their chief.

Bishop R. R. Wright, chairman of the Colored Division of the Democratic Party for the Midwestern Region, sent Steve Early a report on Oct. 10, 1940 on how the Negro voter viewed the government. He told of considerable excitement on a national scale among Negroes over NAACP criticisms of the War Department's segregation program approved by FDR. Wright then proposed that the Administration regain lost ground among Negro voters by making an unprecedented appointment. "It would be the greatest stroke of the year," he told Early, "if it could be announced that Col. B. O. Davis, who is the outstanding Negro Army officer, had been promoted to brigadier general, which will be the first time in the history of America that a Negro is so promoted." Wright predicted that such an announcement would "sweep public opinion among Negroes as nothing I know."

It was undoubtedly more than a coincidence when the news of Davis' promotion to general was released on Oct. 25, two weeks after Bishop Wright's frankly political proposal was made. The first reaction to the promotion of Davis to reach FDR was a telegram from a Charleston, W. Va. man which read, "Mr. President, are you crazy, appointing a nigger as general in the United States Army?"

As Negroes began to express greater indignation over their limited role in the war effort, FDR began to feel some pressure from certain liberal-minded members of his own cabinet. These men wanted to allay rising alarm of Negroes over their virtual exclusion from both defense industries and combat branches of the services. In the Spring of 1941 he received a curious little note from Harold L. Ickes enclosing a scholarly memorandum by Saul K. Padover of the Department of the Interior.

Padover's memorandum consisted of an interesting excursion into American history, recalling the pressure brought to bear on President Lincoln during the Civil War to give Negro slaves and freedmen a share in fighting the Confederacy. Ickes' diligent young researcher had dug up some data showing that Joseph Medill through his Chicago Tribune had urged the Union Government to free the slaves at the outset of the Civil War, confiscate Confederate property and to arm the freed slaves so they could make a contribution to the winning of the war. One is immediately struck by the apt analogy. In citing a Civil War precedent, was Ickes drawing a historical parallel to help FDR deal with the Negro's demand for equality of sacrifice as well as glory in World War II?

The gravity of the war situation forced FDR to concentrate on the crushing burdens of top-level strategy and to devote decreasing time to purely domestic affairs. He allowed aides like Marvin McIntyre to take over the handling of troublesome disputes like the Sojourner Truth Defense Homes incident in January, 1942.

This project, originally intended for Negroes, was transferred to white occupancy by the Detroit Housing Commission, a move which was protested as a "great blow to Negro morale." McIntyre went into action using the well-known hush-hush technique. McIntyre later admitted that his whole purpose was "to avoid an open fight at this time," an idea that met with the wholehearted approval of the President.

Later in 1942 FDR placed on record his belief that the Negro's status constituted the biggest public relations problem faced by the U.S. in selling the nation and its allies that the war was being fought for the freedom of all mankind. The President read a personal letter from an old friend, Lester Walton, U.S. Minister to Liberia, objecting to an Associated Press dispatch from Northern Ireland reporting the arrival there of the first U.S. troops to be sent to Europe. The A.P. story described Negro troops with the first contingent as "intended for service of supply."

FDR promptly got in touch with Elmer Davis, chief of the newly-created Office of War Information, and told him how damaging unintelligent publicity concerning the Negro could be to America's total war effort. "This is your No. 1 headache," he advised Davis. "The Army people are dumb when it comes to a matter of information that Negro troops landing in Ireland are for 'service of supply.' In other words, it is the same old story of publicizing the fact during the World War that the Negro troops were sent to France as 'labor battalions'."

As the war dragged on and took its dreadful toll of his health, FDR's preoccupation with the progress of war operations and relations with America's allies cut him off almost entirely from direct contact with Negro issues like the lynching of Negro soldiers at Flagstaff, Ariz., lynchings at Texarkana, Tex., and Sikeston, Mo., and gathering complaints of racial bias in the services and in government and industry. He was urged on Aug. 10, 1942 to publicly condemn the poll tax, but made no comment.

Though she knew his mind was crowded with hundreds of other pressing matters, Eleanor Roosevelt often brought the Negro into her personal discussions with her husband and helped secure White House consideration for various projects and problems submitted to her by colored contacts like Mrs. Bethune. According to John Gunther's *Roosevelt in Retrospect* Mrs. Roosevelt was instrumental in having FDR write "a very strong letter" to the Governor of Virginia asking a stay of execution for Odell Waller, a Negro sharecropper convicted of murdering a white man.

Surveying FDR's record on the Negro, one conclusion emerges with startling force: his failure to fight for civil rights can be ascribed to his conviction, mistaken or not, that such action would have split his party down the middle and torpedoed the entire edifice of social legislation for which he strove. Action on Negro rights was to him something to be deferred until the time was ripe, always an unspecified date. Harry S. Truman of Independence, Mo., on the other hand, not only drafted a comprehensive civil rights program but challenged the Southern Democrats, who bolted the party rather than support measures distasteful to them.

No president since Lincoln was so revered by Negro Americans. They regarded his New Deal as a tremendous step forward in their long battle to become first-class citizens in a working democracy.

FDR's death in Warm Springs, Ga., was mourned throughout the length and breadth of Negro America with a massive outpouring of feeling.

It was a spontaneous recognition of his service to "the forgotten man."

THE CIVILIAN CONSERVATION
CORPS AND THE NEGRO

JOHN A. SALMOND

The Act of March 31, 1933, creating the CCC, contained this clause: "That in employing citizens for the purposes of this Act, no discrimination shall be made on account of race, color, or creed." In this selection John A. Salmond accounts for the inability of President Roosevelt, who appears here as motivated more by political realities than by racial justice, and administrators such as W. Frank Persons, the Department of Labor's director of CCC personnel selection, to implement this clause in the face of determined resistance inside and outside the government and in all parts of the nation.

*

On March 31, 1933 President Franklin D. Roosevelt signed a bill authorizing the creation of the Civilian Conservation Corps, an agency designed to help relieve poverty and provide training for young men by employing them in conservation work on the nation's forests, parks, and farms.[1] The new President had experience and a personal interest in conservation of land and resource programs. His own Hyde Park estate was a laboratory in forestry techniques and as governor of New York he had fostered a scheme to put ten thousand unemployed men to work in the state forests and parks.[2] Now, the social chaos of the Depression gave him the opportunity to institute a national plan.

The CCC became one of the most popular and successful of all New Deal experiments. Before it was abolished in 1942 more

Reprinted by permission from the *Journal of American History*, LII (June 1965), 75–88.

than two and one half million young men passed through its ranks,[3] a major battle was fought against the ravages of a century of waste and depredation upon the land, and in regenerating the land the enrollees improved their own condition. Life in the CCC brought corpsmen better health and a second chance to get the education and training necessary for better employment. It also made better Americans. City and farm youth worked side by side. New Yorkers spent time in Iowa and South Carolinians in Vermont.[4] The result was a more national outlook and a greater understanding of the American people. The present purpose, however, is not to enumerate the CCC's successes, but rather to examine one of its few areas of failure—the official policy which prevented full participation by Negroes.

Operation of the CCC involved four federal departments and a national director. The Department of Labor, working through state and local relief agencies, selected the members. The Department of War administered the work camps or companies and placed Army officers in command. The departments of Agriculture and Interior were responsible for organizing and supervising the work projects. And at the center of the entire endeavor the director of the CCC formed policy and coordinated all operations.[5] For this important post Roosevelt selected a prominent labor official, Robert Fechner. Some organized labor leaders expressed fear that the CCC was the forerunner of an attempt to regiment the labor force, and Fechner owed his appointment as much to the need to pacify organized labor as to his administrative ability. The tall, slow-spoken, high-booted Tennesseean, who once quipped that his clerks were better educated than he, was not the archtypical New Deal administrator.[6]

The Act of March 31, 1933, which gave the CCC legal existence, contained the clause: "That in employing citizens for the purposes of this Act, no discrimination shall be made on account of race, color, or creed."[7] The intention was clearly to protect the rights of Negro citizens in the matter of selection for the CCC organization, but these mere words did not ensure them full equality.

Certainly no group needed help more. The Depression had added further misery to the Negro's normal condition of chronic poverty. In 1933 Negro unemployment rates were double the national average and more than two million were on relief. In northern states Negro laborers found that the adage "first fired, last hired" rang bitterly true, while in the South the Depression had erased even the structure of traditionally "Negro" jobs. White men now cleaned the streets in Atlanta, or collected garbage in Memphis, and Negro deprivation increased. Federal relief schemes were almost all that was left for the Negro.[8]

Scarcely had selection begun for the CCC camps when reports from the South indicated that in that desperately poor region local selection agents often sought to exclude Negroes from participation in CCC activities. Particularly deplorable were events in Georgia where the Negro population in 1930 was 1,071,125, or 36.8 percent of the total.[9] On May 2, 1933 an Atlanta resident, W. H. Harris, protested to Secretary of Labor Frances Perkins that no nonwhites from Clarke County had been selected for CCC work even though the population was 60 percent Negro.[10] W. Frank Persons, the Department of Labor's Director of CCC Selection, immediately demanded an explanation from the Georgia State Director of Selection, John de la Perriere. The Georgia director replied that all applications for CCC enrollment in Clarke County were "classed A, B and C. All colored applications fell into the classes B and C. The A class being the most needy, the selections were made from same."[11] Persons reiterated his insistence that selections be made regardless of race, but reports trickling in from other Georgia counties indicated that de la Perriere was making little effort to comply. Jessie O. Thomas, secretary of the Atlanta branch of the National Urban League, complained on May 9 that no Negroes were included in the first fifty men selected from Washington County although in that county too the population was more than 60 percent colored.[12] Persons was reluctant to take stronger action at that time. He stressed to Fechner the importance to the success of the CCC in the South of adjusting the matter locally "without any apparent intervention from Washington." The extent of his action, then, was to write to de la Perriere and Georgia officials asking firmly that they treat Negro applicants fairly.[13]

On May 19 a long telegram from Will Alexander, widely respected southern liberal and director of the Committee on Interracial Co-operation in Atlanta, spurred Persons to more positive action. In his plea for more decisive federal action Alexander claimed that local committees in Georgia were not registering Negroes, nor did they believe that the federal government was serious in directing them to do so. "Rural politicians," devout adherents to the dogma of white supremacy, administered Georgia's relief programs, he contended, and as a result of their discrimination the Communists had been given a strong opportunity "for further agitation" in their drive for Negro support.[14]

Upon receipt of the telegram Persons immediately telephoned de la Perriere, who admitted that Negroes were not being selected but denied that this was due to racial discrimination. Rather, he insisted that "at this time of the farming period in the State, it is vitally important that negroes remain in the counties for chopping cotton and for planting other produce. The negroes in this way are able to obtain work on farms throughout the state."[15] Since this optimistic picture of full Negro employment did not coincide with figures on the state of Negro joblessness in Georgia, Persons asked de la Perriere for a definite committment to increase Negro enrollment. When this was not forthcoming he called Governor Eugene Talmadge. At first Talmadge showed few signs of cooperating, but when Persons threatened to withhold Georgia quotas entirely unless Negroes were selected the Governor reluctantly agreed to "instruct Mr. de la Perriere" to proceed with their enrollment.[16]

The Selection Division had won its first battle, but executing the agreement was not without further tribulations. Indeed, de la Perriere protested to Persons on June 1 that county committees believed that "there are few negro families who . . . need an income as great as $25 a month in cash."[17] Hence their reluctance to enroll them. Nevertheless, Fechner was able to report to the President that Negroes were at last being enrolled in Georgia, though "not as many as the Department of Labor would like."[18] Persons, however, realized the basic weakness of his position and was satisfied with what small gains he had made. He knew that the attitudes of local communities in Georgia could not be revolutionized "by means of our own transitory contacts with the race problem in that state."[19]

Georgia was not the only southern state to balk at the selection of Negroes on the same basis as white enrollees. The relief director of Florida, John C. Huskisson, reported that "on the basis of merit, no negroes have yet been selected for the CCC." After Persons applied pressure, he agreed to "lower his standards" enough to accommodate two hundred Negroes, though he refused to select them at the same depots as whites.[20] Similarly, after investigating an NAACP complaint of discrimination in Arkansas Persons again threatened to withhold quotas. The state's indignant relief director, William A. Rooksbery, unequivocally denied the charge that no Negroes had been selected. No less than three had in fact been enrolled, he protested, but Persons was unimpressed. The chastened state official promised to induct more within the following few weeks.[21] In Alabama Persons won the cooperation of the state director of relief, Thaddeus Holt, who was willing to select Negroes, but found that some local councils were "trying to force" them not to enroll. Persons once more threatened to withhold quotas pending compliance with the law.[22]

Gradually, by combining pressure and persuasion Persons was able to insist that southern state directors enroll at least a token number of Negroes in their CCC quotas. By June 12 Georgia had selected 178 and Alabama 776. Mississippi, with a Negro population of over 50 percent, had the poorest record with 46, or only 1.7 percent of the total enrollment, and South Carolina, also with a Negro population of over 50 percent, established the best record with Negro enrollment accounting for 36 percent of the state's total.[23] The unusual exertion required to effect this meager enrollment portended what was to follow as the CCC tried to place its Negro enrollees in work camps throughout the country.

It was never the policy of CCC officials to attempt to create a nationwide system of integrated camps. Given the customs of the era, to do so would have invited trouble. From the first the mixing of the races was permitted only in those regions where Negro enrollment was so slight that no colored company could be formed. Elsewhere Negroes were assigned to all-Negro camps. Scarcely had Negro camps been established when angry complaints began to flood Fechner's office insisting that they be filled with white enrollees or be removed.[24] Not all the agitation came from the South. In fact, Fechner attested that "there was far less protest" from southern communities than from other regions.[25] He complained that "there is hardly a locality in this country that looks favorably, or even with indifference, on the location of a Negro CCC camp in their vicinity."[26] Recognizing that the success of Negro camps was conditional on winning the acquiescence of the local communities in their establishment, the director moved to relieve local tensions by ruling that no Negro was to be transported outside his own state and that all-Negro campsites were to be selected by the state's governor. But despite these changes local apprehension persisted.[27]

The reasons for the disinclination to accept Negro camps varied in detail from locality to locality but were similar in general trend. Residents feared the effect of a large body of Negroes on the social values of their community. They anticipated great increases in drunkenness and other social vices and, in particular, they feared for the safety of white women and children. The citizens of Thornhurst, Pennsylvania, for example, hearing a rumor that a Negro CCC camp would be established in their area, petitioned Fechner "righteously and vigorously" for its removal. While "truly disavowing any prejudice against those people on account of race and color," the petition pointed out the social danger of "isolating so great a number of unattached Negro males" in an area occupied "permanently and exclusively by white people."

> Many of these, especially unescorted women of various ages, are obliged . . . to travel by the site of these camps and along the highways thereabouts at all hours of the day and night. Among the families who live . . . at Thornhurst . . . are to be found scores of boys and girls just attaining youth and early womanhood who should not be exposed to dangers that are possible, if not indeed, probable.[28]

Similar protests came from most parts of the country. Residents of Washington, D.C., protested the establishment of a Negro camp near a residential area where "women are left alone."[29] Citzens of Contra Costa County, California, noted that members of a Negro company there were frequently "in an intoxicated condition," and that the camp was "a menace to the peace and quiet of the community."[30] In vain Fechner countered that there had not been "one single case where the conduct of Negro enrollees in the CCC camps had disturbed the peace and quiet of any community."[31]

Most of the examples of moderation on the issue came, somewhat paradoxically, from southern communities, particularly in Alabama where a well-rounded Negro CCC program developed by Governor Bibb Graves performed much useful work.[32] Arkansas citizens, too, accepted with equanimity many Negro camps. Residents of Laurens County, Georgia, considering themselves "above prejudice" in racial matters, successfully petitioned Fechner for the establishment of a Negro camp to combat soil erosion in their vicinity. White citizens of Morton, Mississippi, declared that they had had no trouble with the two colored camps in their district and predicted that if other communities could see the high standard of the work accomplished they "would be glad to get them instead of some white camps."[33] But such isolated gestures could not balance the widespread hostility toward Negro camps. Fechner himself never attempted to force communities to accept them. He frequently said that he was "a Southerner by birth and raising" and "clearly understood the Negro problem."[34] If protests showed no signs of abating he usually removed the camps either by cancellation or by transfer to an Army reservation.

At the same time Fechner was being petitioned to remove Negro camps, other sources pressured for expanded Negro participation. The NAACP and other Negro action groups complained about discrimination in CCC selection, and although not all their assertions were well founded, they clearly demonstrated that Persons had not convinced most selection agents that Negroes should be given an equal chance to enroll.[35] Some malcontents sought to effect reform by appealing to the President. Alton Wright, Superintendent of the Colored Rescue Mission Incorporated in Kansas City, complained to Roosevelt that "Negroes can't get into the CCC," and "no one seems to care."[36] "Just a Colored Mother" asked the President: "if war was declared, would they pick all the white boys first and leave the negro boys as the last called for service? This is what they do in the CCC."[37] In at least one state the relief director sought a change in discriminatory practices. Delaware's potential Negro enrollment was insufficient to justify a separate Negro company, yet racial feeling did not permit integrated camps. Therefore no Negroes at all could be enrolled. Fechner told the protesting relief director that the nonexistence of CCC opportunity for Delaware's Negroes was a fact "she would have to accept."[38]

An investigation by the Julius Rosenwald Fund confirmed what was only too well known by that time. The Fund found that "Negroes have not been placed in CCC jobs at anything like their proportion of the population, to say nothing of their greater need of employment as indicated by relief statistics." The Fund's report asked Persons if he "could select 863 white juniors in the State of Florida, and only 18 Negro juniors without discrimination against Negroes. . . ."[39]

Negro complaints were not confined solely to matters of enrollment policy. The Corps administration had decided that Negroes would not be widely employed in colored camps in any position of authority other than that of educational advisor, a ruling predictably opposed by the leading Negro spokesmen.[40] Fechner justified the policy on the grounds that the only way to get communities to accept Negro companies "was on the assurance that white supervisors would be in charge of the camps. Because of the practical difficulties of the situation it has not been felt desirable to extend the appointment of Negroes to include any large responsibilities."[41] These protests were laid before the President,

who decided in 1936 that colored officers and supervisory personnel should be used in the camps "wherever possible," a statement
vague enough to permit wide interpretation yet representing at
least a partial victory for Negro interests.[42] Some white groups, of
course, bitterly opposed the extension of any responsibility in the
camps to Negroes as "detrimental to the best interests" of Corps
and country.[43]

In 1934 Fechner, in an attempt to draw together the tangled
skeins of the Negro problem, ordered a full investigation of Negro
enrollment and placement by the War Department. The Army
reported varying practices in each Corps area. In the New England
states, for example, there were about 250 Negroes assigned to 68
white companies, and similar conditions prevailed in most other
areas. Strict segregation was maintained in the South, but in all
other regions, though segregated camps predominated, Negroes
were attached to many white companies. Some had even been
sent out of their home state, strictly contrary to Fechner's ruling.
The Army report recognized the situation as unsatisfactory but
recommended against change. The maintenance of segregated
camps in all Corps areas would only increase the number of
Negro units and compound the problem of placement.[44]

Fechner's response, however, was unequivocal. On September
10 he ordered that all Negroes in camps outside their home states
be repatriated as soon as possible, that they be replaced by white
enrollees, and that strict segregation be maintained in all Corps
areas.[45] There was to be absolutely no latitude allowed. He
claimed that by maintaining rigid segregation he would check
racial violence within the camps. Such violence, however, had
been a negligible factor in the context of the whole Negro problem.[46] What Fechner had done, in fact, was to increase greatly his
own difficulties by increasing the need for colored campsites without doing anything to lessen the prejudice in local areas against
their establishment. His policy on placement would therefore have
to be firmer, or else Negro enrollment would surely have to be
curtailed. It is difficult to understand why he made this decision
contrary to Army advice unless he was strongly influenced by personal beliefs and prejudices. His absorption of southern social
mores may have been so complete that he preferred not to act as
head of an organization which permitted even the smallest
amount of racial intermingling.

The Army report also confirmed what reports from the field
had long indicated: specifically, that in defiance of the provisions

of the CCC act and Persons' repeated instructions local authorities were using a definite quota system in the selection of Negro CCC enrollees. Negroes were chosen in most areas only as vacancies occurred in Negro camps. Furthermore this quota system had been established with the direct cognizance and encouragement of area and district military authorities. Several state selection agents reported to Persons that Army authorities had refused to accept colored selectees because they had "no vacancies for colored men,"[47] and actually had notified selection agents how many, if any, colored enrollees were required from each particular district.[48]

To Persons such policies clearly contravened both the spirit and letter of the CCC legislation. He strongly emphasized to the Advisory Council that "the Department of Labor is responsible for the enforcement and observance of the law. The law definitely states that there must be no discrimination, and it [the Department] cannot be put in the position of discriminating against the negro [sic] race. We have been placed in an intolerable position."[49] In his dealings with state directors, Persons insisted that the Labor Department's position on the matter be observed. To the Missouri state director, Wallace Crossley, he wrote, "Arbitrary colored quotas are not to be established by the selecting agencies, nor are limitations amounting to discrimination to be placed in the way of qualified applicants voluntarily desiring the privilege of enrollment."[50] To a New Jersey official he stressed that all colored eligibles were to be accommodated even if it meant camp reorganization.[51]

But for all Persons' blustering Fechner's ruling of September 10, 1934 still held, and state directors could only promise to enroll more Negroes when more Negro camps were established in their states.[52] By insisting on the dual policy of rigid segregation and confinement to the home state Fechner had closed the two safety valves selection agents could use, while his reluctance to override local protests in placing colored camps put definite limits on their expansion. These restrictions forced state directors to use a quota system, in spite of Persons' strong protests. Fechner himself was leaning more and more to authorizing a definite restriction of Negro enrollment as the easiest solution to the problem. He told the CCC Advisory Council: "I think we can easily defend and justify a policy of making replacements in accordance with the color of the vacancy existing. The practical thing is to maintain the organization we've got. Everytime we make a change, it constantly brings up more friction."[53] Against such a tendency Fechner's tacit commitment to uphold the intent of the original act was of little consequence. He now needed only an incident of sufficient import to enable him to establish his policy of curtailing Negro enrollment on a national basis.

The chance came in July 1935 when there was serious unrest among white communities in California, Arkansas, and Texas over the proposed establishment of new Negro camps as part of a general plan of CCC expansion. To Senator Joseph T. Robinson, Fechner wrote that he was "completely at a loss to know what I can do in handling these protests. The local welfare boards select the Negroes, and under the law we are compelled to take them. Something should be done to regulate the number of Negroes who are selected. . . ."[54]

"Something should be done," he had written, and immediately he resolved to do it. He accordingly instructed Persons to stop all colored enrollment in Texas on the grounds that there were no more camps planned for Negroes there. Negroes were to be accepted only as vacancies occurred in existing camps. Incensed, Persons refused to comply. He considered the director's request to be "a direct violation of the law," especially since "the CCC has never adequately fulfilled its opportunities for the selection of colored enrollees. For us now to expressly deny the right of selection to such men when there are eligible and qualified applications available and when state quotas cannot be filled would be an indefensible procedure."[55] But Fechner was not to be stopped. After Persons' refusal to order the curtailment of Negro enrollment he put the whole position before the President. Roosevelt termed the situation "political dynamite" and decided to approve Fechner's policy though he asked that his name "be not drawn into the discussion."[56] Since Persons still refused to issue the required instructions Fechner was forced to do so himself.[57] In his announcement that henceforth Negroes would be selected only as vacancies became available in already established Negro companies, he indicated that the policy had the President's approval. The order applied not only to Texas but to the entire country.[58]

The Selection Division, though objecting bitterly, was forced to acquiesce in the new policy. Dean Snyder, Persons' assistant, angrily told the Advisory Council that the decision was clearly "a violation of the basic act," but the Council, unmoved, upheld the director.[59] Persons made no further attempt to investigate alleged instances of racial discrimination. He had lost his fight and now turned all such matters over to Fechner rather than deal with them himself according to a policy personally repugnant to him. Fechner, courteous but definite, had no interest in reopening the question. He expressed regret that he could not "accept every person who wanted to enroll in a CCC camp," but, he added, this was not possible.[60] That the "degree of impossibility" varied according to the color of the applicant's skin was conveniently overlooked.

Fechner's decision to restrict Negro enrollment did not end agitation for fairer treatment of colored youths, but it rendered it more fruitless. When the slowly improving economy permitted some curtailment of CCC activity Fechner ordered that white and Negro camps be cut in strict proportion.[61] Walter White, Executive Secretary of the NAACP, protested without effect that the new jobs went almost exclusively to white youths and that Negroes needed the CCC as much as ever.[62]

Nor did Fechner permit any compromise on camp segregation, despite the fact that he was forced to break another of his own injunctions in the process and send Negroes outside their home states. Philip La Follette, governor of Wisconsin, requested in 1938 that some Wisconsin Negroes be enrolled in integrated camps within the state rather than be sent to segregated camps in Illinois.[63] The Director's Office refused, claiming it would be "contrary to official policy,"[64] a reply which the executive secretary of the Milwaukee Urban League characterized as "a decided disappointment, coming as it did from a Federal agency." "To my knowledge," he wrote, "there are no units in Wisconsin designated as Italian, Polish, German, or Jewish. Therefore we feel it well within the fitness of things to raise the question as to why Negroes are being set aside into so-called Negro units."[65]

Only in the employment of colored supervisory personnel were significant gains made. Building on an agreement of 1936 to use some Negroes as supervisors in colored camps it was decided in 1938 that all white supervisors were to be replaced.[66] In spite of the vigorous objections of some white selection agents and Army officers the policy was immediately implemented and sustained.[67]

It was not until late 1941 that a substantial increase in the number of Negroes selected was ordered. In that year, white youths, attracted by jobs in the booming war industries or needed at home because of a shortage of farm labor, could not be persuaded to join the CCC. Enrollment dropped from 300,000 in

January to 160,000 in October,[68] and the need to continue the Corps was called into question. In an attempt to boost sagging enrollment figures the director, now James McEntee, Fechner's former assistant, authorized increased Negro selection,[69] a move which Persons had insisted on from the beginning.[70] Thus considerations of expediency and survival, not moral pressure, induced the CCC belatedly to provide some measure of equality for colored enrollees. The move, however, came too late to be of much use. The CCC was ended in July 1942.

The outcome of the controversy over Negro enrollment is a blot on the record of the CCC. The Negro never gained the measure of relief from the agency's activities to which his economic privation entitled him. The clause in the basic act prohibiting discrimination was honored far more in the breach than in the observance. Much of the blame for the curtailment of Negro enrollment must, of course, lie firmly with the director. His southern attitudes influenced his approach to Negro policy. Unwilling to permit integrated camps or to allow the Negro the latitude of interstate travel permitted to white enrollees, and only too ready to heed the demands for removing Negro camps, he made little enough attempt to extend to Negroes the fullest benefits of CCC life.

Fechner, however, can by no means be held solely culpable. President Roosevelt himself made no attempt to ensure fairer treatment for Negroes and acquiesced in the restriction of their enrollment. And much of the responsibility must lie with the local communities, northern and southern, which refused to accept Negro CCC camps. Without community good will some curtailment of Negro selection was probably inevitable, even if Fechner had adopted a stronger line. Negroes could be enrolled only to the extent that there were camps in which to place them; therefore, in a sense, by restricting their selection Fechner was merely reflecting a strong section of prevailing white opinion. Moreover, the director's main purpose was to reduce unemployment and accomplish useful conservation work, not to further the cause of American race relations. However desirable, the fullest employment of Negroes was only a matter of subsidiary concern. It should also be remembered that only 10 percent of the population was colored and although their economic state was indeed parlous, Fechner owed an obligation to numerous white youths whose position was little better. A public outcry every time he tried to place a Negro camp was hardly good for public relations, nor did constant bickering with selection agents make for efficient selection policies. Viewed in this light Fechner's decision appears perhaps more understandable.

In its nine-year life span the CCC enrolled about two and a half million men. Almost two hundred thousand of these were Negroes.[71] Though their economic state certainly warranted better treatment, the Corps did provide relief for a considerable number. In so doing it fed many of them better than ever before, provided them with living conditions far superior to their home environments, and gave them valuable academic and vocational training. About 87 percent of all Negro enrollees participated in the CCC education program which developed a variety of skills particularly apposite to their own job opportunities. Some left the Corps to become gardeners, poultry farmers, or cooks; more were placed by Corps officials as janitors, table waiters, or chauffeurs. "Negro jobs" they may have been, but in an era when any employment was prized, training for such fields represented the best practical approach to the problem.[72]

To look at the place of the Negro in the CCC purely from the viewpoint of opportunities missed or ideals compromised is to neglect much of the positive achievement. The CCC opened up new vistas for most Negro enrollees. Certainly they remained in the Corps far longer than white youths.[73] As one wrote, "as a job and an experience for a man who has no work, I can heartily recommend it."[74] In short, the CCC, despite its obvious failures, did fulfill at least some of its obligations toward unemployed American Negro youth. The failure was not so much one of performance as of potential. Much had been accomplished, but much more could conceivably have been done.

NOTES

1. *Statutes at Large*, XLVIII, pt. 1, 22–23.
2. Nelson C. Brown, "The President Has Long Practiced Forestry," New York *Times*, April 30, 1933, VIII, 1; Bernard E. Bellush, *Franklin D. Roosevelt as Governor of New York* (New York, 1955), 94–98.
3. Arthur M. Schlesinger, Jr., *The Age of Roosevelt: The Coming of the New Deal* (Boston, 1958), 339.
4. *Ibid.*, 338–340. See also Kenneth Holland and Frank Ernest Hill, *Youth in the C.C.C.* (Washington, 1942).
5. Schlesinger, *Coming of the New Deal*, 337. For a detailed account see Charles P. Harper, *The Administration of the Civilian Conservation Corps* (Clarksburg, W. Va., 1939).
6. Labor leaders opposed to the CCC included William Green, president of AFL; Alex F. Whitney, president of the Brotherhood of Trainmen; and

Michael J. McDonough, president of the Building Trade Department of the AFL. New York *Times*, March 24–26, 1933; *Time*, Feb. 6, 1939, 10.

7. *Statutes at Large*, XLVIII, pt. 1, 22–23.

8. Dixon Wecter, *The Age of the Great Depression, 1929–1941* (New York, 1948), 162; Arthur M. Schlesinger, Jr., *The Age of Roosevelt: The Politics of Upheaval* (Boston, 1960), 425–438; Searle F. Charles, *Minister of Relief, Harry Hopkins and the Depression* (Syracuse, 1963), 26–27.

9. Will Alexander to Persons, June 12, 1933, Records of the Civilian Conservation Corps; Selection Division, Correspondence: Negro Selection (National Archives). Cited hereafter as SDC, NS. U. S. Bureau of the Census, *Fifteenth Census of the United States: 1930. Population*, Vol. III, pt. 1, 455.

10. Harris to Perkins, May 2, 1933, SDC, NS.

11. de la Perriere to Persons, May 5, 1933, *ibid*.

12. Thomas to Perkins, May 9, 1933, *ibid*.

13. Persons to Fechner, May 5, 1933, *ibid*.

14. Alexander to Persons, May 19, 1933, *ibid*. Alexander meant, no doubt, "selection" when he wrote "registration." Registration or enrollment was the final stage in the selection process. Youths registered with local relief agencies acting in their capacity as CCC selection agents. Then applicants were processed, and some weeks later the prospective enrollees, if successful, were taken to a military post, formally "enrolled" as a CCC member, and sent to camp. This registration or enrollment was a part of the selection process, though all terms were used very loosely. See U. S. Department of Labor, *Handbook for Agencies Selecting Men for Emergency Conservation Work* (Washington, 1933), 2–5.

15. Persons to de la Perriere (telephone conversation report), May 19, 1933, SDC, NS.

16. Persons to Talmadge (telephone conversation report), May 19, 1933, *ibid*. Talmadge later became a violent critic of CCC work.

17. Persons to Perkins, June 1, 1933, *ibid*.

18. Fechner to Roosevelt, June 1, 1933, *ibid*.

19. Persons to Perkins, June 1, 1933, *ibid*.

20. Persons memo files, May 19, 1933, *ibid*.

21. Rooksbery to Persons, June 2, 1933, *ibid*.

22. Holt to Persons (telephone conversation report), May 20, 1933, *ibid*.

23. Alexander to Persons, June 12, 1933, *ibid*.

24. Records of CCC: Minutes of the Advisory Council, 1933–42, June 26, 1933 (cited hereafter as Advisory Council Minutes). The Advisory Council was a body which met regularly with the director to discuss matters of policy and operations.

25. Fechner to W. G. Steel, Sept. 16, 1935, Records of the CCC, Correspondence of the Director (cited hereafter as Director Correspondence).

26. Fechner to James G. Polk, Oct. 30, 1934, *ibid*.

27. Fechner to Polk, Oct. 20, 1934; to Herbert H. Lehman, April 3, 1937, *ibid*. In addition to Fechner's desire to relieve local tensions one suspects him of "buck passing" here.

28. H. S. Sage to Fechner, Aug. 1, 1935, *ibid*.

29. Petition to Fechner, Oct. 26, 1934, *ibid*.

30. William G. McAdoo to Fechner, Aug. 30, 1935, *ibid*.

31. Fechner to H. S. Sage, Aug. 5, 1935, *ibid*.

32. Fechner to Persons, April 18, 1935, SDC, NS.

33. Joseph T. Robinson to Fechner, June 6, 1935; Laurens County Chamber of Commerce to Fechner, Aug. 14, 1935; W. G. Still to Fechner, Sept. 14, 1935, Director Correspondence.

34. Fechner to Robinson, April 22, 1935, *ibid*.

35. Roy Wilkins to Fechner, Nov. 8, 1933; June 7, 1934; July 31, 1934, *ibid*.

36. Alton Wright to Roosevelt, Nov. 2, 1935, *ibid*.

37. "Just a Colored Mother" to Roosevelt, June 16, 1935, SDC, NS.

38. Fechner to Miss Ethelda Mullen, Director, Delaware Emergency Relief Association, Oct. 13, 1934, *ibid.*

39. Garth H. Akridge to Persons, March 10, 1935, *ibid.* "Junior" was the term used to describe enrollees between 18 and 25 years of age, as distinct from veterans, Indians, or other special groups.

40. Fechner to Louis Howe, April 4, 1934, Director Correspondence.

41. Fechner to Thomas C. Hennings, Sept. 3, 1935, Franklin D. Roosevelt Papers, Official File 268, Box 6 (Franklin D. Roosevelt Library, Hyde Park, New York). Cited hereafter as FDRL.

42. Stephen Early to Fechner, Nov. 13, 1936, FDRL, O. F. 268—Misc., Box 18.

43. R. T. Sessions to Robinson, Sept. 23, 1935; John H. Overton to Fechner, Dec. 7, 1936, Director Correspondence.

44. C. P. Gross to Fechner, Aug. 27, 1934, *ibid.* For administration purposes the country was divided into nine CCC "Corps areas."

45. Fechner to Gross, Sept. 10, 1934, *ibid.*

46. Often those Negroes who were placed in predominantly white camps were among the most popular enrollees there. See Holland and Hill, *Youth in the C.C.C.*, 112.

47. J. Fred Kurtz to Persons, March 19, 1935, SDC, NS.

48. Persons to Col. Duncan Major, Nov. 2, 1933, *ibid.*

49. Advisory Council Minutes, Nov. 1, 1934.

50. Persons to Crossley, Aug. 10, 1935, SDC, NS.

51. Persons to Chester Barnard, June 28, 1935, *ibid.*

52. Crossley to Persons, July 26, 1935, *ibid.*

53. Advisory Council Minutes, Nov. 1, 1934.

54. Fechner to Robinson, July 19, 1935; to Adjutant General, July 16, 1935; to Dayton Jones, July 16, 1935, Director Correspondence.

55. Persons to Perkins, July 19, 1935, SDC, NS.

56. Fechner to Persons, July 24, Aug. 1, 1935; Hopkins to Persons, Aug. 6, 1935, *ibid.*

57. Persons to Fechner, July 25, 1935, *ibid.*

58. Fechner to Major, July 24, 1935, Director Correspondence.

59. Advisory Council Minutes, Sept. 24, 1935.

60. Fechner to Persons, May 15, 1936, SDC, NS.

61. Fechner to Persons, March 23, 1938, Director Correspondence.

62. Walter White to Fechner, Dec. 28, 1938, *ibid.*

63. La Follette to Fechner, Dec. 19, 1938, *ibid.* At that time there were no Negro camps in Wisconsin.

64. C. Taylor to La Follette, Feb. 21, 1939, *ibid.*

65. William Kelly to Taylor, Feb. 23, 1939, *ibid.*

66. James J. McEntee to Fred Morrell, March 16, 1938, Records of the CCC, Chronological Reference Material by Subjects, No. 784, Project Assistants.

67. Persons to C. C. Graham, March 16, 1940, Director Correspondence.

68. New York *Times*, March 29, Oct. 5, 1941.

69. Advisory Council Minutes, Sept. 23, 1941. Most of the new Negro companies were put to work on military reservations.

70. *Ibid.*, April 22, 1941.

71. Schlesinger, *Politics of Upheaval*, 434.

72. Howard Oxley to Fechner, June 30, 1938, Director Correspondence.

73. Fechner to Joseph F. Guffey, March 17, 1939, *ibid.* White enrollees remained in camp for about a year. Negroes stayed an average of six months longer.

74. Luther C. Wandall, "A Negro in the C.C.C.," *Crisis*, XLII (Aug. 1935), 244–253.

SUPREME COURT BEHAVIOR
IN RACIAL EXCLUSION CASES,
1935–1960

S. SIDNEY ULMER

In this selection S. Sidney Ulmer, applying quantitative analysis to Supreme Court decisions, arrives at generalizations about the conditions under which the Court has judged total or partial exclusion of Negroes from a state jury system to be in violation of the Fourteenth Amendment. Ulmer's study shows the complicated computations the Court has made in order to achieve in practice at least minimal realization of the constitutional principle of "the equal protection of the laws." The case of Norris v. Alabama (1935), discussed by Ulmer, arose in connection with the Scottsboro cases, which are treated later in the article by Hugh T. Murray, Jr. In Powell v. Alabama (1932) the Court had ruled that the "Scottsboro boys" had been denied "a fair opportunity to secure counsel of [their] own choice" in violation of the due process clause of the Fourteenth Amendment.

In the period 1930–1945 the Supreme Court handed down several decisions in the field of political activity favorable to Negroes. In Nixon v. Condon (1932) the Court held unconstitutional an action by Texas to provide for a white primary. In United States v. Classic (1941) and United States v. Saylor (1944) the Court upheld indictments against election officials who had engaged in fraudulent practices in the counting of votes. Negroes suffered a setback in Grovey v. Townsend (1935), in which the Court decided that the Texas Democratic state convention's exclusion of Negroes from primaries was not unconstitutional because the state was not involved. In Smith v. Allwright (1944), however, the Court reversed the Grovey v. Townsend decision, considering the "action of the party as the action of the state" when party membership is required for voting in a primary. In several cases—New Negro Alliance v. Sanitary Grocery Company *(1938) and three other cases in 1944 and 1945—the Court confirmed the equal rights of Negroes, under federal labor-relations law, to engage in collective labor action and to enjoy nondiscriminatory representation by unions chosen by employees as bargaining agents.*

The Supreme Court's decision in Missouri ex rel. Gaines v. Canada *(1938) was significant, representing a gain for Negroes while indicating the limitations of the context within which this advance was achieved. The Court insisted that the separate facilities permitted under its previous "separate but equal" ruling in* Plessy v. Ferguson *(1896) had really to be equal, but it was not until sixteen years later that the Court declared, in* Brown v. Board of Education *and three other cases, that "separate educational facilities are inherently unequal."*

*

The United States Supreme Court is often guided by rules of law which make the disposition of cases depend upon singular combinations of circumstances. It is a relatively simple procedure to go through the cases in a subject matter area and compile a list of the facts the justices seem to have considered material to their solution of the issue at hand. But the identification of the peculiar combinations of events which push the decisions in one direction or the other is more difficult. The number of possible combinations is almost endless: with as few as twenty specified circumstances there are more than one million possible combinations. And the weight of a particular circumstance may depend on the combination of factors in which it appears.

Fred Kort has pointed to the "concrete differentiation of factual elements" which seem decisive in cases involving such procedural civil rights as protection against unreasonable searches and seizures, coerced confessions, and unfair trial procedures.[1]

This paper does not employ the methods developed by Kort, but its point of departure is also a recognition of the fundamental importance of factual elements in certain kinds of cases. The subject area here is the type of unfair trial procedure at issue in cases involving the exclusion of Negroes from jury service in state

Reprinted by permission from *American Political Science Review*, LVI (June 1962), 1325–1330.

courts. Supreme Court decisions on this issue are well known and the general topic has been well plowed by students of constitutional law. My purpose is to see whether inferences about Supreme Court behavior in racial exclusion cases can be sharpened by a shift from the traditional method of analysis. The shift in method involves no change in focus since my investigation will use the same facts chosen as material by those employing other workways. But my aim is quantitative generalization.

I

Racial exclusion in the Federal courts has been barred by a congressional statute for many years and since 1875 state officials discriminating against Negroes in determining jury service in state courts have been subject to a fine of not more than $5,000.[2] But the vindication of Negro rights in this area has depended not on prosecutions under this statute but primarily on appeals to the Supreme Court invoking the Fourteenth Amendment against convictions in state courts obtained from juries from which Negroes are said to have been systematically excluded. In deciding these appeals the Court has developed the concept of a "representative" jury that is "an impartial jury drawn from a cross section of the community."

As Black put it in *Smith v. Texas*:

It is part of the established tradition in the use of juries as instruments of public justice that the jury be a body truly representative of the community. For racial discrimination to result in the exclusion from jury service of otherwise qualified groups not only violates our Constitution . . . but is at war with our basic concepts of a democratic society and a representative government.[3]

The Court has held that this principle entitles the Negro to a jury system in which Negroes are not intentionally and systematically excluded solely on account of race or color. But whether exclusion is intentional and systematic and solely on the basis of race or color must be determined on the facts.[4] If the facts suggest a *prima facie* case of discrimination, the burden is on the state to rebut the presumption. In deciding whether a *prima facie* case has been made out the Court has chosen to focus on a particular type of fact, *i.e.*—as David Fellman has expressed it—"Usually it is a matter of numbers."[5] The crucial facts, in short, seem to be qualitative variables, the variations in which may be represented numerically. A judgment as to discrimination is a rebutta-

ble inference from a particular combination of numerically expressed facts or factual relationships. The lawyer, by necessity,
must be interested in identifying the criteria which guide the formulation of such a judgment. The political scientist specializing
in public law may equally have an interest if he would explain the
Court's actions. The test which the Court has used to distinguish
the combinations of circumstances which show unconstitutional
exclusion seems to have been clearly stated on several occasions
by several different justices.

In *Smith v. Texas*, for instance, Justice Black declared that
"Chance and accident alone could hardly have brought about the
listing for grand jury service of so few negroes from among the
thousands shown by the undisputed evidence to possess the legal
qualifications for jury service."[6] Stone remarked in *Hill v. Texas*
that ". . . chance or accident could hardly have accounted for the
continuous omission of negroes from the grand jury lists for so
long a period as sixteen years or more."[7] And as late as 1958,
Black, speaking for a unanimous Court in *Eubanks v. Louisiana*,
said, ". . . the uniform and long-continued exclusion of Negroes
from grand juries shown by this record cannot be attributed to
chance [or] to accident . . ."[8]

These statements, and others like them, suggest that while the
Court sees the event of exclusion as a juncture of innumerable
forces, a distinction is made between determinative and chance
factors. When convictions have been upset in exclusion cases, the
Court has found that intentional and purposeful racial discrimination has determined the exclusion. It seems perfectly clear at
the same time that exclusion resulting from chance factors con-
stitutes no violation of the Fourteenth Amendment. In deciding
whether a particular exclusion of Negroes from some part of the
jury system is a chance occurrence, the Court has been careful to
note two types of statistics. One is the ratio of qualified Negroes to
qualified whites in the jurisdiction involved. In determining this
ratio the Court has utilized such measures as the percentage of
Negro taxpayers, the percentage literate, the percentage of Negro
males 21 years and older, and the percentage of Negroes in the
total population of the county. It has not, however, considered
all these factors in every case. In fact, the only statistic running
through all cases is the raw population figure.

The second type of statistic the Court has looked at is the ratio
of Negroes to whites in the area of service from which exclusion
is charged. The ratio chosen for emphasis usually depends on the

nature of the claim, since exclusion from petit juries, grand juries, or jury lists may be involved.

Evidently, we have here an application of the statistical concept of sampling, and it suggests a testable hypothesis, namely, that the outcome in racial exclusion cases depends upon the relationship of a sample to a population on a particular attribute— racial heterogeneity (RH). The population consists of the Negroes and whites from which the sample (read jury or jury list) is drawn. The play in the joints of the judicial machine is of great importance here. For whether the racial heterogeneity of a sample is representative of a population is a meaningful question only if the population and sample are relevant for each other.

The racial heterogeneity of a population or a sample may be measured by an index of qualitative variation. This method essentially counts differences. The greater the number of differences among a set of items, the more heterogeneous the aggregate and hence the greater the variation in it. By counting the differences between each item and every other item in a set, we get a total number of differences in the aggregate. This becomes meaningful when we relate the observed differences to the maximum number of differences possible. The index of qualitative variation is the ratio of total observed differences to maximum possible differences, a ratio that can vary between zero and 100 per cent.

II

An idea of what the court has been doing in exclusion cases can be gained by comparing the racial heterogeneity of the populations and samples to which the court has paid attention. RH values for populations and samples are presented in Table I for the 13 cases decided in the period 1935–1960. The table shows that the court has often used the racial composition of a total county population as a basis for comparison with the racial composition of juries and jury lists. Yet, it is safe to say that in no county or state is the total population the relevant base for determining jury service. Total population always needs refining by the elimination of those who lack the requisite qualities and characteristics specified by the statutes. There is some tension between the notion of a representative cross-section of the community and the long lists of requirements and exemptions which characterize jury selection procedures in many states.[9] But as long as the Supreme Court has not seen fit to prohibit such disqualifications, the

TABLE I

Comparative Racial Heterogeneity in Selected Populations
with Associated Probabilities for Bi-Racial Samples*

Case	Year	Out-come	RHP %	RHS %	P	Vote
Norris v. Alabama	1935	+	29.8(M)	0		8–0
Hale v. Kentucky	1938	+	41(Tx)	0		8–0
Pierre v. Louisiana	1939	+	88.8(R)	0		8–0
Smith v. Texas	1940	+	36(PT)	13.4(JL)	< .001	9–0
Smith v. Texas	1940	+	13.4(JL)	4.5(GJ)	< .05	
Hill v. Texas	1942	+	52.3(R)	0		9–0
Akins v. Texas	1945	−	52.3(R)	23(JL)	< .05	6–3
Patton v. Mississippi	1947	+	92.1(R)	0		9–0
Brunson v. N. Carolina	1948	+	9.3(JP)	3.1(JL)	< .001	9–0
Cassell v. Texas	1950	+	24.3(PT)	25(GJ)	> .7	7–1
Cassell v. Texas	1950	+	24.3(PT)	24(GJ)	P_{21} < .01	
Brown v. Allen	1953	−	53.7(Tx)	53.3(JL)	> .8	6–3
Brown v. Allen	1953	−	53.7(Tx)	34.4(JL)	> .16	
Speller v. Allen	1953	−	94.2(Tx)	26(JB)	< .001	6–3
Reece v. Georgia	1955	+	37.5(M)	4.3(JL)	< .001	9–0
Eubanks v. Louisiana	1958	+	88.8(R)	.07(GJ)	< .001	9–0

* Distinguishing Negroes and Whites only.

Legend: + = decision for the Negro claimant
           − = decision against the Negro claimant
        RHP = racial heterogeneity of the relevant population
        RHS = racial heterogeneity of the relevant sample
           M = males, 21 and over
          Tx = total tax paying population
           R = raw population
          PT = poll tax paying population
          GJ = grand jury
          JL = jury list
          JP = jury pool
          JB = jury box
           P = probability of the difference between RHP and RHS occuring by chance

representative jury should be interpreted as one which represents fairly the population of qualified prospects. And indeed, the justices have at times used a refined rather than a raw population count as a basis for their computations, though they have not been as careful to distinguish the one from the other as might be wished.[10]

In five of the 16 relationships examined, the court used total population statistics. In four of these the racial heterogeneity of the sample population over extended periods of 16 years or more was zero. In the fifth case, the court used the county tax list to identify the qualified population, but here again exclusion was total over a period of 30 years. Since all five cases were decided against the state, it seems fair to conclude that where the Negro population is substantial (7.2 per cent or more), and exclusion from the sample absolute, the court has required no further test. Indeed, the language in the opinions occasionally suggests that proof of total exclusion alone may be sufficient for showing racial discrimination, assuming there were some qualified Negroes in the county. Typical of this view is the comment of Black in *Patton v. Mississippi* that

. . . whatever the precise number of qualified colored electors in the county, there were some. . . . We hold that the state wholly failed to meet the very strong evidence of purposeful racial discrimination made out by the petitioner upon the uncontradicted showing that for thirty years or more no Negro had served as a juror in the criminal courts of Lauderdale County.[11]

Total exclusion cases, therefore, appear to require no further analysis, though problems could arise if the period of exclusion is sufficiently shortened. For the court has often asserted that exclusion of a race from a small enough sample is not sufficient for showing intentional and purposeful discrimination on a racial basis.[12]

The remaining cases raised problems of the type likely to plague the court in the future. In these cases the sample was racially heterogeneous as was also the population with which it was compared. The question the court has been asking is whether the differences in degree of heterogeneity are due to chance or intentional racial policy. As Frankfurter put it in *Cassell v. Texas*, the question is whether there was "a purposeful non-inclusion of Negroes because of race or a merely symbolic representation, not the operation of an honest exercise of relevant judgment or the uncontrolled caprices of chance."[13] While the court has not publicly used statistical tests of significance for the differences observed, nothing prevents us from doing so in our search for a standard. Associated probabilities have been calculated for each of the bi-racial distributions in Table I.[14] In *Smith v. Texas*, the grand jury list was rated 13.4 per cent on the RH factor as compared to 36 per cent for the relevant population, composed of those paying poll taxes in the county. The chance expectation of such a difference is much less than 1 in 1,000. But when the grand jury list and the grand jury are compared on the same factor, the former exceeds the latter by a three-to-one-ratio

—a difference expected by chance less than five times in a hundred. In *Brunson v. North Carolina*,[15] *Reece v. Georgia*[16] and *Eubanks v. Louisiana*,[17] the differences observed have associated probabilities of considerably less than .001. In *Brown v. Allen*[18] on the other hand, the observed differences in drawing grand jury and petit jury lists would be expected by chance about nine times in ten for the latter and approximately 17 times in 100 for the former. Social scientists analyzing these data would be likely to reject chance as an explanation in the first three cases but not in the *Brown* case since .05 is the usual cutting point. In these cases, the Supreme Court consciously or unconsciously has chosen to use a region of rejection consistent with established statistical procedures. And in *Brown*, the decision is for the state, racial discrimination not having been proved.

The remaining three cases do not fit the same pattern. In *Cassell v. Texas*, the difference between the racial heterogeneity of the poll tax population and that of the grand jury is so minimal that its associated probability of occurrence is about eight times in ten. On that basis, we might expect a decision for Texas. In *Akins v. Texas*,[19] the disparity between the RH of the poll tax population and the jury list would be expected by chance less than five times in a hundred. We should therefore anticipate a decision for the Negro claimant. Contrary to these expectations, Texas won the decision in *Akins* but lost it in *Cassell*. The difficulties of squaring the two cases in terms of legal doctrine have been recognized. Herman Pritchett says that "the authority of the *Akins* ruling was subsequently impaired by the somewhat confused decision in *Cassell v. Texas*."[20] And it is true that the seven members of the majority in Cassell split 4–3 in choosing a rationale for their decision. The behavior of this majority, however, is entirely consistent with the statistical considerations previously introduced. For Reed, speaking for the court, was no more impressed by the differences in the racial heterogeneity of the poll tax population and that of the grand jury population than we are. And he declared, "Without more it cannot be said that Negroes had been left off grand-jury panels to such a degree as to establish a *prima facie* case of discrimination."[21]

The decision in the case turned, therefore, on the second charge that "the Dallas County grand-jury commissioners for 21 consecutive lists had consistently limited Negroes selected for grand-jury service to not more than one on each grand jury."[22] While the justices split 4–3 in agreeing with this charge, the decision for the Negro can be explained statistically since the associated probability of no more than one Negro on 21 consecutive grand juries is less than .01. This explanation eliminates the confusion in Reed's opinion and makes the outcome in *Cassell* consistent with the outcome in the other cases. In *Akins*, on the other hand, the Negro claimant failed because his sample was too small, not because the observed differences between sample and population were insignificant. As Reed pointed out for the court, the only complaint was said "to consist of an arbitrary and purposeful limitation by the Grand Jury Commissioners of the number of Negroes to one who was to be placed upon the grand jury panel of sixteen for the term of court at which the indictment against petitioner was found. This is petitioner's only complaint as to racial discrimination."[23] If this is viewed as a claim for proportional representation, it would have no standing. If it is viewed as a claim of intentional racial discrimination, a sample of 16 persons containing one Negro was not sufficient to prove racial discrimination where Negroes constituted 15.5 per cent of the population sampled. The court, indeed, seems to have found the sample inadequate even when doubled to 32 persons including two Negroes. It may be surmised that had no more than one Negro name appeared on 21 consecutive lists, the sample would have been sufficiently large to support an inference consistent with that drawn in *Cassell*.

While the court has not been prone to use such terms as "sample size," an inference that such a factor is important in exclusion cases is entirely consonant with the data we have examined. The sample size in the 13 cases studied varied from 16 in *Akins* to 2,126 in *Speller*. And the sample in *Akins* was only about one-fourth the size of the next smallest sample. This alone is sufficient to put *Akins* in a class by itself. But even more striking is the fact that the court has decided no case in favor of a Negro claimant where the sample available numbered less than 252 names. It is also worth noting that a total of 25 different justices have compiled, over a period of 24 terms, a record of remarkable consistency in racial exclusion cases. For, as Table I shows, the 25 justices cast a total of 113 votes; all but 10 of these were cast consistently with the statistical explanations here advanced. This record shows that the liberal-conservative dichotomy which often characterizes the Supreme Court has not been operative in this area of litigation. It also shows that the court did not wait for Earl Warren to bring unanimity to one area of decision making of vital importance to those subjected to racial discrimination.

The final case, *Speller v. Allen*, is the only one not decided consistently with the statistical formulations we have advanced. In *Speller* no Negro had served on a Vance County, North Carolina, jury in "recent" years. In examining the jury box, it was found that of 2,126 names, only 145 were those of Negroes. The majority of six justices (Vinson, Reed, Jackson, Burton, Clark and Minton) failed to find racial discrimination. Yet the probability of such an observed difference in the racial composition of the tax list and the jury box would be less than .001. *Speller*, therefore, is a deviant case not explained by our formulations. In terms of the standards seemingly used by the court before and after that decision it would appear, as Black and Frankfurter agreed, that there was "unconstitutional discrimination" in the makeup of the jury box in *Speller*.

III

What may be concluded from all this? Basically, that it is now possible to formulate a set of explanatory hypotheses as follows:

(1) The total absence of Negroes from a state jury system or a part thereof is a violation of the Fourteenth Amendment given two conditions:

(a) The proportion of Negroes in the qualified population is substantial (*i.e.*, 7.2 per cent or more).

(b) The period of exclusion is long (*i.e.*, 16 years or more).

(2) Partial absence of Negroes from a state jury system or a part thereof is a violation of the Fourteenth Amendment given two conditions:

(a) The racial heterogeneity of a sample population (read jury or jury list) differs from that of a qualified population to an extent expected by chance less than five times in one hundred.

(b) The sample is sufficiently large (60 or more cases).

These hypotheses are not offered as final explanations or as complete explanations or as the only explanations for the Supreme Court's decisions in racial exclusion cases. They are submitted as explanations consonant with the data examined and are stated with sufficient precision to make empirical testing possible.

NOTES

1. Fred Kort, "Predicting Supreme Court Decisions Mathematically: A Quantitative Analysis of the Right to Counsel Cases," this REVIEW, Vol. 51 (March, 1957), pp. 1–12.

2. 18 USC at 243.

3. 311 U.S. 128, 130 (1940).

4. As Black expressed it in Patton v. Mississippi: "Whether there has been systematic racial discrimination . . . in the selection of jurors is a question to be determined from the facts in each particular case." 332 U. S. 463 at 466.

5. David Fellman, *The Defendant's Rights* (1958), p. 103.

6. *Loc. cit.*, p. 131.

7. 316 U.S. 400, 404.

8. 356 U.S. 584, 587.

9. For example, Alabama excludes those who are under age, habitual drunkards, permanently diseased or unfit because of physical weakness, illiterates (except property holders), and those convicted of any offense involving moral turpitude. Alabama exempts from jury service judges, attorneys, officers of the United States, officers of the Executive Department of the state, sheriffs, deputies, clerks of court, county commissioners, physicians, dentists, pharmacists, optometrists, teachers, actuaries, boat engineers, bus drivers, truck drivers (under jurisdiction of the Public Service Commission), railroad engineers, firemen, conductors, train dispatchers, bus dispatchers, railroad station agents, telegraph operators, reporters, embalmers, radiobroadcasting engineers and announcers, superintendents, doctors and regular employees of Bryce and Searcy Hospitals, officers and enlisted men of the National Guard and Naval Militia, convicts and prison guards. See Anderson v. Alabama, pending before the U. S. Supreme Court, 1961 Term, Docket No. 326.

10. It is only fair to say that the necessary distinction with supporting statistical data has not often been presented in the parties' briefs. On several occasions, the court has apparently found it necessary to take judicial notice of census data in order to reach a determination.

11. 332 U.S. 463, 468–469. This comment was in response to an attempt by the Mississippi Supreme Court to play the role of statistician. "Of the 25 qualified Negro male electors there would be left, therefore, as those not exempt, 12 or 13 available male negro electors as compared with 5,500 to 6,000 male white electors as to whom, after deducting 500 to 1,000 exempt, would leave a proportion of 5,000 non-exempt white jurors to 12 or 13 non-exempt negro jurors, or about one fourth of one per cent negro jurors,—400 to 1. . . . For the reasons already heretofore stated there was only a chance of 1 in 400 that a Negro would appear on such a venire and as this venire was of 100 jurors, the sheriff, had he brought in a negro, would have had to discriminate against white jurors, not against negroes,—he could not be expected to bring in one fourth of one Negro." (p. 467).

12. *E. g.*, Cassell v. Texas, 339 U.S. 282, 286; Akins v. Texas, 325 U.S. 403.

13. *Loc. cit.*, p. 291.

14. Unless otherwise indicated, all probability statistics used in this paper are two-tailed and were computed with the binomial expansion if N

was small and with the binomial test and the Yates correction for continuity if N was large. The formula for the binomial expansion is

$$P(x) = \binom{N}{x} P^x Q^{N-x}$$

where P = proportion of cases expected in one category,

$$Q = 1 - P \text{ and } \binom{N}{X} = \frac{N!}{x!(N-x)!}.$$

For large samples

$$(N > 25)Z = \frac{(x \pm .5) - NP}{\sqrt{NPQ}}$$

15. 333 U.S. 851 (1948).
16. 350 U.S. 85 (1955).
17. 356 U.S. 584 (1954).
18. 344 U.S. 443 (1953).
19. 325 U.S. 398 (1945).
20. C. Herman Prichett, *The American Constitution* (1959), p. 546.
21. *Loc. cit.*, pp. 285–286.
22. *Ibid.*, p. 286.
23. *Loc. cit.*, p. 400.

THE ATTITUDES OF
AMERICAN PROTESTANTISM
TOWARD THE NEGRO,
1919–1939

ROBERT MOATS MILLER

*In 1937 the General Assembly of the Presbyterian Church, U.S.A.,
adopted this resolution, "only one of many" such strong statements, according to Robert Moats Miller, the author of this selection:*

We accept completely the ideal of the brotherhood of all races, as all
are the children of God. We therefore call upon Christians everywhere
to practice mutual good-will and cooperation among all racial groups,
to eliminate every form of discrimination, and to work actively for the
recognition of civil and religious rights of all minority groups.

*Miller considers the attitudes and actions of various Protestant
denominations in race relations in the light of their own precepts.
"Now, if the churches were ordinary institutions, they could be
excused from bowing to society's pressures." Unlike labor unions,
business groups, and fraternal organizations, however, "Christian
churches are not judged by frail human standards but by the uncompromising ideals of the Christian creed." Miller concludes
that from 1919 to 1939 the gap between Christian profession and
practice narrowed. This does "not absolve American Protestantism of the charge that it all too often accommodated itself to
prejudice at the peril of its own soul," and the gap remains far
from closed.*

❋

"If the treatment of the Negro by the Christian Church is called 'divine,' " wrote W. E. B. Du Bois, "this is an attack on the conception of God more blasphemous than any which the church has always been so ready and eager to punish."[1] His harsh evaluation has been echoed by far too many scholars—Negro and white—to be easily dismissed. There was in truth a vast gulf between the Christian creed and the actual deeds of Protestants.[2]

In the first place, Protestant churches were segregated and segregating institutions. White Protestants, while they professed to worship a God who was no respecter of persons, did their worshipping in buildings where the color of skin and not the purity of heart was the entrance test. At the end of the Depression Decade there were approximately eight million Protestant Negroes in America. About seven and a half million were in separate Negro denominations. Of the remaining half million in predominantly white denominations, about 99 per cent were in segregated congregations. Thus about one-tenth of one per cent of all Negro Protestants in the United States—eight thousand souls—actually gathered together with whites for worship.[3]

This searing fact rests with the whites. It is true that perhaps many Negroes prefer to worship in their own churches. It is true that perhaps many Negroes would be reluctant to unite with whites even if the invitations were warmly extended.[4] But why? Because they believe they would not be accepted as equals. There could hardly be a more devastating indictment of white Christian America. And what fate threatened white congregations that accepted Negroes? If the Negroes were poorly treated they left. If well treated, they were perhaps joined by others until the whites, being gradually outnumbered, started to leave. In time the church ended up just as it had started—a segregated institution only now with a congregation entirely black rather than white. Such were often the bleak alternatives facing even those ministers who wanted to do the right thing.

Now, if the churches were ordinary institutions, they could be excused for bowing to society's pressures. So deeply ingrained is prejudice against the Negro that even with the *best well wishes* in the world it has been difficult for labor unions, business groups, fraternal organizations, and even historical societies to break down the barriers. What man is so wise as to possess an easy and quick solution to the Negro problem?

Reprinted by permission from *Journal of Negro History*, XLI (July 1956), 215–240.

But—and this is the point—Christian churches are not merely groups of individuals banded together for fraternal or cooperative purposes. They are not judged by frail human standards but by the uncompromising ideals of the Christian creed. However noble the aims of other institutions, only the churches claim a divine mandate to glorify Almighty God. Other groups may falter and equivocate, but the churches cannot excuse the gulf between their professions of faith and their practices of paganism. A segregated church *content in its segregation* cannot claim to speak for Christ.

Since segregation is such an irrefutable fact, there remains only the question of how many white Protestants were content with its existence. The evidence is very ugly.

"Of all the groups devoted to social uplift," wrote a Negro leader, "I have least hope in the white Christian ministers."[5] This view is accepted wholly or in part by almost all students of race relations in the United States. Their findings are well known and it would serve no useful purpose to burden the narrative with quotations from a score of authorities. One or two important examples must suffice. Gunnar Myrdal, the author of the most exhaustive study of the Negro problem in America, wrote:

> Southern whites usually succeed in keeping the Christian challenge of religious brotherhood off their minds. The observer feels that the very incompatibility between the uncompromising Christian creed, on the one hand, and the actual caste relations, on the other, is a reason why white ministers in the South keep so aloof from the race problem and why the white church in the South has generally played so inconsequential a part in changing race relations. It is also a reason why the white minister has been closely watched by his congregation so that he does not start to draw practical conclusions from Christian doctrine that would favor the improvement of race relations.[6]

Frank S. Loescher, author of what many consider to be the definitive study of the interracial principles, practices, and policies of the Protestant churches, believes that "Protestantism, by its policies and practices, far from helping to integrate the Negro in American life, is actually contributing to the segregation of Negro Americans."[7]

Myrdal and Loescher presented their findings in published studies which are well known. Narrower in scope but probing much deeper into the thought of a single denomination are three unpublished studies of Southern Baptists.[8] Together they represent a searching analysis of the racial attitudes of Southern Baptists as revealed in regional, state, and district association meetings and in the press. Southern Baptists, with only pitiful exceptions, accepted and defended the racial caste system; they accorded priority to the prevailing cultural climate rather than to the commandments of Christ. Racial pride cuts the heart out of the Christian ethic. It is enough to say that Southern Baptists defended Negro degradation in the mid-twentieth century as fervently as they had Negro slavery in the mid-nineteenth.

Further, when an investigator sent out over three hundred letters of inquiry to people from one end of the South to the other asking for examples of particularly good practices in race relations, less than a dozen replies referred to any known instance of organized church action. "So little does the Christian church," sadly commented the writer, "exemplify any practice better than that of the world to which it conforms."[9]

These examples are from the findings of other students. Independent research also revealed instance after instance of the racial pride of white Protestants. A few illustrations covering the decades of the 'twenties and 'thirties must serve to drive this point home.[10]

A New England minister suggested to his congregation that they invite the members of a neighboring Negro church to a church supper, whereupon the ladies of his flock served notice that they would not attend such an affair, much less help prepare the meal. The first national student-faculty conference of the Council of Christian Associations, meeting in Detroit in 1931 was racked by the race issue. The hotel, reneging on its signed agreement, segregated the Negro delegates, refusing them access to the same facilities as the whites. The whites voted to remain at the hotel. The Negroes bolted the conference.[11]

Segregation at church meetings was always a problem. William Joseph McGlothlin, president of the Southern Baptist Convention, refused to attend a banquet to be given in his honor by the Rochester, New York, Baptist Association, when he discovered that by unhappy chance the banquet chairman was Dr. James E. Rose, Negro moderator of the Rochester group. In 1928 Southern Presbyterians in General Assembly went on record in favor of interracial good will and understanding—*after carefully segregating the Negro delegates*.[12]

Resolutions or reports on the Negro problem were not infrequent, but they were not always conclusive. For instance, the *complete* report of the Committee on Interracial Relationships to the Northern Baptist Convention in 1929 read:

The Committee on Interracial Relationships for the last few years has found nothing definite to do, and has had no appropriation for its work. During the last year it has, therefore, done no work and has no report to make, unless it should reiterate the very true and important principles which it has presented before. It is doubtful whether such repetition would be of value; the committee therefore begs leave to be excused from making a report.[13]

In 1929 Reverend William S. Blackshear of St. Matthew's Protestant Episcopal Church, Brooklyn, informed the Negroes in his congregation that they were not welcome. When, on the other hand, an Episcopal minister in New York insisted upon permitting Negroes to worship, his vestry, by a vote of seven to four, had the church closed "for repairs" and locked. Similarly, the pastor of the Bethel Evangelical Church in Detroit resigned when two Negroes were denied membership.[14]

When the National Preaching Mission reached Atlanta, Georgia, in 1936, the local church authorities decided that the Negro member should be excluded from the proceedings. It is instructive that the Chinese member, Dr. T. Z. Koo, promptly left the caravan in protest. Five years earlier Atlanta had been host to a conference of world Methodism. There was no segregation of delegates. However, when an attempt was made to report on the color problem it was blocked by the chairman on the grounds that reports could not refer to "specific evils." Whereupon a delegate with a sense of consistency immediately offered a resolution to the effect that any and all references to the enforcement of prohibition be expunged from the record in order fully to comply with the chairman's ruling.[15]

Of greater moment to American Methodism is the fact that the Negro question was a major factor in delaying unification until 1939. Scores of Southern Methodists, including such leaders as Bishops Candler and Ainsworth, made clear their reluctance to accept any merger that would bring them into familiar contact with Negroes. The relative tolerance of Northern Methodists toward "people of color" was repeatedly chided by Southerners. And when unification was consummated, most Methodist Negroes were placed in a Central Jurisdiction, an arrangement believed by many to mark a retrogression in race relations.[16]

There are accounts of ministers leading their congregations in hunting down Negroes like wild animals, of Negroes being lynched in church yards, of ladies selling grisly pictures of mutilated lynch victims in order to raise church funds, and the like.[17]

The evidence is irrefutable, however, regarding the position taken by some churchmen at the time of the savage race riots following the First World War. In some of these riots the churches remained shamefully silent. In other cases, Negro agitators were blamed and the whites excused for resorting to violence. This myopic explanation for the cruel bloodshed was held by several responsible church journals and by a number of individual clergymen, including even such leaders as Methodist Bishop Mouzon and Episcopal Bishop Thurston.[18]

And what could whites do to prevent race riots? "Let our Christian people," suggested a Southern Episcopal journal,[19] always conscious of propriety, "set the example of never occupying a seat in the street car reserved for colored people, no matter how crowded that car may be. . . . When certain seats are set aside for colored people in the street cars, they should be guarded and reserved for that purpose just as scrupulously as are the seats kept for white people."

The church press provides the clearest indication of Protestantism's acceptance of the racial status quo. Literally hundreds of editorials and articles, the great majority of them appearing in Southern journals, reflected the myth that a peaceful and harmonious relationship existed between the races. There was no need to trouble oneself about the "race problem" for the simple reason that the problem was nonexistent. The black and white each had his place in the scheme of things, and it was suggested that this plan was part of God's orderly design for the races. On the one hand, Negroes should be content, law abiding, hard working, peaceful, and happy in their subordinate but not onerous status. On the other, it was the white man's duty to be patient, understanding, helpful, kindly but firm in his relations with his child-like, simple, and often mischievous colored wards. In a word, the black should be proper and the white paternalistic.

The "good" Negro, then, played the rôle assigned to him in antebellum days—a faithful, cheerful, banjo-plunking clown who could, on occasion, be made to work hard. If, however, the Negro displayed the traditional American virtues of independence, ambition, pride, aggressiveness, resourcefulness, he did not "know his place." He was getting "uppish." The severest strictures of the whites were reserved for such aggressive Negro leaders as Du Bois, and for "meddling Yankees" who did not "understand" the black man and who encouraged him in his ambitions. And apparently the ultimate ambition of all blacks was to marry a white woman. Every attempt to break the existing caste system was answered with the charge that it would lead to the "amalgamation of the races." Social equality—there was the enemy!

It is important to remember that the clerical proponents of the racial status quo were hardly ever vicious or brutal in their arguments. Only very rarely was the Negro referred to in hostile tones. And there is the rub! Except for a few "radical" Negroes, the black man was considered a rather humorous and child-like individual hardly worthy of serious thought. Nature and Nature's God had placed upon earth the black and the white, the one to serve and the other to rule. This relationship was to endure forever and if there was such a thing as a "race problem"—which few admitted—it was unsolvable. Save for the deletion of the word "slavery," there had been no change since Civil War days in the white man's arguments of superiority. Even those who recognized that all was not perfect fell somewhat short in their analysis of the problem. For instance, a Kentucky Baptist began his discussion of race relations by recalling his beloved "ebon mammy" who crooned over his cradle and then concluded that

the race problem of the South can be composed, if we shall show the spirit of Christian helpfulness to the children of the child race whom our ancestors brought from slave ships to do their farm work for them.

The Negro is no angel. His weaknesses, sins and foibles are known to all men. But he also has good points that many other races have not. He is a patriot. He loves the South. He loves his "white folks." He understands the Southern white. He has a genius for religion. He does not hate or retain malice. The mean things sometimes said about whites by Negro writers will be found nearly always to be written by Negroes with white blood in them.

The Negro is a thousand times better for the South than the white Bolshevists, Radical Socialists and Atheists that are a curse in some other sections of America. Let us be faithful to God and help the Southern Negro to work out to wholesome and worthy ends the strange destiny which has placed him here among us.[20]

The church press was not always the most eloquent testimonial to either the physical or mental superiority of the white. For instance, an editorial in the *Arkansas Methodist* gleefully chided a Negro journal for carrying silly advertisements, some of the products designed to bleach dark skin and straighten kinky hair. How absurd of these Negroes, believed the editor. In the *same* issue, it may be observed, readers of the *Arkansas Methodist* were urged to buy St. Jacob's Liniment, Capudine for gripp-aches, Palmer's Blood-Success Tablets, Pinex, Camphoroza, MR, Jad Salts to unclog uric acid in the kidneys, catarrh cures, Bitro-Phosphate

for the nerves, Mr. Booth's Wonderful Discovery, Mrs. Winslow's
Syrup to make baby coo and crow, Dr. Miles Heart Treatment,
Swamp Chill Tonic, NUXated Iron, Peptron for the nerves, Lydia
E. Pinkham's Vegetable Compound, Calotabs, Foley Kidney Pills,
Ramon's Liver Pills, Sage Tea to darken hair, Granger's Liver
Regulator, and Cowans-Rub-It-On.[21]

There was enough evidence of a different nature, however, to
permit the hope that the churches had not entirely forsaken their
redemptive mission. Timid and faltering as these formal, organized institutions often were, it was nevertheless through them
that the teachings of Christ were preserved, perpetuated, and
disseminated. It is absurd to claim the churches were unspotted;
it is blindness to ignore their positive rôle in American history.
The American Dream is based upon Christian foundations, and
the active presence of Christian faith has given a quiet strength
and sustaining courage to millions of unremembered men and
women. And Christian teachings have inspired many of the great
reform and humanitarian movements in the nation's past. Even
those crusaders for justice who disavow formal religion must ac-
knowledge their indebtedness to the spiritual foundations of society which alone make justice possible. In a sense, all those
questing decency in human relations draw upon the faith proclaimed by the churches, however unfaithful the churches may be
to their own ideals. The churches are democratic in their fundamental values and, as even so critical an observer as Myrdal
realized, by their very *being* they serve to lessen racial pride. Try
as it may, the conscience of America cannot ignore the Christian
creed.

This point is illustrated by George L. Collins who sent out fifty
questionnaires to young people asking if they had overcome their
racial prejudice and the influences contributing to this change.
His findings were reported in the *World Tomorrow* of February,
1928.

The connection between vital religion and social pioneering is realized when one reflects that practically all the leadership in interracial
student activity in the South comes from those who are active in
Christian organizations. Either the liberal without religious affiliation
is absent from the scene or he does not dare to risk social disapproval.
But the organized church can take little comfort from these conclusions. As an institution it seems to have directly influenced the recipients of the questionnaire very slightly. The work of the ministry, the
services of the church, the Sunday School, and the Young People's Society were seldom if at all referred to. . . . It is the old story that has

occurred so often through the ages, of pioneering to which the church has been indifferent or which it has even opposed, but for which it has been fundamentally responsible because of the gospel which it has taught and half believed.

In the second place, before judging the churches too harshly it is well to remember their charitable contributions. Thousands of Negroes owe their education or their health to schools and hospitals founded and supported by Protestant denominations. It is true that expenditures to succor the American Negro were not large in relation to total church budgets. It is true that sometimes the churches concentrated on bringing the gospel to the "heathen Chinese" or the natives of "darkest Africa" to the neglect of America's own second class Negro citizens. And it is further true that charitable works are no substitute for justice, for the giving of alms from one's pocketbook does not excuse racial pride in one's heart. It is interesting to speculate on what proportion of the funds given by churchmen to aid the Negro was in the form of "conscience money." Having made these admissions, the fact still remains that the Protestant churches did important work in bettering the education and health of the Negro. This sort of charitable work is sometimes deprecated by sophisticated liberals, but it must be placed in the scales when weighing the churches' contributions to racial justice.

It is not irrelevant to observe also that the important Commission on Interracial Co-operation, while not the instrument of any particular denomination, was born and led by devout churchmen. It worked closely with church groups and over 25 per cent of its members were ministers. In a very real sense the Commission, as the Association of Southern Women for the Prevention of Lynching, represented the leading Christian forces of the South.

The churches worked directly for racial justice.[22] The record of the Federal Council, for example, was honorable. In the tension-fraught year, 1919, the Administrative Committee issued a special statement urging justice for the Negro. Included in the eight-point appeal were protection from mob violence, opportunity to hold the same work on the same terms as other men, the sanctity of the Negro home, equal traveling, education, and recreational facilities, political equality, and closer cooperation between the races. These demands were reiterated in the Council's statement on "The Church and Social Reconstruction." The 1924 meeting of the Council held that the "assumption of inherent racial superiority by dominant groups around the world is neither sup-

ported by science nor justified by ethics." The removal of discriminations in housing, schools, travel, and industry was urged, in
addition to the equal protection of the law and other reforms.
Repeatedly in the 'thirties the Council spoke on the Negro issue,
especially in regard to segregation at church meetings. Putting
precept into practice, the Council refused to fix definitely upon
Indianapolis for its 1932 quadrennial until assurance had been
given that all the delegates would be received without discrimination in the matter of race and color.[23]

The attitude of the Council was also reflected in its two journals. The *Federal Council Bulletin* carried hundreds of references
to the Negro question, and at least a score of issues of *Information
Service* were devoted entirely to race relations. A contributor
seemed to express the general tenor of these items. The good
Christian, he believed, should not be willing to stop with justice
alone, "But justice is a good starting point and, if we follow the
road honestly, we shall have quite enough to do for a while."[24]

In addition, a Commission on the Church and Race Relations
(later the Department of Race Relations) was organized in 1921.
It held hundreds of interracial conferences, sought the birth of
local interracial committees, encouraged the exchange of pulpits,
printed thousands of posters and pamphlets, sent out speakers,
established a Race Relations Sunday (first observed in 1923) and
a Brotherhood Month. This group was headed by a Negro and
seemed to rely on education to lessen friction between the races.[25]

Northern Methodism also assumed a relatively advanced position on the Negro question.[26] It is fitting that this should be so for
Methodism's interest in the Negro dated back to the first General
Conference of 1784 when the question was asked: "What methods
can we take to extirpate slavery?"[27]

The Episcopal Address to the 1920 General Conference pointed
out that this is not a white man's world nor was the church a
white man's church. Talk of "lesser breeds," inferior castes and
"white man's burdens" is not for Methodists. Jesus came to destroy the spirit of racial pride. He must not be denied. Further, the
race problem is not confined to the United States, but is world-
wide in nature, and the yellow and black peoples will not long
submit to white overlordship.[28]

Four years later the Bishops again spoke on the race question.
The Conference also adopted a resolution introduced by E. Stanley
Jones rejecting "as unchristian and untrue the idea that certain
races are born to inherent and fixed superiority and rulership,

while others are born to inherent and fixed inferiority and sub-ordination. We stand for the life of open opportunity for all."[29]

In 1927 when the Methodist Board of Bishops met in Washington, three Negro bishops, quite unknown to their white comrades, were excluded from a dinner given by the Washington Methodist Union. To assuage the wound, the bishops unanimously adopted a statement regarding future meetings, declaring it to be their desire that no invitations to social functions be accepted, unless the invitations were broad enough to include them all.[30]

The 1928 General Conference adopted a report reaffirming the oneness of humanity and calling for equal opportunity in religion, education, citizenship, and industry. In addition, a long statement on social ideals included a demand for the elimination of racial discrimination and for the equal rights of all. Bishop Robert E. Jones, a Negro, presided over a conference session, and the delegates adopted a resolution thanking Bishop Jones for his courtesy and skill, finding much pleasure in this new relationship.[31]

The world service agencies of the Methodist Episcopal Church issued a New Year's message for 1931 which contained a strong statement on race relations.[32] A more significant action took place at the 1932 General Conference. It was here that Northern Methodists adopted the following resolution introduced by Reverend Ernest Fremont Tittle:

WHEREAS, "There cannot be Greek and Jew, circumcision and un-circumcision; barbarian, Scythian, bondman, freedman, but Christ is all and in all"; therefore, be it
Resolved, That the General Conference of the Methodist Episcopal Church shall hereafter meet only in cities where hotels, sufficient in number to accommodate its Delegates, shall in writing agree to meet the following conditions:
(1) No segregation of specific groups in room assignments.
(2) No discrimination against any Delegates in the use of hotel entrances, lobbies, elevators, dining rooms and other hotel services or facilities.
(3) Specific instruction of hotel employees by the hotel authorities regarding the interracial character of the Conference and the treatment of all Delegates with equal courtesy.[33]

The Committee on Entertainment took this resolution seriously and in 1936 told each inviting city plainly of the conditions upon which invitations would be accepted. Columbus, Ohio, observed the agreement in both spirit and letter, and the 1936 General Conference was unmarred by segregation. At this meeting the Bishops once again condemned racial intolerance.[34]

From time to time Methodist conferences at the local level issued pronouncements on the Negro question. Certain it is that the Methodist Federation for Social Service assumed an unequivocal position regarding the sinfulness of racial pride.[35] Encouraging too is the fact that the National Council of Methodist Youth, in 1934 and 1935, adopted statements on race relations that could hardly have been stronger.[36] The Epworth League also gave evidence of lessened prejudice among Methodist young people.

Southern Methodists were conscious of a Negro problem. In 1919 the Committee on Temperance and Social Service called for cooperation and helpfulness between the races and cautioned whites to accept the child-like infirmities of the Negro with tolerance. By 1922 the tone had become less patronizing. The Episcopal Address of that year observed the great strides made by Negroes since emancipation and asked that they be accorded justice "where their lawful rights are concerned." An adopted report to this Conference sought the solution to intolerance by the application of "Christian principles." In 1926 Southern Methodists held Christ's teachings concerning human brotherhood required equal justice and opportunity for all persons regardless of race or color.[37]

In 1930 the Bishops issued a strong condemnation of racial pride and pointed out specific disabilities which must be ended. Four years later the Bishops again maintained that Negroes "deserve and should have equality before the law, social, civil, and industrial justice, equitable educational, community, and religious advantages, and a human chance at the finer spiritual realities of American life." These sentiments were echoed in the adopted report of the Committee on Temperance and Social Service, with the additional provision that Negroes "be guaranteed by law the equal protection to life, liberty, and property." The conference as a whole adopted a social creed calling for justice, opportunity, and equal rights for all regardless of race. In 1938 the Episcopal Address indicted the white race for its unchristian and proud attitude toward the Negro and again noted the Negro's needs in the fields of housing, education, the courts, and economic life.[38]

The Uniting Conference of 1939 also demanded justice for the Negro. It is true that the place of Negro Methodists in the new merger was a compromise to white pride. So much so, indeed, that many Methodists felt it was too high a price to pay for unification. Such was the attitude of Ernest Fremont Tittle, the New York East

Conference, *Zion's Herald*, and the National Council of Methodist Youth, to mention a few examples of those who believed that the color line in Methodism should be completely erased.

Southern Methodists in local conferences now and then championed tolerance. The unofficial Council on a Christian Social Order did important work in bettering race relations.

There remains only the task of assessing the attitude of the Methodist press toward the Negro. With the exception of the *Arkansas Methodist*, the record of those papers examined in the course of this investigation was excellent. *Zion's Herald*, published in Boston, was very advanced in its thinking on race relations. It carried scores of editorials and articles on the Negro, many of the contributed items being written by Negroes. From the race riots of 1919 to the unification compromise of 1939, the journal consistently and courageously championed the Negro. Nor was its tone paternalistic. Inherently the white was not the superior of the black. The Negro deserved not merely kindness, but also justice and equality—and equality that was not on a segregated basis.

Perhaps it is unfair to single out this Boston paper for special praise, because actually both the New York and Northwestern *Christian Advocates* were almost as advanced. In countless items these journals sought to end the Negro's second class citizenship. They damned a segregated America and a segregated church.

Of great significance is that these views, somewhat modified, were accepted by the *Nashville Christian Advocate*. In the matter of race relations, this Methodist publication was clearly the most liberal of denominational church journals published in the South. Not only did it demand justice for the Negro, it did so without undue patronage and by specifically pinpointing the inequities suffered by the Negro. "The unavoidable fact is," maintained the editors, "racial prejudice and racial enmity are un-Christian—are now and ever will be."

Or witness this statement:

How often do we hear, "The Negro is all right in his place." As to that matter, the white man is all right in his place, but he is too frequently out of place. We are told that the Negro is inferior and will always remain so. Those who reiterate this seem to doubt it, since they feel impelled to resort to artificial pressure to "keep him down." . . . The fact is any person of one race is only superior to a member of any other race as he is superior.[39]

All in all, if Methodism be judged not by the uncompromising

Christian ethic but by the prevailing attitude of white Americans, it need not be too ashamed of its record on race relations.

Northern Baptists spoke frequently on the Negro problem. In 1922 the Northern Baptist Convention adopted a resolution deploring unchristian discrimination of race against race, and favored legislation to remedy matters. The following Convention resolved to organize interracial committees at the local level. In 1925 the American Baptist Foreign Missionary Society held the "most ominous sign on the world horizon is the apparent growth of white prejudice." In this year also the Convention believed America could not survive "if racial lines continue to separate us into groups that misunderstand and despise one another." In 1926 the Committee on Interracial Relationships slashed at the "barbarous assumption of racial superiority" which caused whites to disdain and neglect their Negro neighbors. The Committee suggested that "so long as Negroes cannot get lodgings or food in some towns, and have in many places, North and South, inferior wages, housing, police protection, street lighting, and schools, and are treated by many professing Christians as the Jews treated the Samaritans; there is need of emphasizing the spirit of Christ in race relations." Two years later this same Committee reported to the Convention that the superiority of any one race was a shibboleth. Moreover, since racial antipathy is not inborn or innate, but inherited and communicated, all Christians should avoid by word and deed the passing on to the younger generations the racial hatreds acquired from the past. The 1929 Convention passed a resolution on race relations.[40]

The opening year of the Depression Decade found the Northern Baptist Convention terming race prejudice the greatest hindrance to the establishment of the Kingdom of God on earth. This view was repeated in 1931 and 1934, with special reference to the desperate economic plight of the Negroes. In 1935 a resolution was adopted calling for equality in education, housing, and labor. Since race prejudice was unchristian, the Convention also voted to hold future meetings in only those cities where accommodations would be available to all delegates regardless of race or color. The delegates to the next Convention promised to boycott restaurants and other establishments that discriminated against patrons. America was guilty of flagrantly unchristian practices toward the Negro, believed Northern Baptists in 1937, and this view was repeated in 1938 and 1939.[41] From time to time also the church press reported local Baptist groups taking a strong stand against racial intolerance.

The Southern Baptist Convention was not silent on lynching, as has been noted, but aside from this there was little to indicate concern with the Negro problem. In 1920 and 1932 calls were issued for a more brotherly treatment of the Negro, but it was not until the report of the Home Missions Board in 1937 that Southern Baptists spoke with vigor. This report emphasized the infinite worth of personality, regardless of color. It flatly stated that the Negro was not divinely doomed to perpetual subordination. And it listed specific disabilities which must be removed in education, housing, the courts, and labor. The report concluded:

> In making these assumptions it is recognized that our conventional attitudes toward other races, our assumption of superiority, our consequent arrogance and lack of consideration, the limitations of opportunity which we lay on those whom we count inferior, the petty humiliations which we visit upon them, constitute some of the greatest paradoxes of all times. For it is, or should be, assumed that Christians neither would nor could be guilty of such; but the facts are too well known to be denied.

In 1939 the Southern Baptist Convention adopted a very vigorous resolution calling for the ending of inequalities.[42] Occasionally Baptist state and district conventions assumed an advanced position on race relations.

The Southern Baptist press was not noted for its tolerance on the race question. True, a few excellent articles thundered for justice and now and then editorials pointed out grievances suffered by Negroes. But these were exceptions. *On the whole* the Southern Baptist press appeared satisfied with the racial status quo.

In the North, the *Baptist* had a particularly fine record. It pointed out the sinfulness of racial pride with Garrison-like bluntness. The Baptist World Alliance also issued strong statements on race relations and did not segregate the delegates to its congresses.

To generalize, it can be said that Northern Baptists displayed a greater awareness of the unchristian nature of race relations in America than their Southern brethren, but that toward the end of the 'thirties even Southern Baptists began to speak rather strongly.

Northern Presbyterians were not silent. In 1919 the General Assembly condemned mob violence and in 1920 the Standing Committee on Freedmen rather patronizingly urged the extension of a brotherly hand to the colored people. A resolution of 1922 called upon Presbyterians to aid the Negro in securing better education, health, housing, recreation, and all other necessities of a Christian community. The 1928 General Assembly adopted a strongly worded protest against racial intolerance.[43]

In the Depression Decade almost everyone of the General Assemblies discussed the Negro issue. A resolution of 1937 catches the spirit of these discussions.

> We accept completely the ideal of the brotherhood of all races, as all are the children of God. We therefore call upon Christians everywhere to practice mutual good-will and coöperation among all racial groups, to eliminate every form of discrimination and to work actively for the recognition of the civil and religious rights of all minority groups. Conscious of our failures in the past to act upon this accepted principle, we urge that particularly in all conferences under the sanction of the church the utmost care be taken to avoid discrimination.[44]

From time to time presbyteries went on record in support of racial justice and, occasionally, in Omaha and Pittsburgh, for instance, a Negro was elected moderator of a presbytery. The Presbyterian Board of Christian Education, through special pamphlets and its regular journals, *Moral Welfare* and *Social Progress*, spoke in a very vigorous fashion. It is difficult to see how its criticism of racial pride could have been made stronger. Further, the unofficial Presbyterian Fellowship for Social Action fought to end racial disabilities in the 'thirties.

Apparently Southern Presbyterians did not have a deep sense of guilt concerning the treatment of Negroes in America. The 1921 General Assembly requested justice and righteousness in race relations, but it did not speak again until 1936. The Assembly of that year, however, heard an effective presentation of the Negro's plight by the Committee on Moral and Social Welfare. Citing statistics, the report showed how the Negro suffered in education, health, politics, the courts, and economic life. The committee again reported to the Assembly in 1937. It was perhaps the ablest presentation of the Negro's grievances ever read before a church conference in the South. It was specific and it was excellent.[45] A few instances appeared in the church press of local groups of Southern Presbyterians taking a liberal stand on the race issue, but they were neither very frequent nor very vigorous in expression.

What was the record of the Presbyterian press? The *Christian Observer*, published in Kentucky, confined itself almost exclusively to religious news and items on the Negro were rare. It did comment harshly on mob violence and from time to time pointed out examples of Negro progress, but there was little indication of real dissatisfaction with existing Negro-white relationships. On the other hand, the *Presbyterian Advance*, published in Nashville, assumed a quite liberal attitude. On the whole, this journal could be termed a strong defender of Negro rights even if it never urged full equality. Certainly its position was far ahead of general Southern white opinion. It is significant also that the official monthly of Southern Presbyterians, *Program Builder*, carried a series of lessons for young people in which a more Christian treatment of the Negro was urged.

In the North, the *Presbyterian Tribune* was probably the most advanced. And yet the record of such papers as the *Continent* and *Presbyterian Banner* was quite good also. A half-dozen other Presbyterian journals were less vigorous in their arguments, but even they realized the Negro suffered injustices.

Speaking broadly, Northern Presbyterians could be cited as an influence for breaking down racial barriers, and Southern Presbyterians were perhaps a shade in advance of the general thinking of their section.

Congregationalists, historically the Negro's friend and geographically concentrated north of the Mason-Dixon line, displayed dissatisfaction with the existing race relations. In 1919 they pledged themselves to fight "race prejudice and every means by which men rob our neighbor of his good name." They further requested for the Negro equal rights before the law and the complete citizenship guaranteed by the Constitution, and called attention to the acute problems confronting the black in housing, industry, education, and social justice. The 1921 National Council urged Congregationalists to form local interracial committees and steps were taken to promote these groups. Twice again this Council spoke on the need for racial justice.[46]

The famous social creed of Congregationalism, adopted in 1925, requested the elimination of racial discrimination. To augment this view a Commission on Inter-Racial Relations, with Albert W. Palmer as chairman, was established. This group promoted Race Relations Sunday, worked with the Federal Council, published a quarterly bulletin, sent forth speakers, and investigated specific cases of racial injustice.[47]

At the next Council, church groups were urged not to meet in any hotel or club that practiced segregation. The 1931 General

Council of the now united Congregational and Christian Churches resolved not to meet in any city or any hotel that could not promise in advance equal treatment of all delegates. And in 1934 the General Council spoke on specific abuses and stated that racial prejudice was rooted in a competitive economic order. The idea of Nordic superiority, the report continued, is a rationalization growing out of the desire to keep other races in subjection.[48]

In the meantime, the Commission on Social Relations, through seminars and its publication, *Church and Society*, attacked race prejudice in an outspoken fashion. The official Congregational Council for Social Action, formed in 1934, had a Committee on Race Relations as one of its four major departments. The *Congregationalist*, the denominational journal, did its bit in the cause of racial justice.

The Protestant Episcopal Church is one of the distinctly national churches. Although most of its congregations are all white or all Negro, it is not divided into racial branches. It frequently spoke on lynching and mob violence and forwarded race relations through the American Church Institute for Negroes, the authorized agency responsible to the General Convention. Having said this, it still remains true that only rarely—in 1919 and 1934—did the General Convention indicate an interest, aside from lynching, in the Negro. This gap was compensated somewhat by the fact that the unofficial Church League for Industrial Democracy and the Episcopal press were generally advanced in their thinking on the Negro question.

Without presenting the evidence in detail, it can be said that other denominations forwarded the cause of racial justice. The Disciples of Christ, for example, resolved not to meet in International Convention unless assurance was given that there would be no discrimination against Negro delegates. A special advance guard traveled to the city in question to confirm these arrangements. The United Lutheran Church, the Unitarians, and the Evangelical and Reformed Church spoke on the Negro question,[49] as did other denominations.[50]

Denominational journals, in varying degrees, urged racial justice. The *Reformed Church Messenger*, *Christian Register*, and *Universalist Leader* had excellent records, as did the *Christian-Evangelist* in the 'thirties. The *Lutheran*, however, ranks as something less than a warm friend of the Negro.

The undenominational journals examined in the course of this inquiry had an enviable record. The *Christian Work* and the *Chris-*

tian Herald spoke rather frequently and rather strongly, while the *World Tomorrow* and the *Christian Century* displayed a sensitivity toward the Negro probably unmatched in any papers in the country, religious or secular. This is important, particularly in the case of the *Christian Century*. The most influential Protestant periodical in the land, it devoted scores of items to the race question. Without exception, these editorials and articles were characterized by courage, candor, and compassion.

Similar praise can be bestowed on a number of unofficial cooperative religious organizations. The Fellowship of Reconciliation and the Fellowship of Southern Churchmen provide happy examples of Negroes and whites working together to further the cause of Christ, which meant, in part, the end of racial pride. It is to the credit of the whites in these organizations that they accepted the brotherhood of man, fully aware that in so doing they were inviting contempt and even physical violence from other whites. Other groups such as the National Religion and Labor Foundation and the Fellowship of Socialist Christians, although primarily concerned with economic matters, worked to better the lot of the Negroes in America.

And what can be said of the individual churchmen? Many examples could be cited—albeit mostly from the North—of a minister bolting a conference or resigning a pastorate or signing a petition or preaching a sermon in the interest of racial justice.

To cite chapter and verse for these instances would not absolve American Protestantism of the charge that it all too often accommodated itself to prejudice at the peril of its own soul. Christ must weep at the frailty of His church. And yet, as the years between 1919 and 1939 passed, Protestantism came increasingly to the recognition that a segregated church *content in its segregation* was wrong. And as the years passed, also, the gulf between Christ's ideal of brotherhood and men's practices narrowed.

NOTES

1. *Christian Century* (Dec. 9, 1931), 1556.
2. The attitude of the Roman Catholic Church is outside the scope of this study.
3. Frank S. Loescher, *The Protestant Church and the Negro* (N. Y., 1948), 76–77.

4. Jesse Howell Atwood, *The Attitude of Negro Ministers of the Major Denominations in Chicago Toward Racial Division in American Protestantism* (unpublished Ph.D. dissertation, University of Chicago, 1930), 105.

5. *Christian Century* (April 16, 1925), 507.

6. Gunnar Myrdal, *An American Dilemma. The Negro Problem and Modern Democracy* (2 vols., N. Y., 1944), II, 868.

7. Loescher, *The Protestant Church and the Negro*, 15.

8. George D. Kelsey, *The Social Thought of Contemporary Southern Baptists* (unpublished Ph.D. dissertation, Yale University, 1946); Hugh A. Brimm, *The Social Consciousness of Southern Baptists in Relation to Some Regional Problems* (unpublished Th.D. dissertation, Southern Baptist Theological Seminary, 1944); Foy Dan Valentine, *A Historical Study of Southern Baptists and Race Relations, 1917–1947* (unpublished Th.D. dissertation, Southwestern Baptist Theological Seminary, 1949). These three studies, drawing upon a mountain of evidence, were far more convincing to the present writer than anything else he has seen in print. Broader in scope but equally gloomy in their conclusions concerning the gulf between Christian theory and actual practice are Martin Kieffer, *The Attitudes and Practices of the Major American Protestant Denominations Toward the Negro Problem* (unpublished M.S.T. thesis, Union Theological Seminary, 1947) and Trevor Bowen, *Divine White Right. A Study of Race Segregation and Interracial Co-operation in Religious Organizations and Institutions in the United States* (N. Y., 1934).

9. Charles S. Johnson and Associates, *Into the Main Stream. A Survey of the Best Practices in Race Relations in the South* (Chapel Hill, 1947), 282.

10. The reader is reminded that this inquiry covers only the years 1919–1939. Undoubtedly the shadows would be fewer in more recent years.

11. *Christian Century* (May 28, 1930), 683; (Jan. 14, 1931), 62–63; *Christian Evangelist* (March 27, 1924), 416.

12. *Time* (June 13, 1932), 41; *Christian Century* (June 21, 1928), 785.

13. *Annual of the Northern Baptist Convention* (1929), 153.

14. *Information Service* (Sept. 28, 1929), 3; *Christian Century* (Nov. 2, 1932), 1325; *Literary Digest* (Jan. 11, 1930), 30–31.

15. *Christian Century* (Oct. 21, 1936), 1380; (Nov. 11, 1931), 1409.

16. The debate over unification raged in the Methodist press for over two decades.

17. *Chicago Defender,* July 20, 1935, clipping in files of the American Civil Liberties Union (Vol. 820) in New York Public Library; *Chicago Defender,* Nov. 25, 1933, clipping in files of the American Civil Liberties Union (Vol. 639) in NYPL.

18. Although the race riots of East St. Louis, Illinois, Phillips County, Arkansas, and Tulsa, Oklahoma, took a frightful toll of life and property, the Southern Baptist Convention, the state conventions of Arkansas and Oklahoma, and the district associations which convened soon after the riots remained silent. Brimm, *The Social Consciousness of Southern Baptists,* 48. For Bishops Mouzon and Thurston see *Arkansas Methodist* (June 16, 1921), 9–10, and *Living Church* (June 25, 1921), 249.

19. *Southern Churchman* (Aug. 9, 1919), 13.

20. *Western Recorder* (Aug. 23, 1923), 11.

21. (Nov. 13, 1919), *passim.*

22. The Protestant churches spoke frequently and vigorously against lynching. The evidence supporting this assertion is so abundant that it cannot be included here.

23. *Federal Council Bulletin* (June, 1919), 128; (Oct., 1919), 169–170; *Quadrennial Report of the Federal Council of Churches* (1916–1920), 111; (1920–1924), 82–83; (1928–1932), 69; Department of Research of the International Council of Religious Education, *Social Pronouncements by Religious*

Bodies Affiliated with and Related to the International Council of Religious Education, 1930–1939. Research Bulletin No. 16 (Chicago, 1939), 15; *Reformed Church Messenger* (June 23, 1932), 5.

24. *Federal Council Bulletin* (March, 1927), 16.

25. The annual reports of the group are on file in the New York headquarters of the present National Council of Churches. These reports are long on detail but short on interpretation. That is, one is informed that in 1939 exactly 10,320 posters and 82,349 pieces of other literature were distributed, but the effectiveness of this activity is not made clear.

26. Frank Loescher, *The Protestant Church and the Negro* (N. Y., 1948) is not a trustworthy guide for denominational pronouncements. He did not examine the denominational minutes and hence his conclusions are incomplete, inaccurate, and unfair to the churches.

27. Francis Emner Kearns, *Changing Social Emphases in the Methodist Episcopal Church* (unpublished Ph.D. dissertation, University of Pittsburgh, 1939), 59.

28. *Journal of the General Conference of the Methodist Episcopal Church* (1920), 171–179.

29. *Ibid.* (1924), 188, 295.

30. *Northwestern Christian Advocate* (May 20, 1926), 460.

31. *Journal of the General Conference of the Methodist Episcopal Church* (1928), 616–617, 622–623, 399.

32. *Christian Century* (Jan. 7, 1931), 36.

33. *Journal of the General Conference of the Methodist Episcopal Church* (1932), 259–260.

34. *Ibid.* (1936), 146; *Northwestern Christian Advocate* (May 28, 1936), 707–708.

35. This conclusion is based upon an examination of complete files of the Federation's *Social Service Bulletin* and *Social Questions Bulletin*.

36. Miron A. Morrill, ed., *Methodist Youth Council* (Chicago, 1934) and *The National Council Meets Again* (Chicago, 1936).

37. *New York Christian Advocate* (Oct. 9, 1919), 1282–1283; *Journal of the General Conference of the Methodist Episcopal Church, South* (1922), 237–238, 356; F. Ernest Johnson, *The Social Work of the Churches* (N. Y., 1930), 155.

38. *Journal of the General Conference of the Methodist Episcopal Church, South* (1930), 377–378; (1934), 294–295, 369; (1938), 246–247.

39. (Feb. 28, 1936), 287; (Nov. 12, 1937), 1444–1445.

40. *Annual of the Northern Baptist Convention* (1922), 183; (1923), 245; (1925), 190, 428; (1926), 168–169; (1928), 88; (1929), 105.

41. *Ibid.* (1930), 152; (1931), 463; (1934), 701–702; (1935), 182, 276–277; (1937), 103; (1938), 248–249; (1939), 269, 180–181; *New York Times*, Feb. 16, 1936, 9.

42. *Annual of the Southern Baptist Convention* (1920), 97; (1932), 91; (1937), 271–272; (1939), 141.

43. *Minutes of the General Assembly of the Presbyterian Church, U. S. A.* (1919), 170; (1920), 78; (1922), 185; (1928), 153.

44. *Ibid.* (1937), 223. This is only one of many strong statements.

45. *Minutes of the General Assembly of the Presbyterian Church, U. S.* (1921), 80, 114; (1936), 99–100; (1937), 105–107.

46. *Minutes of the National Council of Congregational Churches* (1919), 36, 40; (1921), 385, 74–75, 236.

47. *Ibid.* (1925), 47–48, 52.

48. *Ibid.* (1927), 56–57, 230; *Minutes of the General Council of Congregational Christian Churches* (1931), 197; (1934), 110–111.

49. *Christian-Evangelist* (Oct. 29, 1936), 1413–1414; *Federal Council Bulletin* (Jan., 1936), 3–4; *Minutes of the Convention of the United Lutheran*

Church in America (1932), 412; *Christian Register* (Feb. 7, 1935), 87–89; *Minutes of the General Synod of the Reformed Church in the United States* (1932), 154–155; *Acts and Proceedings of the General Conference of the General Synod of the Evangelical and Reformed Church* (1936), 253.

50. See Johnson, ed., *The Social Work of the Churches*, 154–155; *Social Pronouncements*, 15–17.

ORGANIZED LABOR
AND NEGRO WORKERS[1]

HERBERT R. NORTHRUP

In this selection Herbert R. Northrup examines the policies toward blacks of American trade unions, concluding that the favorable effect of unionism on the welfare of Negro workers, evident since 1936 when "the pendulum began to swing the other way," will persist and that "trade unions will perform a real service in helping to alleviate the race problem." Studies made two decades later show Northrup's prediction to have been overoptimistic. (See Herbert Hill, "Racism Within Organized Labor: A Report of Five Years of the AFL-CIO, 1955–1960," Journal of Negro History [Spring 1961]; Ray Marshall, "The Negro and Organized Labor," Journal of Negro Education [Fall 1963].)

✻

The racial policies[2] of American trade-unions vary from outright exclusion of Negroes by some organizations to full acceptance of them with all privileges of membership by others. Moreover, union poliices toward Negroes are somewhat fluid and subject to change if the circumstances so warrant. For example, the appearance of a rival union with a liberal racial policy may result in a reversal of the policies of its competitor, which had, up to that time, discriminated against colored workers. The presence of an exclusionist union in the same jurisdiction with one which usually tolerates no discrimination may cause the latter organization to relax its principles for fear that it might alienate its predominately white membership.

Reprinted by permission from *Journal of Political Economy*, LI (June 1943), 206–221.

The attitude of unions toward Negroes also often varies within the same organization from region to region, depending upon local customs and the type of leadership which is selected. It sometimes happens that Negroes are refused membership in an organization in one part of the country, while received freely by it in another. In one local union a sympathetic president or business agent may play an important role in cementing good feeling between the white and colored workers; in a neighboring local of the same national union a prejudiced leader may cause the whites to exclude the Negroes.

Dynamic elements such as these prevent any clear-cut categorizing of American labor unions according to their racial policies. This fact should be borne in mind for the discussion which follows, in which (1) union racial policies will be classified and analyzed; (2) the position of the American Federation of Labor and (3) that of the Congress of Industrial Organizations will be set forth; and (4) an examination will be made of what the spread of union organization can mean to colored workers, using as illustrations the aircraft industry, and the International Association of Machinists and the United Automobile Workers, the unions which have jurisdiction in that industry.

I

At least[3] fifteen American trade-unions specifically exclude Negroes from membership by explicit provisions in either their constitutions or rituals. Of these, six—the Airline Pilots, the Masters, Mates and Pilots, and the Wire Weavers,[4] all A.F. of L. affiliates, and the Train Dispatchers, the Railroad Yardmasters of America, and the Railroad Yardmasters of North America, which are unaffiliated—are of no great importance in barring Negroes from jobs, since none of them has a membership exceeding 3,000. Quite different, however, is the effect of the remaining nine exclusionist unions, for they include some of the larger and more influential organizations in the American labor movement, namely: the International Association of Machinists, the Commercial Telegraphers, the Railroad Telegraphers, the Railway Mail Association, the Switchmen, the Locomotive Engineers, the Locomotive Firemen and Enginemen, the Railroad Trainmen, and the Railway Conductors. The first five of these larger exclusionist unions are A.F. of L. affiliates; the last four are independent.[5] In addition, five unions (all A.F. of L. affiliates)—the Flint Glass

Workers; the Brotherhood of Electrical Workers;[6] the Plumbers and Steamfitters; the Asbestos Workers, Heat and Frost Insulators; and the Granite Cutters usually deny admittance to Negroes by tacit consent. Nine others—the Boilermakers, Iron Shipbuilders, Welders, and Helpers;[7] the Railway and Steamship Clerks, Freight Handlers, Express and Station Employes;[8] the Railway Carmen;[9] the Maintenance of Way Employes;[10] the Blacksmiths, Drop Forgers and Helpers;[11] the Sheet Metal Workers;[12] the Federation of Rural Letter Carriers; the Rural Letter Carriers' Association,[13] and the American Federation of Railroad Workers (the constitution of this union bars Negroes, but they are admitted to an auxiliary with no voting rights)—permit Negroes to join and give them the privilege of paying dues, but limit their participation to segregated, "Jim Crow" auxiliary bodies which in one way or another prohibit them from having a voice in the affairs of the union, from negotiating their own agreements, or from having an opportunity to advance in the occupational hierarchy. All but the last two of these organizations are likewise A.F. of L. affiliates.

To summarize the above in tabular form:

I. *Union which excludes Negroes by provision in ritual:*
Machinists, International Association of (A.F. of L.)

II. *Unions which exclude Negroes by provision in constitution:*
   A. A.F. of L. affiliates:
      Airline Pilots Association
      Commercial Telegraphers Union
      Masters, Mates and Pilots, National Organization
      Railroad Telegraphers, Order of
      Railway Mail Association
      Switchmen's Union of North America
      Wire Weavers' Protective Association, American
   B. Unaffiliated organizations:
      Locomotive Engineers, Brotherhood of
      Locomotive Firemen and Enginemen, Brotherhood of
      Railroad Trainmen, Brotherhood of
      Railroad Yardmasters of America
      Railroad Yardmasters of North America
      Railway Conductors, Order of
      Train Dispatchers' Association, American

III. *Unions which habitually exclude Negroes by tacit consent:*
All A.F. of L. affiliates:

Asbestos Workers, Heat and Frost Insulators
Electrical Workers, International Brotherhood of
Flint Glass Workers' Union, American
Granite Cutters, International Association of
Plumbers and Steamfitters, United Association of
    Journeymen
IV. *Unions which afford Negroes only segregated auxiliary*
status:
   A. A.F. of L. affiliates:
      Blacksmiths, Drop Forgers and Helpers, Brotherhood
      of
      Boilermakers, Iron Shipbuilders, Welders, and Help-
      ers, Brotherhood of
      Maintenance of Way Employes, Brotherhood of
      Railway Carmen of America, Brotherhood
      Railway and Steamship Clerks, Freight Handlers, Ex-
      press and Station Employes, Brotherhood of
      Rural Letter Carriers, Federation of
      Sheet Metal Workers' International Association
   B. Unaffiliated organizations:
      Rural Letter Carriers' Association
      Railroad Workers, American Federation of

In most instances the exclusionist and discriminatory practices of these unions have been in effect for several decades, and there can be no doubt that they represent the desires of the majority of the membership of the unions. Despite the efforts of a number of members in several of these organizations to have the discriminatory provisions erased, they continue to remain in force.[14] Nor does it seem necessary to discuss at great length the underlying motives which bring them into being. Undoubtedly, racial prejudice plays a part, particularly on the railroads, where a majority of the exclusionist unions are found. Most of the railroad unions came into being as fraternal and beneficial societies. To admit Negroes to their ranks on an equal footing would be, in the minds of many white members, tantamount to admitting that the colored man is a social equal; and this the majority of white railroad workers have always refused to countenance.[15]

But it is much more important to note that nearly all the unions practicing discrimination—and railway labor organizations are certainly no exception—are organizations of skilled craftworkers. In view of the well-known work-scarcity consciousness of most craft unionists, it seems more likely that economic self-interest, or, as Spero and Harris so well put it, "the desire to restrict competition so as to safeguard job monopoly,"[16] is the major contributing factor. To exclude Negroes, these craft unionists have discovered, is a convenient and effective method of limiting the number of sellers of a particular type of labor or skill, and that, in turn, enables the white craftsmen to obtain a larger share of the avaliable work for themselves and/or to command a higher wage.

A few other craft unions which do not exclude Negroes or confine them to inferior status do, nonetheless, tolerate, if not sanction, discrimination by their local bodies. Thus, the Carpenters and Joiners and the Painters, Decorators and Paperhangers, neither of which has any rules or stipulations providing for exclusion or segregation of colored artisans, follow a policy of organizing Negro workers into separate local unions. While it is true that these separate Negro locals have equal status with the white locals, and while it is also true that in certain instances, notably among longshoremen, Negroes seem to prefer a separate setup, it is an undeniable fact that in the building trades, as in most other industries, the Negro workers segregated into separate local bodies are at a distinct disadvantage. Unless, as is seldom the case, the white and Negro locals co-operate in the allocation of union jobs, the members of the two local groups will be competing for work. Since the white local is usually the larger and more powerful, and since its business agent, because of his race, is able (especially in the South, where segregation is most common) to contact employers much more easily than his Negro rival, the result is usually that the colored unionists are unable to obtain a proportionate share of the employment. Moreover, discrimination resulting from separate local unions, as featured by the Carpenters and the Painters, is, although very effective in eliminating Negro workers from job opportunities, quite difficult to prove. Once a national trade-union adopts a policy of segregation, the way is open to white locals to deal with the situation as they wish, however much the national officers may deplore the results.

In some industries, notably textile manufacturing, the printing trades, and clerical and white-collar pursuits, Negroes are largely excluded from employment by the decisions of management. Undoubtedly, however, such decisions meet with the approval, if not the assistance, of the majority of the white unionists in these fields. On the other hand, in some of the rare instances when Negroes have obtained employment in these industries, they have been admitted to the unions.[17]

There are also, it should be pointed out, craft unions which have on a number of occasions endeavored to enforce economic equality upon their locals and which officially condemn discrimination in all its forms. Foremost among these organizations are the Bricklayers, Masons and Plasterers and the Operative Plasterers and Cement Finishers. Both these unions have constitutional stipulations providing for $100 fines to be assessed against members who discriminate against fellow-members because of race, creed, or nationality; and both give the national officers discretionary power to grant a local charter to a body of craftsmen if the objection of the subordinate union to the establishment of a second local is based on race or national origin.[18] It is worthy of note that in the South about 50 per cent of the tradesmen over which these two organizations have jurisdiction are Negroes. Had the Bricklayers and Masons and the Plasterers and Cement Finishers not offered an equalitarian program to Negroes, they would have had considerably more difficulty in organizing the workers in their crafts in the South.

Besides these "liberal" craft unions, those organizations having jurisdiction over workers engaged primarily in unskilled or semi-skilled labor,[19] e.g., the Hod Carriers, Building and Common Laborers and the International Longshoremen's Association, and the unions organized mainly on an industrial basis,[20] e.g., the Ladies Garment Workers and the Hat, Cap and Millinery Workers, all of which are A.F. of L. affiliates, and the unions which are members of the C.I.O., by and large, afford colored workers equal treatment, both on the job and in the union.

The fact that some trade-unions use the color bar to restrict competition for jobs should not be regarded as too extraordinary. A great many barriers against economic opportunity are sought by a wide variety of organized groups—farmers, business and professional men, and consumers, as well as labor organizations—and this is only one of several. That is not to say that the writer condones any of these attempts to create barriers. Each must be considered on its merits, and the use of a color bar by workers' organizations to limit the job opportunities of a minority race is one of the most difficult of all to justify.

But, whatever one may think of the ethics of trade-union discrimination, there is a fundamental inconsistency between the racial policies of most of the organizations in question[21] and the oft repeated principles of their parent-body, the A.F. of L., which never tires of "reiterating, re-endorsing, and reaffirming" the fact that the A.F. of L. has no color bar, or of proclaiming that the "workers must organize and unite under its banner, without regard to race, color, creed, or national origin."

II

For the first few years after its formation the leaders of the A.F. of L. apparently made a real effort to adhere to their expressed policies of racial equality. Candidates for affiliation were forced to pledge "never to discriminate against a fellow worker on account of color, creed, or nationality," and the 1890 convention refused to sanction the admittance of a machinists' union because the organization excluded Negroes from membership by constitutional provision.[22]

These sentiments, however, were of short duration. The Knights of Labor, with its ideal of solidarity irrespective of race, was rapidly disappearing as a rival of the A.F. of L., and the Federation heads soon came to realize that their ideals were standing in the way of expansion. Hence, when in 1895 this same machinists' union removed its color bar from its constitution and transferred it to its ritual, it was allowed to affiliate and became the International Association of Machinists. So the A.F. of L.'s policy of racial equalitarianism came to an abrupt end. One year after the Machinists affiliated, the Boilermakers and Iron Shipbuilders were welcomed, despite a similar method of excluding Negroes. Since then, A.F. of L. officials have not troubled to insist on this questionable ruse, but have admitted as affiliates organizations which exclude Negroes by constitutional provision.[23]

After 1000 the Federation adopted the explicit policy of organizing Negroes into separate locals or directly affiliated "Federal" unions when they were refused admission to an affiliated national union because of their color. The A.F. of L. constitution was further amended to permit the Executive Council to charter separate city central labor unions "if the situation warranted"— meaning, if a local central body refused to seat colored delegates.[24]

This method of compromise has proved quite unsatisfactory to Negro workers. The A.F. of L. Executive Council is supposed to act as the "international" for Federal locals; but, as a matter of fact, it is rarely in a position to do so. Usually it refers matters pertaining to these locals to the national union which has jurisdiction in the field. But, since the national union to which the affairs of the Federal locals are referred excludes Negroes, it is not surprising that colored workers organized in Federal locals have lacked competent assistance in settling grievances and in negotiating contracts and have failed to receive adequate support in preventing the encroachment of white workers on their job opportunities. Moreover, when, as in the cases of the Railway Clerks and the Railway Carmen, the exclusionist unions have amended their rules so as to permit the affiliation of Negroes in a subordinate, Jim Crow status, the A.F. of L. Executive Council has not hesitated to revoke the Federal charters, despite the opposition of the affected colored workers, and to transfer the locals to national unions under rules which deny to Negroes even the autonomy which they enjoy under Federal local charters.[25]

The Negro migration into northern industry during World War I brought the color question to the fore in several A.F. of L. conventions. Most important for our purposes was the discussion at the 1920 meeting. Federal locals of railway-coach cleaners introduced a resolution demanding that the Railway Carmen, which had jurisdiction over that group of workers, either remove its color bar or permit the coach-cleaners to establish a national union of their own. The same resolution demanded that the A.F. of L. take action on the refusal of the Machinists, the Boilermakers and Iron Shipbuilders, and the Blacksmiths and Drop Forgers to admit Negroes. A resolution, similar in content to the one introduced by the coach-cleaners, was offered by Federal locals of Negro freight-handlers, who demanded that the A.F. of L. take action on the refusal of the Railway Clerks to admit Negroes.

Reporting on the resolution of the coach-cleaners, the resolutions committee found that the Machinists and the Boilermakers had "no law in their constitution prohibiting the admission of colored workers following the trade" and that the "Blacksmiths issue charters to colored workers of the trade and have no law denying admission to colored workers." The committee did find that the Railway Carmen excluded Negroes; therefore, it could "only recommend" that the Carmen "eliminate from their constitution all reference to the admission of colored workers." The resolution of the freight-handlers was referred to the committee on organization. It "non-concurred" on the ground that the A.F. of L. could not interfere with the autonomy of an affiliate, but, after one of the most vigorous debates on the race question in the history of the Federation, an amendment was carried recommending that the Railway Clerks remove the color bar.[26]

The report of the resolutions committee on the resolution of the coach-cleaners contained a significant number of factual omissions. It is true that neither the Machinists nor the Boilermakers have clauses denying Negroes admission in their *constitutions*. But both at that time excluded Negroes by provisions to that effect in their *rituals*.[27] It is inconceivable that the members of the resolutions committee did not know this. It is also true that the Blacksmiths issue charters to Negroes. But a glance at footnote 11 will show that the purpose of these charters is to control the competition of Negroes, to prevent them from advancing in the occupational hierarchy, and to deny them a voice in the affairs of the union.

The action taken by the conventions of the Railway Carmen and the Railway Clerks on the 1920 A.F. of L. convention's recommendation that they remove the color bars from their constitutions is also revealing. Meeting in 1921, the Railway Carmen amended their constitution so as to permit the chartering of Negro auxiliary locals with rules not unlike those imposed on colored workers by the Blacksmiths. This the A.F. of L. Executive Council found quite satisfactory. It revoked the charters of the Federal locals of Negro coach-cleaners and turned them over to the Carmen's union. Thus Negro coach-cleaners lost the right to run their own unions and to attend A.F. of L. conventions without being granted anything worthy of mention in return.[28]

The Railway Clerks' convention of 1922 did not even go as far as the Carmen's conclave of the previous year. When a resolution urging the elimination of the "white only" clause was introduced, it created such an uproar that it was declared out of order. No action was taken on the question,[29] but the A.F. of L. exacted no penalty on the Clerks' union for ignoring its recommendation. Having once admitted as autonomous affiliates organizations excluding Negroes, the A.F. of L. was powerless to force equalitarianism upon a recalcitrant international except by expelling it from the Federation, and this has never been done.

As membership in A.F. of L. unions declined in the twenties, interest in organizing Negroes also died down. The Federation did not trouble to give serious heed to proposals of Negro leaders or other socially minded individuals interested in achieving a greater organization of colored workers.[30] It was not until the resurgence of trade-unionism during the decade of the thirties was coupled with the presence of a recognized spokesman for Negro labor at A.F. of L. conventions in the person of A. Philip Randolph, president of the Brotherhood of Sleeping Car Porters, that the debate on the minority race question again became a feature of A.F. of L. conventions. Yet the results continue to be disappointing.

At the 1934 convention, for example, Mr. Randolph demanded expulsion from the A.F. of L. for "any union maintaining the color bar."[31] The resolutions committee voted adversely on the grounds that the "American Federation of Labor . . . . cannot interfere with the autonomy of National and International unions."[32] However, an amendment to this report was adopted which authorized the appointment of a five-man committee "to investigate the conditions of the colored workers of this country and report to the next convention."[33]

The committee, composed of John E. Rooney, of the Operative Plasterers and Cement Finishers, John Brophy, of the United Mine Workers, John Garvey, of the Hod Carriers and Common Laborers, Jerry L. Hanks, of the Journeymen Barbers, and T. C. Carroll, of the Maintenance of Way Employes, held open hearings in Washington and recommended a threefold plan: (1) that all international unions which in any way bar Negroes or afford them only inferior status take up the "Negro question at their next convention for the purpose of harmonizing constitution rules and practices to conform with the oft-repeated declaration of A.F. of L. conventions on equality of treatment of all races within the trade union movement"; (2) that the A.F. of L. issue no more charters to unions practicing discrimination; and (3) that the A.F. of L. inaugurate a campaign of education "to get the white worker to see more completely the weakness of division and the necessity of unity between white and black workers to the end that all workers may be organized."[34]

Although this report would by no means have solved the A.F. of L.'s race problem, it might have provided a workable method whereby significant reform could have been accomplished had not the Executive Council effectively sabotaged the whole thing. Instead of allowing this committee to report its findings to the 1935 convention, as it had been directed by the resolution which created it, William Green, president of the A.F. of L., handed over the report to George M. Harrison, an A.F. of L. vice-president and president of the exclusionist Railway Clerks. In so doing, Mr. Green followed a very unusual and, without doubt, unconstitutional procedure. The committee had been ordered by a convention, the A.F. of L.'s highest governing body,[35] to report directly to it the following year. Yet Mr. Green permitted a member of the Executive Council to substitute a document more pleasing to himself. In fact, one wonders whether *any* report would have been presented to the delegates had it not been for the continual prodding of A. Philip Randolph. As it was, Mr. Harrison delayed action until about 10:00 P.M. on the eleventh and last day of the convention. By then the delegates had already become exhausted and divided by the craft-industrial union controversy.[36] And so, when President Green submitted a totally innocuous document, which Mr. Harrison had substituted for the original committee report, advocating no action except "education," it was adopted by the tired delegates over Mr. Randolph's protests.[37]

Despite the fact that the suspension of the C.I.O. unions by the A.F. of L. Executive Council provided Randolph and his supporters with an excellent argument with which to demand the expulsion of unions violating the A.F. of L. constitution by excluding workers because of race, they have been unable to convince that body that it is guilty of any inconsistency.[38] Moreover, the departure of the more liberal industrial unions into the C.I.O. renders it very unlikely that either the A.F. of L. or its constituent unions will take any action on their own initiative to remove color bars. On the other hand, however, is the fact that increased publicity has been given both union affairs and the rights of minority peoples by the war, and this has supplied new ammunition to those who are demanding the end of union exclusion. Bolstered by the appointment of the President's Committee on Fair Employment Practices, a development for which he was in no small way responsible, Mr. Randolph introduced two resolutions at the 1941 A.F. of L. convention. The first called for the appointment of a seven-man committee to investigate discrimination by affiliated unions and to report back to the next convention.[39] When the resolutions committee reported adversely, Randolph rose to cite case after case in which A.F. of L. unions were preventing Negro workers from obtaining employment on defense projects. The Boilermakers and Shipbuilders and the Machinists drew his heaviest fire for preventing the employment of Negroes in shipyards and airplane plants; but the building trades—the Carpenters, the Painters, and even the Bricklayers and the Plasterers and Cement Finishers—were also prominent on his list.[40] Some of the presidents of the unions mentioned in his report attempted to answer his charges, but none of them was able to refute his facts.[41] The official A.F. of L. attitude was clearly stated once more in the speeches of three Federation spokesmen: John P. Frey, president of the Metal Trades Department, Matthew Woll, a vice-president,

and President William Green. In brief they stated (1) that discrimination existed before the A.F. of L. was born and that human
nature cannot be altered; (2) that such a committee as proposed
by Randolph would violate the sacred doctrine of autonomy of the
Federation's affiliates; (3) that the A.F. of L., per se, does not
discriminate, because it gladly accepts Negro workers into its directly affiliated Federal locals. Besides, the A.F. of L. hopes that,
"if there is any barrier" in the way of organizing Negroes, it will
ultimately be broken down; and (4) that the Negroes should be
grateful for what the A.F. of L. has done for them.[42]

To which Mr. Randolph and his supporters replied (1) that,
condoning existing discrimination, the A.F. of L. had nurtured its
growth; (2) that Randolph's proposal would not violate trade-
union autonomy but would only investigate a means of ending
discrimination (Mr. Woll's claim that it would do otherwise was
merely an appeal to the delegates to vote against the proposal by
misstating the intents and purposes of the resolution); and (3)
that not only does the policy of organizing Negroes into Federal
locals give tacit approval of discrimination, but the A.F. of L. only
recently had itself committed an act of discrimination against
Negro freight-handlers and station porters who had been so
organized. The exclusionist Brotherhood of Railway Clerks had
amended its rules so as to permit the organization of Negroes in
segregated Jim Crow auxiliaries, the members of which are not
allowed to negotiate with their employers or to have a voice in the
affairs of the Brotherhood. Over the protests of the leaders of
these Negro workers the A.F. of L. Executive Council revoked the
Federal local charters of these workers and allowed the Railway
Clerks to assume jurisdiction over them[43] (an action on the part of
the Executive Council which duplicated the one twenty years
earlier in the case of the Negro coach-cleaners and the Railway
Carmen.)[44] The last point (4) brought out by Mr. Randolph and
his supporters was that the Negro workers are grateful for what
the A.F. of L. has accomplished, but they feel that it could and
should do far more.[45]

Defeated in this attempt to force at least a study of A.F. of L.
discrimination, Randolph attempted to have the A.F. of L. convention go on record as opposed to Jim Crow auxiliaries. But John P.
Frey declared that, if the resolution was passed, it would forbid
unions to establish ladies' auxiliaries, composed of the wives and
daughters of union men. On the basis of this pretext the resolution
was defeated.[46]

Similar resolutions introduced by Randolph at the 1942 convention met a like fate.[47] The tenor of the debates at both the 1941 and the 1942 conventions offers little hope to Negroes that the offending unions will relax their discriminatory rules and practices. Fortunately, the racial policies of the C.I.O. and its affiliates, to an examination of which we now turn, are, in general, much more liberal.

III

One of the main objectives of the C.I.O., according to its constitution, is to ". . . . bring about the effective organization of the working men and women of America regardless of race, color, creed, or nationality. . . ." Thus far, there can be little doubt that both the C.I.O. and its constituent unions have sedulously adhered to this nondiscrimination policy in organizing Negroes. Of course, this is not to say that colored workers have never been accorded unfair treatment by either C.I.O. members or local unions; but, in so far as this writer has been able to determine, no national C.I.O. union excludes Negro workers from membership or segregates its colored members into separate local unions. Moreover, the national officers of the C.I.O. unions have, by and large, a consistent record of practicing what they preach in regard to the treatment of Negroes.

It is not especially difficult to comprehend why the C.I.O. has pursued its liberal racial policy. Unlike craft unions, which are organized on an exclusive and narrow basis and which depend upon their control of a few highly skilled and strategically situated jobs for their bargaining power, industrial unions acquire their strength by opening their ranks to all the workers in an industry.[48] The United Mine Workers, the Amalgamated Clothing Workers, and the Ladies Garment Workers[49] had been organized on an industrial basis for many years prior to 1935, the year their leaders founded the C.I.O. Few, if any, labor unions had better records for fair treatment of Negroes than did these three.[50] Besides, their officers foresaw that the projected campaigns to organize the workers of the iron and steel, the automobile, and the other mass-production industries would be doomed to failure unless the unions in these fields opened their doors to workers of all creeds and colors. Finally, the C.I.O. contains within its ranks most of the left-wing elements of the American labor movement. These groups have always most vociferously opposed all forms of racial discrimination. For these reasons, then, the C.I.O. has attempted to enroll workers regardless of race, creed, color, or nationality.

True economic equality, however, involves more than organizing workers into one union regardless of race. It entails also the establishment of some standard by which jobs may be allocated without prejudice. The general principle adhered to by most unions in this respect is that seniority of tenure, with certain qualifications for ability, should be the governing criterion. But it makes little difference, for the purposes of this discussion, what the standard is, as long as it is applied without discrimination. The question is whether this standard has been applied fairly (*a*) with respect to layoffs and rehirings and (*b*) with respect to promotions.

The application of racial equality to seniority in layoffs and rehirings has not caused very serious difficulties. The fairness of such action is too obvious for either management or white workers to protest, and the principle now has fairly general acceptance in a large segment of American industry.

On the other hand, however, the question of literal application of the equalitarian policy to seniority in promotions has caused serious difficulties. Because few Negroes have been promoted to the better-paying jobs in the past, white workers have come to regard white priority as the established order of things. At the same time, the Negro workers have justly pointed out that, if the principle of equal treatment is to have real meaning, it must be applied to this, as well as to other, aspects of the collective-bargaining agreement.

The manner in which this issue has been resolved has varied considerably from place to place and from region to region. But it may be said that the national officers of such unions as the Steelworkers, the Automobile Workers, the Aluminum Workers, and the Marine and Shipbuilding Workers have made praiseworthy attempts to enforce a literal application of promotion seniority regardless of race; and in the North, despite some opposition from their white members and local leaders, they have been able to open up a sizable number of new employment opportunities to Negroes. In the South, however, these same national union leaders have felt it necessary to act more slowly in altering the status quo. For there they have encountered a far more determined opposition from their white membership. Consequently, they have felt that to force the issue would result either in wrecking their southern locals by internal dissension or in inducing predominantly white memberships to transfer allegiance to rival unions the leaders of which are not committed to a policy of racial equality. To give a few examples:

The Marine and Shipbuilding Workers' union has collective agreements with the Federal Shipbuilding Corporation of Kearny, New Jersey, and with the Alabama Dry Dock and Shipbuilding Company of Mobile, Alabama. At the former, the union has opened up the company's apprentice training school and many top-bracket jobs to Negroes, who compose approximately 10 per cent of the employees there. At the latter, however, Negroes continue to be barred from advancing beyond semiskilled levels, a policy inaugurated by the company many years ago and left largely unchanged during the four years in which the union has had contractual relations. Should the union officials attempt to alter this long-standing policy, they declare "disruption" would result. What they mean is that the white membership, about 85 per cent of the Alabama company's employees, would swing over to a rival union, the A.F. of L. Metal Trades Department, which in two National Labor Relations Board elections has unsuccessfully attempted to wrest bargaining rights from the C.I.O. union. In both these elections most of the Negroes supported the Marine and Shipbuilding Workers—the second time, despite its failure to improve their occupational status, but for very good reasons nonetheless. The Metal Trades Department includes the Machinists, the Boilermakers and Shipbuilders, the Electrical Workers, and the Plumbers. None of these unions usually welcomes Negroes on equal terms. The Metal Trades Department has a contract with a neighboring Mobile yard, and there the only Negroes employed, out of approximately 10,000 workers, are 22 porters. Had the Metal Trades Department won bargaining rights at the Alabama company's yard, the Negroes feared that they would have been entirely displaced, just as were most of the colored employees of the Tampa Shipbuilding Corporation, Tampa, Florida, soon after the Metal Trades Department signed a contract in 1938. Consequently, the Negro workers at the Alabama company gave their support to the union which had by far the better record for fair dealing with members of their race.[51]

The writer's field notes contain many other illustrations, although few are so clear and vivid. The Aluminum Workers union has a strict seniority rule governing promotions in its contracts with the Aluminum Company of America. In northern plants Negro workers have derived much benefit from this provision. At the Alcoa, Tennessee, plant, however, concessions have been made to the white workers at the expense of the Negroes. In the Pittsburgh iron and steel industry Negroes have been advanced to skilled production jobs as a result of the contracts of the United Steelworkers. Formerly, it was not unusual for many qualified colored workers to be passed over. In the Birmingham, Alabama, area, however, there has been no great change in the racial-occupational picture. No two unions have a better record in practicing equality than the Automobile Workers and the Ladies Garment Workers (to take a case from the A.F. of L.). Yet neither of these organizations has prevented its locals in Atlanta, Georgia, from depriving Negroes of rights guaranteed by their respective union constitutions.[52]

It was to be expected that so radical a change in industrial mores as the application of racial equality to promotions would meet with considerable opposition. It is not, therefore, remarkable either that the principle has been applied imperfectly or that it has been less rigidly adhered to in the South than elsewhere. Nevertheless, in a very short period significant progress has been accomplished in extending to Negroes the right to advance in the occupational hierarchy in accord with their ability. Whether unionism will one day lead the way to a fairly general acceptance of nondiscriminatory promotion—which this writer believes to be an acid test of the workability of equality in the labor movement—only the future can reveal. If, however, this practice is to become widespread, it is imperative at this time that equalitarian-minded, and not exclusionist, unions win bargaining rights in new and expanding industries. Nowhere is this fact better illustrated than in the manufacture of aircraft—surely one of the great industries of the future.

IV

Before the current expansion in aircraft production was induced by World War II, the industry was noted for its "almost universal prejudice against Negroes."[53] This was the result of management decisions, for at that time the workers in the industry were, for the most part, unorganized. Today, despite acute manpower shortages, the numerical participation of Negroes in aircraft production is woefully small, since only a few companies have tapped the Negro labor reserve to any great extent.[54]

Since the beginning of the American rearmament program a

substantial number of workers in the aircraft industry have been organized by the International Association of Machinists and the United Automobile Workers, which have been given exclusive jurisdiction in the industry by the A.F. of L. and the C.I.O., respectively. The reader will recall that the Machinists' union excludes Negroes by a provision in its ritual. In localities where the I.A.M. has been recognized as the workers' bargaining agent—e.g., Nashville, Tennessee, or Seattle, Washington—the exclusionist pattern has been strengthened, if not institutionalized.[55] The I.A.M. has also organized the Lockheed Vega plant at Burbank, California, which is one of the few companies employing a large number of Negroes. The local there has even admitted a few Negroes, and this has been hailed as an encouraging sign by the Negro press.[56] So it is. It should not be forgotten, however, that the local union could be forced to dismiss its colored members by the national officers—and, indeed, should be so ordered, according to the I.A.M.'s rules. That the national union has taken no action is probably ascribable to its officers' reluctance to invite censure by the President's Committee on Fair Employment Practices. Any statement that the I.A.M. has changed its racial policy is premature at this time and will be as long as the exclusionist clause remains in the union's ritual.[57] Moreover, the Lockheed Vega case is more than offset by instances of discrimination elsewhere.[58] Consequently, if the I.A.M. should obtain bargaining rights in a majority of the plants in the aircraft industry, it is difficult to see how Negroes can expect anything but strengthened opposition in their attempts to gain employment. And, if the I.A.M. is able to obtain closed-shop contracts, Negroes may be entirely excluded from a large sector of the industry.

The experience of the colored workers with the United Automobile Workers has been much more pleasant. The U.A.W. actually facilitated the introduction of Negroes in the industry. Prior to the defense program, the U.A.W. had enrolled Negroes on an equalitarian basis but had made little effort to improve their occupational standing. As a result, 75 per cent of the 30,000 Negroes in the automobile industry, who comprise about 6 per cent of all automobile workers, remained concentrated in the tough, dirty work of the foundries.

With the outbreak of the war and the conversion of the automobile industry to aircraft production, much of the foundry work disappeared. Except at the Ford River Rouge plant, where, besides the usual concentration in the foundry, Negroes were also employed in production and assembly-line jobs, little provision was made to retrain and reclassify Negro workers. The national officers of the U.A.W., however, demanded that Negroes be retrained and upgraded. National and local interracial committees were established to enforce the union's nondiscrimination policy.[59]

Discrimination in U.A.W. locals has not disappeared; but, as a result of the action on the part of the national officers, Negroes who would have been displaced have instead been retrained and upgraded into better-paying jobs. When white workers conducted illegal stoppages in protest against the assignment to machines of former Negro janitors who had taken war-training courses, R. J. Thomas, U.A.W. president, ordered the strikers to return to work or suffer loss of union membership and employment. The Negroes have remained at their machines, and the ringleaders of the disturbances have been dismissed.[60] If, then, the U.A.W. should obtain bargaining rights in a majority of the plants in the aircraft industry, Negroes may expect sympathetic treatment in their attempts to gain a more equitable share of the industry's jobs. And if the U.A.W. is able to obtain closed-shop contracts, the national leaders will be in an even stronger position to enforce their equalitarian principles on recalcitrant local memberships.

V

This brief survey of Negro-union relations has shown that labor organizations can be a great force either in imposing severe obstacles upon Negro workers or in assisting them to overcome the difficulties which they face in their efforts to obtain greater economic opportunities. It would seem that, prior to 1935, unionism was more of a hindrance than a help to Negro workers. Since 1936, however, the pendulum seems to have swung the other way, and thousands of Negro workers have benefited from increased wages, improved working conditions, and job security as a result of collective agreements. Moreover, it seems likely that unionism will continue to affect the welfare of Negro workers favorably. With the exception of the Machinists, and possibly of the Boilermakers and Shipbuilders, the Electrical Workers, and the Plumbers and Steamfitters,[61] most of the unions which habitually discriminate against Negroes either are relatively small or else are confined to industries in which the trend of employment had been declining, particularly the railroad industry. If our optimism proves correct, trade-unions will perform a real service in helping to alleviate the American race problem.[62]

NOTES

1. Anyone familiar with the penetrating analysis of this subject by S. D. Spero and A. L. Harris, *The Black Worker* (New York, 1931), esp. pp. 53–115, will realize my debt to them. In addition, I have benefited from an unpublished manuscript by Dr. P. H. Norgren and from suggestions from Professor S. H. Slichter and Drs. J. T. Dunlop and J. Shister.

2. The term "racial policies" as used here refers to policies directed at the Negro race. No attempt has been made to investigate policies toward the other colored races. However, the evidence at hand indicates that unions generally treat Orientals, Indians, and often Mexicans in the same manner as they treat Negroes. On the other hand, the A.F. of L. Journeymen Barbers' Union, which admits Negroes, excludes Orientals.

3. "At least" is said advisedly. During the last few years many independent, quasi-independent, and company unions have been formed, mostly local in jurisdiction. No effort has been made in this article to examine the racial policies of these organizations.

4. The Wire Weavers Association admits to membership only "white Christian males" and subjects aliens to an admission fee of $1,000. To the writer's knowledge, it is the only union in America which excludes non-Christians. Having a membership of less than 500, its influence is negligible.

5. The last four are the "Big Four" railroad-operating brotherhoods. During the last few years, two small exclusionist unions, the independent Dining Car Conductors, and the A.F. of L. Sleeping Car Conductors, merged with the Railroad Trainmen and the Railway Conductors, respectively.

6. In recent years some locals of the Electrical Workers in the electric light and power and the electrical machinery industries have begun to accept Negroes. But in building construction, shipyards, and railroad shops, where the bulk of the union's membership is employed, exclusion continues to prevail.

7. Before 1938 the Boilermakers excluded Negroes, and the "white" clause is still retained in the ritual. The 1937 convention amended the union's rules to permit the chartering of Negro auxiliary locals. The auxiliaries are limited to localities where a white local exists and where there are sufficient Negroes employed to maintain a local. Negroes have no voice in national union affairs but must obey all union laws. They cannot transfer except to other auxiliary locals. They are dependent upon the business agent of the "supervising" white local for job assignments. And, although they pay the same dues as white members, they receive only half as much in death and disability benefits and are not eligible for voluntary insurance plans to which white members may subscribe (cf. Brotherhood of Boilermakers, etc., *Subordinate Lodge Constitution* [ed. 1937], with *idem, By-Laws Governing Auxiliary Lodges* [ed. 1942]).

8. Before 1939 the Brotherhood of Railway Clerks excluded Negroes, and the "white" clause is still retained in the union constitution. The 1939 convention empowered the Executive Council to establish a Negro auxiliary. Auxiliary members must abide by all the rules of the Brotherhood and pay the same dues as the white members, but have no voice or representation in

the governing bodies of the Brotherhood (see Brotherhood of Railway Clerks, *Regulations for the Government of Lodges of the Auxiliary* [ed. 1940]).

9. "On railroads where the employment of colored persons has become a permanent institution they shall be admitted to membership in separate lodges. Where these separate lodges of negroes are organized they shall be under the jurisdiction of and represented by the delegate of the nearest white local in any meeting of the Joint Protective Board Federation or convention where delegates may be seated" (Brotherhood Railway Carmen, *Subordinate Lodge Constitution* [ed. 1941], sec. 6, clause C).

10. "Rights of membership of the colored Maintenance of Way Employes . . . . shall be under the direct control of the System Division. . . . . They shall be entitled to all the benefits and protection guaranteed by the Constitution to its members and shall be represented in the Grand Lodge by delegates of their own choice selected from any white Lodge on the System Division . . . . where employed. Nothing in this section operates to prevent the colored employes from maintaining a separate Lodge for social purposes and to receive official communications and information from, the Grand Lodge and the System Division . . . ." (Brotherhood of Maintenance of Way Employes, *Constitution* [ed. 1940], Art. XIII, sec. 1).

11. "Where there are a sufficient number of colored helpers, they may be organized as an auxiliary local and shall be under the jurisdiction of the white local having jurisdiction over that territory. . . . . Colored helpers shall not transfer except to another auxiliary local composed of colored members, and colored members shall not be promoted to blacksmiths or helper apprentices and will not be admitted to shops where white helpers are now employed" (Brotherhood of Blacksmiths, Drop Forgers, and Helpers, *Constitution*, quoted in U.S. Bureau of Labor Statistics, *Handbook of American Trade Unions* [Bull. No. 618 (1936)], p. 175).

12. Negro sheet metal workers may be organized in separate locals "with the consent of the white local" of the locality or else in "auxiliary locals" if consent of the white local is not obtained. Negro locals are under the supervision of the white locals. See U.S.B.L.S., *op. cit.*, p. 110.

13. Both the rural letter-carriers' unions prohibit Negroes from holding office or from acting as delegates to conventions (*ibid.*, p. 309).

14. A notable exception to this statement was the action taken by the Hotel and Restaurant Workers (A.F. of L.) at its 1936 and 1938 conventions. Before 1936 the constitution of this union stipulated that Negroes must be organized either in separate locals or as members-at-large. Colored workers were, however, given all other rights and privileges; and in actual practice the national union permitted locals to accept Negroes on a basis of full equality, if they so desired. The 1936 convention removed these restrictions as a preliminary move to an organizing campaign among railroad dining-car workers, and the 1938 convention inserted the following paragraph into the constitution (sec. 3a): "Any local law prohibiting the admission of any competent person, male or female, 'because of race, religion or color' is . . . . null and void."

On the other hand, in recent years attempts to remove the restrictive clauses from the rituals or constitutions of the Machinists, the Boilermakers and Shipbuilders, the Railway Carmen, and the Railway Clerks have failed.

15. Spero and Harris, *op. cit.*, pp. 66–67, 284 ff.

16. *Ibid.*, p. 56.

17. Material from the writer's files, based on field work. See also Spero and Harris, *op. cit.*, pp. 347–351, and C. L. Franklin, *The Negro Labor Unionist of New York* (New York, 1936), pp. 192, 214–215, 251–252, 271–274, 371–375.

18. Bricklayers, Masons and Plasterers' International Union, *Constitution* (ed. 1936), Art. XIII, sec. 1; Art. XVIII, sec. 14; Operative Plasterers' and

Cement Finishers' International Association, *Constitution* (ed. 1941), secs. 64, 22, 25.

19. Apparent exceptions to this rule are the Maintenance of Way Employes and the Railway . . . . Clerks, Freight Handlers, etc. But the former was organized by an all-white group, the track foremen, who at first entirely excluded Negroes. Later, when they extended their jurisdiction to cover all track workers, they had to organize Negroes who predominated on the southern roads; but, in order to prevent them from controlling the unions in the South, they segregated them into auxiliaries. Similarly, the latter union was organized by an almost all-white group and did not extend its jurisdiction over sections of the industry employing many Negroes until some time later.

20. The leading exception to this rule is the exclusionist American Federation of Railroad Workers, which claims jurisdiction over all workers in the industry. However, it was organized in 1901 as a union of shop craftsmen and did not claim its larger jurisdiction until ten years later. Eugene Debs's short-lived American Railway Union was another industrial union which excluded Negroes.

21. This, of course, does not apply to the unaffiliated exclusionist unions. However, when one examines the official pronouncements of any of them on "brotherhood," "progressive unionism," etc., one can unearth a multitude of inconsistencies.

22. Spero and Harris, *op. cit.*, pp. 87–88.

23. *Ibid.*, pp. 88–89.

24. U.S. Congress, *Report of the Industrial Commission* (Washington, D.C., 1901), XVII, 37.

25. See below, pp. 213, 215–216.

26. A.F. of L., *Proceedings, 1920*, pp. 307–310 and 351–352; and Spero and Harris, *op. cit.*, pp. 93–94, 101–102, 104–107.

27. In 1937 the Boilermakers amended their rules so as to give the national officers the power to establish auxiliary locals for Negroes (see n. 7, above). The Machinists still exclude Negroes.

28. Spero and Harris, *op. cit.*, pp. 89–91; n. 9, above; and Brotherhood Railway Carmen of America, *Proceedings of the Fourteenth Convention* (1921), pp. 5–6, 351–355, 383–385.

29. Brotherhood of Railway . . . . Clerks, etc., *Proceedings of the Tenth . . . . Convention* (1922), p. 163. For action of a later convention of the Clerks in amending their rules so as to give Negroes auxiliary status, see below, pp. 215–216.

30. Spero and Harris, *op. cit.*, pp. 107–112.

31. A.F. of L., *Proceedings, 1934*, pp. 330–331.

32. *Ibid.*, p. 331.

33. *Ibid.*, p. 332.

34. *Ibid., 1935*, p. 809.

35. "The Annual Convention is the supreme authority of the American Federation of Labor. . . . . When the majority will of labor is expressed in the convention it becomes law by which the whole of the American Federation is bound" (William Green, *Labor and Democracy* [Princeton, N. J., 1939], p. 175).

36. This was the convention that led to the formation of the C.I.O. and to the split in labor's ranks.

37. A.F. of L., *Proceedings, 1935*, pp. 787, 807–808, 814.

38. *Ibid., 1936*, pp. 235–238. The act of the A.F. of L. Executive Council in suspending the C.I.O. unions from membership was, of course, unconstitutional. Article IX, section 12, of the A.F. of L. constitution states that such action can only be taken by a two-thirds majority vote of an A.F. of L. convention.

39. *Ibid., 1941*, pp. 475–476.

40. *Ibid.*, pp. 476–481.

41. *Ibid.*, pp. 481–485, 489–490.

42. *Ibid.*, pp. 482–484, 486–489, 491–492.

43. Twenty-three Federal locals of Negro freight-handlers, red caps, and station employees protested to the A.F. of L. Executive Council against transferring their local unions to the Railway Clerks Auxiliary. After considering these protests, the Executive Council disallowed them because of "no justified reason." The A.F. of L. also refused the offer of these Negroes to pay dues both as Federal locals and as members of the Auxiliary for a trial period during which they could determine if the Brotherhood of Railway Clerks would really protect their interests. (See *ibid., 1940*, pp. 645–649.) Rather than join the Clerks' Auxiliary, several locals of Negro freight-handlers attempted to form a separate union, the National Council of Freight Handlers, Express and Station Employees; but they were almost entirely unsuccessful in obtaining recognition from management or in persuading the National (Railway) Mediation Board to establish a separate class for themselves. In August, 1942, the Negro freight-handlers dissolved their organization and affiliated with the Utility Workers Organizing Committee of the C.I.O. The revolt of the red caps, however, has been fairly successful. Several locals of these workers joined the then independent (now C.I.O.) United Transport Service Employees of America instead of applying for Railway Clerks Auxiliary charters. In elections conducted by the National Mediation Board, the U.T.S.E.A. overwhelmingly defeated the Railway Clerks for the right to represent these workers.

44. See above, p. 213.

45. A.F. of L., *Proceedings, 1941*, pp. 484–486; 490–492.

46. *Ibid.*, pp. 536–537.

47. *Ibid., 1942*, pp. 574–580, 646–649.

48. Of course, today the C.I.O. and the A.F. of L. can no longer be differentiated along craft versus industrial lines. But it is fair to say that the policies of the former have been, and still are, made by industrial union-minded leaders, and those of the latter, by craft union-minded leaders.

49. The Ladies Garment Workers later returned to the A.F. of L., and the Mine Workers appear about to do likewise.

50. For an analysis of the racial policies of the two garment unions and of the Mine Workers, see Spero and Harris, *op. cit.*, pp. 337–347, 352–382, and the present writer's article, "The Negro and the United Mine Workers of America," *Southern Economic Journal*, April, 1943, pp. 313–326.

51. See *In the Matter of the Alabama Dry Dock and Shipbuilding Co.*, 5 NLRB 149, 7 NLRB 9, 39 NLRB 954, 40 NLRB 280; Robert C. Weaver, "Racial Employment Trends in National Defense," *Phylon*, II (1941), 357–358; *ibid.*, III (1942), 23; A.F. of L., *Proceedings, 1940*, p. 509; *ibid., 1941*, pp. 478–479; *Crisis*, XLVI (1939), 273; and Committee on Fair Employment Practices, "Hearings, Birmingham, Ala.," (typed manuscript, June, 1942), I, 71; II, 207–243, 300–345.

52. Material from the writer's files, based on field notes.

53. "Half a Million Workers," *Fortune*, XXIII (1941), 98.

54. Robert C. Weaver, "With the Negro's Help," *Atlantic Monthly*, CLXIX (1942), 702.

55. A.F. of L., *Proceedings, 1941*, pp. 477–478; and Committee on Fair Employment Practices, *op. cit.*, I, 107 ff.

56. See, e.g., the Associated Negro Press dispatch in the *Kansas City Call*, March 12, 1942.

57. Attempts of some members of the Machinists' union to have the restrictionist clause deleted from the union ritual were defeated at the 1940 convention. Because the ritual is "secret," all debate on this question is held

in executive session, and discussion is not reported in the convention proceedings.

58. When Negroes demanded the end of exclusion at the Boeing Aircraft Plant in Seattle, the I.A.M. agent declared this entailed "too great a sacrifice." Writing to the secretary of the Louisville, Kentucky, Urban League on April 28, 1941, a vice-president of the I.A.M. declared that the I.A.M. opposed any plan to train Negroes as machinists because such a program was "designed for the purpose of creating cheap labor for employers even though it is disguised as the National defense program." In January, 1942, President Roosevelt had to intervene to force a San Francisco local of the I.A.M. to give working permits to competent Negro shipyard labor. And in July, 1942, the Committee on Fair Employment Practices forced an I.A.M. local to cease distributing cards urging white workers to join to prevent the use of Negroes in skilled jobs, and another one to cease using the closed-shop provision of its contract to bring about the discharge of Negroes.

59. Weaver, "Racial Employment Trends . . . ," *Phylon*, III, 24–26; and Lester B. Granger, "Negroes and War Production," *Survey Graphic*, XXXI (1942), 544.

60. Granger, *loc. cit.* At least three such stoppages occurred. See the forthright discussion of the issues by Mr. Thomas in the *United Automobile Worker*, July 1, 1942.

61. The reader will recall that the Electrical Workers and the Plumbers have no rules prohibiting the admission of Negroes, but that they generally do not admit them in actual practice.

62. It is interesting to note that on two occasions Philip Murray, president of the C.I.O., has declared that one of the issues which must be discussed in the current peace negotiations between the C.I.O. and the A.F. of L. is the discriminatory practices and rules of certain A.F. of L. unions (see *C.I.O. News*, August 10, 1942, and *New York Times*, November 10, 1942).

THE DECADE OF HOPE

CLARK FOREMAN

This selection by Clark Foreman is a participant's brief history of the Southern Conference for Human Welfare, formed in 1938 and disbanded in 1948. The history of the SCHW, an organization composed entirely of Southerners, white and black, and the recipient of vital support from the CIO and Southerners in the Roosevelt administration, points up the inaccuracy of generalizations about white Southern uniformity of opinion on either the New Deal or race relations. (A full-length account of SCHW is Thomas A. Kreuger, And Promises to Keep: The Southern Conference for Human Welfare, 1938–1948 *[Nashville: Vanderbilt University Press, 1968].)*

❁

For ten years—1938 to 1948—an organization composed entirely of Southerners existed for the sole purpose of establishing political and economic democracy in the South. The Southern Conference for Human Welfare brought together for the first time many elements of the South on a basis of unsegregated equality.

The history of the Southern Conference causes one to conjecture what might be the present state of democracy in this country if the attention of the government had not been deflected from the domestic to the foreign field. Yet, in a way the Southern Conference for Human Welfare marks the peak of the New Deal, as it was so clearly the outgrowth of the efforts of President Roosevelt to help the people of the South escape from the feudal economic conditions which made it in Roosevelt's words, "The Nation's No. 1 economic problem."

Reprinted by permission from *Phylon*, XII (Second Quarter 1951), 137–150.

In 1938 neither the prospect of a third term nor the war in Europe had turned the President's attention from the need of making the Democratic Party of the South a more adequate expression of the economic and political needs of the people. The 1937 "recession" had convinced the President and others in Washington that there was still need to make a continuing fight for liberalism and the South was the "nation's largest untapped market."

The two factors which merged to make the Southern Conference for Human Welfare a remarkable expression of the fight for democracy in this country were, first, the organization of the Congress of Industrial Organizations and, second, the group of southern liberals whom Roosevelt had brought together in his administration. Both of these groups believed in the necessity of reforming the economy of the South and both believed that Negroes must be included on a fair basis if this reform was to take place.

The rise of the C.I.O. had a tremendous effect on the southern people. Although W. E. B. Du Bois had written in his Atlanta University studies at the beginning of the century that the only hope for the southern people was for the white and colored workers to unite, little progress had been made in that direction. In fact, the extent to which organization had taken place in the South was largely on a craft basis, and in these craft unions Negroes were excluded or discriminated against. The all-white craft unions were often the most vociferous force against Negroes, whom they considered as non-union competitors for the existing jobs.

The big exception was the United Mine Workers which was organized on an industrial basis and included all workers, regardless of color. The strength which this fact has given to John L. Lewis has too often been overlooked. It made Lewis the natural leader of the movement to organize more industrial unions under the protection of the Wagner Act, and Lewis saw to it that the policy of integration was carried over into the C.I.O. when it was organized in 1936.

The organization of the steel workers was one of the first jobs undertaken by the C.I.O. In Alabama this effort was met by tremendous opposition from the subsidiaries of U.S. Steel and Republic Steel, which form the principal industrial backbone of the state. The testimony before the La Follette Committee[1] gives a valuable record of how these big northern-owned industries exploited southern prejudice to prevent the Negro and white workers from coming together in the same union.

The big corporations did not limit themselves to the encouragement of superstition and hatred; they actually hired thugs to serve as company goons for physical assaults on the union organizers. One of the victims of these goons was a young Alabaman named Joseph Gelders, who gave up his job as Assistant Professor and head of the Physics Laboratory at the University of Alabama in order to help the workers organize. Because of his activity on behalf of civil rights and labor unions, Gelders was severely beaten by company thugs who also jumped on his stomach and left him for dead. He never entirely recovered from the internal injuries, which later caused his death.

Joseph Gelders survived the beating, however, and was more determined than ever to fight the company violence which was seeking to prevent the workers of Alabama from organizing. As a part of his campaign he went in the spring of 1938 to Hyde Park, New York, to see Mrs. Roosevelt, to whom he told the need for a conference in the South which would call to the attention of the country the things which were happening in Alabama. Gelders told Mrs. Roosevelt that he would like to call the conference the Southern Conference for Human Welfare. Mrs. Roosevelt thought the idea was a good one and assured Gelders that he might expect the cooperation of the President and herself. This cooperation continued as long as the President lived, and Mrs. Roosevelt still helps the Southern Conference Educational Fund.

When Gelders returned to Alabama he secured the invaluable support of William Mitch, the President of District 20 of the United Mine Workers, and at that time the Alabama Director of the C.I.O. Mitch played a leading role in the creation of the Conference and took a most important part in the organization throughout its history. His convictions on the necessity of including Negroes on a fair and equal basis put the labor support of the Conference on a solid basis from the beginning.

The initiating sponsors called together by Mitch and Gelders to launch the Conference decided that instead of confining the agenda to civil rights they would broaden it to include the general economic problems which had been raised in a pamphlet just published by the National Emergency Council: *The Report to the President on Economic Conditions in the South*. In fact, it was decided to take advantage of the great publicity which that report had received and to make the Conference the South's answer to the report.

The circumstances leading up to the publishing of the report illustrate the concurrent working of the southerners in the New Deal as the other factor behind the creation of the Southern Conference for Human Welfare. Roosevelt's long residence in Georgia made him aware of the evil of discrimination as well as the political necessity of caution in seeking a remedy. Soon after his election he was approached by a committee headed by Edwin R. Embree, then President of the Julius Rosenwald Fund, and asked to appoint some one in the Federal government whose job it would be to see that Negroes were treated fairly by the New Deal. Roosevelt welcomed the suggestion and agreed that the best place for such a person was in the office of the Secretary of the Interior, Harold Ickes.

In 1933 I was offered and accepted the job of Adviser to the Secretary of the Interior on the Economic Status of Negroes. It was the first time that the Federal government had recognized the need for such an activity and as there was no provision for it in the budget my salary was paid by the Julius Rosenwald Fund. With the help of Miss Lucia Pitts as my secretary and Dr. Robert C. Weaver as an assistant, a beginning was made in a fair inclusion of Negroes in all Federal activities. Miss Pitts was the first Negro woman to serve the government as a secretary. Other Departments soon added Negroes to their staffs and there grew up what was referred to in the press as the "Black Cabinet."

The Southern Policy Committee, organized by Francis Pickens Miller, held a number of small meetings over the South during the Thirties to discuss southern problems. They also promoted in Washington regular dinner meetings of liberal southern Congressmen and New Dealers. These meetings at Hall's Restaurant were presided over by Congressman Lister Hill of Alabama until he was elected Senator in 1938. They served to bring together a nucleus of liberal southerners and to promote the discussion of controversial issues.

The President had frequently said that the Democratic party could stay in power only so long as it continued to be "the party of militant liberalism." The southern Congressmen were the chief reactionary forces threatening the liberalism of the party. On March 23, 1938 President Roosevelt made a speech in Gainesville, Georgia, which presaged his campaign to improve economic and political conditions in the South. In the presence of Senator George he spoke bluntly about the poor wages and low purchasing power of the southern people. He attacked the feudal economic system of the South and said, "When you come down to it, there is little difference between the feudal system and the Fascist system. If you believe in the one, you lean to the other." Even in this speech Roosevelt did not mention the discrimination against Negroes directly. He did say, however, "the American system calls for the elimination of special privilege."

Soon after his return to Washington in the spring of 1938 President Roosevelt called me to the White House and asked my advice about a suitable candidate to oppose Senator George in the Democratic primary in Georgia. I did not have any suggestions on that score but I did take the opportunity to urge the President to authorize a pamphlet on the economic conditions in the South. He liked the idea, made some suggestions and told me to talk with the Administrator of the National Emergency Council, Lowell Mellett.

I talked with Mellett, who prepared a letter authorizing the study for the President's signature and then asked me to undertake it. I was at that time the Director of the Power Division of the Public Works Administration. I brought together a group of southerners to work out a very concise statement of the economic conditions in the South.

On the fourth of July, 1938 this statement was presented to another group of Southerners at a Conference on Economic Conditions in the South in Washington. The group under the chairmanship of Dr. Frank P. Graham, then President of the University of North Carolina, suggested certain changes and agreed to serve as an advisory committee for the report. It was in a letter to this Conference that the President used the phrase that later became so well known: "The South presents right now the Nation's No. 1 economic problem."

The report was issued in August and President Roosevelt recommended it to the southern people on August 11th in his speech at Barnesville, Georgia, when he called for the defeat of Senator George.

Many papers in the South and North reprinted the report in full. It was logical then that the sponsors of the Southern Conference for Human Welfare, which had been called for November of 1938 in Birmingham, should decide that the Conference should provide the South's answer to the report.

Judge Louise Charlton of Birmingham was selected by the sponsors to preside over the conference. In the Proceedings she describes the preliminary arrangements made at the organizational meeting of sponsors in Birmingham in September, 1938:

One of the first requirements voted upon at the earliest organization meeting was that no one could be a delegate to this Southern Conference unless he or she was southern by birth or residence; that visitors were cordially invited, but that the decisions of the Conference would be the decisions arrived at by southerners. No other effort was made to restrict membership, no limit was placed upon the number of delegates any organization might send, but a free and urgent invitation was extended to every one interested in a liberal, honest effort to consider ways and means of lifting the level of life for all. This invitation was made daily through the press, the radio and by word of mouth. Two hundred sponsors left no stones unturned to assure the southern public that this was their conference and to urge the South to attend.

The chairman and vice-chairman of the Sponsorship and Participation Committee were, respectively, Congressman Luther Patrick of Birmingham and Brook Hays, then the Democratic national committeeman from Arkansas and now a member of Congress from that State.

Twelve hundred people from all parts of the South came by every conceivable form of transportation to that first conference. Workers, farmers, writers, government workers were there as well as bankers, editors, Congressmen and Senators. All faiths and all colors were represented. It was unquestionably the most all-inclusive meeting of southerners which had ever been held. President Roosevelt sent his greeting to this conference and to all later ones held during his lifetime.

Arrangements had been made in advance with the municipal authorities for the delegates to seat themselves as they chose regardless of the pattern of segregation which existed in Birmingham. Nevertheless, as the conference got under way city police appeared with instructions to enforce the separation of the white and colored delegates.

Although the emphasis of the conference was intended to be on the broad economic problems, this action by the city authorities forced the group to face at once the most controversial issue possible for southerners. The delegates discussed the matter thoroughly. They voted a strong censure of the city authorities but decided to go ahead with the meeting rather than disband. The delegates voted, however, never again to hold a segregated meeting, and this cardinal principle was adhered to throughout the ten years of the Conference's existence.

Mrs. Roosevelt, who was one of the principal speakers at the conference and who attended many of the panel discussions, refused to observe the segregation order. She had her chair placed in the center aisle which the police had decided must separate the white from the colored delegates. By doing so she symbolized the determined opposition of the Conference to the practice of segregation.

In addition to Mrs. Roosevelt the speakers at this first conference included Senators Bankhead of Alabama and Pepper of Florida. Justice Hugo L. Black received the Conference's Thomas Jefferson Award for outstanding service to the South.

At this conference it was decided to form a continuing organization. Dr. Frank P. Graham was elected President and Professor H. C. Nixon of Alabama was elected Executive Secretary. A Civil Rights Committee was established with Joseph Gelders as Executive Secretary and began at once to dramatize for the country the evil of the poll tax.

In 1940 a second conference was held in the city auditorium of Chattanooga, Tennessee. The absence of segregation was accepted calmly by both the delegates and the city. The Executive Committee had decided that the theme of the Chattanooga conference would be Democracy in the South. There was pressure by some of the delegates, however, to take a stand against Russia's invasion of Finland. This was opposed not only by the pro-Communists but by those who felt the Conference should confine itself to strictly southern questions.

William Mitch was the Chairman of the Resolutions Committee and he called upon Dr. Frank Graham to suggest a resolution expressing the views of the Conference. Dr. Graham wrote the resolution which was adopted by the Committee and the Conference. As an expression of the views of the Conference it was never changed. The resolution as passed and published makes interesting reading in view of the attempts to smear the Conference. It condemned all aggression as follows:

We deplore the rise of dictators anywhere, the suppression of civil liberties, the persecution of minorities, aggression against small and weak nations, the violation of neutral rights and the democratic liberties of the peoples by all fascist, nazi, communist and imperialist powers alike which resort to force and aggression instead of to the processes of law, freedom, democracy and international cooperation.

The great emphasis of the Chattanooga conference was, as planned, on the fight for more democracy in the South. Economic problems such as the equalization of freight rates, electoral problems such as the poll tax were discussed along with the general social and educational issues.

Reverend John B. Thompson, then of Norman, Oklahoma, but now Dean of the Rockefeller Chapel of the University of Chicago, was elected President at the Chattanooga conference. The Thomas Jefferson Award was given to Dr. Will W. Alexander of Georgia, who addressed the conference.

Howard Lee of Arkansas had succeeded Nixon as Executive Secretary but in the days following the Chattanooga conference the financial condition of the organization was in bad shape. Crucial assistance was given the Conference at this time by organized labor. Miss Lucy Randolph Macon of the C.I.O. and a member of the Southern Conference Board worked hard on a volunteer basis to make the Chattanooga conference a success. When Howard Lee had to take a better paying job Labor's Non-Partisan League loaned the Conference the service of Alton Lawrence of North Carolina. Later Mr. Lawrence was succeeded by Dr. James A. Dombrowski of Florida who did much to keep the Conference going during the difficult war years.

The third conference was held in the State Auditorium in Nashville, Tennessee, on the theme of The South's Part in Winning the War. There was considerable factionalism at this conference, but both an effort by Socialist Party members to split the Conference and an effort by pro-Communists to get the Conference to take action on the creation of a second front in Europe were defeated.

The great emphasis of the third conference was to mobilize the South fully behind the war against fascism. It was clearly stated, however, that this meant the fight against fascist tendencies in the South as well as fascist armies abroad. Symbolic of the attitude of the Conference toward the joint participation of both races was the award of the Thomas Jefferson medals to Mrs. Mary McLeod Bethune and to Dr. Frank P. Graham.

The selection of a successor to Dr. Thompson as President was left to the Executive Board. Dr. Homer P. Rainey, the President of the University of Texas, was the choice of the Board. He first accepted and then had to decline because of pressure in Texas. The Board then chose Clark Foreman of Georgia and he served as President for six years except for the time he was abroad during the War. During that period Tarleton Collier of Kentucky was the Acting-President.

In the fall of 1942 as a part of the program adopted in Nashville, the Conference held a Win-the-War rally in Raleigh, North Carolina. Distinguished speakers came from various parts of the South and the completely unsegregated meeting in the Raleigh auditorium made history in that city.

In 1942 the Conference started the publication of its monthly bulletin, *The Southern Patriot*. During the war years this paper did a great deal to keep the organization alive. The suggestion for starting the *Patriot* was made by Palmer Weber of Virginia. The editor, through most of its life, has been Dr. James A. Dombrowski.

The creation of the C.I.O. Political Action Committee and its affiliated National Citizens Political Action Committee for the purpose of reelecting President Roosevelt in 1944 had a profound effect on the Southern Conference. It seemed that organized labor was ready to enter strongly into political action and many independent citizens welcomed the opportunity of joining them.

At the C.I.O. convention in November of 1944, James Carey, the Secretary of the C.I.O., introduced a resolution endorsing the Southern Conference for Human Welfare as the natural spearhead of liberal action in the South. Carey had attended the Nashville conference and was familiar with the work of the organization. The President of the C.I.O., Philip Murray, gave the Carey resolution his full support and it was adopted by the C.I.O. convention. This resulted in generous contributions from many C.I.O. unions and from some of those of the A.F. of L.

Encouraged by this increased support from organized labor, the officers of the Conference immediately set about trying to improve the electoral conditions in the South. The officers initiated an independent conference of editors and writers of the South on the subject of Voting Restrictions. The conference was held in Atlanta in December of 1944. Mark Ethridge, the publisher of the Louisville *Courier Journal*, was the chairman, and the delegates included the leading writers and editors of the South, white and colored, meeting without segregation in the Atlanta Biltmore Hotel. The report of the conference greatly stimulated electoral reform throughout the South. The first achievement was the repeal of the poll tax in Georgia a few months after the conference.

The growing interest in political action on the part of the Southern Conference caused the establishment of various state committees. The Executive Board of the Conference appointed a Committee on Reorganization headed by Dr. Frank P. Graham to recommend appropriate changes in the by-laws. Early in 1946 a south-wide membership meeting was held in Durham, North Carolina, to act on the report of the reorganizing committee.

The Southern Conference for Human Welfare had been incorporated in 1942 as an educational organization. The charter did not provide for the political action which the Board now wished to undertake. This situation was met by the formation of two organizations, one of which kept the charter and the other the name. The Southern Conference Educational Fund, Inc., continues to this day and is primarily interested in the problem of segregation in the South. The political action organization was known as the Southern Conference for Human Welfare.

The fourth and last large south-wide conference was held in New Orleans in November of 1946. It was a coincidence that about twelve hundred delegates, the same number who attended the first conference in Birmingham, attended the meeting in New Orleans. Like the conference in Birmingham the one in New Orleans was also plagued by the hostility of the city officials to a policy of non-segregation. The city auditorium, which had been reserved for the Conference, was withheld at the last minute because the officers would not agree to their sudden demand that the audience be segregated. The conference was held in Carpenters Hall.

Although all political parties had members at this conference, as in the past, the New Orleans conference was by far the most harmonious. It was as if the members had learned something vital from the fight against fascism. The resolutions were confined to domestic issues and were adopted unanimously.

The speakers at the New Orleans conference included Mrs. Mary McLeod Bethune, Senator Claude Pepper, and Walter White, Executive Secretary of the N.A.A.C.P. The Thomas Jefferson award was given to Governor Ellis Arnall of Georgia who addressed the conference.

In 1947 Henry A. Wallace had become the outstanding champion of Roosevelt's thesis that the Democratic Party could stay in power only if it continued militantly liberal. Under the auspices of the Southern Conference Wallace made a number of speeches in southern states. All of these meetings were unsegregated, despite the efforts of some municipalities to enforce segregation. The meeting in Norfolk, Virginia was an important victory in the fight against segregation. The State of Virginia had, and still has, a law which prohibits public meetings which are not segregated. The Committee for Virginia of the Southern Conference was confident that the law could not stand up in the courts and decided to defy it. As the crowd filled the city auditorium to hear Wallace the city police stood guard on both sides of the platform to see that no one entered on to it. They said that they had orders from City Hall not to allow any one on that platform until the audience was segregated according to color.

With the auditorium jammed and Wallace expected to arrive at any minute, the President of the Conference forced the issue by mounting the platform from the audience and calling the meeting to order. The police, taken by surprise, had to allow the meeting to proceed or face the challenge of the law in the courts. They chose to preserve the law in name and to allow the meeting to proceed. The Chairman of the Committee for Virginia, Henry Wallace, and the other speakers came to the platform from the orchestra stairs as the police continued to stand guard at the wings, and the meeting was held without segregation. The next day the Norfolk papers announced that the Southern Conference had effectively killed the segregation law.

Out of all the conferences and meetings there came a coherent program for southern advance. This program provided the basis for action by the Conference and by the state committees. It stands as a guide for those who wish to work for a prosperous and democratic South. In essence it can be stated in the three following points:

I. The development of agriculture and industry so that the full advantage of the natural wealth of the South may accrue to the workers of the South. If the South is to raise itself from the position of the Nation's No. 1 economic problem there must be an end to usurious farm loans and confiscatory charges to tenants. There must also be an end to freight rates which discriminate against southern industry.

During its ten years the Southern Conference gave great attention to the economic backwardness of the southern states. The low wages of the workers, the meager social security, the miserable status of large sections of its farm land are all related to the social and political backwardness of the people. Prejudice permitted disfranchisement and disfranchisement encouraged backwardness.

II. Full political democracy for all the people of the South regardless of color. This means the abolition of the poll tax as a prerequisite for voting, and also the elimination of all discrimination in the registration and voting of the people.

Largely owing to the conscientious devotion of Joseph Gelders and Virginia Foster Durr the poll tax was brought to the attention of the country as a major evil. The first bill to be introduced into Congress to abolish the poll tax as a prerequisite for voting was introduced by Congressman Lee Geyer of California. In introducing it he said that he was doing so at the request of the Southern Conference for Human Welfare. The fact that the bill several times passed the House but was defeated in the Senate by southern filibusters illustrates the importance of the issue. Even so the publicity and continued fighting on the part of the abolitionists has succeeded in getting the poll tax annulled in Florida, Georgia, South Carolina and Tennessee. It remains in five southern states but even there it is under constant attack.

Owing largely to a series of sweeping decisions by the Supreme Court in the years after the Conference was started, Negroes now participate in the Democratic Party primary elections which still determine the politics of most southern states. During the decade of the Southern Conference the voting of the Negroes in the South increased about tenfold, from approximately 100,000 in 1938 to approximately a million in 1948. Discrimination against Negroes seeking to register continues in many places. So far the evil and fraudulent practice of registration boards asking Negroes to qualify by telling how many drops of water go over Niagara Falls each day, and similar impossible questions, has not been stopped by the courts.

Nevertheless in the past ten years over forty Negroes have offered themselves for municipal office in the South. Others have run for the Senate, House of Representatives and for gubernatorial offices. In North Carolina and Virginia Negroes have been elected to city councils. In several southern cities Negroes now serve on school boards.

III. Full civil rights for all the people of the South regardless of color or occupation. This means not only an end to lynching but also to the general intimidation for which lynching is the enforcing menace. It means the right of all workers to organize freely and bargain collectively. It means also an end to segregation and all forms of discrimination against workers, Negroes, Mexicans, Jews and others.

It was in this third field that the work of the Southern Conference was most conspicuous. This is perhaps due to the fact that every effort to improve conditions in the South is opposed by some people on the grounds that it might lead to "social equality." The Southern Conference had to face that opposition at its very first meeting. The fact that the delegates refused then and later to be frightened by the conventional bugaboo is one of the principal achievements of the Conference.

For ten years there was an active, broad popular southern movement that would not compromise on the question of full civil rights for all the people. This fight on the part of the Conference undoubtedly facilitated the peaceful acceptance of Negro students in southern universities, once the courts had forced the institutions to open their doors.

The clear and consistent program of the Southern Conference for Human Welfare was unquestionably a challenge to many vested interests. It was opposed bitterly from the very beginning. In fact even before the first conference the big corporations in the South attacked the *Report on Economic Conditions in the South*. The principal attackers were southern agents of northern owned corporations, outstanding among them the power companies, the railroads, the steel mills and the textile factories.

The House Committee on Un-American Activities from the beginning kept a close watch on the activities of the Southern Conference. We know this from the testimony of Ex-Congressman Joseph Starnes of Alabama, who testified at the hearings before the Senate Committee on the confirmation of David Lilienthal as Chairman of the Atomic Energy Commission. Starnes said he was the chairman of the sub-committee of the Un-American Activities Committee responsible for watching the activities of the Southern Conference and that he had had the Committee's best detectives on the lookout from the time the Southern Conference held its first meetings. They failed to find any evidence of Communist or subversive control.

Nevertheless after the War, when the forces of reaction had been greatly strengthened, the Un-American Activities Committee issued a report on the Conference just before a large public meeting in Washington. The Committee announced at the same time that it would have "observers" at the meeting. It is equally significant that in June of 1947 when this action was taken the people of Washington still could not be intimidated by such tactics and an overflow meeting was held at the Watergate Stadium.

After nine years of "observation" and investigation the Un-

American Activities Committee made a report so fraudulent and unfair as to have become the standard illustration of unfair committee tactics and smear-by-association. The Committee's report was analyzed in a masterly way by Dr. Walter Gellhorn, Professor of Law at the University of Colorado, in the *Harvard Law Review* in the October, 1947 issue.

The critical change which occurred after the War was that some of the leaders of organized labor began to say the same things which their chief opponents had been saying for years. The tactics which the textile and steel companies had used in the Thirties to prevent labor organization were now used by some of the C.I.O. unions in their raids on others. Appeals to race prejudice and violence were excused on the basis that the unions which were raided were leftist—the same excuse which the steel companies had made ten years before in opposing the organizing drives of the C.I.O.

In 1946 the A.F. of L. had a southern meeting in Asheville to launch an organizing drive. The Negro delegates surprised the officials in charge of the meeting by refusing to abide by the segregated seating arrangements. Rather than face the unfavorable publicity which would have resulted from the walk-out of the Negro delegates the officials dropped their plans for segregation in the meeting. This was a great advance on the part of the A.F. of L. and was undoubtedly due to the stiff competition which the C.I.O. unions had been giving them in the last decade.

It is ironical that in this same year the leadership of the C.I.O. began giving ground on this all-important issue. The selection of Van Bittner to head the organization drive that was hailed as "Operation Dixie" proved to be a great mistake. Instead of following the firm precedent set by John L. Lewis, the leaders of "Operation Dixie" resorted to opportunism in the hope of making the C.I.O respectable in the South.

Any experienced C.I.O. organizer in the South could have told Bittner that such tactics were doomed to failure. William Mitch of the Mine Workers and Paul Christopher of the Textile Workers, C.I.O., had repeatedly stated that prejudice against Negroes is subsidized by the corporations to keep labor from uniting. Every meeting of the Southern Conference had heard testimony that the only way to be respectable in the eyes of the forces which dominate southern industry and politics is to discriminate against Negroes and thus betray trade unionism.

The futile results of the compromising, confused tactics of the

C.I.O. in its "Operation Dixie" are illustrated in the testimony of
Emil Rieve, the President of the Textile Workers of America,
before the Senate Labor and Public Welfare Committee in 1951.
Rieve testified that in the last few years the southern membership in his union had declined from twenty per cent of the textile
employees to fifteen per cent. The textile industry is the largest in
the South. So the loss of a quarter of the Union's membership is
a sizable loss indeed, and we can leave unmentioned the significance of such a low percentage of the total workers who were
organized even in the peak period.

The southern leaders of the Textile Workers, C.I.O., were
among the first to succumb to the hysteria and divisive tactics of
the reactionary corporations. For example, in 1947 North Carolina officials of the Textile Workers approached the Chairman
and Executive Secretary of the Committee for North Carolina of
the Southern Conference for Human Welfare and complained
about the participation of Negroes in the meetings of the Committee. The Chairman quite properly replied that all were welcome to participate in the work of the Committee and that if the
Textile Workers thought that Negroes played too important a role
the answer must be that the Textile Workers were themselves
playing too small a role, and the cure for that lay in their own
power.

The cooperation of the Textile Workers and the Southern Conference for Human Welfare declined from the time of that interview. It was not long after that that the officials of the Textile
Workers were joining with the reactionaries in denouncing the
Conference as communistic.

One after another of the leaders of the unions which had provided the principal backing of the Conference adopted the smear-
ing tactics which prepared the way for the Taft-Hartley Law. The
decline of militancy on the part of the unions was followed un-
avoidably by a decline in the strength of the Southern Conference.

Next to the financial support provided by the unions, the chief
source of funds was from liberal northerners who understood
the importance to the whole country of having real democracy in
the South. A committee of prominent New Yorkers, many of them
with Southern backgrounds, did an heroic job of raising funds.
Dinners were held in New York, Chicago and California. Letters
of solicitation and even a tag day in New York were used to raise
the necessary funds to keep the organization going in the South.

It was inevitable that this appeal for northern funds would

provide ammunition also for the Conference's enemies in the South. The objection to northern funds for progressive causes in the South is part and parcel of the southern chauvinism which espouses segregation. The two attitudes help to keep the people divided, prejudiced, ignorant and poor. The proof of the casuistry of the objection is the fact that hardly ever is there a protest against northern support for reactionary causes in the South. It is sad but nevertheless true that no liberal or progressive southern movement has been able to finance itself on southern funds alone.

The attacks of the reactionaries and the changing attitudes of the unions greatly decreased the financial support and made it unavoidable that the political activity of the Conference come to an end. The candidacy of Henry Wallace also caused a division in the membership. The Conference as such endorsed neither Truman nor Wallace, which was in itself a symptom of the weakened condition of the Conference, and it was about the last act before the disbanding in November, 1948.

The experience of ten years with the Southern Conference taught the leaders certain lessons, the statement of which seems an appropriate ending for the article. Let us hope that these lessons, learned in long and heated struggle, will be of assistance to those who in the future may seek to carry on the work which the Southern Conference started:

1. The chief instrument of exploitation, and therefore the chief cause of poverty, is segregation.
2. Organized labor cannot win adequate protection for its members until it effectively abolishes segregation and other forms of discrimination in its own ranks.
3. A fairly organized labor movement is the necessary basis for social organization strong enough to overcome the economic and political ills of the South.
4. The progressive forces of the South must have the support, financial and moral, of the progressive forces of the rest of the country. Prejudice and hate in the South are amply subsidized from within and without. If the decent elements of the South are to win against such forces the democratically-minded people of the rest of the country must help.

NOTES

1. Report of the La Follette Committee on Violations of Free Speech and Rights of Labor—Hearings before Senate Subcommittee on Education and Labor, 75th Congress, 1st Session 803–806, 1937.

STRUGGLES OF THE
THIRTIES IN THE SOUTH

JOHN WILLIAMS

*John Williams here recalls the activities of Communists in the
South and suggests the general theme of radical protest in the
1930's. The particular form which dissent took under the sponsorship of the Communist party was frequently an eerie amalgam
of courageous, humane individual conduct rooted in genuine indignation at social injustice, combined with the subordination of
individuality to the doctrinaire requirements of an organization
with headquarters in Moscow and a tendency to manipulate
men coldly in order to realize purportedly humane ends. (Of the
great many writings that shed light on this "eerie amalgam," one
of the most illuminating is George Charney,* A Long Journey [Chi-
cago: Quadrangle Books, 1968].) Williams' article also evokes the
efforts of the American Communist party to recruit Negroes, who,
as victims of segregation and discrimination and as members of
the working class, should have responded to Marxist appeals—
according to Marxist doctrine. Although the CIO was able, to a
significant degree, to submerge white and black workers' racial
antagonisms in a sense of common economic interest, the enduring of poverty in common by white and black small farmers in
the South had a limited impact on race relations: in the organization of the Southern Tenant Farmers' Union, "of 103 locals, 73
were all-Negro or all white; of the remaining 30, 7 had only one
Negro or white member." In any event, the Communists' quest for
support among black workers and farmers came to almost nothing, and there was heated conflict between the American Communist party and the NAACP. (See Philip Murray, chairman,
Steel Workers Organizing Committee, address, National Negro
Congress, 1937, in Gilbert Osofsky, ed.,* The Burden of Race: A*

Documentary History of Negro-White Relations in America [*New York: Harper and Row, 1967*], *pp. 364–369; Samuel Lubell, The Future of American Politics* [*New York: Harper Colophon Books, 1965, 3rd ed. rev.*], *p. 59; Jerold S. Auerbach, "Southern Tenant Farmers: Socialist Critics of the New Deal," Labor History* [*Winter 1966*], *p. 17n; Wilson Record, The Negro and the Communist Party* [*Chapel Hill: University of North Carolina Press, 1951*], *and* Race and Radicalism: The NAACP and the Communist Party in Conflict [*Ithaca: Cornell University Press, 1964*].)

✿

In celebrating Negro History Week, it is important to give due consideration and credit to the role played by the Communist Party during the past 35 years in the struggle of the Negro people for their freedom, particularly in the South. It was the Communist Party that forged its way into the South in the early thirties, and especially into Alabama, and forced the brakes to be applied to the lynchers' car. It was the Communist Party that led the fight to save the nine Negro youths of Scottsboro, Alabama, first from the lynch rope and then from the electric chair, and so opened up the only real iron curtain—the iron curtain of the South, U.S.A.—and let the whole world see how the Negro was being lynched and denied all rights as an American citizen.

Many of the people who are taking part in today's great civil rights struggles are entirely unaware of these early battles, led by Communists, which laid groundwork for them. Many don't know, for instance, that in the very same park in Birmingham in front of the 16th Street Baptist Church, where Bull Connor had the water hoses and police dogs turned on the Negro people in May, 1963, a big unemployed demonstration took place in May, 1933 —thirty years before.

The Unemployed Demonstrate

The unemployed committee got a permit from the city officials to hold a meeting in this park and put out leaflets announcing it. These brought out thousands from all over Birmingham, the great majority of them Negroes. The leaflets not only raised demands for the unemployed. They also demanded the right of Negroes to

Reprinted by permission from *Political Affairs*, XLIV (February 1965), 15–25.

vote, serve on juries and hold office. They came out against the poll tax and demanded the freedom of the Scottsboro Boys and an end to lynching of Negroes.

The city officials told the press that the meeting would not be held, that it had been canceled. But these unemployed Negroes were well organized. They had formed a Women's Sewing Club in the community, and unemployed block committees. These clubs had delegated captains and sub-captains—each captain had three to four people that he was responsible for—and at 3:30 when the meeting was called and the people gathered at the park, they told them where to assemble. It was considered that 3,000 people assembled outside the park.

No sooner did the people gather on the corner of 5th Avenue and 16th Street than the police began to swarm to break up the meeting. They had plainclothesmen in the crowd, and as soon as the first speaker began to speak, a motorcycle cop rolled up and told her: "Come down!" When he said that, the people began to yell: "Let that woman speak! Let that woman speak!"

There were instructions not to have any knives, sticks or pistols, to come completely unarmed. But there was an old man by the name of Ned Goodman who came with a hickory walking stick, against the instructions. When the police came up to take this woman speaker down, he hit a policeman on the side of the head with the stick, and then the struggle began. Two policemen grabbed Ned Goodman on each side, and another got the stick out of his hand and attempted to beat him over the head. But a Negro snatched the stick out of his hand, and another cop hit this Negro on the head with his pistol and grabbed him by the back of his collar. Then a Negro woman hit the policeman across the eyes with her parasol. The Negroes began coming across the street intersection. The police were telling them to get back, but they kept crowding in and a free-for-all battle took place right at the intersection that lasted about ten minutes.

Thirty years later a great struggle again took place there. This struggle planted the seed for it. It built confidence among the Negro people that if they stood together they could be counted, they could have strength.

Some whites friendly to the Negroes reported that fifteen policemen went to a meeting with the officials that night to decide how they could handle the Negroes in case another such meeting took place. They told the officials that if they couldn't shoot the Negroes with their pistols, they didn't want the job any longer. But they were told: "You're not supposed to shoot." And according to the reports, they laid their guns and badges on the table and quit their posts.

That was the first time that the Police Department of Birmingham had come to know that a policeman wasn't supposed to shoot a Negro whenever he felt like reaching for his gun. Before that time, not a Saturday night passed without at least one Negro being shot down, murdered in cold blood by the police. In those days the billy sticks were short, about eight inches long and wrapped in leather. But today the Birmingham police carry long sticks, and this change started with that meeting in May, 1933.

That was the first time that Negro women came to know that they could stand up and fight back and defend themselves. So from then on everyone wanted to know, "When are we going to have another such meeting? I want to fight some more." We must say, of course, that we are against violence. Just like the non-violent organizations today, the Communist Party has always been against violence. But the Party did raise the question, and does raise the question today, of the right of self-defense. And that's what those Negroes felt, and that's what they learned that day—that they had the right to defend themselves.

Things have been bad since that time, but before that day the Negroes saw no way of stopping the police from shooting whenever they felt like it. They were happy-jack with the pistol. But it was the Communist Party that turned the tide, and whatever is said about Negro history, we have to take note of the role the Party played in building this courage among the Negro people in 1933.

Struggles on Many Fronts

It was the fight for the Scottsboro Boys and the Party program on the Negro question that awakened the Negro people in the South to the consciousness that they could fight for their freedom. Before that time, the working Negro masses knew nothing about organization and had no one to speak in their behalf. When the lynchers were running the Negroes from the swamps and forests, the Negroes felt hopeless because they had no security. Before the Party came to the South, the talk was always: "Negro, stay in your place." But after the Party came and raised the slogan of the right of self-determination for the Negro people of the Black Belt and the right to secure ownership of the land, it was different.

When the Party raised the demand for the right of Negroes to vote, the Negroes began to get into action, and the political officials of Alabama saw that they were listening to the Party. So in Birmingham, in the early thirties, the Democratic Party officials called the Negro leaders together and told them that the Party was agitating among the uneducated Negroes for the right to vote. They said: "We want to give you the privilege of organizing a Democratic voters' club, and we will prepare some of your best people to become qualified voters. We will give you a charter, and we want you to keep your people from going over to the Communist Party."

They said they would qualify only fifty Negro voters a year, and these had to be "the best type of Negroes," ones that they would recommend. "Now don't bring down any ordinary workers," they said, "because we are not going to accept them."

As late as 1938 there were still less than 400 Negroes on the rolls of qualified voters in Jefferson County. But the Party had launched the fight for the right to vote. The Party also put forth slogans of the right to serve on juries and to hold public office, against the poll tax, for equality in education. And it tied all these slogans up with the struggle for the freedom of the Scottsboro Boys. It showed that it was not only nine Negroes but the whole Negro people who were on trial, that all the rights of the Negro people as American citizens were tied up with the freedom of the Scottsboro Boys.

Before that time the Negroes did not have any decent schoolrooms. The schoolhouses for the Negro children in Alabama and the Black Belt were falling apart. You could look out through the shingles and the holes in the roofs. They were leaky and cold. But after the Party raised the slogan of equality in education and fought for this demand, the officials of Alabama began to try to improve these old schoolhouses.

Negro Sharecroppers Organize

It was the Communist Party in 1931 that raised the slogan of the right of Negro sharecroppers and tenant farmers to sell their products themselves. Up to that time, in many parts of the South and particularly around Camphill, Railtown and Selma, Alabama, the sharecroppers would make their crop and the landlords would sell it and give them whatever they pleased. Many Negroes didn't know what price the landlord got. It was the Party that called on the Negro sharecroppers and tenant farmers to organize and demand the right to sell their product.

The Party also demanded $1.00 a day pay for farm laborers. Before that time the landlords were paying 50 cents a day and sometimes less for working from sunup to sundown. Eventually the Party was able to win this demand.

After the appeal to organize, the Negroes in Camphill, Alabama formed what was known as the Sharecroppers' Union. As they began to meet in the church to discuss their problems, the landlords and deputy sheriffs began to rise against them. One night they were holding a meeting in the church and the landlords threatened to break it up. So the Negroes put out watchmen, some of them armed with shotguns.

One night after that, the landlords hailed Ralph Gray, who was on his way to the church, and demanded that he drop his shotgun. He refused, and there was a shooting battle. Ralph Gray and a number of deputy sheriffs were wounded. Some of the tenants and sharecroppers took Ralph Gray home and went to his home to defend him against the lynchers who were coming to kill him. The Negroes held the fort at the house and exchanged shots with the landlords and the deputy sheriffs and the other lynchers. But eventually their ammunition gave out and they had to retreat. The landlords went into the house and lynched him right in his own home. They also put 30 or 40 Negro tenants in jail—those who couldn't give an account as to where they were that night.

The International Labor Defense, fully supported by the Communist Party, fought for the freedom of these sharecroppers and tenant farmers, and eventually forced the release of all of them. Some were held in jail so long that they weren't able to make a crop that year. One farmer named Drakes, who was one of the most militant in the group, they wanted to hang anyway because they considered him the leader. But eventually, through mass pressure led by the Party and protests from all parts of the world, all were freed.

A Mass Funeral

In Railtown, in December of 1932, the landlords went in to take the livestock of Clifford Jones. There the Negroes also had a sharecroppers' union and many of them were members of the Communist Party. The Negroes refused to let the landlords take his stock. In the battle between them and the deputy sheriffs, Joe Moss was killed, another farmer, Marlow Bentley, was wounded. Some of the deputy sheriffs were also wounded. The farmers were forced to retreat.

Late that afternoon, when Clifford Jones went back to see what had happened to the house and his livestock, he too was wounded. They got into Tuskegee and went to the family doctor to be treated. But the doctor called the deputy sheriffs. They took Marlow Bentley and Clifford Jones and put them in Kilby prison in Montgomery. There, it was claimed, they both died of pneumonia. It is said they were put on a cold concrete floor in cells without beds. But whether this is what happened or whether they were actually beaten to death, no one has ever been able to find out.

The ILD had the bodies brought to Birmingham where the Welch Brothers undertakers had agreed to embalm them. But when the train arrived, they refused to do so, saying they had been visited by their white friends who had warned them not to handle the bodies. These were then taken to Hickman Jordan in North Birmingham, who told the leaders of the organization that if they would take care of the living, he would take care of the dead.

Across each of the caskets was a beautiful red ribbon with a hammer and sickle on it. An official came and demanded that Jordan take the hammers and sickles off. He refused. He said he was being paid to bury the dead, that those who paid him put the hammers and sickles there and if they wanted them removed they would have to do it themselves.

The Party had issued leaflets calling on everybody to view the bodies and attend the funeral that Friday. When the handbills went out, the officials went to Jordan to force him to bury the bodies immediately. He refused to bury them or to close the caskets. He said, "If you want them buried, you bury them yourselves. These people want these bodies buried Friday and I'm going to bury them when they say bury them."

Friday at 11:00 o'clock the funeral was held. It was in the heart of the depression, and many had to walk down the railroad tracks to get there. The police said there would be no funeral and told people to go back home. But the crowd continued to grow and some of the militant Negroes in the group said: "These dead are Negroes and we're going to the funeral." They walked on by the police and the crowd got so angry that the police had to back up and let them by. It was reported that about 7,000 people attended that funeral, that it was the biggest mass funeral ever known to be held in Birmingham—the funeral of these two sharecroppers that were killed in Alabama.

All this action took place around the right of the Negro sharecroppers to sell their product and the right of the Negro people to defend their homes and their families against the attacks of the landlords and their kind.

Battle for Work and Relief

In the days before WPA, the city relief in Birmingham had a number of unemployed projects, such as East Lake Park. And on many of the open fields which had lain fallow for years, Negroes were digging up the land with picks. They raked the land and planted gardens. They opened up water sewers in and around Birmingham. They opened up the highway from Birmingham to Montgomery, doing heavy manual labor and blasting to widen the highway.

In those days when Negroes were suffering on these relief jobs it was the Communist Party that raised the question of free rent for the unemployed workers and their families, as well as other demands. The workers on the mountain, building the highway, were being paid only in food checks to turn in at the supply house for canned tomatoes, dried beans, white potatoes and rice, with no butter, no milk and no shortening to season this food with. Three Negro leaders who were Party members walked down the mountain and called on these workers to assemble at the Kingston schoolhouse in Birmingham, and to demand cash pay for their work.

About 250 or 300 workers gathered at noon on the school grounds. The three leaders pointed out how by organized action they could gain money for their work, and they made a motion to march on City Hall and send a committee to see Jimmy Jones who was then president of the City Commission. The next morning, which was on a Saturday, around 125 or 130 assembled on the school grounds, all Negro except one, and started to march to City Hall. By the time they got there, the group had dwindled to around 50.

They elected a committee of six to go in and see Jimmy Jones, among them the one white worker. As they started up the steps a city detective went up ahead of them and asked where they were

going. They said they were going to see Jimmy Jones about getting
paid for their work and getting more relief for the unemployed.
He pulled out a pistol and told them to get back down the steps,
saying: "You're not going to see Mr. Jones." He asked the white
worker, "Are you with this crowd?" He said, "No, I'm going up to
the Welfare Department." So he let him pass, while the Negroes
went back to the sidewalk.

The leader, a young Negro YCL member 19 years old, said:
"Fellow workers, we're going back to reorganize and reinforce,
and we're coming back and we *are* going to see Mr. Jones." When
he said that, the detective hit him on the side of the head with his
fist and said: "I told you to get away from here."

He walked away and all the Negroes walked up the sidewalk
behind him, back to the school grounds from which they had
started. They didn't go back to City Hall right then. The officials
thought the Negroes were coming back next day, and they reinforced the police around City Hall. They had them on top of the
building, it was reported, with machine guns and sawed-off shotguns.

But the Negroes didn't march back until November 7, and when
they did, it was estimated that 7,000 were there, including whites.
A mass meeting was called by the Party on the county courthouse
steps to demand relief for the unemployed. A committee went in to
lay the demands before Jimmy Jones. On it was a young, militant,
Birmingham-born white woman. They wanted to know if she believed in social equality for the Negro people. She said, "Yes, why
not? The Negroes are just as good as you and I."

When she said that, Jimmy Jones said to the detectives standing around: "Go to the courthouse and have that crowd move
away from there. I won't listen to that any longer." They came to
the courthouse, about 10 or 15 big, husky white lynchers, and
they stood on the courthouse steps and said: "Everybody get out of
here." There were Negro women and children with baskets thinking food was going to be given out. There was quite a struggle that
followed, with much pushing between the police and many of the
Negro people, as well as many of the whites in the crowd—coal
miners, steelworkers and others.

Organizing the Coal Miners

In the early part of 1933, John L. Lewis sent organizers into Birmingham to organize the coal miners. The first local meeting was

held at the Saryton Mine, one of the Republic Steel mines in North Birmingham. This was the first local in the area organized into the United Mine Workers. After this locals began to crop up like wild-fire in the various mines—Lewisburg, Hampton Slope, Edgewater and others. All the mines had what they called "mine dicks," and there was a constant struggle between them and the union members.

The Communist Party played a major role in exposing to the public the conditions under which the miners worked. One of the main battles was over "washer's loss." The coal dug by a miner each day was examined by a company man for rock, and if he found more than a certain number of cans of rock, the balance of the coal was taken to make up for "washer's loss"—an outright robbery.

Most of the miners were Negroes, and the Party members in the mines would get them together to compile all their complaints. They were overcharged for "stoppage"—halts for sharpening the picks or the drills for dynamiting coal. They were made to pay for caps and powder, and when they got through with all of this and with being docked for washer's losses, the miners had nothing to take home for food and clothing on pay day. What little they did get, they had to spend in the company commissaries at company prices. At that time the miner left home before daylight and came home after dark, and when the week was over he often didn't draw any money because he was in debt at the commissary. Many miners didn't make over $1.50 or $2.00 a day.

It was the Communist Party in Birmingham that continually exposed these rotten conditions, and was able to bring about the unity of white and Negro miners in the struggle led by the Ne-groes to change them through the United Mine Workers in the early years from 1933 to 1941–42—it took that long before they were able to break down the practice of "washer's loss."

From these struggles there came forward such leaders as Henry O. Mayfield from the Hamilton Slope Mine. Formerly an unem-ployed leader, he was on the mine grievance committee where he battled for the miners' rights, against the Ku Klux Klan elements in the local, and against the tricks and pitfalls of the company. There were many other Negro leaders such as John Bedell in the Lewisburg Mine, and others not in the mines—Joe Howard, Fred Walker and Eb Cox. Cox worked his way into the top staff of the United Steelworkers in Birmingham but had gotten his early schooling in the Party.

A Courageous Fighter

We must also give credit to the role played by Hosea Hudson in the United Steelworkers in Birmingham. He was one of the first Negro recording secretaries to be elected in any of the big steel lodges. That was in 1937, at the Ansley Steel plant, Local 1489.

Hudson had come up as a sharecropper from the cotton fields of Georgia, and eventually became a molder in a stock pipefitting company in Birmingham. When the CIO steel union first began organizing around Birmingham, they would accept workers from any shop for membership so long as it had something to do with steel. Hudson was working at the Walward Foundry and became a member of Local 1489.

In the election of officers in 1937, the local membership meeting was attended by a packed house of Negro steelworkers and only four or five whites. As a rule during that period, the union officials would appeal to the Negro workers: "We can't get the poor white devils to come into this union. They won't sit in meetings with Negroes. They will only join the union if they can join by themselves, but not with Negroes." And they would say: "If you stick with us, we'll stick with you. If these poor white devils come into the union, they will have to come into the meeting hall where you are."

When it came to election of officers the president of the local, who was white, said: "Here is a member and I'm going to appoint him recording secretary." He asked Hosea Hudson if he would accept the nomination, and Hosea Hudson told him: "My education is very poor. I didn't have much chance to go to school. But I will not decline the appointment." The president offered to show him how to keep minutes, and Hudson took the books and served as recording secretary until the next election of officers in 1938.

Later he became unemployed, and was one of the first to enjoy unemployment compensation in 1938, though it was only $9.50 a week. Then he got on WPA, which had just come into being.

The WPA workers were organized in the Workers' Alliance, and Local 1 met in the Birmingham courthouse. Hudson was elected vice-president and Edwina Collins, a young Negro woman, was elected recording secretary. The meeting room had a balcony and the Negroes sat there while the whites sat on the main floor. But Hosea Hudson and Edwina Collins would not serve as officers while sitting in the balcony. So they went down and sat with the rest of the officials.

But then the county officials told the white local officers that if Negroes met with them they would have to quit meeting in the courthouse. The officers reported this to the membership, which was made up largely of Negro and white workers including some students, teachers, and small business people forced into the ranks of the unemployed and onto WPA. These white workers voted for a motion empowering the officers to find a place where Negro and white could meet together, saying that the county officials could not dictate to them how they should hold their meetings. They found a hall, seating 600, on 22nd Street and Second Avenue, after which a county council was organized of representatives from 27 locals. Hudson became vice president of the council also.

The Workers' Alliance put up a fight for the right of its members to become qualified voters in 1938, because they found that the politicians in Washington were against having WPA projects in Birmingham and were against a raise in wages for WPA workers, who were getting only $40.80 a month. They realized that they had to put men in Congress that would work for the interests of the unemployed and the working people of Birmingham.

A Right-to-Vote Club was organized, under the leadership of Hudson and one or two other young Negro leaders. It was set up in competition with the Negro Democratic Club in which only those could be members who were eligible to vote. They charged only 25 cents to join and took up collections for anything needed, such as stationery. Classes were held every Tuesday night. School teachers and coal miners came in to learn how to fill out the necessary blanks to become voters. When the books opened for registry at the courthouse, truckloads of Negro miners and steelworkers came in to register.

The Negroes piled in with their overalls on, something the officials had never seen before. They wanted to know who had sent them there. The Negroes said they wanted to elect officials who would do something for their people. This created quite some excitement among the white politicians and they began questioning the Negro Democratic Club. Why were they allowing these Negroes to meet and put out material without consulting them? The Negro Democratic Club was up against the wall. They had no answer, and began trying to find a way to get the Right-to-Vote Club to unite with them. But these rank-and-file Negroes who had been left out in the cold in the past would not unite. They remained independent, and continued to exist until the Southern

Negro Youth Congress came to Birmingham under the leadership of James and Esther Jackson, Ed and Augusta Strong, and later Louis Burnham and many other young Negro fighters. When this organization took over the responsibility for educating the Negro people on how to become qualified voters, the Right-to-Vote Club dissolved and joined in its activity.

These are some of the things that happened in the Birmingham area in the thirties. There were great strides made in those years, and one cannot for one moment see these without seeing the groundwork that was laid and the seed that was planted in the consciousness of the Negro people by the Communist Party throughout the South in that period. So when we celebrate Negro History Week, we must recognize this as part of the history of the Negro people's struggles.

III

Black Reaction

The activism described in the articles by Robert L. Zangrando, Erwin D. Hoffman, and August Meier and Elliott M. Rudwick occurred at a time when the leading Negro organizations, the NAACP and the National Urban League, both middle class in origin, strove to bring blacks into the main stream of American life. They came under the fire of separatists, or advocates like W. E. B. Du Bois of certain forms of separatism (economic in Du Bois' case), and impatient critics like Ralph Bunche, who deplored their conciliatory approach and gradualism and the NAACP's virtual failure to take an interest in economic problems. The Urban League, it is true, had long concentrated on securing greater employment opportunities for black workers and at an early date had urged them to join the emerging unions of the 1930's, but the NAACP did not come out forthrightly for Negro-union solidarity until 1941. The organizations that later sponsored the direct, nonviolent action of the Negro Revolution, moreover, were not formed until near the end of the period of our concern or later: the Congress of Racial Equality (CORE) in 1942, the Southern Christian Leadership Conference (SCLC) in 1957, and the Student Non-Violent Coordinating Committee (SNCC) in 1960.

The inquiries into the Negro in politics in the articles by James H. Brewer, John M. Allswang, and Ernest M. Collins emphasize urban politics. This should not lead one to overlook the single most important fact about the Negro in politics in the period 1930–1945. As Ralph Bunche put it in 1941, ". . . it is in the South that the overwhelming majority of Negroes reside, and, within the framework of democratic analysis, enforced non-voting is far more meaningful than voting."[1] Nor should one forget that "the Negro voter in the North is much more thoroughly assimilated politically than he is socially or economically."[2] It should be noted too that the growing activity and importance of the Negro in urban politics emerged at the same time the urban electorate as a whole was playing an increasingly influential role in politics.[3]

1. Ralph Bunche, "The Negro in the Political Life of the United States," *Journal of Negro Education* (July 1941), p. 579.

2. *Ibid.*; William R. Keech, *The Impact of Negro Voting: The Role of the Vote in the Quest for Equality* (Chicago: Rand McNally, 1968), explores the question whether equal voting rights bring equal social and economic opportunity for blacks.

3. Carl N. Degler, "American Political Parties and the Rise of the City: An Interpretation," *Journal of American History* (June 1964); Samuel J. Eldersveld, "The Influence of Metropolitan Pluralities in Presidential Elections since 1920," *American Political Science Review* (December 1949); Norman A. Graebner, "Depression and Urban Votes," *Current History* (October 1952); Samuel A. Lubell, *The Future of American Politics* (New York: Harper Colophon Books, 1965, 3rd ed. rev.), pp. 43–68.

THE NAACP AND A
FEDERAL ANTI-LYNCHING BILL,
1934–1940

ROBERT L. ZANGRANDO

In the 1930's the NAACP, concentrating on action in the courts, attacked the poll tax and the white primary. The campaign against the poll tax failed, but in 1944 the Supreme Court handed down a decision on white primaries ending Southern sophistry on that issue. "The heart of NAACP litigation in the 1930's was the beginning of a long-range battle against segregation. For tactical purposes, the main emphasis was placed on educational discrimination." (See August Meier and Elliott M. Rudwick, From Plantation to Ghetto: An Interpretive History of American Negroes *[New York: Hill and Wang, 1966], p. 215.) A black child, of course, could survive while awaiting integration in the schools, but a victim of the evil practice of lynching, needless to say, could not benefit from continued litigation. (See Arthur F. Raper,* The Tragedy of Lynching *[Chapel Hill: University of North Carolina Press, 1933].) In this selection Robert L. Zangrando deals with the NAACP's persistent but futile effort to obtain an anti-lynching law. Although this attempt was unsuccessful, it brought the organization national attention and considerable prestige. (Gilbert Ware, in a brief, comprehensive summary of the NAACP's activities, "Lobbying as a Means of Protest: The NAACP as an Agent of Equality,"* Journal of Negro Education *[Spring 1964], discusses the organization's opposition to filibustering and to the confirmation of President Hoover's nomination of Judge John J. Parker to the Supreme Court, its campaigns for FEPC and for voting rights, and its efforts to obtain enactment of an anti-lynching law.)*

❖

Historians have never satisfactorily discussed and analyzed the role of the National Association for the Advancement of Colored People in campaigning for a federal anti-lynching bill. The present article will examine the subject from 1934 to 1940, when the Association's efforts were the most intensive in its entire experience at Congressional lobbying. Limitations of space prevent a detailed examination of each development, but a representative sampling of NAACP tactics clearly establishes the nature and intent of its program throughout those years.

Actually the organization had long concentrated on the lynching problem; as far back as 1911, two years after its inception, the NAACP developed a systematic campaign to bring lynching to national awareness.[1] Thereafter, the techniques included the investigation of mob violence, the compilation and publication of statistics, the sponsoring of conferences and mass meetings, and a generalized program of public education on the causes, enactments, and subsequent, minimal prosecutions characteristic of lynchings.[2] The Association had sought federal legislation as early as 1922,[3] and its later efforts drew heavily on this backlog of experience.

In November, 1933, the Association announced that its legal council had drafted an anti-lynching bill for presentation to the Senate; in the ensuing session Colorado's Edward Costigan and New York's Robert Wagner stepped forward as co-sponsors.[4] The objective of the bill was to destroy the usually complacent acceptance of mob murder and to make lynching too hazardous as a local pastime. S. 1978 sought ". . . to assure to persons within the jurisdiction of every State the equal protection of the laws, and to punish the crime of lynching." The measure would penalize with a fine or a jail term those state and local officials found delinquent in protecting citizens or in arresting and prosecuting violators of the law; five years to life would await lawmen who aided the mob in its work. In deference to the concept of local police power, federal agencies would be empowered to act only if a lapse of thirty days proved state and area officials ineffective or indifferent. Finally, a $10,000 fine would be levied against the county(s) wherein the victim was seized and put to death.[5] The NAACP understood the need to pressure enforcement agencies: there had been no indictments whatever in fifteen of the twenty-

Reprinted by permission from *Journal of Negro History*, L (April 1965), 106–117.

one lynchings of 1930, and in the remaining six instances only four of forty-nine defendants were ultimately convicted. All too frequently coroners' inquiries closed with the disclaimer that death had come "at the hands of parties unknown."[6] Years later Walter White declared federal action an appropriate mechanism to shield officials, judges, and jurors from the community prejudices which had customarily nurtured the lynching practice.[7]

On February 20, 1934, NAACP spokesmen appeared before a Senate Judiciary subcommittee, and White testified that since 1882, 5,053 lynchings (involving 3,513 Negroes) had occurred. Not only had 94 of these been women, but in only one-sixth of the cases had rape—the traditional rationalization for lynching—been even the *alleged* cause of mob action. How then could the eternal charge of Negro sexual perversion be sustained by the bill's opponents? Moreover, Southern politicians had long defended the capacity of the separate states to solve the lynching problem. White challenged this; 277 lynchings over the past twelve years confirmed the need for national protection against mob violence. He also raised the then-timely issue of Communism's attraction for twelve million members of America's most depressed and downtrodden minority. Could the Negro continue to believe in the American dream when his government seemed powerless—or unwilling—to guarantee the basic right of life?[8] Before concluding, Mr. White offered articles and editorials from the nation's press, some of Southern origin, which favored the anti-lynching bill. Moreover, he displayed copies of letters from a dozen governors, including Florida's David Sholtz, all of whom sustained the measure in question.[9]

The next NAACP witnesses were Arthur B. Spingarn, chairman, and Herbert K. Stockton, member, of the Assocation's National Legal Committee. The former reported that since 1899 less than one percent of lynchings had resulted in any punitive measures by local and state authorities; and this despite the fact that, starting with Georgia in 1893, state after state had enacted anti-lynching laws.[10] Mr. Stockton examined legal, constitutional points raised by the bill's critics and demonstrated that sufficient precedent for action did exist. He presented the subcommittee a brief by Moorfield Storey, former president of the American Bar Association and onetime chief counsel for NAACP-sponsored cases before the Supreme Court. The statement argued that the Fifth and Fourteenth Amendments and the power of Congress to legislate for the peace of the country all justified the proposed act.[11]

The Association's testimony proved decisive, for on March 28 the Judiciary committee recommended passage of the Costigan-Wagner bill with minor amendments[12]—none of which was objectionable to the NAACP. Incorporation into the report of Supreme Court decisions cited by the Association indicated the organization's impact; indeed, they were the same cases mentioned by James Weldon Johnson in his 1926 defense of the Dyer bill before a Senate subcommittee.[13] With S. 1978 moving to the floor, White and his colleagues hoped next to arouse support for passage.

Accordingly, Senator Wagner introduced an open letter to Congress from the Writers' League Against Lynching, an organization under NAACP sponsorship. Dated April 24, the letter employed the Association's data concerning the numbers and supposed causes of lynchings and bore the signatures of two dozen outstanding authors and scholars.[14] The use of endorsements by prominent figures remained a typical NAACP tactic. In December, 1934, for example, the Association sent President Roosevelt a petition from nine governors or ex-governors, twenty-seven mayors, fifty-eight bishops and churchmen, fifty-four college presidents and professors, and one hundred nine lawyers, editors, writers, and jurists, all asking that the Costigan-Wagner bill be made a piece of "must" legislation in the coming session. The signers included John J. Tigert, President of the University of Florida, Mayor T. A. Penny of Tulsa, and the Right Reverend E. Cecil Seaman, Episcopal Bishop of North Texas.[15]

The Association conducted a vigorous campaign for public support. Its monthly publication, *The Crisis*, devoted the January, 1935, issue to a series of articles outlining the latest bill, listing organizations which had pledged their endorsement, and advising readers to procure transcripts of committee hearings. The magazine pleaded that letters be sent to Washington and funds to the Association and noted that copies of the published report on the Claude Neal lynching were available for distribution.[16] That incident and the NAACP's reaction merit examination as an illustration of the attempts to affect public and governmental opinion.

On October 19, 1934, a young Negro, Claude Neal, was arrested for murder in Marianna, Florida. To avoid the angry public mood, officials moved Neal from jail to jail. On Friday, October 26, however, he was seized by mob action at Brewton, Alabama and transported back to Marianna where a crowd of over four thousand awaited the lynching. Subjected to the most brutal treatment, Neal was finally hanged by the neck in the courthouse square. Local police failed to maintain order, and one deputy sheriff—who a week later announced his candidacy for sheriff in 1936—reportedly stated, "In my opinion, the mob will not be bothered, either before or after the lynching." An eight page pamphlet entitled *The Lynching of Claude Neal*, which appeared about five weeks after his death, and which was reprinted in December, 1934 and in February, 1937, recounted the entire episode. Beyond the rioting and murder, the pamphlet documented the more bizarre fact that newspapers throughout the country had run the story of the *anticipated* lynching even before it occurred. Fifteen such papers were identified. The NAACP stressed the inability and/or reluctance of local and state officials to protect Neal, and requested the Justice Department in Washington to intervene on the grounds that Neal's abduction from an Alabama jail and murder in Florida involved a violation of the Lindbergh Law. With no federal act specifically drafted against lynching, the government denied jurisdiction.[17]

Simultaneously the Association exposed lawmakers and the public each to the reactions of the other. In January, 1935 *The Crisis* printed replies from Senators and Representatives asked to state their positions on the anti-lynching bill,[18] and at Senate hearings in February Walter White emphasized the growing popular approval for the anti-lynching bill. After discussing the Claude Neal affair, he handed committee members copies of petitions and resolutions from state legislatures, politicians, professional people, over 2,800 Southern white college students from thirty-one institutions, and some 700,000 Catholics, Protestants, and Jews represented at a mass meeting in Cleveland earlier that month.[19]

From February 15 through March 2, the Association sponsored "An Art Commentary on Lynching" at New York City's Arthur U. Newton Galleries. NAACP activities had not gone unnoticed: the exhibit nearly failed when the Jacques Seligmann Galleries, the original site, asserted four days before opening that "political, social, and economic pressure" prevented it from handling the event. As it developed, though, three thousand persons thronged the Newton Galleries to view the collection of oils, black-and-

whites, wood carvings, and sculpture. Pearl S. Buck addressed
the opening, and Sherwood Anderson joined Erskine Caldwell in
writing forewords for the exhibit catalogue. Thirty-seven artists
participated—George Bellows, Thomas Benton, John Steuart
Curry, E. Simms Campbell, and Reginald Marsh among them.
Commenting on the effectiveness of the event, the New York
World-Telegram declared: "It is an exhibit which tears the heart
and chills the blood. If it upsets your complacency on the subject
it will have been successful."[20] This, of course, was the Association's avowed purpose.

With similar intent, the organization supplied Senators and
journalists with detailed statistics on lynching and with political
and constitutional arguments for legislation; colored newspapers,
NAACP branches, and co-operating groups received a steady
stream of information, as well.[21] Through these varied activities
the Association maintained a complex network of communications designed to inform and to create its own feedback.

The core of opposition lay with Southern Congressmen who
relied on the strategy of delay and felt no need to disguise their
contempt for the Association's aspirations. These critics fully recognized the NAACP's role as a lobbying force. Senator Connally
of Texas, for example, observed that several members of the
Judiciary committee had met with ". . . this colored man . . . a
fellow named White. He runs the Association for the Advancement of Colored People."[22] South Carolina's James Byrnes was
more explicit:

> One Negro, whose name has heretofore been mentioned in the de-
> bate—Walter White, secretary of the Association for the Advancement
> of Colored People—has ordered this bill to pass. If a majority can bring
> about a vote, the bill will pass . . .

The Senator feared that Mr. White, "who from day-to-day sits
in the gallery," and who "For years . . . has worked for this bill,"
would use his influence to make further demands and exact additional legislation.[23]

Hatton Sumners of Texas, chairman of the House Judiciary
committee, thought obstruction more effective than denunciation:
he attempted to counter the Association-sponsored Gavagan bill
by expediting the progress of the weaker Mitchell anti-lynching
bill. This created a feud between the NAACP and Representative Mitchell, the Congress's only Negro, and prompted organization officials to wire Democratic House leaders and the party chair-

man, James Farley, that rushing the Mitchell bill to a vote would be "bitterly resented," because the measure was "emasculated, ineffective and virtually worthless."[24] Subsequent developments demonstrated the results of the Association's labors. While Congressman Gavagan employed a discharge petition to force his bill to the floor, the House refused (257 to 123) to consider the Mitchell bill which had been reported favorably by the Judiciary committee.[25] Within a week, the House resolved itself into a Committee of the Whole for consideration of the Gavagan bill. During debate, Mr. Robison of Kentucky discussed the NAACP's endorsement of the measure and its condemnation of the Mitchell bill; the former passed by a vote of 277 to 120.[26]

Friends of anti-lynching legislation enjoyed less success in the Senate, where filibusters and the threats of filibusters kept the NAACP from its goal. Josiah Bailey of North Carolina had said at one point: ". . . this bill is not going to pass . . . We will be here all summer . . . We will speak night and day."[27]

Early in 1938 Southern Senators and their allies consumed nearly six weeks filibustering the anti-lynching bill.[28] Realizing their measure could not survive both the filibuster and the pressing demands of additional legislative business, Senators Wagner and Van Nuys (the latter had joined as co-sponsor when Mr. Costigan left the Senate) tried in late January to compel a vote on the bill by securing cloture. Their efforts fell terribly short of the necessary two-thirds approval: 37 to 51.[29]

As the speechmakers persisted, the New York Democrat made a final move: in mid-February he sent another cloture petition to the chair.[30] The following day, Vice President Garner laid before the Senate telegrams from citizens' meetings affiliated with the NAACP offices in New York and Tulsa, Oklahoma. Though timely and helpful, these communications could not reverse the earlier balloting; a vote of 42 to 46 signified the hopeless position of the anti-lynching bill. Indeed, even Senators Wagner and Van Nuys conceded the necessity of attending to other matters. The filibuster ended; the bill was dead and unlamentedly buried.[31]

It is evident in retrospect that the climax had passed. Nevertheless, Walter White assured the press that "Nothing has happened to change our opinion that a federal anti-lynching law is needed if lynchings are to be checked and lynchers punished." Tenaciously, the organization's leaders conferred with Congressmen on new legislation and sought to expand Senatorial consent to limit debate. The tempo of investigations, reports, and press releases showed no decline.[32] Yet, the bill was never to become law.

Early in 1939 Senator Connally confirmed the Association's vigor by informing his colleagues of a new campaign for cloture: "I hold in my hand a statement from the National Association for the Advancement of Colored People. This seems to be the parent organization of all these movements. . . ." That particular communication had been issued by Walter White to all branches; it pleaded for renewed exertions on behalf of an anti-lynching bill and carefully outlined procedures by which members could rouse governmental and popular support.[33] Nonetheless, a year elapsed before the Association got another bill out of committee and through the House (252 to 131),[34] and again the Senate barred the way.

In October, 1940 Warren Barbour of New Jersey rose to read a letter from Mr. White. Would the Senator be willing to ask on the floor about the status of the anti-lynching bill? Could a vote be secured before adjournment? Although much of the letter reflected the tenuous condition of a dying cause, the enclosure of data on the year's lynchings and investigations symbolized the NAACP's persistent involvement with these issues.[35] In reply to Senator Barbour's inquiry, Majority Leader Barkley confessed that a busy legislative schedule, the previous filibusters, and the inability to obtain cloture made the prospects too dim to be practicable. While noting the Association's efforts, the Kentucky Democrat admitted he and Minority Leader McNary of Oregon had polled their followers and found little enthusiasm. "I do not feel it would be possible at this time," he confided, "to take the bill up and dispose of it before some form of recess is taken. . . ."[36] There matters rested; during 1941 and 1942 no anti-lynching bills were reported from committees.[37]

The lack of formal passage need not depreciate NAACP efforts. The depression and the New Deal responses jointly fashioned a vibrant sense of national-community spirit,[38] and the Association both capitalized on and contributed to this sentiment. In leading the first broadly organized Northern concern for the Negro since Reconstruction, the NAACP generated widespread interest in lynching and helped significantly to right and purify the public conscience. Suggestive of this sharpened awareness were the results of a Gallup poll:[39]

"Should Congress enact a law which would make lynching a federal crime?"

	Yes	No
Nation	70%	30%
New England	75%	25%
Middle Atlantic	72%	28%
East Central	77%	23%
West Central	70%	30%
South	65%	35%
Mountain	65%	35%
Pacific Coast	59%	41%

Surely the Association's emphasis upon popular understanding and political-legal redress supplied a therapeutic exposure badly needed in American racial relations.[40]

It is impossible to measure precisely the NAACP's influence upon the lynching problem. The organization maintained that just the threat of federal action bred caution in the South. Walter White reminded a Senate subcommittee in 1935 that during the first six months of 1934—when the Costigan-Wagner bill was pending—no reported lynchings occurred; there were sixteen, however, during the remainder of that year.[41] Gunnar Myrdal has agreed that the discussion of federal legislation hastened the decline in mob violence, while Senator Wagner reported the Montgomery (Ala.) *Adviser* as crediting an averted lynching, in part, to the threatened bill in Washington.[42] Actually, lynchings did decrease markedly during the second half of the 1930's and never again returned to the customary double-figure totals of previous years.[43]

The over-all effects of the lobbying proved beneficial for the NAACP itself. Suppression of the Mitchell bill signified what prominence the Association had acquired as the leading Negro protest group. Furthermore, the campaign served indirectly to publicize the organization and accelerate the activities of the branches. *Time* magazine acknowledged this trend by featuring Walter White's picture on the cover of a January, 1938 issue, and one scholar has recently traced the positive consequences of the anti-lynching debate for Negro movements in South Carolina during the late 1930's.[11] Fully aware of these broader implications, *The Crisis* declared in December, 1937 that the bill's passage would elevate respect for law and order and ". . . give us a more solid footing from which we can attack the other obstacles in our path." Similarly, the group's long-time president, Arthur Spingarn, agreed that attempts to achieve federal anti-lynching legislation had been of considerable assistance to the Association and its general objectives.[45]

The ultimate failure in Congress, therefore, fades before the contributions made to the reduction in lynchings and to the emergent, national acceptance of Negro rights. In this sense, the role of the NAACP was frequently central, consistently contributory, and rarely insignificant.

NOTES

1. Mary White Ovington, *The Walls Came Tumbling Down* (New York, 1947), 112. Even the famous "Lincoln's Birthday Call" of 1909, written by Oswald Garrison Villard and instrumental in the NAACP's founding, included the demands of equality before the law and an end to mob violence.

2. Ovington, *op. cit.*, 113–115, 153; Ovington, "The National Association for the Advancement of Colored People," *Journal of Negro History*, IX (April, 1924), 113; NAACP, *Thirty Years of Lynching in the United States, 1889–1918* (New York, 1919), which was subsequently added to each year. In 1917 Dr. J. E. Spingarn, the Association's chairman, announced a fund of ten thousand dollars for use in the study of four lynchings, *New York Times* (January 3, 1917), 5:4. Furthermore, it was through his work as an investigator of mob-inflicted deaths that Walter White, executive secretary during the 1930's and 1940's, made his initial contributions to the Association's program. Walter White, *A Man Called White* (New York, 1948), 49–51; *Times* (January 3, 1927), 3:5.

3. The Dyer bill passed the House, 230–119, on January 26 of that year, but it never secured favorable Senate action. Ovington, *op. cit.*, 236–237; *Times* (January 27, 1922), 17:8; Ovington, *loc. cit.*, 113.

4. *Times* (November 30, 1933), 2:6; *The Crisis*, XLI (January, 1934), 66.

5. *Congressional Record*, 73 Cong., 2 Sess. (February 2, 1934), 1820–1821.

6. George Fort Milton (chairman), *Lynchings and What They Mean; General Findings of the Southern Commission on the Study of Lynching* (Atlanta, Ga., 1931), 49.

7. Senate Subcommittee of the Committee on the Judiciary, 76 Cong., 3 Sess., *Hearings on a Bill . . . to Punish the Crime of Lynching* (H.R. 801) (February 6, 7 and March 5, 12, 13, 1940), 68–70.

8. Nathan Glazer has discussed the unsuccessful and often insincere efforts of Communists to build a following among American Negroes: *The Social Basis of American Communism* (New York, 1961), chapter five.

9. For a full reading of White's testimony, see: Senate Judiciary Subcommittee, 73 Cong., 2 Sess., *Hearings* (S. 1978), (February 20, 21, 1934), 10–20.

10. *Ibid.*, 64–67.

11. *Ibid.*, 261–270.

12. Senate Judiciary Committee, 73 Cong., 2 Sess., *Report No. 710* (March 28, 1934), 2.

13. *Ibid.*, 6–7; Senate Judiciary Committee, 69 Cong., 1 Sess., *Hearings* (S. 121), (February 16, 1926), 29–36.

14. *Cong. Rec.*, 73 Cong., 2 Sess. (April 28, 1934), 7597.

15. *Times* (Decmber 30, 1934), 4:2. In the crucial spring of 1935 the

President told Walter White he regretted having to pacify Southerners vested by seniority with key committee positions, but to do otherwise would jeopardize important New Deal legislation. White, *op. cit.*, 168–170.

16. *The Crisis*, XLII (January, 1935), 10, 11, 29.

17. All remarks and quotations relative to the Neal incident come from the Association's pamphlet: *The Lynching of Claude Neal* (New York, November 30, 1934).

18. *The Crisis*, XLII (January, 1935), 14, 25.

19. Senate Judiciary Subcommittee, 74 Cong., 1 Sess., *Hearings* (S. 24), (February 14, 1935), 32–54, 64.

20. *The Crisis*, XLII (April, 1935), 106.

21. NAACP, *26th Annual Report* (New York, 1936), 21; *Cong. Rec.*, 75 Cong., 1 Sess., Appendix, 2302.

22. *Cong. Rec.*, 75 Cong., 2 Sess. (November 17, 1937), 68.

23. *Ibid.*, 75 Cong., 3 Sess. (January 11, 1938), 310.

24. *The Crisis*, XLIV (April, 1937), 113; *Times* (April 5, 1937), 4:3. A comparison of the two measures explains Mr. Sumner's tactics and the NAACP's apprehensions. The Mitchell bill was less extensive in its application to seizure of the victim, to penalties against delinquent officials, to the role of the federal government, to the responsibilities of counties involved, and to the disposition of damages allotted survivors. *Cong. Rec.*, 75 Cong., 1 Sess. (April 7, 1937), 3252 and (April 13, 1937), 3423.

25. *Cong. Rec.*, 75 Cong., 1 Sess. (March 29, 1937), 2856–2857, and (April 13, 1937), 3439; (April 7, 1937), 3252–3253.

26. *Ibid.*, 75 Cong., 1 Sess. (April 13, 1937), 3423, 3441, and (April 15, 1937), 3563–3564.

27. *Ibid.*, 74 Cong., 1 Sess. (April 25, 1935), 6369.

28. *Ibid.*, 75 Cong., 3 Sess. (January 7–February 17, 1938), 138–161, 253–275, 305–318, 362–386, 430–442, 447–452, 493–511, 571–590, 610–632, 682–691, 703–705, 752–771, 813–835, 873–896, 964–1001, 1033–1054, 1098–1138, 1168–1182, 1197–1213, 1339–1347, 1385–1407, 1450–1464, 1490–1497, 1502–1512, 1533–1562, 1623–1643, 1683–1712, 1924–1927, 1945–1961, 2022–2037, 2090–2118.

29. *Ibid.*, 75 Cong., 3 Sess. (January 27, 1938), 1166.

30. *Ibid.*, 75 Cong., 3 Sess. (February 14, 1938), 1887–1888.

31. *Ibid.*, 75 Cong., 3 Sess. (February 15, 1938), 1924; (February 16, 1938), 2007–2008; and (February 21, 1938), 2209–2210. The failure of local officials to protect Negroes and the success of Southern filibusters were, as the NAACP well knew, both products in large part of the same phenomenon: the disfranchisement of Southern Negroes.

32. NAACP, *29th Annual Report* (New York, 1939), 5, 6; *30th Annual Report* (New York, 1940), 4–5; *The Crisis*, XLVI (December, 1939), 372; *Cong. Rec.*, 76 Cong., 1 Sess., Appendix, A2678–2679.

33. *Cong. Rec.*, 76 Cong., 1 Sess. (January 20, 1939), 559–560.

34. *Ibid.*, 76 Cong., 3 Sess. (January 10, 1940), 253–254.

35. *Ibid.*, 76 Cong., 3 Sess. (October 8, 1940), 13353.

36. *Ibid.*, 76 Cong., 3 Sess. (October 8, 1940), 13353–13354.

37. *Ibid.*, 77 Cong., 1 Sess., Index, 374; 77 Cong., 2 Sess., Index, 292.

38. Mario Einaudi in *The Roosevelt Revolution* (New York, 1959) and Arthur Schlesinger, Jr. in his current series, *The Age of Roosevelt* (Boston, 1958), are two among several scholars who have discussed this phenomenon.

39. *Cong. Rec.*, 75 Cong., 1 Sess. (April 15, 1937), 3523. The impact of the Association's work may also be judged by the increased number of anti-lynching bills presented in Congress. From 1892 to 1933, there were 61; from 1941 to 1951, 66; but from 1934 to 1940, when the NAACP campaign attracted most attention, 130 bills were offered. Jesse W. Reeder, *Federal*

Efforts to Control Lynching (Cornell University Doctoral Thesis, 1952), 231–236.

40. "To get publicity is of the highest strategic importance to the Negro people," Gunnar Myrdal, *An American Dilemma* (New York, 1944), I, 48.

41. Senate Judiciary Subcommittee, 74 Cong., 1 Sess., *Hearings* (S. 24), (February 14, 1935), 32–59.

42. Myrdal, *op. cit.*, I, 565; *Cong. Rec.*, 75 Cong., 3 Sess. (February 3, 1938), 1449.

43. Over the period 1933–1941, the yearly totals were 28, 15, 20, 8, 8, 6, 3, 5, 4, respectively. U. S. Bureau of the Census, *Historical Statistics of the United States, Colonial Times to 1957* (Washington, D. C., 1960), 218. NAACP efforts were nicely complemented by reactions against lynching in many important sectors of Southern life. Milton, *op. cit.*, 1–8; Senate Judiciary Subcommittee, 76 Cong., 3 Sess., *Hearings* (H.R. 801), (February 6, 7 and March 5, 12, 13, 1940), 52, 60–61; Robert M. Miller, "The Protestant Churches and Lynching, 1919–1939," *Journal of Negro History*, XLII (April, 1957), 118–131.

44. *Time*, XXXI (January 24, 1938); Edwin D. Hoffman, "The Genesis of the Modern Movement for Equal Rights in South Carolina, 1930–1939," *Journal of Negro History*, XLIV (October, 1959), 363–369.

45. *The Crisis*, XLIV (December, 1937), 369; Arthur Spingarn in an interview with the author, December 9, 1960. Symbolizing this newly-augmented national status, the NAACP shifted from mandamus action in state courts and began in late 1938 seeking injunctions and damage suits in federal courts for equalization of educational opportunities and teachers' salaries. *Times* (August 9, 1940), 13:5.

THE GENESIS OF THE
MODERN MOVEMENT FOR EQUAL
RIGHTS IN SOUTH CAROLINA,
1930–1939

ERWIN D. HOFFMAN

*In 1930 the NAACP was partly responsible for the Senate's failure
to confirm President Hoover's appointment to the Supreme Court
of John J. Parker, who in 1920 had voiced his approval of the
exclusion of Negroes from politics. (See Richard L. Watson, Jr.,
"The Defeat of Judge Parker: A Study in Pressure Groups and
Politics,"* Mississippi Valley Historical Review *[September 1963].)
The NAACP campaign was successful despite the lack of a significant body of NAACP members in Parker's state, North Carolina, to lend support to the national office. This selection by
Erwin D. Hoffman recounts the growth of the NAACP and the
creation of black civic organizations in the other Carolina in the
years 1930–1939. These developments are placed in a setting that
included the plight of rural and urban Negroes; the impact on
blacks of the Great Depression, of employed and unemployed
workers' movements, and of the New Deal; and white indifference, slight white help, and white hostility, especially as expressed
by the Ku Klux Klan. In 1939 the NAACP in South Carolina had
eight branches with a total membership of less than one thousand,
but, Hoffman concludes, "in the Thirties trends were established
and personalities emerged that were to make such meaningful
history in the field of equal rights in the years that followed." (The
membership of the NAACP increased nearly tenfold in the South-
east between 1940 and 1945.)*

❖

One of the South's most dynamic and successful movements for Negro rights flourished in South Carolina during World War II and the postwar decade. Striking victories were won by a complex of aggressive organizations which were deeply rooted in both the cities and countryside of the Palmetto State. Negro teachers attained pay equal to that of their white colleagues in 1944–45 and the "white primary" was opened to colored voters in 1947–49. In 1954, the Supreme Court decided in favor of the Negro plaintiffs of Clarendon County, South Carolina, and ruled that segregated schooling was unconstitutional. In a decade, from 1939–48, the National Association for the Advancement of Colored People grew from 800 members to 14,237. In 1954 it had eighty-six branches in the state, as against three in 1930. A Negro voters movement, the Progressive Democrats, was organized in 1944 and claimed over forty-four thousand members that year. By 1952 it announced it had seven hundred and fifty chapters and claimed to have registered 125,000 Negro voters. Civic welfare councils pressed to end local inequities in almost every major town, and a hard-hitting Negro weekly, the Columbia *Lighthouse and Informer,* spurred on the people to ever-increasing attainments.[1]

Not since Reconstruction days had South Carolina Negroes demonstrated such determination, unity and ingenuity for equal rights and opportunities. Indeed, the people were dormant so long that, at first glance, the era of mass militancy appears to have been born full grown during the war years. Since such a development is usually contrary to historical experience, the writer undertook an intensive study of the preceding decade to test his thesis that the modern movement had its origin in the years of the Great Depression and the New Deal.

Going back a quarter century before the Clarendon case was won and looking at the life and lot of South Carolina Negroes in the early Thirties, one gets the impression of a people trapped in a morass. The high hopes of Reconstruction had long faded, and the complete triumph of white supremacy in the Tillman era had mired the Negroes in the bogs of Jim Crow and a grinding economic exploitation. Only the older folk recalled those freer days when a colored man's voice could challenge Pitchfork Ben Tillman in the legislative halls or when the two races sat side by side on a Charleston streetcar or in a Columbia theater. Sharecrop-

Reprinted by permission from *Journal of Negro History,* XLIV (October 1959), 346–369.

ping and the crop-lien system, the drudgery of the white woman's kitchen and the white man's fields, lynching and the harsh hand of police and courts all seemed to possess an eternal life for the Negroes of the Palmetto State.

If South Carolina by 1930 saw industry dotting its piedmont, employment opportunities there were as restricted as were the voting booths. In a state where the Negro population almost equaled the white (793,681 Negroes, 944,040 whites in the census of 1930), four times as many whites as Negroes worked in factory, shop and mill. By law, no Negro was allowed to work in the same room, use the same stairway or even share the same factory window as the white worker in the textile mills. When a Negro did work in the mills, it was as a furnace man, porter or truck driver, and never at the cotton machines. In Greenville colored labor was used extensively in a candy and a mayonnaise factory, an iron foundry and a shirt plant, always at wages far lower than those earned by white workers in the piedmont. The Negro worker in town and city was most often the common laborer or the inevitable helper of the white mechanic or craftsman. Since the building trades, involving vigorous physical effort, were traditional Southern Negro occupations, he was allowed a tenuous role beside white journeymen there. In Charleston he could find employment as a longshoreman, and in the federal Navy yard a few highly skilled jobs were available. Over fifty thousand women were domestics earning wages so low that even the white mill hands could afford their hire.[2]

The Negro middle class was woefully small and usually defined in terms of vocations rather than incomes. Doctors and dentists, some morticians and part of the clergy in the larger towns might be counted as prosperous, especially in comparison to the mass of working people. Davis Lee, after touring Charleston in 1934 for the Baltimore *Afro-American*, describes its colored ministers as "living on the fat of the land." He caustically noted that "they have fairly decent homes and ride in sumptuous automobiles, while those who support them live in houses not fit for dogs to live in." Most of the state's Negro preachers, of course, enjoyed no such luxury and their low salaries had to be supplemented by manual work or school teaching. Other professions, most of the highly skilled trades and the major fields of business enterprise were barred to ambitious Negroes by custom, law, lack of capital or denial of opportunity for training. There was a sprinkling of struggling shopkeepers, hairdressers, insurance agents, and service station operators. State and local governmental positions were for whites only and rarely did a colored South Carolinian enjoy a federal white-collar job. Teaching was the dominant professional calling, but the low salaries and inadequate training in this field barely lifted it above the category of the farm hand and the domestic. The stipend of the Negro teacher best illustrates the fallacy of readily applying the term "middle class" to any considerable group of Carolina Negroes. In 1930 the colored male teacher earned an average of thirty-four dollars a month (less than one-fourth of the pay of his compeer in the white public schools) while the Negro woman teacher earned considerably less.[3]

Most often, almost as if by definition, a Negro was one who earned his living on the land. South Carolina had almost twice as many colored farmers as white, if one can use as unprecise a term as "farmer" in the Southern milieu. The 1930 census listed 61,362 Negro tenant farmers to 11,937 Negro farm owners, with more than half of these tenants sharecroppers. White owners held over six times as much land as colored owners, and their land was worth over eight times as much. Still worse, the majority of South Carolina Negroes were listed as farm laborers, mere wage workers upon the land. Women, to the number of 63,414 toiled in the fields beside their men folk and often their children. Only domestic service in the towns was an equally large sphere of employment for those Carolina women who never have enjoyed idealization as "Southern womanhood" or the "fair sex."[4]

The ubiquitous chain gang was an especially noxious feature of the Carolina scene. It not only had Negro convict labor doing most of the road maintenance work in the state, but it also was a means by which white landowners secured exceptionally cheap labor. Poor Negroes, readily convicted of alleged misdemeanors and sentenced to the chain gang unless they payed the fines imposed, saw white farmers paying their fines and having them repay the sum by laboring on their lands. And when a Negro farmer borrowed from a white landowner (at outrageous rates of interest), he faced a term on the chain gang if he could not repay the loan and would not work off the debt on the lender's land.[5]

Rural poverty was extreme. The Negro's unpainted shack often lacked window panes, to say nothing of electric lights or proper sanitary facilities. Even wells and outhouses were absent in many a country home. Not only did midwives deliver almost all babies, but the rural Negro commonly received no medical care.[6]

Except for the fundamental fact that the Negro has been so valuable a source of labor to the South Carolina economy, one would hardly gather that the Palmetto State was his land as well as the white man's. The beautiful state parks and beaches, supported by public funds, were barred to him. In the towns and cities, he got little or no share of the libraries, playgrounds or other recreational facilities. Even the policemen who patrolled his neighborhoods were white. His streets were naturally left unpaved and unlit by the white city councils and only at white schools were there traffic lights or policemen to protect children at street crossings.

To this brief sketch of the wretched degradation imposed on the Negroes of South Carolina, a description in no way different from those of every other deep Southern state and one that has so slowly changed since 1930, must be added the complacency of the white community. Whether the injustice was economic discrimination, exclusion from the white primaries, niggardly appropriations for Negro education, or the all-pervasive system of segregation, it failed to stir the conscience of any appreciable segment of the whites. Only lynchings might be singled out as a feature of the Carolina landscape that was seen as a blight by any noticeable body of white leaders. When in the summer of 1930 the notoriously demagogic South Carolina senator, Cole L. Blease, boastfully told the nation to expect still more lynchings and fulminated about "the protection of the virtues of the white womanhood of the South," he was effectively challenged by the foremost newspapers in the state. *The Columbia Record* praised the National Association for the Advancement of Colored People for its sincere efforts against lynchings. It condemned the political demagogues inciting race hatred on the stump and said that the majority of sober thinking whites have not believed their rantings. That these ideas on lynchings were shared by many white voters was clearly demonstrated by the defeat of Blease in his effort to win renomination in the 1930 Democratic primary. The Senator found his sensational defense of lynching so damaging that he was never able to make a political comeback.[7]

That such white support to the anti-lynching cause did not reflect a mood of equality and democracy was made clear in an editorial in Charleston's *News and Courier* on May 30, 1930.

The *News and Courier* wishes to defend the Negro from injustice, and to stop lynching; in doing so it is opposing a powerful mob element. The task is a dangerous and difficult one. Nevertheless, the *News and Courier* and its followers want, in self defense, to make Negroes industrious and productive; they want to protect Negroes' property and their persons; they want to oppose beating, killing and cheating colored people; they want to improve their health and give them some education.

In this effort they are accomplishing something. But they do not propose to invite Negroes to take part in Government, and when anyone asks this, the South is going to oppose a solid and unyielding front. The question whether we are right or wrong in this attitude, whether or not it is savage or civilized, we decline to discuss.

One white and one interracial group, both small and struggling, were all that the state could muster in behalf of better race relations and an alleviation of the Negro's plight. In February, 1931, perhaps encouraged by the defeat of Senator Blease, a group of white ladies active in church and civic circles met in Charleston and formed a South Carolina Council of the Association of Southern Women for the Prevention of Lynching. "We abhor and repudiate the use of the expressed protection for the white women of the South as a cloak for mob violence," the founding resolution declared. Headed by Mrs. George E. Davis of Orangeburg, the organization worked to influence public opinion against lynching and to put pressure on peace officers and the governor that they should safeguard prisoners who were in danger of mob action. The primary technique of the ASWPL during the Thirties was to secure written pledges from sheriffs and lay citizens that they would help avert lynchings. In 1935 six sheriffs, 1966 women and twenty-one men signed such pledges. The State Federation of Women's Clubs and the women's missionary societies of the white Baptist and Methodist churches affiliated with the group. Lynchings did not cease, but they definitely were decreasing under the persistent pressure.[8]

Beyond the issue of lynching, the Charleston Interracial Committee stood alone as an organization in which white South Carolinians could shake off the general complacency and seek to help the Negro. The committee's history went back before 1930, and it was affiliated with the Southwide Commission on Interracial Cooperation. Most of the small group of whites within the local organization were members of Charleston's aristocracy, and they exuded an attitude of noblesse oblige toward the Negroes with whom they associated. Mrs. Celia P. McGowan, the elderly lady who dominated the group, worked on the premise that the whites should listen to the Negro members but that the colored people had not yet "come of age" and needed her to speak in their behalf.

In 1931 the committee succeeded in attaining a Negro branch of the Charleston Public Library, but no Negro was placed on the county library board. Mrs. McGowan, Secretary of the Board, was satisfied that they were represented there through her presence.[9]

The major project of the Charleston Interracial Committee was its annual unsegregated public meeting on Race Relations Sunday, held during the week of Lincoln's birthday. The event was alternately held in the largest white and Negro churches, with a Negro speaker when in a white church and a white speaker when in a colored church. Choirs from the white and Negro high schools sang. Race Relations Sunday was always a popular and most respected event and undoubtedly became a ritual by which the patricians of the city showed they had a more "civilized" attitude toward "their" colored folk than did the less well-bred whites in other parts of the state.[10]

As if the Negro's burden, under which he struggled with such slight white help, were not enough, he soon had the weight of the Great Depression to bear as well. By the spring of 1931 the agonies of economic collapse had travelled from Wall Street all the way to "Chittlin' Switch." Wages of farm hands in Sumter county fell to twenty-five cents a day for adults and half that for children. These pitiful sums were not paid in cash but represented credit at the plantation store. In nearby Clarendon county farmworkers made fifteen cents a day hoeing cotton. A cropper with a family of nine was allowed $2.50 a week advance credit for food. Even such meager credits were often unavailable as merchants lost their ability to extend them. Pellagra, of course, was widespread on the unbalanced diets of corn pone, fatback and molasses. A landlord was an exceptional humanitarian if he allowed his tenants a garden patch for fresh vegetables, for every available space outside the tenants' shacks was to be planted in cotton. As the ever-deepening depression wrecked the state's finances, its anti-pellagra program often saw the state distributing cotton seed meal in place of the customary yeast, and destitute country people would stir the cotton meal into soups to make up for the lack of vitamins in their unchanging diet. If there was one brighter spot on the Carolina countryside, it was the fact that the Southern creditor was lackadaisical in collecting debts, and foreclosures were less common than in the North.[11]

In the towns unemployment was widespread and the soup kitchen commonplace by the time Roosevelt was swept into office. Unemployed whites were able to demand many jobs then held by

Negroes and get them. In Greenville, where Negroes were the only skilled building trades craftsmen, they had to "kick back" a large part of their wages to the contractors who told them that this made it possible to enter successful bids for construction work and thus provide the men with some work. There were no fixed rates of pay, and before WPA the Negro worker always had to haggle over wages. The Negro domestics, of course, lost their employment as the white mill workers were laid off. Teachers were paid in scrip to be held until the counties collected sufficient tax money to redeem it. This scrip became a severe cut in pay in addition to announced salary reductions because the needy teachers were forced to cash in their scrip at a fraction of its face value.[12]

When interviewed in 1957, South Carolina Negro leaders first recalled the Thirties as a dreary period of lethargy and inaction. They thought of the modern movement for equal rights as born in the years of World War II, with the twin victories of equal teacher pay and entry into the Democratic primaries the first breakthrough in the solid wall of white supremacy. But upon reflection they remembered enough incidents of organization and struggle in the pre-war decade to suggest that the seeds of revolt were germinating and sometimes sprouting in the earlier years. Undoubtedly during the war a qualitative change from sporadic to systematic activities occurred and the ranks so swelled that the pioneering efforts dimmed by comparison. Still, the days of the depression and the New Deal were ones of primary schooling for the present-day movement and a considerable portion of the modern leadership entered the arena at that time.

Race Relations Sunday in Charleston in 1932 furnishes us with a dramatic example of early ferment. The meeting that year was at St. Andrews Lutheran Church and the mixed audience heard an address by the new Negro principal of Simonton public school, J. Andrew Simmons. Simmons remarked that before he had left Charleston to study at Fisk University, there was no segregation on the city's streetcars or at the Battery and Colonial Lake Park. While away, he noted, the Kiwanis club had marked the park benches "No Negroes Allowed to Sit Here." Simmons boldly denounced these conditions and the readiness of his audience to accept them without complaint. The inevitable reaction to his forthright criticism followed. Three white school board officials went to the young principal asking whether he was advocating racial equality. No, said Simmons, he was simply deploring unjust conditions. He pointed out that the three men belonged to different social groups but all had equal privileges. One of them was a blue blood, one a liquor dealer, one a rabbi. They did not associate with one another in their private lives but they enjoyed the same privileges. Those same privileges were what he wanted. The outcome of the incident was that Simmons had to resign his post at the end of the school year, but he was fortunate in getting a better position as principal of the Negro high school in Columbia.[13]

That this episode was atypical of the times is suggested by a report of Reverend Robert W. Bagnall, national Director of Branches of the NAACP. After touring South Carolina he wrote that "Charleston Negroes are noted . . . for their complacent satisfaction with 'good race relations.' " He noted that only one percent of them voted, that they had no first class high school nor any museum. Columbia, with equally discriminatory conditions, was just as dormant. Only a few young men, and still fewer older men who were young in spirit, were articulate and determined to have their rights. The traditional organizations of the Negro communities, their churches, colleges, civic welfare leagues and a scattering of NAACP chapters, were generally quiescent.[14]

J. Edward Arbor, a young Southern Negro writer, bitterly charged in 1935 in *The Crisis*, the national magazine of the NAACP, that the militant Southern Negro was "hog-tied by the fundamentalist, do-nothing colored churches." He spoke of a timorous "Preachocracy" advising humility and patience, and he characterized the Negro newspapers as "cheaply printed prayer books" that breathe "praise of those who exploit them." Langston Hughes, after touring South Carolina and other Southern states, condemned Negro higher education in equally scathing terms. In a *Crisis* article entitled "Cowards from the Colleges," he charged that Southern Negro colleges were "doing their best to produce spineless Uncle Toms," and concluded that they were "Jim-crow centers built on the money docile and lying beggars have kidded white people into contributing" in which he saw only the rarest examples of student militancy. Undoubtedly, these *Crisis* articles reflected somewhat the radicalism and irreligion found among many depression-bruised Negro intellectuals in the North, but in harsh words or gentle ones, the basic complaint had validity. The Negro churches and colleges in South Carolina generally failed to generate protests in the early thirties against either the traditional pattern of discrimination or the new hardships brought on by the economic crisis.[15]

On the other hand, the visiting writers did overlook instances of unrest in church circles of real import. Many Negro churches in Greenville were stirred up by the struggles of the unemployed there in 1931, and the African Methodist Episcopal Church gave evidence of a tendency to remonstrate against injustice, albeit a weak one. This denomination had been the most forthright sector of Negro religious life in the nineteenth century, and it was to become still more militant under the leadership of Bishop Frank Madison Reid (1944–56). Evidence that it too suffered from the general trend of church immobility in the early thirties is the appearance of ex-Senator Cole Blease as guest speaker at Bethel A.M.E. Church in Columbia in 1933. *The Pittsburgh Courier* reported that the pastor told a meager crowd that the notorious Negro baiter had become a new man and "that it is his intent to make as many friends for the church and its people as he can." In truth, the speech lacked the old vituperativeness and Blease used the term "darky" only once. Cole Blease was voted "a staunch friend to suffering humanity and a champion of Negro advancement," and his remarks were punctuated by loud "Amens." But the African Methodists were capable at times of more clear-cut support for the cause of Negro rights. When the NAACP in Darlington opened a drive for membership in 1934, A.M.E. Bishop Noah Williams was credited with giving such support to the group that the drive was most successful. The Bishop also cancelled an annual church conference in Clinton the previous year in protest against the lynching there of Norris Dendy.[16]

Around 1930, the National Association for the Advancement of Colored People was far from the militant organization it was to become. Columbia, Charleston and Greenville did have three of its older chapters. They made no attempt to end segregation or to win a voice in Carolina politics but satisfied themselves with occasional efforts to get fair play for Negroes under the Southern white man's rule. Protest against the most outrageous cases of police brutality and against lynchings were their most aggressive actions. In the former instances, their technique was limited to the sending of delegations to public officials, often with "knees bowed and body bent." In the event of a lynching in the state they tended to trail after the national office and played no conspicuous independent role. Occasionally a national officer would visit the state to stimulate a membership drive in the chapters, but no campaign was organized to create branches in the smaller cities or rural areas. A few Negro intellectuals around the state did subscribe to *The Crisis* and so kept informed of the nationwide activities of the group. The weakness of the NAACP in South Carolina is demonstrated by the report of the national treasurer in 1936 that only one percent of the total branch payments came from that state.[17]

A brighter moment in the early history of the NAACP in South Carolina came with the formation of a fourth chapter in the town of Darlington in 1934. Following an address by William Pickens, the national field secretary, at a local Negro public school, six prominent white men and some thirty Negroes joined the branch. Darlington's mayor, city clerk, the clerk of the court along with a physician, a druggist, and an insurance underwriter apparently became the first white citizens in the state to embrace the Negro rights group. There is no record of how long they remained members or how long the chapter lasted but it seems likely that the interracial chapter was short-lived.[18]

The severe hardships brought on by the depression, like the traditional indignities to which the Carolina Negroes were subjected, failed to result in a general mass movement for redress or relief. The relatively secure middle class, when not indifferent to the plight of their less fortunate fellows, usually did not dare to jeopardize their status by helping to organize the common people. The NAACP chapters, with one possible exception, never became instruments of struggle or protest, and they even failed to show cognizance of the plight of the needy. (In Columbia, when Mayor Marshall instituted vagrancy pickup drives to force jobless Negroes to go into the countryside and pick cotton for impossibly low pay, a visit by a delegation of leading Negroes persuaded him to halt this practice. This delegation may have been organized by the local NAACP chapter.)[19]

In marked contrast to the general passivity throughout the state, a unique and dramatic movement to allay the bitter hardships of the depression was instituted in the textile center of Greenville in 1931. The National Textile Workers Union, affiliated with the left-wing Trade Union Unity League, was then active among the local mill workers. It organized a bi-racial Unemployed Council which led thousands of Greenville's jobless in a series of militant protests. Here were whites and Negroes standing side by side, unflinchingly demanding relief and jobs in the face of intense intimidation by the vociferous Ku Klux Klan and by the Greenville police.

At eight o'clock in the morning of February 16, 1931, two thousand unemployed, chilled and troubled, assembled in downtown Greenville. In the ranks were two hundred Negroes, for no color line was to be drawn that day. Led by a white steam shovel operator the march began. Out the Paris Mountain road the long procession of jobless headed. Five miles out, to the construction project of Reid and Abee. Bitter talk was in the air of how North Carolinians were getting jobs there while so many local people were needy. *The Greenville News* was to call the two thousand a "mob," but the march was orderly, the appeal for work made peacefully. Then the long walk back to town and a demonstration before the courthouse. Heads nodded in affirmation as spokesmen told the assembled crowd that the marchers "were cold and hungry and demanded their rights." Anxious to protest still further, five hundred of the workers, mainly jobless ex-servicemen, next gathered in front of the South Carolina National Bank. There the bank president, who had publicly opposed the idea of a bonus for World War I veterans, was vehemently denounced.

On March 2, the still restless unemployed demonstrated once again as over one thousand of them gathered to demand work. Yet another mass rally may have occurred on March 16, but other tactics than the outdoor rallies became the vogue. One was direct protests made at the American Red Cross headquarters. The work of this earliest relief group was subjected to severe criticism by the Unemployed Council. The ARC was giving aid to 905 families out of Greenville's ten thousand unemployed. The Unemployed Council complained that only seventy-five Negro families were aided and that colored workers applying for Red Cross loans had to submit to the indignity of being fingerprinted. They charged that when workers asked for coal they were told to "stay in bed and keep warm"; when wanting food, the Red Cross retort was "go on the farm and raise some." Apparently the Unemployed Council succeeded in getting the Red Cross to issue more food to the needy.

Another tactic used to arouse support for the jobless was mass representations made to the city council. In March the council was confronted by biracial committees demanding relief. Negro and white delegates sat side by side in Council Hall, the men in overalls, some of the women in cheap cotton dresses. Their spokesman, Mrs. Fanny Herbert, asked the sleek, well-dressed mill owners and other members of the council for work and cash relief. "Every day when I tramp the streets looking for work," she charged bitterly, "they tell me 'Sorry, come back later.' I hate that word 'sorry.' And when I die at least Christ won't say 'Sorry, come back Monday.'"

The obvious unity of Negroes and whites and the militant radicalism of their leaders was not to go unchallenged. On April 8, the headline in *The Greenville News* read "KKK Present As Unemployed Make Demands before Town Council." The scene was the meeting of the town council of West Greenville the night before. Twenty-two Klansmen were already in the council hall when the biracial delegation from the Unemployed Council entered. While the spokesmen for the jobless made known their demands for free house rent, the abolition of chain gangs and ten dollars a week work relief, the fully robed and masked Klansmen "took charge," as *The Greenville News* smugly put it. The committeemen were warned to leave the Unemployed Council if they hoped to get aid or jobs. Klan intervention was obviously intended primarily as a move to intimidate the Negroes present. The *News* reported that the Klansmen scared them away, but *The Southern Worker*, which reflected the outlook of the Unemployed Council, praised the Negroes present for remaining in the hall to the last and leaving with the white workers.

Two nights later, about one hundred robed and masked Klansmen raided the hall of the Greenville Unemployed Council just before a regular meeting was to take place. Once again the press accounts in *The Greenville News* and *The Southern Worker* were poles apart. The former reported sixty to seventy-five Negroes and whites present and said the Klan "gave the Negroes present the scare of their lives." The white leaders were ordered to leave town. The Negro jobless were described as "wild-eyed and frantic" and ready to flee, but the Klansmen told them no violence was intended and had them stay and listen. *The Southern Worker* report said the Klansmen drove out of the hall the twenty-five white and Negro members present. The Negro workers were beaten up as were the whites who sought to protect them. Both papers agreed that Greenville police were on the scene and that they did not interfere with the Klansmen. The *News* reported that the police felt that KKK action would end the activities of "communist" organizations in the city.

Greenville's police and its Klansmen apparently complemented each others' efforts to smash the biracial Unemployed Council on numerous occasions. *The Southern Worker* carried a letter on April 18, 1931, from a Negro worker relating how the police went from house to house in the colored section of Greenville warning the people that they would break up any future meetings. The writer reported that one meeting was held despite the warning, with fifty white mill workers coming to the Negro community and meeting there with some fifty Negroes. The police failed to show up. In late April the KKK increased its intimidation as hundreds of Klansmen paraded through the colored section of town. Then on May 1, the police broke up an attempted May Day rally while telling the participants that "niggers and whites cannot meet together." Following the abortive May Day meeting, the combination of police and Klan antagonism forced the left-led unemployed to convene secretly. But in September the Klan learned of an Unemployed Council meeting in the home of a Negro worker and struck again. Eighteen carloads of armed Klansmen, in full regalia, took part in the raid, in which they abducted and badly beat two colored Council members.[20]

No further news of the activities of the Greenville jobless appeared in the press and the movement apparently died. There is no indication that other South Carolina towns followed in Greenville's footsteps. The dramatic events of 1931 appear to have been the fruit of a seed blown in from sections of the nation where the radicalism and militancy of the unemployed were more normal and where the unity of Negro and white were not inhibited by deeply rooted race prejudice. Yet the stray seed did sprout and thus give evidence that in economic crisis the traditional race and class patterns in South Carolina could undergo considerable change. Indeed, as will be noted below, the appearance in 1937 of an energetic branch of the Workers Alliance in Greenville suggests that the soil there remained fertile for seeds of dissent.

With the elevation of Franklin D. Roosevelt to the Presidency, new leavening was added to the slowly fermenting Negro movement for a better life. Federal relief programs gave fresh hope to the needy, and by October, 1933, 218,806 persons (almost 28% of the Negro population of South Carolina) were on the federal relief rolls. With the establishment of WPA projects in 1935, work relief for Negroes became a subject of intense controversy. From the point of view of the white supremacists, the federal policy of equal pay regardless of race made the WPA an intolerable innovation menacing the customary wage patterns of the South. White relief administrators were viewed as Scalawags or Carpetbaggers when they insisted on "spoiling" the Negroes by a non-discriminatory wage system. And undoubtedly, the white supremacists recognized that more was involved in federal relief to Negroes than the wage question. For the first time since Reconstruction, the Southern Negro was receiving sympathetic notice from the national government, and it was bound to stimulate his lagging hopes.[21]

While the coming of WPA gratified South Carolina Negroes, their systematic exclusion from white-collar relief jobs rankled some of them and brought on a new incident of protest. When a meeting was held in Columbia to discuss work projects in the state, a few Negro leaders were invited to attend. The discussion made it apparent that only manual labor was projected for Negroes on relief. Then two Columbians "tore up the meeting." They were Dr. Robert W. Mance and Mrs. Andrew W. Simkins, whose names were to reappear time and again for over twenty years as uncompromising Negro champions of the cause of equality. After listening to the pious talk about helping "underprivileged" Negroes, the fiery-tongued physician arose and told the whites present that all Negroes were underprivileged. "I am a doctor, and since my patients are all underprivileged, I also am underprivileged and you had better give my people some white-collar jobs too." The protests were successful and resulted in a WPA directive that suitable work be found for unemployed Negro teachers. Positions were made available in adult and nursery schools, in anti-tuberculosis work, and even a few in a state history project.[22]

This protest in Columbia may have been the only one of its type. Charlestonians recall no white-collar WPA jobs and Greenville Negroes recollect only two. In neither city did the Negro civic leaders follow the example of Dr. Mance and Mrs. Simkins, though in Greenville a Negro pharmacist, H. H. Gibbs, organized a delegation of colored doctors and dentists that persuaded the city officials to secure a WPA project to lay the first sewers in the Negro sections of town. And in Greenville there appeared the only South Carolina branch of the Workers Alliance, by which WPA workers could themselves speak up for better conditions.[23]

The Workers Alliance, as novel for conservative South Carolina as was the Unemployed Council of six years before, was organized by Greenville whites who had little or no prejudice against Negroes. But in contrast to the earlier movement of the jobless, this union of WPA workers thought it necessary to have separate white and Negro locals. Leaders of the two chapters met together with no friction, but at white Workers Alliance meetings there were occasional flareups of anti-Negro sentiment. These same white workers, however, would go out on strike in behalf of their colored brothers and work side by side with them. The Workers Alliance encouraged the unemployed to register and vote, and white members would accompany Negroes to the registration board. Members of both races would fill up City Hall, demanding low-cost federal housing for Greenville.

The Workers Alliance did not provoke as intense intimidation as did the earlier Unemployed Council, but many arrests were made of Negro and white members and the police would raid houses looking for communist literature. Apparently no arrests resulted in convictions and no red literature was found. But when a national leader of the Workers Alliance frankly admitted his communist membership, the news alienated many members in Greenville. The white chapter soon disappeared, and when its members regained work in the cotton mills, they gave only rare evidence that the period of association with Negro workers had altered their traditional race attitudes. But as late as 1939 the Negro chapter was thriving and claimed two thousand members. In the Greenville vote campaign of that year its chairman conspicuously stood outside the registration office directing Negro applicants for voting certificates.[24]

The stimulation of the New Deal, especially after the Roosevelt administration assumed a far more progressive character in 1935, may well explain the increased tempo of Negro activity in South Carolina on issues beyond that of relief. Several events occurred that suggest a decline of provincialism and an attitude that Negroes could have an influence beyond their state. Interest in the anti-lynching bill pending in Congress and an identification with the national Democratic party were two trends supporting this conclusion.

In 1935 the Costigan-Wagner Anti-Lynching Bill was the subject of widespread controversy. Although the national NAACP was urging its branches to extraordinary activities on behalf of the bill, it was not the South Carolina branches but the State Negro Citizens Committee, an early civic welfare group, which first spoke up in the Palmetto State. Lengthy telegrams, signed by Dr. R. W. Mance, chairman, and Mrs. Andrew W. Simkins, secretary, were sent on April 28 to President and Mrs. Roosevelt, Vice-President Garner, and a number of Senators. Senator "Cotton Ed" Smith was told: "South Carolina, as you know, has not, cannot or will not punish lynchers. We do not believe you represent in your attitudes the enlightened Christian sentiment of South Carolina. Why not let such sentiment show instead of the all too barbarous and brutal one which is the child of a two by four politician?"[25]

By 1937 the campaign for passage of the anti-lynching bill was stirring the NAACP branches in the state to action. Newly organized chapters appeared at Allen University and Benedict College. As Negro college youth awakened under the stimulation of a national protest movement, Allen, Benedict and Claflin College groups joined a nationwide youth demonstration against lynching on February 12. The Charleston branch ordered one thousand "Stop Lynching" buttons for distribution, but its chairman, at least, still seemed reluctant to pursue the issue. This gentleman, John H. McCray, who in the Forties was to become a forthright and militant leader of the equal rights movement, publicly regretted the campaign for a federal anti-lynching bill. Presuming to speak for Southern Negroes he stated on April 13, 1937, "We are content to wait." On April 24, the *Charleston News and Courier* carried a scathing reply to McCray from Walter White, National Secretary of the NAACP. He labeled the statement "incredible" and said "Mr. McCray has misused his position as President of the Charleston branch and will not be permitted to speak in behalf of that branch nor the association any further since his viewpoint is so much at variance with that of the association." It should be noted that McCray felt that the problem of lynching could be met best by mass Negro voting in South Carolina.[26]

If prior to the presidential campaign in 1936, South Carolina Negroes had at best a vicarious interest in national elections, they began to come alive under the appeal of Franklin Roosevelt. While, because of the white primary, Negroes could participate only in the general election and had no hope of influencing the course of state Democratic affairs, political action took on new meaning. No longer would the small handful of diehards who participated in the state's pitifully weak Republican movement represent the sole avenue of political expression. The headline in the *New York Times* on August 22, 1936, announced: "Negro Vote Jumps in South Carolina—Rush to Register Is Ascribed by Officials to Desire to Support Roosevelt," and it predicted more Negroes would vote that November than in the past forty years. The *Times* quoted a Columbia registrar who clearly pointed up the reasons for the quickening of Negro interest. "Every Negro I have registered so far has said he would vote for President Roosevelt. They say Roosevelt saved them from starvation, gave them aid when they were in distress, and now they were going to vote for him. Then, too, many of the Negroes registering are old, and they have hopes of the old age pension."[27]

A characteristic type of organization of South Carolina Negroes in the last generation was the civic organization, often called a citizens committee or a civic welfare league. Such groups were primarily interested in improved municipal conditions for colored residents and were composed mainly of members of the Negro middle class. In 1938, such a group, the Civic Welfare League of Columbia, was formed by forty-five citizens. The preamble to its constitution pointed up the strength that comes through unity and stated that because "common sense seems to dictate such a policy by virtue of the fact that elsewhere our people seem to be making progress by such procedure, it has dawned upon the gentlemen who called such a meeting for organization that the economic and civic conditions of the colored people of the city of Columbia and Richland County might be improved." The group pressed for playgrounds, better housing, an end to brutality of the police and measures to reduce crime. In March, 1939, it voted to publicize firms whose stated policy was to refuse employment to Negroes. In November its leaders reported more than fifty splendid and important contacts had been made relating to a Negro playground, the deplorable conditions at the boys' reform school, and the securing of information on Ku Klux Klan activities. A committee was formed that included members of the Interdenominational Ministerial Union, the National Negro Business League chapter and the local NAACP to investigate the rise of homicide, felonious assault and juvenile delinquency among Columbia Negroes. It noted a "marked disregard" for the law due to the fact that the courts often dealt too leniently with Negroes who harmed other Negroes. On November 9, a city-wide protest meeting was called to condemn brutality of the police and to demand the addition of Negroes to the police force. Despite its vigorous program of activities, the group remained small and complained of a poor response to its appeal for support. During 1939, the League received only $18.80 in membership dues. As W. H. Harvey, chairman of its executive committee, remarked, "It takes time to make a man, to create sentiment, and to make inroads against evils that have been years in developing."[28]

As the Thirties came to a close, the NAACP had clearly come alive in the Palmetto State. In the summer of 1939, the Greenville Negro community was aroused over the failure of the city council to accept $800,000 in federal aid for low cost, slum clearance housing. The local NAACP branch chairman, J. A. Briar, an elderly school teacher, appointed a committee of twelve to organize a voters club to lead a drive to get Negroes to register and vote in the municipal election. The Greenville Negro Youth Council and the colored Workers Alliance chapter also became active in the campaign. A goal was set of registering one thousand Negro voters in the textile city, and five thousand in the county. The Negro clergy backed the drive by frequent appeals to their congregations. An unprecedented registration followed with as many as sixty Negroes a day, mostly women, receiving certificates.

The Ku Klux Klan reacted with its traditional pattern of intimidation. It announced that the Klan would ride again in South Carolina and made copies of the names of Negro registrants. KKK advertisements in the Greenville papers called on Klansmen to prevent Negro registration and to rally to the support of "white supremacy." Especially fearless in the face of the Klan was nineteen-year-old William Anderson, a janitor in a white junior high school, who headed the Youth Council. On July 6, while at the city hall directing colored citizens where and how to register, he openly argued with the KKK leader and went so far as to shake his finger in the Klansman's face. Eleven days later Anderson was arrested on the improbable charge of trying to date a white girl student on the telephone. After a quick trial behind locked doors he was sentenced to thirty days in jail or a one hundred dollar fine for breach of the peace and disorderly conduct. The Negro community charged that he was framed. Another youth leader, J. C. Williams, was arrested in August and was twice visited in jail by the local Klan leader who sought to intimidate him for his role in the vote campaign. The colored businessmen saw their property in jeopardy and were ready to shoot anyone attempting to destroy it. A Negro druggist gave Briar, the NAACP leader, a gun when Klan violence threatened, and both of them sent out word to the Klan that they could be found in an undertaking parlor fully armed and ready. On December 1, Briar was arrested and charged with carrying a concealed weapon. He was convicted and fined.

The intense intimidation by the Klan and the police kept Negro registration well below the goals set, but it failed to destroy the will to vote. The Greenville campaign continued into the Forties, and voting rights became a central issue throughout the state. Greenville itself was to bear the scars of the struggle until a wartime need for unity had its healing effects. Mr. Briar was denied suitable employment for years and a considerable exodus of Negroes from the city took place.[29]

In 1939, there were only eight branches of the NAACP in the state with a total membership of less than one thousand. The min-

ute books of the Cheraw chapter, organized that year, have been
preserved, and they offer an excellent insight into branch thought
and activities. A plumber, Levi S. Byrd, who had it "on his heart to
try getting up an organization of this kind," initiated the effort to
institute the local group. At the organization rally held in the
Cheraw high school, the first chairman, J. L. Dickson, pointed out
that "We have been sleeping on our rights and we should be awake
and about our business for we have a long distance to go as to accomplishments and we need to prepare ourselves." Members were
urged to be race conscious but not to "resent the people of any
race." There was much discussion of the persecution of Negro
leaders in Greenville, and the branch raised funds for the defense
of Anderson and Briar.

The meetings of the Cheraw branch were characterized by an
intensely conscientious attitude and a basic dignity. Members
were invariably respectful toward one another and never frivolous. Although many of the 160 members were women, they customarily let the men dominate discussions. The Negro ministers,
perhaps because they were economically more independent than
the laymen, and surely because they were the traditional community leaders, played a conspicuous role in the branch life. Meetings, as was the pattern in the state, were held on "Third Sunday,"
and the meeting place was deliberately rotated among the several
Negro churches. Understanding the fundamental role of religion
in Negro life, the branch patterned its meetings after those of
their church groups. Prayers and hymns were invariably as much
a part of the agenda as the guest speaker, the offering and the
business items.[30]

It was out of Cheraw in 1939 that the impetus came for the unification of the state's branches into the South Carolina Conference
of the NAACP. At an executive committee meeting in the modest
home of Levi Byrd on October 3, he proposed that the branch arrange a state-wide meeting. In the branch minute book appears a
record of that first state meeting held in the library of Benedict
College on November 10, 1939. Twenty-five delegates from the
branches in Cheraw, Charleston, Columbia, Florence, George-
town, Greenville and Sumter attended, and the state organization
was started with a freewill offering of fifty cents a branch. Only
the Reverend James M. Hinton of Columbia, who in the Forties
and Fifties was to be the notable state president of the South Carolina NAACP, opposed the creation of the state conference. An
executive board of fourteen was elected, with S. J. McDonald of

Sumter as chairman, and Reverend A. W. Wright became the first state president. Among the fourteen were J. A. Briar of Greenville, Hinton and Byrd.[31]

The conclusion may be fairly drawn that in the Thirties trends were established and personalities emerged that were to make such meaningful history in the field of equal rights in the years that followed. Simkins, Hinton, Mance, McCray, Byrd, Simmons, McDonald—names of prominent Negro spokesmen of the Thirties—are still well known today for their leadership in a generation of struggle. Their rising mood of equality perhaps was best expressed in a manifesto of the Cheraw branch at the end of the germinal decade.

. . . To be set aside as a subject group by social prejudice and government sanction; subject to the dominance of all and any who might assume authority to command, is to be robbed of the same native rights which others demand and for which they barter their lives. Incidentally ours are tossed in for full measure when the time comes.

What the Negro needs is INTEGRATION, instead of SEGREGATION. These conditions are exact opposites. They are to each other as plus is to minus. The one affirms, the other denies. All the blessings of life, liberty, and happiness are possible in integration, while in segregation lurk all the forces destructive of these values.

Reason and right deny us nothing. When these prevail, all will be well. . . .[32]

NOTES

1. NAACP membership records courtesy NAACP national office; Jessie Parkhurst Guzman (ed.), *Negro Year Book 1941–1946* (Tuskegee, 1947); Columbia *Lighthouse and Informer*, October 18, 1952, January 10, 1953.

2. Interviews with H. H. Gibbs and Dr. E. A. E. Huggins, Greenville, October 31, 1957; *Fifteenth Census of the United States: 1930, Population,* Vol. III, Part 2, pp. 775, 783.

3. Baltimore *Afro-American,* November 24, 1934; William Nixon, Chairman of the South Carolina Teachers Association, in *Pittsburgh Courier,* February 7, 1931.

4. *Fifteenth Census, Agriculture,* Vol. II, Part 2; *Population,* Vol. III, Part 2, p. 783.

5. Interview with John McCray, Columbia, March 2, 1958.

6. Interview with John Bolt Culbertson, Greenville, October 31, 1957.

7. Columbia *State,* July 8, 1930; *Columbia Record,* September 25, 1930; *The Spartanburg Journal,* December 30, 1930.

8. Norfolk *Journal and Guide,* February 21, 1931; ASWPL *Bulletins:* "Are the Courts to Blame" (February, 1934), "This Business of Lynching" (January, 1935), "Death by Parties Unknown" (January, 1936); ASWPL, *Southern Women Look at Lynching* (Atlanta, 1938); *The Crisis* (New York), April, 1931.

9. Interviews with John Harris and Mrs. St. Julian Childs, August 30, 1957; with Mrs. Susie Dart Butler, Charleston, August 10, 1957.

10. Harris interview.

11. *The Southern Worker* (Chattanooga), June 27, 1931; interview with Mrs. Andrew W. Simkins, October 31, 1957.

12. Gibbs and Simkins interviews.

13. Interview with Robert Morrison, Charleston, August 20, 1957; with J. W. Brawley, August 21, 1957.

14. *The Crisis*, April, 1932.

15. *The Crisis*, April, 1935 and August, 1936.

16. *Pittsburgh Courier*, September 16, 1933.

17. Gibbs and Simkins interviews; *The Crisis*, 1930–1932 and April, 1936.

18. NAACP *Press Service*, 1934.

19. Simkins interview.

20. No South Carolinians could be found who recalled these events in Greenville in 1931. The press accounts were in the *Greenville News*, February 17, April 8, 10, and in the *Southern Worker*, February 28, March 21, April 4, 18, May 2, June 6, July 4, 18, 25, September 12.

21. Monroe N. Work (ed.), *Negro Year Book 1937–1938* (Tuskegee Institute 1937); Interview with Rebecca Reid, Sumter, August 17, 1957; McCray interview.

22. Simkins interview.

23. Gibbs and Morrison interviews.

24. Culbertson interview; Charleston *News and Courier*, July 16, 1939.

25. State Negro Citizens Committee, copies of telegrams to President and Mrs. Roosevelt, Vice President Garner, Senators Byrnes and Smith, April 28, 1935.

26. NAACP *Press Service*, 1937; *The Crisis*, January and February, 1936; Charleston *News and Courier*, April 24, 1937; McCray interview.

27. Charleston *News and Courier*, August 16, 1936; *New York Times*, August 22, 1936.

28. Minute book of the Civic Welfare League of Columbia, 1938–1941; Civic Welfare League press release, November, 1939.

29. Charleston *News and Courier*, July 8, 16, 1939; Gibbs and Culbertson interviews; NAACP *Annual Report* for 1939; NAACP *Press Service*, 1939, 1940; Norfolk *Journal and Guide*, July 22 and August 5, 1939; *The Crisis*, October, 1939 and January, 1940.

30. Interview with Levi S. Byrd, Cheraw, December 4, 1956; Minute book, Cheraw branch NAACP, 1939–1941.

31. Byrd interview; Minutes, "State Meeting, November 10, 1939" (in Cheraw minute book); *Official Program of the First Annual Conference of the South Carolina Conferences of Branches NAACP*, Columbia, May 17, 1940.

32. Cheraw Branch, NAACP, *Exhortation for Solid Voluntary Action by All the People of Cheraw, South Carolina* (Probable date: June, 1939).

NEGRO PROTEST AT THE
CHICAGO WORLD'S FAIR,
1933–1934

AUGUST MEIER AND
ELLIOTT M. RUDWICK

*In this selection August Meier and Elliott M. Rudwick describe the
NAACP's efforts to abolish discrimination in employment and
services at the Chicago World's Fair. The NAACP took legal action
against discrimination in public accommodations such as restaurants, but neither the courts nor the Democratic officeholders of
Chicago provided redress. Satisfaction was obtained from the
Republican-dominated state legislature, and this experience indicated to Negroes the strategic possibilities of their political action.*

*(Six years later, in connection with the New York World's
Fair, which had as its theme "The World of Tomorrow," Negroes
employed the technique of direct action as a means of protest.
The most historically significant and "the most dramatic aspect of
their [the blacks'] struggle against discrimination," Meier and
Rudwick conclude in "Negro Protest at the World's Fair, 1939–
1940," New Politics, III (1964), 2–8, "was the use of mass picket-
ing in an effort to obtain equal employment opportunities." The
resultant gains in jobs for Negroes and in impact on public
sentiment were slight, but the very fact of the demonstration
"foreshadowed 'tomorrow's world' of the Civil Rights Revolution.")*

✿

The Chicago world's fair of 1933–1934, celebrating the one hun-
dredth anniversary of the city's birth, had as its theme "A Century

Reprinted by permission from *Journal of the Illinois State Historical
Society*, LIX (Summer 1966), 161–171.

of Progress." But if the fair was any index to the nation's progress in race relations, it simply indicated that Negroes were still largely "invisible men," and that the race would have to fight for recognition of even the most elementary rights.

During the year before the fair opened some Negroes expressed fears that they might be excluded from everything within the gates of the exposition grounds, or if admitted, that the official programs would ignore them.[1] However, in answer to queries from Negro leaders, the fair's president, Rufus C. Dawes, gave assurance that discrimination would not be tolerated. Determined to obtain "long sought race recognition," Negro leaders cooperated wholeheartedly with city officials to beautify the city that would soon welcome visitors from all over the world. The *Chicago Defender* sponsored a "Plan Beautiful and Dress-Up Campaign" to transform Negro neighborhoods into a "veritable flowery way."[2]

Negroes across the country were planning to visit the fair, and in 1933 Chicago became the convention city for organizations such as the National Association for the Advancement of Colored People, the National Medical and Bar associations, and the National Association of Colored Women's Clubs.[3] Sharing in the "booster" enthusiasm of Chicago's leaders, the *Defender* publicized the exposition week after week. As a promotional device the paper launched a nationwide contest to select the twenty-one "most popular Race girls in the United States," the winners to receive expense-paid trips to Chicago.[4] The fair's official opening day on May 27 was marked by a parade down Michigan Boulevard to the exposition grounds, and the *Defender* reported that the "greatest honor for the Race" was a color guard of Negro policemen.[5]

Of the few displays by or about the race, Chicago Negroes were especially proud of the replica of the log cabin originally built in 1779 by Jean Baptiste Point du Sable. This exhibit, financed by the city council and staffed by "intelligent and interesting Race Women who tell the story of Chicago's first settler," was the one most popular with Negroes.[6] Visitors returned again and again to hear the lecturers describe how Du Sable, a French-speaking Negro, built the "first house in Chicago," at the mouth of the river when "Eschicagou" was a wilderness. The lecture produced considerable race pride. As one observer put it, he expected a conspiracy to "'read De Saible out of the party,' and make him a creature of the North pole, or something, but the record stands."[7] Although Negroes flocked to the exhibit's dedication ceremonies in June, evidently the event was not considered sufficiently important to assure the presence of the governor of Illinois, the mayor of Chicago, or even the president of the exposition.[8]

Scattered here and there on the fairgrounds were a few other exhibits touching on Negro life. The United States Department of Interior exhibit included a film about Howard University.[9] The Florida Hall had photographs of manual training classrooms and laboratories at Bethune-Cookman and Florida A. & M. colleges, and a chart illustrating Negro land ownership in the state.[10] Negroes varied in their reactions to a midway sideshow titled "Darkest Africa." Some were evidently entranced by the Congolese, Ashanti, and Nigerians who presented allegedly native music, ceremonial dancing, and fire-eating. Though the promoters claimed they were attempting to be "educational," the emphasis of the show was on the strange and picturesque aspects of these "primitive people." One fairgoer commented: "You will come away with the thought that Africa is not dark after all . . . but brilliant and sparkling like the unpolished gems found in its regions." But others considered the dancers offensive in their animal skins and ostrich feathers and regarded the show as patronizing. As one observer put it, "A troupe of native Africans put on stunts for the edification of our good white folks who have never been to Africa."[11]

Two exhibits suggested that race discrimination had limited the progress of the past century. The Western Reserve University exhibit showed large drawings of a Negro man and a white man, captioned, "These men are defeated by life." The text noted that though both were victims of the economic depression, the Negro's defeat—reflected in a shorter life expectancy—was greater because of discrimination.[12] The National Urban League display at the Hall of Social Science consisted of an oil painting, "The Exodus," by the Negro artist, Charles C. Dawson. It portrayed the great migration from the rural South to the urban North. To its left were statistical tables emphasizing the concomitants of the Negro's low economic status—disease, bad housing, unemployment, and delinquency; on the right side were graphs depicting race progress in economics, education, and culture.[13] Ironically, the league's executive secretary, Eugene Kinckle Jones and other speakers at a conference sponsored at the fair by the Chicago Urban League, seemed to forget discrimination and stressed the belief that everywhere in the nation solutions to intolerance were at hand.

Some Negroes, disappointed that there was no big Negro exhibit devoted to illustrating the Negro's progress and achievements, charged discrimination. A *Defender* columnist not only considered such a display desirable but scathingly blamed Negroes for failing to finance one.[14] However, the NAACP doubted the wisdom of a "purely 'Negro' exhibit . . . to blare forth to the world the progress of colored Americans."[15]

A similar division of opinion arose over the advisability of commemorating Negro achievements through a special Negro Day at the fair, as Italians, Jews, Greeks, and other ethnic groups were doing. But because of jealousy among some of Chicago's Negro political leaders, and an ideological conflict over the advisability of a segregated celebration, Negro Day became a shambles.

The Negro promoters of the event, led by Chandler Owen, formerly associated with A. Philip Randolph on the *Messenger*, a Negro socialist magazine, prevailed upon Governor Henry Horner to proclaim August 12 as official Negro Day at the Century of Progress, and to arrange for the Negro Eighth Regiment to lead a gigantic parade. Posters appeared all over the South Side announcing "The Greatest Day in the Life of the Negro." In addition to the parade the festivities were to include a beauty queen contest crowning Miss Bronze America, a track meet featuring the "great stars of 'Negro Athletic History,' " and a pageant in Soldier Field.[16] But in Chicago Republican politics Chandler Owen was a threat to Congressman Oscar De Priest, and De Priest therefore charged that the celebration was being used for personal and financial aggrandizement.[17] Others criticized the event on the grounds that it smacked of Jim Crowism. Placed on the defensive, some of Owen's supporters took the view that since segregation was forced on Negroes, "why not let us put up a good front?" They noted that various ethnic groups were allocated days to commemorate their achievements, and held that a Negro celebration could boost the morale of the race. However, because Owen lacked the support of many of the Negro ministers and community leaders, he had difficulty raising enough funds to give his pageant a professional production.[18] What had previously been advertised as a "mammoth" parade was boycotted by civic, fraternal, and business groups whose participation had been expected. The evening pageant, "Epic of a Race," started an hour late with crudely constructed scenery and an unprepared cast.[19] The *Defender*, which had helped publicize the event as the "Greatest Day in Race History," reported that it was a "flop."[20]

During the fair's second season, in 1934, Chicago Negroes held another pageant, and this time the self-segregation issue was not seriously raised—at least partly because the occasion was not billed as Negro Day. N. K. McGill, general manager of the *Defender*, headed the sponsoring committee and President Franklin D. Roosevelt at the White House ceremonially pressed an electric button signaling the start of the program.[21]

For months a cast totaling five thousand people had rehearsed in various churches, and among the entertainers who performed were Bill "Bojangles" Robinson, W. C. Handy, and Richard B. Harrison, "De Lawd" of the play "Green Pastures." The pageant, called "O Sing a New Song," depicted the development of the race from African beginnings. The audience thrilled to African songs, spirituals of the cotton field, and ragtime ballads, and the evening was fulsomely praised as "the greatest pageant ever staged by members of the Race."[22]

More blatant, however, than the inadequate recognition in the fair's exhibits were the patterns of discrimination in employment and public accommodations. With the exception of a handful of Negro policemen and clerks, members of the race received only "boot black jobs."[23] Early in 1933 exposition president Dawes gave assurances that qualified Negroes would receive consideration for positions as skilled workers, clerks, and watchmen.[24] Nevertheless, few Negroes were allowed to rise above menial labor. A "Race entrepreneur" received the washroom concessions, and shortly afterwards Negroes had "a monopoly on all porter jobs in the toilets." The *Defender* noted that all the model house exhibits "are equipped with Race maids along with other modern articles. They seem to go with the furniture."[25] A number of Negroes did gain employment as entertainers in stereotyped roles. On the midway Negroes appeared in the "Midget Village," the "Show Boat," and especially in the "Old Plantation Show." Elsewhere on the fairground the celebrated Mundy Choristers gave a hundred concerts during the 1933 and 1934 seasons.[26]

In 1934, as the fair was preparing for its second season, a Negro Republican representative from Chicago, Charles J. Jenkins, told the Illinois legislature that although the Chicago relief rolls were bulging with Negroes, concession operators were hiring whites from all parts of the nation. Hundreds of white men were also employed to repaint the exposition buildings, but not one Negro.[27] The only consolation for Negroes was that more of them were hired in unskilled positions than during the first season.[28] For example, a reporter made the following comment after visiting the automobile exhibits:

I see a dark boy sweeping the floor, another one polishing some machinery, and still another one applying a soft cloth to a 1908 model Ford touring car. . . . This is something. Last year there wasn't a black man picking up paper in the General Motors exhibit.[29]

Negroes in responsible positions were so scarce that race papers were ecstatic when a mechanic joined the staff at the Ford building and gave brief lectures in the museum section of the exhibit. The NAACP's *Crisis* commented: "There is now at least one concrete, unmistakable, but unlabeled bit of evidence of Negro ability. . . . Without any trumpets, headlines, placards, pamphlets or oratory, without any 'race' propaganda, he is proving daily to millions of visitors from every corner of the earth the skill and ability of his race."[30]

Some Negro visitors who arrived at the fairgrounds were apprehensive and hesitant because they feared hostile white reaction. Their "pitiful 'Uncle Tom' and 'Aunt Jemima'" timidity was scathingly condemned by a Chicago Negro businessman: "We want men and women . . . who are unafraid of whites . . . and who refuse to cringe and apologize when they enter their places of business. . . . We need men and women . . . to assert their rights."[31] On the whole, however, Negroes were treated courteously at the various exhibits. One observer commented that attendants were "as polite and deferential as Frenchmen."[32] Another fairgoer, expecting insulting treatment, expressed pride and pleasure after having been taken for a test drive at the Ford "Roads of the World" exhibit: "Strange as it seems, there was absolutely no difference shown those who stood in the line—as a car pulled up to the loading point, the next persons in line were given seats."[33]

But when Negroes entered restaurants on the fairgrounds, they frequently met all kinds of evasions to discourage their patronage, despite the prior assurances that no racial discrimination would be allowed. At such establishments as Pabst Brewery's Blue Ribbon Casino, the Adobe House, and Casino de Alex, waiters first ignored Negro customers and then frankly informed them that the management did not cater to colored people. At the Century Grill, Negroes were told that vacant tables "were reserved for employees."[34]

The *Defender,* declaring that a Century of Progress in arts

and sciences was worth little "unless our spiritual advancement
has kept pace," advised persons experiencing discrimination to
obtain redress in the courts on the basis of the Illinois civil rights
act.[35] However, when the Chicago branch of the NAACP took
legal action, neither the Chicago police department nor municipal
judges showed much interest in enforcing the public accommodations law. For instance, in one case, police officers "lost" a warrant
they were to serve against a cafe owner. After the NAACP attorney appeared in court to request a second warrant, the judge retorted that he "would not issue a warrant for a business man on a
charge of this kind without first calling him in and asking him
about it."[36]

In July, 1933, Representative Jenkins sought the cooperation
of the Illinois General Assembly to compel the Cook County state's
attorney to enforce the civil rights law. Jenkins reminded his colleagues that the discriminatory restaurants were located on public land which, under provisions of a special legislative act, had
been leased to the Century of Progress Corporation. The General
Assembly agreed to pass a resolution requesting the state's attorney in Chicago to conduct a grand jury investigation "to determine whether or not there is a general conspiracy among [the
restaurants] to persist in said criminal violations."[37] Almost immediately the Chicago NAACP announced its willingness to fur-
nish evidence concerning these allegations of a conspiracy.

About a month later, Representative Jenkins and A. C. Mac-
Neal, president of the Chicago NAACP, requested an interview
with Thomas Courtney, Cook County state's attorney. Courtney
was unavailable when a large delegation arrived, but its members
conferred with his assistant, Grover C. Niemeyer. After reciting
numerous instances of discrimination at the fair, the Negroes
requested a grand jury inquiry. Niemeyer replied that he would
take legal action on the public accommodations cases after receiving "sufficient detailed information." Pressed by MacNeal to state
what kind of action he would take and when it would be taken,
Niemeyer became angry and accused the Chicago NAACP leader
of trying "to pin him down and put the State's Attorney's Office on
the spot." The delegation was informed that the county prosecutor
would act "in due course, and in the order of importance to other
matters pending in the office." After this unsatisfactory interview,
Negroes pessimistically concluded that the restaurant cases would
be handled only after the fair had ended.[38]

Although Mayor Edward J. Kelly once again promised to use

his good offices to protect all visitors to the fair, Jenkins decided that only stronger legislation would solve the problem. Consequently, after officials announced that the exposition would be held over for another year, Jenkins and two other Negro legislators threatened to block passage of an enabling act to promote the 1934 fair, if Negroes were not guaranteed the same rights as whites in all public accommodations.[39] By a House vote of 98–2 and a Senate vote of 27–0, a new law provided that racial discrimination in public accommodations at the fairgrounds would result in the guilty concessionaire's establishment being declared a public nuisance. In the event of violations, the circuit court or superior court would issue injunctions as "emergency matters . . . [taking] precedence over any other action pending in said court."[40]

After the Illinois legislature had acted, the *Defender* advised Negroes "to get into the habit of eating wherever you wish to eat and have money" to do so. Readers were told that racial discrimination should be reported to the newspaper and to the police.[41] The new law appeared to be quite effective, with only a few violations reported.[42]

Negroes had failed to obtain redress from Democratic officeholders in Chicago, but were successful in the Republican dominated legislature, because in 1933 Negroes by and large still voted for the party of Abraham Lincoln. The Negro political machine in Chicago, headed by Congressman De Priest, was still in Republican hands. But the victory in the state legislature did suggest that with the Negro vote increasing in northern cities, the race could use its political power to secure redress of its grievances and the recognition of its legal and constitutional rights. The Chicago fair of 1933 indicated that white America had made very little progress in its treatment of colored Americans. But the experiences of those who fought its discriminatory policies indicated that militant use of political action was to be an important strategy for achieving progress toward recognition of the Negro's citizenship rights in the future.

NOTES

1. *Chicago Defender*, June 3, 1933, p. 1.
2. *Ibid.*, Jan. 7, p. 13, Jan. 21, p. 24, Feb. 18, p. 4, May 20, pp, 2, 4, June 3, p. 1, 1933.
3. *Ibid.*, April 29, 1933, p. 17.
4. *Ibid.*, Feb. 4, p. 1, Feb. 11, p. 1, Feb. 18, p. 1, July 22, p. 1, 1933.

5. *Ibid.*, May 27, p. 5, June 3, p. 2, 1933.
6. *Ibid.*, June 3, p. 17, Sept. 9, p. 15, 1933.
7. *Ibid.*, June 3, p. 17, July 29, p. 3, 1933.
8. *Ibid.*, June 17, 1933, pp. 1, 12.
9. *Ibid.*, June 24, 1933, p. 16; *Pittsburgh Courier*, June 24, 1933, p. 2.
10. *Chicago Defender*, Sept. 9, 1933, p. 15.
11. *Ibid.*, July 29, p. 16, Aug. 5, pp. 13, 24, 1933.
12. *Ibid.*, July 15, 1933, p. 15.
13. *Ibid.*, June 10, 1933, pp. 1, 12; *Opportunity*, XI (Aug., 1933): 230, 252.
14. *Chicago Defender*, Feb. 18, p. 2, July 22, p. 16, Aug. 26, p. 11, 1933.
15. *Crisis*, XLI (Sept., 1934): 275.
16. *Chicago Defender*, Aug. 5, p. 3, Aug. 19, p. 10, 1933.
17. *Ibid.*, Aug. 5, 1933, p. 2; *Pittsburgh Courier*, Sept. 30, 1933, p. 4; *Cleveland Gazette*, Aug. 12, 1933, p. 2.
18. *Chicago Defender*, July 22, p. 4, Aug. 5, p. 17, Aug. 26, p. 11, 1933; *Pittsburgh Courier*, Aug. 13, 1933, p. 4.
19. *Chicago Defender*, Aug. 19, 1933, p. 10.
20. *Ibid.*, July 29, p. 12, Aug. 19, p. 2, 1933.
21. *New York Times*, Aug. 26, 1934, p. 18.
22. *Chicago Defender*, July 21, pp. 1, 2, 19, Sept. 1, pp. 1, 2, 1934; *Baltimore Afro-American*, Sept. 1, 1934, p. 1.
23. *Chicago Defender*, May 20, 1933, p. 24, July 21, p. 3, Nov. 10, p. 11, 1934.
24. *Ibid.*, Jan. 28, pp. 1, 2.
25. *Ibid.*, July 21, p. 3, Nov. 10, p. 11, 1934.
26. *Ibid.*, June 24, pp. 12, 16, Oct. 7, pp. 2, 16, 1933, June 30, p. 9, Nov. 3, p. 10, 1934.
27. *Ibid.*, April 14, 1934, p. 4; *Baltimore Afro-American*, April 28, 1934, p. 9.
28. *Chicago Defender*, Dec. 1, 1934, p. 11.
29. *Ibid.*, June 23, 1934, p. 10.
30. *Crisis*, XLI (Sept., 1934): 275. See also *New York Age*, Aug. 11, 1934, p. 2.
31. *Chicago Defender*, Oct. 28, 1933, p. 13.
32. *Ibid.*, June 24, 1933, p. 16.
33. *Ibid.*, June 30, 1934, p. 9.
34. *Ibid.*, June 24, pp. 2, 4, July 1, p. 24, 1933; *Pittsburgh Courier*, June 17, 1933, p. 3.
35. *Chicago Defender*, May 27, p. 4, June 10, p. 14, 1933.
36. *Ibid.*, May 27, p. 4, June 24, p. 4, July 15, p. 5, 1933.
37. *Ibid.*, July 8, 1933, p. 24.
38. *Ibid.*, Aug. 26, 1933, pp. 1, 2; *Pittsburgh Courier*, Aug. 5, p. 2, Aug. 12, p. 5, 1933.
39. *Chicago Defender*, Feb. 17, pp. 1, 4, Feb. 24, p. 2, 1934; *Pittsburgh Courier*, Feb. 17, 1934, p. 10.
40. *Chicago Defender*, April 28, pp. 1, 2, May 5, p. 14, 1934; *Baltimore Afro-American*, May 5, 1934, p. 15.
41. *Chicago Defender*, Sept. 22, 1934, p. 11.
42. *Ibid.*, Sept. 1, p. 4, Nov. 10, p. 11, 1934; *Pittsburgh Courier*, June 15, 1935, p. 2.

ROBERT LEE VANN,
DEMOCRAT OR REPUBLICAN:
AN EXPONENT OF
LOOSE-LEAF POLITICS

JAMES H. BREWER

This selection by James H. Brewer is about the publisher of the
Pittsburgh Courier, *the largest Negro weekly, who campaigned for
Roosevelt in 1932 and 1936 but supported Wendell Willkie in
1940, charging that "Roosevelt has strayed from his original principles and policies towards the Negro." As succeeding articles by
John M. Allswang and Ernest M. Collins demonstrate, this de-
fector from the New Deal was not typical of black voters.*

*

When Robert Lee Vann concluded his celebrated campaign
speech[1] many National Democratic party leaders were convinced
as to the wisdom of the choice of the Pittsburgh journalist as their
chief Negro spokesman. The strong appeal of this speech, along
with numerous others, to the Negro voter during the presidential
campaign of 1932 left little doubt that editor Vann's political
career was in the ascent. Where it would eventually lead to within
the Democratic party machinery was a matter of much specula-
tion by both Vann's friends and his political acquaintances. However, Vann's political astuteness coupled with his unique political
philosophy, contributed immeasurably to his sudden rise to national prominence.

Reprinted by permission from *Negro History Bulletin*, XXI (February
1958), 100–103.

Vann's early political activities were local. In Pennsylvania politics the Negro editor had little influence prior to 1920. Attorney Vann served as the Assistant City Solicitor of Pittsburgh from 1917 to 1921. His steady rise in Pennsylvania political circles rested to a marked degree upon his ownership and control of *The Pittsburgh Courier*, the nation's largest weekly Negro newspaper. Prior to 1932, Vann utilized his newspaper to espouse the Republican cause. He served as publicity director for the Negro newspapers during each presidential campaign from 1920 to 1932.

His celebrated speech, "The Patriot and the Partisan," one of the best in his distinguished journalistic career, projected him into the arena of national politics. Its bitter denunciation of the Negroes' allegiance to Republican leadership attracted the attention of high political circles to this unheralded Pittsburgh editor. In Vann, the Democrats envisioned one who eventually might deliver to them the crucial northern Negro vote in both the state and the national elections of 1932. At this time many Democrats openly stated that nothing short of a miracle could move the Negro to desert the Republican party. It was apparent that Negroes believed that only the "best people" voted Republican, and they were reluctant to be identified with any party that had strong political ties in the South. Then, too, few blacks outside the State of New York were acquainted with Franklin Delano Roosevelt. Hence Roosevelt had little appeal to the black belts of the northern and border states where the Negro vote might prove to be crucial. Vann's anti-Republican speech was also gratifying to those who had expressed their confidence in his ability to interest the reluctant Negro electorate in Roosevelt's leadership.

For example, the Negro editor's Cleveland speech was particularly pleasing to both James A. Farley, Chairman of the Democratic National Committee, and Senator Joseph F. Guffey, who controlled the puny Democratic machine in Pennsylvania. To Farley it represented the culmination of efforts he put forth as early as 1928 to interest Negro leadership in his party.[2] Like Farley, Senator Guffey had a similar interest in the outcome of Vann's appeal to the Negro voters. At this time Guffey was eager to lure Negro leaders into the Pennsylvania Democratic party. Thus Vann's bitter attack on the Republican policy was viewed by Guffey as an assurance of support by the Negro editor. To cement this relationship Vann and Guffey eventually worked out what was to become known in Pennsylvania political circles as the "Guffey policy." This was an agreement that in so far as patronage was concerned the Negro "was entitled to ten per cent, no more and no less."[3]

During the 1932 presidential campaign Democratic political strategy was designed to encourage the Negro voter to follow Vann's political leadership, and to look to the Negro press for political guidance. Thus excerpts of Vann's September speech condemning Republican leadership were published in many prominent Negro newspapers. In October, Vann launched an aggressive campaign among his people. He spoke in the large metropolitan centers in the North and the border states. Everywhere he charged the Republican party with contempt for the Negro along with bitterly denouncing their political impotence.

The growing interest of the Negro press in the program of the Democratic party was soon apparent. Under Vann's direction numerous editorials were devoted to denouncing Republican leadership. Their weekly news releases not only instructed the Negro how to vote, but explained why the black vote was so important in states where the scales could be tipped in either direction by the Negro vote. In some sections that had traditionally voted the Republican ticket political changes were noticed. For example, George R. Bates, Chairman of the Essex County Republican Association of Newark, N.J., asserted "it was once a rare thing to find colored Democrats, now the woods are full of them . . . Negro newspapers have deserted us."[4] However, the Republican organizational chiefs had ample reason to dismiss the importance of the growing number of Negroes openly supporting the New York governor.[5]

Even before the final votes were tabulated it was apparent that the bulk of the nation's Negro electorate had continued their traditional loyalty to the Republican party. In attempting to explain this Gosnell states that "the Democratic party as a national organization contained elements in 1932 which conscious Negro leaders could not very well defend."[6] Nevertheless, the effect of Vann's oratory, coupled with constant agitation by the Negro press, was sufficient in many areas of the North to deflect a large percentage of the northern vote into the victorious Democratic columns. In Vann's county in western Pennsylvania may be found a typical example. The 35,000 Negro votes cast in Allegheny County, Pennsylvania, were sufficient to place the county into the Roosevelt column. The election returns disclosed that the districts that were predominantly Negro voted the Democratic ticket.[7] Consequently, when the votes were finally tabulated, Allegheny

County Republican party leaders were forced "to rub their eyes with amazement."[8]

The effectiveness of Vann's work in the 1932 presidential campaign caused the victorious Democratic political chieftains to feel assured of his party loyalty. However, the Negro editor's abrupt shift from the Republican party and his subsequent support of the Democratic party, stemmed from motives unknown to either political party. Actually, the political behavior of both the Republican and the Democratic parties from 1920 to 1932 had greatly influenced Vann.[9] Consequently, Vann viewed the presidential election of 1932 as the most opportune time to manifest his militant political philosophy. Although somewhat premature, and lacking the support of other Negro leaders, Vann severed his long established relations with the Republican party chiefs. He then committed his paper, *The Pittsburgh Courier*, to work for a Democratic victory. He termed it "loose leaf politics" for the American Negro. There is no doubt that Vann considered "no political allegiance" as the most expedient political practice for the Negro voter. Vann felt that by doing this the Negro voters could always retain their bargaining power in their struggles for new economic and political horizons.

A careful analysis by Democratic leaders of Vann's September speech would have revealed to them the true motive behind Vann's political actions. In this speech Vann cautioned his hearers that even sympathy for one's political party must be practical. He urged Negroes to change their political philosophy and to select the party which they believe will best fit their immediate needs. He added ". . . to my mind . . . the only party which now has the power to make the necessary changes at Washington is the Democratic party."[10] Vann, moreover, had no interest in any movement or party that endangered the ability of the black electorate to bargain or to demand additional political patronage. However, the Negro editor realized the need for ample support behind one's threat to bolt a political party. Vann immediately proceeded to convert a large bloc of Negro voters behind his "loose leaf" program. Between 1932–1936 the journalistic activities of the Pittsburgh editor alienated him from a segment of party machinery. Vann was continually insisting that Democratic national party leaders show evidence of carrying out pre-election campaign promises. Now many Democrats began to openly question his party loyalty.[11] This doubt was prompted by what conservative Democrats considered Vann's untimely utilization of his newspaper to campaign against the discriminatory practices of the federal government. However, political expediency prevented a general retreat of Democratic party leaders from the Negro journalist.

As the presidential campaign of 1936 approached, Attorney Vann resigned his position in the office of the United States Attorney-General. Vann realized that such action would free both him and his newspaper from party dictates.[12] Two facts about Vann's political thinking were now obvious. First, he was reluctant to make any continual commitment of the Negro electorate to any political party. Secondly, he would not hesitate to utilize his newspaper to rebuke national party organizations. Nevertheless the Democrats were anxious to avoid a breach with Vann and his political fortunes were still in the ascent. Actually, by this time most Democratic factions recognized Vann as their most formidable Negro spokesman. However, Vann awaited the convening of both party conventions and refused to mount the Democratic band wagon. Already he was haunted with the fear that the Negro voter had already jeopardized his bargaining power by his open manifestations of allegiance to Roosevelt and to the Democratic party.

Soon after the close of the Republican and the Democratic conventions the Negro editor once again announced his intent to espouse the Democratic cause. As the campaign progressed James A. Farley found it politically expedient to shift Vann to a state party post. The Negro attorney was assigned to direct the Negro Division of the Pennsylvania State Democratic Committee.[13] Undoubtedly the New Deal leaders counted heavily on the Negro vote to carry Pennsylvania for Roosevelt. Hence, Vann was delegated the responsibility of snaring the black vote in his state. In September Farley announced to the American press "the appointment of R. L. Vann as special advisor to the Democratic National Campaign Committee."[14] A few weeks later Vann was placed in charge of handling publicity for the Negro press.[15] In a news bulletin to the *Pittsburgh Post Gazette* Vann stated that the colored press of the country was divided as follows:[16]

Supporting Roosevelt	*Circulation*
The Pittsburgh Courier	174,000
The Afro-American	70,000
Norfolk Journal and Guide	24,000
Amsterdam News	16,000
Philadelphia Independent	14,000
TOTAL	298,000

Supporting Landon	Circulation
Chicago Defender	50,000
Saint Louis Argus	15,000
Kansas City Call	16,000
TOTAL	81,000

Continuing, Vann asserted that "I know of nothing that has happened since 1932 to change my opinion of the Republican party and its leaders."[17] It is significant that throughout the 1936 presidential campaign, editor Vann frequently reiterated the motives behind his campaigning. He assured his readers that he regarded it politically expedient at this time to work for a Democratic victory.[18]

His effectiveness is attested by the favorable results of his campaign responsibilities. Under Vann's leadership the Negro press launched a successful campaign. Hence eighty per cent of the northern Negro electorate was lured into the Democratic columns. However, it should be noted that the master voice and the pleasing personality of Roosevelt had convinced an array of blacks as to the value of voting the Democratic ticket.

Roosevelt's overwhelming victory in the 1936 presidential race had no pronounced effect on Vann's loyalty to the Democratic party. In a post-election news release he carefully defined his "loose leaf" political philosophy. He asserted "our political fortune rests, not in the Democratic party alone, but in full participation of our political rights."[19] This prediction was to soon prove valid. By 1938, Vann saw ominous signs that the re-enslavement of the Negro electorate was rapidly approaching. No Negro leader saw this more clearly than he. To Vann, Roosevelt's New Deal measures were the one thing that could eventually enslave the Negro vote. Consequently, he refused to support party plans to exploit such measures of Roosevelt as the WPA and relief. This refusal was prompted by the actions of some politicians to utilize Roosevelt's popularity to corral the Negro vote. To Vann's dismay Roosevelt's New Deal program had enticed Negroes to blindly follow Democratic leadership. Vann, like other Negro leaders, had no legitimate claim to assert control over the Negro vote.

Between 1938–1940, editor Vann took positive steps to (a) Regain control of the Negro vote, and (b) Impede Democratic strategy geared toward corralling the black vote. In February, 1938, he launched a journalistic campaign calling for equality in the army, navy, and air force. Such a program, he felt was necessary, and it would also disclose publicly the attitude of the Democratic party toward liberal social legislation. Then, too, if his campaign failed, Vann hoped to awaken many Negroes to the fallacy of blind political allegiance to any political party. An open letter making an appeal to the President of the United States marked the opening of his campaign.[20] This was followed by hundreds of letters sent to Congressmen, newspaper editors, and national leaders in various aspects of American life. However, no immediate executive or party endorsement was forthcoming. Vann then called upon his political allies to aid him in his fight. A letter to Senator Guffey, Democratic leader of Pennsylvania, mentioned the merits of having "the present administration create a Negro division."[21] He informed Guffey that "Hon. Hamilton Fish is going to handle the thing in the House and I want you to pick out a Senator to handle it in the Senate."[22] Early in April both Vann and Congressman Fish announced to the press the provisions of H.R. Bill 10065 calling for equality in the armed forces.[23] A few days later the Negro editor accompanied by Senator Guffey talked with the President. At the conclusion of their conference Vann happily announced Roosevelt's endorsement of his program.

However, between 1938–1940 the schism within key Democratic circles over Vann's journalistic activities was obvious. Other factors were to also prove disconcerting to his Democratic constituents. For example, not only did Republican support enable him to gain some definite results, but his militant fight had attracted national attention.[24] The Negro editor was waging an all-out war for what he believed in; namely, the acquisition of sufficient voting strength to apply, if necessary, his "loose leaf" philosophy. Thus, by the time of the presidential campaign of 1940 Vann had accomplished three things. First, he had disclosed the unwillingness of a vital element of the Democratic party to support liberal legislation. Secondly, many Negro leaders were now conscious of the folly of chauvinistic party loyalty and began to realize the tremendous bargaining power of Vann's political philosophy. Finally, his activities stimulated Republican party chiefs seriously to consider plans for the formulation of a liberal party platform.

During the early months of 1940, both the Democratic and the Republican party leaders were eager to place Vann in their camps. Vann realized that his actions were being closely observed. Writing to Emmett J. Scott on January 1, 1940, editor Vann stated:

I am writing you at your home because I want you to keep this letter home . . . I hope you will understand and appreciate that I cannot and will not commit myself to a presidential candidate or a national party platform so far in advance. You understand and appreciate my position. I am being watched like a hawk, and I know it, and I am not going to say anything until I am ready to state my position and defend it throughout the campaign. . .[25]

Continuing, Vann asserted that "here in my own state, the Republican leadership is headed pell-mell back into conservatism." This attitude forced Vann to conclude that the "Republicans are determined to stay right where they are rather than give up some of their beloved traditions."[26]

During the spring months, political discussions with both Democratic and Republican party leaders still found the Pittsburgh editor unwilling to commit his newspaper to either party. At the opening of their National Conventions both party leaders recognized the tremendous danger of Vann's "loose leaf" political philosophy. Needless to say each was anxious for the Negro editor to contribute his prestige to their party's political fortunes. Unfortunately, Vann was not in the best of health, but he managed to keep close contact with the party machinery of each major party.

With the closing of both National Conventions, Attorney Vann had to make known his political decision. Subsequently, in October 1940, the *Pittsburgh Courier* announced to its readers that "Roosevelt has strayed afar from his original principles and policies towards the Negro."[27] Vann asserted that it was a mistake for the Negro to "help elect a Northern Democrat to the Presidency."[28] He then espoused the cause and "urged the election of Wendell L. Willkie and the restoration to power of the Republican party."[29] The jubilant Republican party leaders were soon destined to experience a great political loss. Late in October Vann's condition became critical, and he was rushed to the Shadyside hospital in Pittsburgh, Pennsylvania. News of his death on October 24, 1940, was immediately forwarded to Republican headquarters.

Both Vann and his controversial political philosophy have become a casualty of history. Historians today either neglect or accord this eminent journalist the barest of mention. Yet, to his contemporaries, he had few peers in political astuteness. To Vann, once the Negro electorate renounced its blind political allegiance to any party, it would tremendously enhance its power to bargain successfully. Even at death, the Pittsburgh editor was still fighting for what he sincerely believed in; namely, the correct application of his "loose leaf" political philosophy.

NOTES

1. This address was delivered before the St. James Literary Forum in Cleveland, Ohio, on September 11, 1932.

2. MS. Letter from Robert L. Vann to J. A. Farley, July 22, 1940. In possession of Mrs. R. L. Vann. Through Farley, Vann met Louis McHenry Howe, Roosevelt's personal secretary and political advisor. As a result of this meeting the trio discussed plans to snare the Negro vote. Farley also introduced Vann to other notables such as Guffey of Pennsylvania, Vice President Garner and Senator Patrick Harrison.

3. MS. Letter from R. L. Vann to J. F. Guffey, September 12, 1938. In possession of Mrs. R. L. Vann.

4. *The Pittsburgh Courier*, October 1, 1932.

5. *The Pittsburgh Courier*, October 8, 1932.

6. See Harold F. Gosnell, *Negro Politicians: The Rise of Negro Politics in Chicago* (University of Chicago Press: Chicago, Ill., 1935), p. 32.

7. *The Pittsburgh Courier*, November 12, 1932. The Negroes of the third and the fifth wards in the "Hill District" of Pittsburgh along with those in the city's tenth, twelfth, and thirteenth wards voted in the Democratic ticket. In Allegheny County the black belts of Penn Township, Rankin, Braddock, Swissvale, Wilmerding, etc., also voted the Democratic ticket.

8. *The Pittsburgh Courier, op. cit.*

9. See Dayton D. McKean, *Party and Pressure Politics* (Houghton Mifflin Company: N. Y., 1949), p. 76, for a discussion of the reaction of Negro Republicans to the "lily-white" movement. For comments on the political behavior of national parties toward the Negro in their National Conventions see Gosnell, *op. cit.*, pp. 32–33.

10. MS. *The Patriot and the Partisan*, Speech of R. L. Vann, September 11, 1932. In possession of the writer.

11. R. L. Vann to J. A. Farley, July 22, 1940. See *Pittsburgh Courier*, July 2, 1932. The pre-election campaign agreements made between Vann and the National Democratic Party leaders included:
    1. End of discrimination in the Civil Service
    2. End of segregation in governmental departments
    3. End of "Jim-Crowism" in the interstate travel
    4. Enforcement of the 14th and the 15th Amendments
    5. Recognition of the Negroes' political support by increasing the number of appointments in the diplomatic service and all other governmentally appointed jobs
    6. Opening up of technical branches of Armed Forces to the Negro
    7. Stopping of segregation and discrimination in citizens' training camps

12. MS. R. L. Vann, *Sketch of My Life*. In possession of Mrs. R. L. Vann.

13. *Pittsburgh Press*, August 1, 1936. Of the 265,000 potential Negro votes in Pennsylvania, two-thirds were concentrated in the cities of Pittsburgh and Philadelphia.

14. *International News Service*, September 4, 1936.

15. *Pittsburgh Post Gazette*, October 22, 1936.

16. *Pittsburgh Post Gazette*, October 22, 1936.

17. *The Pittsburgh Courier*, October 17, 1936.

18. *Ibid.*

19. *The United News*, November 12, 1936.

20. *The Pittsburgh Courier*, February 19, 1938.

21. R. L. Vann to J. F. Guffey, March 7, 1938.

22. R. L. Vann to J. F. Guffey, March 7, 1938.

23. *The Pittsburgh Courier*, April 2, 1938. This bill, along with H. R. 10064 and 10066, was referred to the Military Affairs Committee.

24. The Air Corps Expansion Bill provided that at least one colored school "shall be lent flying equipment for the training of colored pilots." In June 1940, the Adjutant General stated "the War Department plans colored combat troops." Another release from the War Department announced provisions for the training of Negro officers in all branches of the armed forces.

25. Letter from R. L. Vann to E. J. Scott. In possession of Mrs. R. L. Vann.

26. *Ibid.*

27. *The Pittsburgh Courier*, October 26, 1940.

28. *Ibid.* Vann pointed out "that during the eight years under Roosevelt, Congress had been run by Southern Democrats among whom are some of the most vicious type of professional politicians." Vann showed how most important committees of the House and Senate would be changed by southerners if the Democratic party could curtail both Houses.

29. *Ibid.*

THE CHICAGO NEGRO VOTER AND THE DEMOCRATIC CONSENSUS: A CASE STUDY, 1918–1936

JOHN M. ALLSWANG

In the judgment of John M. Allswang, the author of this selection, the Negroes' lag behind other ethnic groups in the swing to the Roosevelt Coalition demands an analysis of black voting behavior prior to 1936, the year of the big shift of black voters from the party of Abraham Lincoln to the party of Franklin D. Roosevelt. In his investigation of Negro politics in Chicago in the years 1918–1936, Allswang focuses on five selected black voting areas. In 1936 Roosevelt received 45 per cent of the two-party vote in these five areas (compared to 21 per cent in 1932), and "it was clear that Negroes were about to follow their leaders into the Democratic Party." What had taken them so long to change parties is Allswang's main concern. (Relevant studies of Negro politics before the Roosevelt era are Richard B. Sherman, "The Harding Administration and the Negro: An Opportunity Lost," Journal of Negro History [July 1964], and Sherman, "Republicans and Negroes: The Lessons of Normalcy," Phylon [First Quarter 1956].)

✷

The reluctance of Negroes to join with other ethnic groups in the swing to the Democratic Party—to the "Roosevelt Coalition"—until well into the 1930's has perhaps led to too little attention being paid to Negro voting behavior prior to that time. That Negroes were remaining Republican while others were switching to

Reprinted by permission from *Journal of the Illinois State Historical Society*, LX (Summer 1967), 145–175.

the Democrats is itself significant in understanding political development in general as well as among Negroes. The question of
basic nonpolitical differences between the Negro experience and
that of other ethnic groups is similarly raised. A case study of the
political behavior of Chicago's Negroes from 1918 to 1936 may
possibly shed light on these and other problems.[1]

The Chicago Negro community was increasing rapidly during those years, rising from 4 percent of the city's population in
1920 to 7 percent in 1930 (in whole numbers: from 109,458 in
1920 to 233,903 in 1930). Primarily, this reflected the continuing immigration of southern Negroes to the city. And they took
advantage of the opportunities offered them by Chicago. Illiteracy, for example, was down to 2.2 percent by 1930 (from 3.8 percent in 1920) and was below the Chicago average.[2] Similarly,
Chicago's Negroes were eager to participate politically, particularly those coming up from the South, where they had been pro-
hibited from doing so.[3] Among those who were able to meet residence requirements, levels of voting were proportionate to those
of whites in the city.[4]

Economically, too, Chicago's Negroes were moving ahead in
this period. The immediate postwar years had seen economic
resentment on the part of whites and the great Chicago race riot
of 1919.[5] And social discrimination continued fierce. But the
period of the 1920's saw real economic advancement for Negroes
in Chicago, with unprecedented levels of employment and the
development of growing business and professional class employment as well.[6]

The Negro political tradition in Chicago was one of adherence
to Frederick Douglass's famous dictum: "The Republican Party
is the ship; all else is open sea." By and large this commitment
would last into the height of the New Deal period, but with some
interesting variations. It is possible to isolate a number of almost
totally Negro areas in Chicago, of varying socioeconomic classes,
as a sample for the study of Negro voting behavior (the five areas
chosen included about 50 percent of the total Negro population of
the city). Voting, along with expressions of opinion by the Negro
press and by Negro opinion leaders, provides the means to seek
an understanding of the political developments of this period.

Among the lowest socioeconomic Negro areas were the Second Ward on the near-south side (hereafter called Area Ia) and
the growing west side ghetto (Area Ib). Slightly higher on the
socioeconomic scale were the Third Ward (Area IIa), and a poor

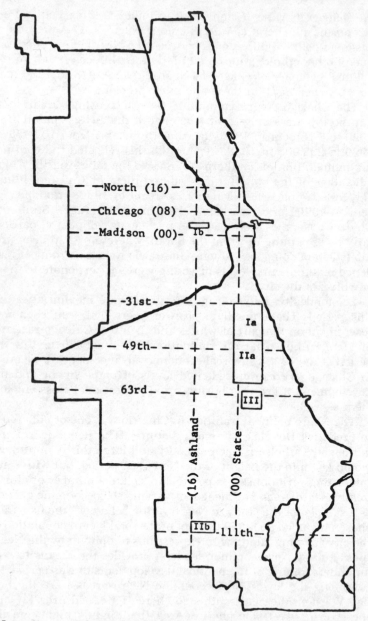

Locations of five selected Negro voting areas in Chicago

but high-home-owning area on the far south side (Area IIb). The remaining area was south of the Second and Third wards with the highest socioeconomic status of any Negro community in the city (Area III). It was the one area out of the five which could be called middle class.[7]

Negro politics in Chicago during the 1920's was largely dominated by the personality and organization of three-time mayor (1915–1923, 1927–1931) William Hale Thompson.[8] "Big Bill" exercised as strong an emotional and organizational hold on Chicago's Negroes as probably any politician has ever exercised on a like group in the history of American politics. And this was a control that affected national and state politics as well as local. In his first try at the mayoralty, in 1915, Thompson demonstrated his great popularity with Chicago's Negroes, and from that point it blossomed.[9] At no time in the 1920's were the Democrats able to come up with a man who could contest this hold.

In the national election of 1918, just before the end of World War I, and in those of 1920 and 1924, Negro Republicanism was hardly threatened. There was a certain hopefulness among Negroes in 1918, based upon the newly augmented numbers of the community and the occupational opportunities that had been provided by the war. As the *Broad-Ax*, a militant but unpredictable Negro newspaper, put it, the war had provided "plenty of all kinds of work," and "places of responsibility and chances of promotion heretofore undreamed of. . . . We are rising."[10] This paper was not, however, very interested in the campaign, although it did recommend the reelection of Democratic Senator James Hamilton Lewis, primarily because he had visited Negro soldiers at the front.[11] The larger and more influential *Chicago Defender*[12] shared this general lack of interest but stuck to its traditional Republicanism in endorsing Lewis's opponent, Medill McCormick.[13]

By 1920 the soldiers had returned, and much of the opportunity the *Broad-Ax* had written about seemed to have disappeared. Particularly grating was the lack of political representation. The *Broad-Ax* complained, for example, that every Chicago ethnic group except "the Japanese, the Chinese and the Colored Race have representatives on the Municipal Court Bench."[14] This factor aided neither party, since both were guilty of the same inconsideration. But there seemed little threat to Negro Republicanism in 1920, when President Wilson's reputation played so prominent a part. As a result of Wilson's policy of segregation in the federal civil service, Negroes had voted against the Democrats in 1916 and 1918.[15] James M. Cox, Wilson's presumptive successor, seemed also to be generally unfriendly to Negroes, while Cox's opponent, Warren G. Harding, echoed the general Republican slogans of equality, although at the same time supporting the idea of segregation.[16] Any apparent contradiction in this stand was not felt in Chicago in 1920. There were some allegations in this campaign that Harding had Negro ancestry, but these received little attention in Chicago, from whites or from Negroes.[17]

To the *Defender*, in 1920, the Republicans were simply the lesser of two evils, but Harding personally was attractive and seemed really to want to abolish the "color line." He was looked upon as the best candidate in a decade for Negroes, and they were strongly advised to support him.[18] Cox had little to recommend him, and his running mate, Franklin D. Roosevelt, deserved to be rebuked for "raping the rights of Hayti [*sic*] when he was Assistant Secretary of the Navy." Consequently, the whole Republican ticket had to be supported, to "Get the South out of the Saddle."[19]

The *Broad-Ax* took a vague but typical stand in 1920. Its curious habit of failing to distinguish between editorials, news stories, and advertisements (a fairly frequent phenomenon in the ethnic press) makes it hard to tell whether it was accepting a Democratic advertisement or endorsing the entire Democratic ticket; the former was probably the case here, but accepting the advertisement might have included the paper's endorsement as part of the price.[20]

The *Defender* did get very excited in this campaign over charges of racism against ex-Senator Lewis, who had lost to McCormick in 1918 and was now the Democratic candidate for governor. Lewis made a statement to the effect that the government was the white man's, and he criticized the "criminal, lawless Negro." The *Defender* was indignant, finding the singling out of the criminal among the Negroes to be supremely unjust. Lewis explained but did not retract.[21] And this sort of thing did not help the Democratic cause.

A profile of the 1924 campaign resembles that of 1920, with perhaps even greater ostensible Negro commitment to the Republicans. A conference of the African Methodist Episcopal Church, meeting in Chicago, endorsed President Calvin Coolidge for reelection, calling him "a ruler who knows justice and whose heart has undergone change, rebirth and Christian regeneration."[22] One could hardly ask for more. The Negro press followed suit. To the *Defender*, Democratic candidate John W. Davis, while an able man, was the representative of the South, as Cox had been four years earlier, and so must be defeated; Progressive Robert M. La Follette was seen as unreliable, and unable to win in any case. Furthermore, the Ku Klux Klan was seen as an issue within the Democratic Party—another reason why the *Defender* again endorsed the entire Republican ticket, state, local, and national.[23] The *Broad-Ax* followed suit, arguing that the Democratic platform said absolutely nothing about Negroes, while the Republicans at least condemned lynching. It, too, endorsed the entire Republican ticket, particularly recommending the reelection of former Mayor Thompson's close ally, Governor Len Small.[24]

Essentially, voting in the 1918, 1920, and 1924 elections in the five areas reflected newspaper coverage, in terms of interest and of voting itself. Like their press, Negroes showed extremely low interest in the election of 1918, with only 13 percent voting.[25] The five areas were more interested in the elections of 1920 and 1924, with 38 percent voting in the former and 43 percent in the latter.

The five areas together voted 65 percent Republican for senator in 1918, 89 percent Republican for President in 1920, and 90 percent Republican for President in 1924. The higher Democratic vote in 1918 was probably a reflection of wartime conditions, and because of the light vote is probably not very significant. In the 1920 and 1924 elections, none of the five areas ever voted more than 21 percent Democratic. The highest area socioeconomically (Area III) was the most Democratic in both presidential contests, followed in 1920 by Area IIa, and in 1924 by Area IIb. Areas Ia and Ib—socioeconomically the lowest—were more than 90 percent Republican in both elections.

These interclass differences were not, in any case, great. Probably the main reason for the difference was that the poorest areas were at the center of Negro population and were under closer control by the local Republican organization. Toward the end of this period, an opposite pattern would emerge: Democratic voting would grow faster in the poorer areas, and Area III would vote more as the higher socioeconomic areas of other ethnic groups voted—more strongly Republican.

At the same time that this commitment to Republicanism was being made in national elections, Mayor Thompson was demonstrating his hold over Chicago's Negroes in local contests.[26]

Thompson campaigned most often on Americanism, something which was never too clear to him, and certainly not to the Negro voters of Chicago. But they were affected by his reputation as a friend of the race, as Robert S. Abbott of the *Defender* would put it, and by the influence of the Negro politicians who had allied with him. Starting his campaign for reelection in 1919 in the Second Ward, Thompson said: "Enemies have tried to divide us— they are trying to divide us now, but we have always stood together and we always will. I've given you a square deal and you've given a square deal to me."[27]

The *Defender* campaigned vigorously for Thompson in 1919, and after the election would proudly note that it was the only Chicago newspaper to have supported him: "It was a victory not only for Mayor Thompson, but for the *Chicago Defender* as well."[28] The *Broad-Ax*, following its less predictable course, and perhaps motivated more by dislike for the *Defender* than anything else, had endorsed Thompson's opponent, Robert M. Sweitzer.[29]

The mayoralty race of 1923 was a greater demonstration of Thompson's power, especially since he was not even running. Scandals in his own administration, and in that of his ally, Governor Small, had persuaded him not to run. Opposing factions in the highly fragmented local Republican organization had prevailed in nominating the little-known postmaster of Chicago, Arthur Lueder; Thompson was alienated. And the Democrats, smelling their first mayoral success in eight years, had nominated a "clean" candidate, Judge William E. Dever.

It seems clear that Thompson was working behind the scenes to defeat Lueder, perhaps because of a deal with the Democrats, but more probably from a simple desire to humble the opposition in his own party and to prepare the way for his own renomination four years hence. Oscar De Priest, a leading Negro politician and close Thompson ally, openly bolted the party and supported Dever, as did Second Ward Alderman Louis B. Anderson.[30]

The *Defender* added to the dissent by refusing to endorse anyone and bemoaning the lack of consensus in the Republican Party.[31] The *Broad-Ax* did continue Democratic, calling Dever a friend of the Negro (and also a longtime subscriber to the *Broad-Ax*), and endeavoring to spite the "Negro-hating sheet, the *Chicago Tribune*," which was pro-Lueder.[32] There was real mobilization of Negro organizational support for the Democratic candidate, and he was successful, as was Thompson.

In 1927 Thompson returned to the wars, with a campaign that

must be considered an American classic. The campaign revolved around America First and opposition to Prohibition (the latter was something on which Thompson's record previously was not completely clear: he had ordered Sunday closing in 1915). In searching for campaign issues, Thompson had concluded: "I have figured it out, the issue will be America First." Asked what this had to do with the mayoralty race, he replied:

That's just it—it hasn't anything to do with it, and that is why it will make a good issue. If anyone opposes us we will say he is not for America First; he is for America second or third or he is perhaps not a good American at all. Everybody is for America First, and if anyone is against us we will say he is disloyal.[33]

This was the great illogic of Thompson's 1927 campaign, and he had perhaps discovered an immutable law of twentieth-century politics: win by obfuscating and stampeding the voting public, particularly its less well assimilated elements. Thus the King of England played a central role in a Chicago election. The second half of the campaign, perhaps more meaningful to Chicago's Negroes, was Thompson's pledge of a wide-open town:

Wherever Bill Dever closes up one [liquor] joint, I will open up two. Wherever he closes up one wet place, I will open two.[34]
I will break any cop I catch on the trail of a lonesome pint into a man's house or car. I will put them on the street and they must catch hold-up men.[35]

Characteristically, Thompson opened his campaign in the Black Belt and told an audience of 10,000 about the "police terror" in Chicago, repeating his promise to keep the cops away from people intent on a peaceful drink.[36] When Mayor Dever stepped up police raids in crime-ridden Negro areas, Thompson supporters in both the city council and the state General Assembly called them "cossacks," and Thompson himself said it was persecution; he told a jubilant Negro audience: "Take those policemen's star numbers, I want those numbers."[37] Daniel M. Jackson, Negro Republican committeeman of the Second Ward, a Thompson appointee with underworld connections, traveled the Black Belt promising that Thompson, if reelected, would reopen policy stations closed by Dever.[38]

Things reached a tumultuous pitch in the campaign of 1927 when Thompson apparently embraced a Negro child (perhaps the nephew of Oscar De Priest). George Brennan, head of the Cook County Democratic Party, tried to build on this incident by printing and distributing a cartoon which showed Thompson kissing a Negro child: "Do you want Negroes or White Men to Run Chicago?" He also sent calliopes through the streets playing "Bye, Bye, Blackbird," and distributed handbills which showed a trainload of Negroes coming from Georgia and piloted by Thompson: "This train will start for Chicago April 6, if Thompson is elected."[39] The Democratic Party was still operating with the idea that an electoral majority could be built through persecution of a minority group.

The *Defender* started its 1927 Thompson campaign early. When the Democrats talked about Black Belt rule, it quoted approvingly Thompson's reply that "the black finger that is good enough to pull a trigger in defense of the American flag is good enough to mark a ballot."[40] The paper gave unceasing publicity to his campaign, confident of victory, and recommended a straight Republican ticket. As the campaign closed, the *Defender* called it "one of the dirtiest campaigns ever held in the city of Chicago," and argued that Thompson was not simply pro-Negro, but rather was for "ALL Chicagoans. We are for him now just as we were for Mayor Dever in 1923 when he took the trouble to look us up and promise us our rights under the Constitution. . . . We received nothing."[41]

The *Broad-Ax*, for its part, remained favorably disposed toward Dever, although it never formally endorsed him. His campaign was extensively covered, and it was noted that his administration had done more for Negroes than the two preceding Thomspon administrations. Dever was seen as a true friend of the Negro, and one who had appointed many of them to "legal and responsible positions."[42] In this context it is worth mentioning that Democratic County Board President Anton Cermak (a man with a very different attitude toward ethnic politics from that of George Brennan, whom he would soon replace) had recently put *Broad-Ax* editor and publisher Julius F. Taylor on his Civic Commission.[43] Some Democrats were learning.

Negro voting in these three mayoral elections of 1919, 1923, and 1927 generally followed the lead of the Thompson organization, and of the *Defender*, in terms of interest and inclination. Voting was low in 1919, at 25 percent, but even this was almost double that of a year earlier in the national elections. The effect of Thompson's opposition to Lueder was seen in a drop in percent voting in 1923, to 22 percent (and in the Second Ward alone, where Thompson's strength was greatest, to 17 percent, from 28 percent in 1919). And in 1927 voting jumped to 49 percent, the highest Negro voting percentage of any election in the 1920's. Thompson was strong! In 1919 he himself won 78 percent of the Negro vote, and in 1927 this figure rose to 93 percent. In 1923 the Negro vote had been 53 percent Democratic, a formidable demonstration of how Thompson and his organization could indeed "deliver" the Negro vote at that time. There were no outstanding socioeconomic variations in the voting. The poor but high home-owning Area IIb was the only one of the five areas to remain Republican in 1923, but this was mainly the result of its geographic isolation from the centers of Negro life and organization. The most striking thing, of course, is the lack of real difference: in 1927, when Thompson was running in a very race-conscious campaign, none of the five areas voted more than 11 percent Democratic.

This devotion to Thompson was demonstrated even more decisively one year later, in the 1928 primaries, when Thompson suffered the defeat that marked the beginning of the end of his political career. The bitter factionalism of the Republican Party culminated in the famous "Pineapple Primary," with its bombings and murders. One result was the unification of all the Republicans who opposed Thompson, Governor Small, and State's Attorney Robert E. Crowe. The groupings were more than clear to the public, and in the primary Small and Crowe were slaughtered, the former receiving 38 percent in the city, and the latter 39 percent. But both received 68 percent of the Negro vote, the highest total they got from any group except the Italians. Thompson had been the central issue of the primary, and Chicago's Negroes made it clear that they still supported their mayor. Once more there was no great socioeconomic variation in the Negro vote, but there was a clear tendency for socioeconomically lower areas to vote proportionately higher for the Thompson candidates (a tendency seen even more clearly in other ethnic groups of Chicago, and a clue to Thompson's overall strength).

There existed, then, in the spring of 1928 a history of long and extremely strong Negro Republican voting, and with it a real alliance between Chicago's Negroes and their mayor—an alliance that could be stronger than the party tie itself.

In the candidacy of Al Smith for President in 1928 we find the only time throughout the pre-New Deal period when Chicago's Negroes seemed susceptible to the same forces affecting the other ethnic groups of the city.[44] This should not be overstated, since the Negro Democratic vote was low, but Negroes did show that they were attracted to the Democratic candidate.

There were no objective reasons for Negroes to be attracted to the Democratic Party, as a party, in 1928. Indeed, the Democratic platform was silent on the problem of the Negro, even refusing to match the Republican demand for a federal anti-lynching law. And the few Negro alternates to the Democratic National Convention in Houston (there were no Negro delegates) were separated from the others by a chicken-wire fence.[45] But candidate Smith, even though he said very little about Negro rights in his speeches, somehow seemed considerably more than just a representative of his party. In fact, one of the more interesting things about this crucial campaign was that it was generally looked upon as a contest between Herbert Hoover as a representative of the Republican Party and Al Smith as an individual standing only on his own record and personality. This conception prevailed among all ethnic groups and is reflected in the *Defender* editorial which endorsed a Democratic presidential candidate for the first time:

> The Republican party, to which we have given our wholehearted support since it came into being . . . has deserted us. . . . The Republican party has allied itself with the Ku Klux Klan. . . . The Republican party in the governmental department is directly responsible for segregation and discriminations. . . .
> On the other hand . . . Governor Smith has denounced in no uncertain terms the Ku Klux Klan; he has denounced racial and religious bigotry; he has been brave enough to speak out plainly for the things for which he stands. . . . The Democratic candidate has proved through his administration . . . in New York that he stands for ALL the citizens of his dominion.[46]

The image of Hoover that emerged among Negroes stemmed from a misunderstanding of his position. In one campaign speech he supposedly agreed (really, failed to disagree) with a comment about keeping the Republican Party in the South "lily white."[47] This did not help him in the Negro press.[48]

Among Negroes interest in the campaign was heightened even further by the fact that Oscar De Priest was running for Congress and would become the first Negro elected thereto in over a generation. As the *Defender* put it, "It is far more important that Mr. De Priest be elected than that either Mr. Smith or Mr. Hoover win."[49] Nonetheless, the *Defender* did endorse Smith and devoted a good deal of attention to his campaign.

The *Broad-Ax* was no longer publishing in 1928, leaving the

Defender as the only really large Negro paper in the city. Its competitor, the *Chicago Eagle*, was not at all race conscious; not surprisingly, it soon went out of business. But the *Eagle* also found Smith extremely attractive and campaigned vigorously for him. It devoted the front page of every weekly issue to his campaign and concluded, in one of those great headlines so popular with the ethnic press, "Not in Sixty Years Has There Lived a Man in This Country Who Has So Thoroughly Gripped the Heart Strings of the American People."[50]

This rather startling change on the part of the Negro press was paralleled in the activities of a number of organizations, political and otherwise. For example, the three presiding elders of the African Methodist Episcopal Church—the same organization that had been so enamored of Coolidge in 1924—endorsed Smith's candidacy as "the most effective blow for the political emancipation of our people."[51] And J. Finley Wilson of the (Negro) Improved Benevolent Order of the Elks campaigned for Smith all over the Chicago Black Belt; Wilson had been elected president of the organization by acclamation when he announced that he had been denied a place on the speakers' committee of the Republican Party.[52] Marcus Garvey, leader of the Universal Negro Improvement Association, commented from his Canadian exile that the time had come to desert the Republican Party and vote for Smith.[53]

Mayor Thompson's role in all of this is unclear. There is no notice of his being active at all, but he had opposed the nomination of Hoover, whom he saw as another "stooge" of the King of England. His close colleague, De Priest, was also strangely silent in the campaign and never did come out openly for Hoover, despite the fact that he was always campaigning for himself as a Republican congressional candidate. And Louis B. Anderson, Negro alderman and Republican committeeman of the Second Ward (Area Ia), formally announced that, while supporting De Priest, he was not officially recommending either presidential candidate. For himself, Anderson would buck the party and support Smith: "The Republican party has shown us the gate. Now let all the colored people walk out of this gate."[54]

The extent of Negro press and organizational support for Smith was certainly greater than the extent of Negro voting for him generally, but the voting switch was there to be seen. The percentage voting dropped from that of 1924—to 37 percent; among an essentially Republican group, this drop was an important sign of disaffection. And Smith received a vote of 23 percent from the five areas combined, certainly not overwhelming, but nonetheless significant when compared to the 10 percent received by Davis in 1924 and the 11 percent received by Cox in 1920 (to say nothing of the 7 percent received by Mayor Dever in 1927). Further, Smith fared better among Negro voters than almost all other Democratic candidates in the national elections of 1930 and 1932, including Franklin D. Roosevelt in the latter year, and without benefit of the Depression. However limited, an important break had been made: Chicago Negroes would never again be so overwhelmingly Republican in national politics.

There was an interesting socioeconomic variation in the voting of the five Negro areas in 1928: lower socioeconomic status tended to correlate with greater Democratic voting. Areas Ia, Ib, and IIa gave Smith 27 to 30 percent, while Areas IIb and III gave him only 16–17 percent. In part, the reason was geographic-political: these poorer areas were in the center of Negro settlement and thus more susceptible to the defection from Republicanism of Negro leaders. There was also, however, the phenomenon of a general lower-class attraction to Smith among all of Chicago's ethnic groups.

The election of 1928, then, did see a swing to a Democratic candidate among the Negro leadership and among Negro voters generally; there remained the problem of winning the Smith followers over to the party if the Democrats were to prevail in Chicago Negro politics.

This last problem would be only partially solved in the three ensuing elections. Most of Chicago's other ethnic groups formed the coalition which made the new Democratic Party. The elections involved were the city election of 1931, in which Thompson was defeated by Anton Cermak, a longtime power in the Democratic Party, in inter-ethnic affairs, and in opposition to Prohibition; the national election of 1930, in which the Democrats swept everything before them; and the 1932 presidential election, in which Franklin D. Roosevelt became the first Democratic presidential candidate to carry Chicago since 1892. In these elections the divergence between Chicago's Negroes and the other ethnic groups became even greater.

If Thompson had ever really understood the intricacies of ethnic politics—something clearly doubtful in an "America First" candidate—he lost this understanding in the 1931 election, in which he campaigned largely by belittling Cermak's foreign origins.[55] He had not, however, lost his ability to campaign successfully among the Negroes.

As the mayor in office, Thompson was held somewhat responsible for the growing severity of the Depression in Chicago. Furthermore, he could no longer run on the issue of the wide-open town, since the town was then too wide-open for comfort; new scandals broke out in the midst of the campaign, alleging Capone control in the mayor's administration,[56] and Thompson tried to stay away from this issue as much as possible. Neither could the Mayor run really as a champion of anti-Prohibition, since his opponent was famous as one of the leading wets in the nation.[57] He would even have some trouble with his campaign among Negroes because of unwise decisions in the national elections of 1930. Thus, from the start, the Mayor faced a difficult situation.

Nevertheless, Thompson took the offensive in the Black Belt, and, as was often the case, his attacks hit home. He reprinted and distributed a page of the 1929 *Report of the Forest Preserve District of Cook County*, wherein it was stated that Negro caddies on the district's golf courses would be replaced with white ones because of "complaints and trouble."[58] The Forest Preserve District was under the control of County Board President Cermak, and thus the Mayor got in a blow.

Another widely distributed Thompson broadside was a copy of a notice allegedly from the Democratic headquarters of the Twenty-third and Twenty-fourth wards, summoning people to a meeting to hear the truth about "The Menace of Thompson and his Negroes"; it noted that many Negroes had been appointed to office under Thompson, thus threatening the white population.[59]

On the whole, however, Chicago's Negroes seemed considerably less aroused by this campaign than by that of 1927, and interest —in terms of press coverage and of organizational activity—was considerably lower, lower too than in the presidential contest of 1928. The *Defender*, for example, reported the publication of the broadside about "Thompson and his Negroes" but did not editorialize upon it, and gave equal coverage to the statement of the Cermak forces that the document was phony.[60] Otherwise, and significantly, the *Defender* barely noticed the campaign, endorsed neither candidate, and in fact acted as if there were no pending election at all.[61] From one of the Mayor's oldest and strongest supporters this stance was a clear sign of changing times in local politics. Negro Republican politicians were strangely silent also, although this too was not noticed amidst the seemingly traditional enthusiasm with which the Negro voters greeted Thompson.

Negro voting dropped in 1931 to 39 percent from the 49 percent of 1927, and this played a small role in Thompson's first loss of a city election; he received only 42 percent of the city's vote. Negroes generally, however, continued to support him strongly; here, as in 1928, they were slower to change than their leaders. He received 84 percent of the Negro vote, 9 percent less than in 1927, but still a landslide by any measurement. To the last, Chicago's Negroes remained loyal to their mayor.

There was a clearer socioeconomic variation among Negro areas in 1931. The higher-income areas (IIb and III) gave Thompson his largest totals—demonstrating the desire of a socially ambitious group to conform to its conception of what middle class people did, even though in this election Chicago's white middle class was all on the Democratic side. Area Ia, where Thompson received 94 percent in 1927, gave him 83 percent in 1931, a decrease that could mean that his lower-class seat of power was beginning to slip away, or that some Negro politicians there were beginning to think about making the party switch that they indeed would make a few years hence.[62] Too much, however, should not be inferred from an election in which the Negro vote for Thompson was still overwhelming.

Newly elected Mayor Cermak readily saw the one important ethnic group in his city which he had failed to dent, and he endeavored immediately to do something about it. The day he took office he fired 2,260 temporary city employees, a large part of whom were Negro. And he threatened to close up the policy stations in the Black Belt unless Negro hoodlums and politicians saw the advantage of changing their party loyalty. As the *Defender* put it, "The Race was hard hit"; "The entire city is closed up like a drum. The lid went on five minutes after it was certain that Mayor Thompson had lost."[63] Thus the tortuous process of change continued, and what Anton Cermak started would be finished by his successor, Ed Kelly.

The national elections of 1930 and 1932 did not seem to affect Chicago's Negroes unduly, and they, almost alone among ethnic groups, remained firmly Republican. In 1930 a rift developed between Thompson and his chief Negro allies that contributed to his declining power. Mrs. Medill McCormick, widow of the senator, daughter of Mark Hanna, and by marriage a member of the *Tribune* family, was the Republican candidate for the Senate, facing James Hamilton Lewis, whom her husband had defeated in 1918. A personal clash of wills with Mrs. McCormick, plus a long-time animosity to the *Tribune*, and perhaps an ill-conceived hope of gaining publicity for his ensuing campaign, persuaded the Mayor to try to deliver the Negro vote to Lewis. He made the effort brazenly, with uniformed Chicago policemen handing out announcements at Negro churches.[64]

Congressman De Priest led Negro politicians in opposing Thompson's effort, calling the Mayor a "sick man" and charging that "no sane man unless ill advised or sick would ask the colored people to vote for a Democrat." He stumped the state for Mrs. McCormick, continuing to question the health of the Mayor and using Lewis's 1920 "white man's government" statement against him again.[65] Even the very nonpolitical Chicago NAACP got into the act, blasting the Mayor.[66] Some of this rancor surely continued to the next April, when Thompson was defeated.

The 1932 campaign, despite the Depression, was relatively quiet in Chicago, particularly among Negroes. The politicians were active, however, especially Congressman De Priest, who apparently took his high office seriously, as he campaigned vigorously for Hoover.[67] Ex-Mayor Thompson was nowhere to be seen.

The *Defender* was more interested than in 1930, when it had given no coverage to the campaign at all. But its fervor of 1928 had disappeared, and it returned to the traditional position: "Every right we . . . enjoy in this country was bestowed upon us by the Republican party."[68] The attraction of Smith, then, had been strictly personal. Roosevelt, personally, was seen in 1932 as in 1920—not a friend of the race. The *Defender* accused him of having furthered segregation when he was Assistant Secretary of the Navy under Wilson.[69] But despite its support of the Republican Party, and thus implicitly of Hoover, it did not endorse the President specifically.[70]

The *Defender*'s lack of interest in the 1930 campaign was reflected in the level of voter interest, with only 27 percent voting, a decrease of 10 percent from 1928. In 1932 the level of voting rose considerably, but with strong differentials between the two areas studied for this trend. The Third Ward (Area IIa) stayed the same as in 1928, at 38 percent; but the Second Ward (Area Ia) jumped from 37 percent in 1928 to 73 percent in 1932. At no previous election had the two wards varied, for reasons that are not truly clear, as much as ten points. Most likely, the activity of Negro politicians, especially De Priest (his congressional district encompassed Area Ia) was responsible; election fraud is also a possibility, but hardly to this extent.

Thompson had slight success in 1930 in switching the Negro vote; the five areas gave Mrs. McCormick 76 percent of their vote, but they were still loyal to Thompson, personally, as 1931 would show. In 1932 Hoover received 76 percent from the five areas, two points better than he had done against Smith in 1928. The lower socioeconomic areas (Ia, Ib, and IIa) remained somewhat more Democratic, as in 1928; but all except one area fell off to a lower Democratic percentage than in 1928. Thus Negro Democratic voting in 1930 and 1932 remained at roughly the same levels forged by Smith in 1928, but beyond this they seemed determined not to go, at a time when other ethnic groups were delivering landslide Democratic votes for the second and third times.

The experience in Chicago through 1932 would reflect, essentially, that of other northern Negro communities also. Certainly, other cities did not have a demagogue of the level of Big Bill Thompson to hold on to Negro votes. But, most important, a real Democratic force was necessary for overcoming traditional Negro voting patterns, and this was simply not provided by the local Democratic Party or by the national organization, up to 1932. As in Chicago, most urban Democratic organizations failed to appoint Negroes to enough positions or to guarantee them enough nominations for office. And, as in Chicago, many of them were controlled by short-sighted leadership that failed to see the political imbecility of prejudice. As other ethnic groups began to flock into the Democratic Party after 1928, it seemed to some that they could do well permanently without the Negroes. But more farsighted leaders were on the horizon—Ed Kelly in Chicago, for example—who would see it differently.

The candidacy of a man like Al Smith could have some effect, in that many Negroes, like members of other disadvantaged minorities, would identify with him and vote for him. But winning their allegiance to the Democratic Party would require a drastic political change.[71] And this was about to come.

When Mayor Cermak was assassinated in 1933, he was replaced by Ed Kelly, who was more determined than even Cermak had been to bring the Negroes into the fold. Ultimately he accomplished this task, drafting first the Negro politicians, and then the voters, into his organization, with a big assist from the national Democratic administration and its anti-Depression activities.

One of the first clear indications of the coming change was the 1934 elections. The Democrats put up a Negro candidate, Arthur W. Mitchell, to contest De Priest's congressional seat in the heart of the Black Belt. The *Defender* remained firmly Republican and supported De Priest with fervor,[72] but Mitchell narrowly defeated him (53 percent to 47 percent), becoming the first Negro Democrat in Congress, and signifying a long step forward for the Democrats.

Otherwise in this election, Negro Democratic voting increased but remained under 50 percent. In the vote for congressman-at-large, for example, the Democratic candidate received over 40 percent from three of the five areas, and 36 percent in one more; only Area III—socioeconomically the highest—still remained overwhelmingly Republican (80 percent). The crack in the wall was spreading.

In 1935 things moved even more rapidly, as Kelly ran for his first full term as mayor. Alderman William Dawson of the Second Ward (presently Democratic congressman from the same congressional district held by De Priest and Mitchell) and Alderman Robert Jackson of the Third Ward both were running for reelection, and both were still nominally Republican.[73] But they both had the public backing of Mayor Kelly, and they both publicly backed the Mayor in return.[74] The *Defender* accurately saw this as a sign that the Democrats were building a Black Belt organization based on and run by Negro politicians and felt that for this reason they would justly succeed. Kelly received the highest accolade: "Black people believe in [Mayor] Ed Kelly and in fact say that the only difference between him and Bill Thompson in respect to them is the name."[75]

The same idea was repeated when the *Defender* formally endorsed Kelly's candidacy, arguing that under him the Second and Third wards would be led politically by Negroes; it also realized that he was sure to win and so thought it purposeless to oppose him.[76]

The *Defender* forecast was correct; Kelly carried the city with the amazing total of 83 percent of the vote. And the Negro voters joined the bandwagon. Area III once more trailed, but voted 52 percent Democratic; the other four areas voted between 71 and 80 percent Democratic—levels they had never remotely approached before. (The level of voter interest was about the same as in 1931, with 37 percent voting; and there was a continuation

of the 1932 phenomenon of strongly different levels for Areas Ia
and IIa—the former had 50 percent voting and the latter 24 percent.)

It was more difficult for the mass of Negro voters to change
political allegiance at the national level than at the local, primarily
because it was at the national level that the Negroes' traditional
commitment to the Republican Party was most deep and meaningful. The voters would take a little longer than the politicians,
however clear it might be by 1936 that this switch was sure to
come. Thus in the 1936 presidential election the *Defender* remained Republican; the Republican Party was still "our Party,"
and so Alf Landon should be supported.[77] Gone, however, were
the old accusations of racism against Roosevelt; now he personally was seen as a friend of the Negro but, unfortunately, as
the representative of a party that was still dominated by the South
and therefore untrustworthy.[78] In its own tortuous process of
change, the *Defender* was articulating the problem of the individual Negro voter.

In the voting in 1936 the five areas produced Democratic totals
slightly greater on the whole than those of 1934, but still shy of
majorities. Area IIa (the Third Ward) did return a bare Democratic majority, with 50.1 percent; Areas Ia, Ib, and IIb were
close behind, from 44 to 48 percent. And Area III again demonstrated its higher socioeconomic status by voting only 36 percent
Democratic.

Thus by 1936 important changes had developed; it was clear
that Negroes were about to follow their leaders into the Democratic Party.[79] By the middle of the 1930's it had become clear to
Negro politicians, as it had earlier become clear to other ethnic
politicians, that their future lay with the Democratic Party—the
Kelly-Nash machine locally and the New Deal organization na-
tionally. Both local and national party leaders had made a concerted effort to attract Negroes, and they were helped mightily by
the employment and status opportunities offered by New Deal
programs.[80]

In retrospect, it is not surprising that Negroes took so long to
change parties. They had been offered so little for so long by either
party, particularly the Chicago Democrats. William Hale Thompson's great contribution to them had been to make it seem that, at
least locally, they were really wanted and respected for their
power; this was no small feat, as Negro voting demonstrated. It
was not easily overcome.

NOTES

1. Most of the materials found in this article are taken from the author's doctoral dissertation, "The Political Behavior of Chicago's Ethnic Groups, 1918–1932," prepared for the department of history at the University of Pittsburgh.

2. All demographic data is taken from the following sources: U. S. Department of Commerce, Bureau of the Census, *Fifteenth Census of the U. S.: 1930* (Washington, 1932) and *Fourteenth Census of the U. S.: 1920* (Washington, 1922); Ernest W. Burgess and Charles Newcomb, *Census Data of the City of Chicago, 1930* (Chicago, 1933) and *Census Data of the City of Chicago, 1920* (Chicago, 1931).

3. Charles E. Merriam and Harold F. Gosnell, *Non-Voting: Causes and Methods of Control* (Chicago, 1924), 82–83.

4. *Ibid.*, 6, 35.

5. See Chicago Commission on Race Relations, *The Negro in Chicago: A Study of Race Relations and a Race Riot* (Chicago, 1922).

6. St. Clair Drake and Horace R. Cayton, *Black Metropolis: A Study of Negro Life in a Northern City* (New York, 1945), 78–80.

7. Because ward lines and numbers changed three times during the period under consideration, and precinct lines and numbers even more frequently, it was necessary to give arbitrary numbers to the essentially non-changing areas used in this study. Area Ia corresponds to Ward 2 throughout. Area Ib corresponds to Pct. 51 of Ward 14 through 1921; Pct. 28 of Ward 28, 1922 through June, 1928; Pct. 32 of Ward 28 from July, 1928, through 1931; Pct. 38 of Ward 28 commencing in 1932. Area IIa corresponds to Ward 3 throughout. Area IIb corresponds to Pct. 106 of Ward 32 through 1921; Pct. 46 of Ward 19 from 1922 through June, 1928; Pcts. 52, 59, 96 of Ward 19 from July, 1928, through 1931; Pcts. 44, 45, 46 of Ward 19 commencing in 1932. Area III corresponds to Pct. 53 of Ward 7 through 1921; Pct. 56 of Ward 6 from 1922 through June, 1928; Pcts. 56, 67 of Ward 6 from July, 1928, through 1931; Pcts. 21, 22 of Ward 6 commencing in 1932.

Socioeconomic class was computed from census data on these bases: percent of homes owned; average rental of apartments; percent of workers employed in white collar industries; percent of families having a radio; geographic region of the city. Areas Ia and Ib can be considered lower-lower class; Areas IIa and IIb, upper-lower class (although IIb would rate above IIa because of high home-owning and region of the city); Area III, lower-middle class.

As noted in the text, those five areas comprised about 50 percent of the Negro population of Chicago.

8. See, for example, Harold F. Gosnell, *Machine Politics: Chicago Model* (Chicago, 1937) and *Negro Politicians: The Rise of Negro Politicians in Chicago* (Chicago, 1935); Charles E. Merriam, *Chicago: A More Intimate View of Urban Politics* (New York, 1929); Lloyd Wendt and Herman Kogan, *Big Bill of Chicago* (Indianapolis, 1953).

9. He received 71 percent of the vote of Area Ia and 67 percent of Area IIa. Methodological limitations preclude knowing his vote in this election for the three other areas.

10. *Chicago Broad-Ax*, Oct. 12, 1918. The *Broad-Ax* was a relatively successful example of the personal, often frivolous, journals found frequently among the ethnic press. Its weekly circulation is indeterminable,

but probably ranged between twenty and thirty thousand; it was well known and often quoted.

11. *Ibid.*, Nov. 2, 1918. One possible reason for this endorsement was that its writer, S. A. T. Watkins, was obligated to Lewis for his appointment as assistant state's attorney when Lewis was Chicago corporation counsel, 1905–1907.

12. The *Defender* was far and away the leading Negro newspaper in Chicago, and one of the foremost in the nation as well. Under the leadership of Robert S. Abbott it had emerged as a highly race-conscious and highly successful organ of Negro opinion and information. Its circulation was rapidly growing during this period, and by 1930 would reach 80,000 to 90,000 weekly in Chicago (*Defender* estimate, 1965), and its national edition would be almost as great.

The question of whether the *Defender* (or other members of the ethnic press) directed or followed the opinions of its readers is essentially indeterminable. But it is clear, in the *Defender*'s case, that it was a pretty accurate gauge of Negro opinion in Chicago. Where it was interested, so too were Negro voters and where it was apathetic, so too were they. And the overwhelming number of its political choices were theirs also, although deviations did sometimes occur. The ethnic press played an important role, but it is one which has received little attention from scholars. Little of note has been added to the pioneering study of Robert Park, *The Immigrant Press and Its Control* (New York, 1922). But see also Roi Ottley, *The Lonely Warrior: Life and Times of Robert S. Abbott* (Chicago, 1955).

13. *Chicago Defender*, Nov. 2, 1918, p. 1.

14. *Chicago Broad-Ax*, Oct. 23, 1920, p. 3.

15. Harold F. Gosnell, "The Chicago 'Black Belt' as a Political Battleground," *American Journal of Sociology*, Nov., 1933, pp. 329–341.

16. Wesley M. Bagby, *The Road to Normalcy: The Presidential Campaign and Election of 1920* (Baltimore, 1962), 152–153.

17. *Ibid.*; *Chicago Tribune*, Oct. 30, 1920, pp. 1, 4.

18. *Chicago Defender*, Oct. 30, 1920, p. 12.

19. *Ibid.*, pp. 1, 12.

20. *Chicago Broad-Ax*, Oct. 16, p. 2, Oct. 30, p. 7, 1920. Park, in *The Immigrant Press and Its Control*, discusses this troublesome problem, which more contemporary historians have ignored.

21. *Chicago Defender*, Oct. 30, 1920, p. 12; *Chicago Tribune*, Oct. 26, 1920, p. 7, Nov. 1, 1920, p. 7; Frances W. McLemore, "The Role of the Negroes in Chicago in the Senatorial Election of 1930" (master's thesis, University of Chicago, 1931), 8.

22. *Chicago Defender*, Oct. 4, 1924, p. 15.

23. *Ibid.*, Oct. 4, p. 16, Oct. 24, p. 12, Nov. 1, p. 1, 1924.

24. *Chicago Broad-Ax*, Nov. 1, p. 1, Nov. 8, p. 1, 1924.

25. Methodological problems precluded making this scale as complete as desired. Particularly, population data for precincts were not available; this could be circumvented for almost all demographic data except the exact population of each precinct. Consequently, the percentage of population voting in each contest could be determined only for Areas Ia and IIa, which were whole wards. The number voting in each ward was divided by ward population figures for 1920, 1921, and 1930, to provide reliable figures. Although there are some difficulties, as noted in the text, I think these are generally reliable figures reflecting voting levels among all Negro voters.

26. An indication of this strength can be seen in a perhaps true story from the 1919 campaign. One Second Ward precinct gave Thompson 271 votes out of 272 cast, and Oscar De Priest said to an assistant: "I know who double-crossed there. Go out and find Most Jackson and give him a raking over the coals." Quote in *Literary Digest*, LXXVI (March 3, 1923): 54.

27. *Chicago Tribune*, March 25, 1919, p. 7.

28. *Chicago Defender*, April 5, 1919, p. 1.

29. *Chicago Broad-Ax*, March 8, p. 1, March 29, p. 1, 1919. Such rivalries were common among the ethnic press of the period.

30. *Ibid.*, March 22, 1923; Gosnell, *Negro Politicians*, 44; McLemore, "The Role of the Negroes in Chicago in the Senatorial Election, 1930," p. 50n.

31. *Chicago Defender*, March 31, 1923; but see footnote 41.

32. *Chicago Broad-Ax*, March 24, p. 1, March 31, p. 1, 1923.

33. Quoted in Merriam, *Chicago*, 290.

34. Quoted in Charles E. Merriam, "Recollections" (MS autobiography, Charles E. Merriam Papers, University of Chicago), Chap. 7, p. 7.

35. *Literary Digest*, XCIII (April 16, 1927): 6. This leads to the question of the role of the gangsters in Thompson's campaigns, and in fact it does seem that he had Capone financing in 1927. See Wendt and Kogan, *Big Bill of Chicago*, 250, 268–269; Fred D. Pasley, *Al Capone: The Biography of a Self-Made Man* (New York, 1930), 181.

36. *Chicago Defender*, March 19, 1927, pp. 1, 3.

37. *Chicago Tribune*, March 10, pp. 1, 14, March 14, pp. 1, 8, 1927.

38. Wendt and Kogan, *Big Bill of Chicago*, 249; Gosnell, *Negro Politicians*, 153–162; McLemore, "The Role of the Negroes in Chicago in the Senatorial Election, 1930," 19–22.

39. *Chicago Tribune*, March 1, 1927, pp. 1, 2; Wendt and Kogan, *Big Bill of Chicago*, 256; Gosnell, *Negro Politicians*, 54; George C. Hoffman, "Big Bill Thompson: His Mayoral Campaigns and Voting Strength" (master's thesis, University of Chicago, 1956), 36–38.

40. *Chicago Defender*, March 5, 1927, p. 2.

41. *Ibid.*, April 2, 1927, p. 1, and Section II, p. 2. As seen above, the *Defender* had not endorsed Dever in 1923; why this was said is unclear.

42. *Chicago Broad-Ax*, April 2, pp. 1, 2, March 26, p. 1, 1927.

43. *Ibid.*, April 9, 1927, p. 1. Perhaps this and the failure of the *Broad-Ax* to join the Negro political mainstream help to explain why the paper shortly went out of business. The *Broad-Ax* was, like many other short-lived ethnic journals, too personal, and perhaps more intent on serving its owner than anyone or anything else.

44. On this election and its effects on the ethnic groups of the United States see Samuel Lubell, *The Future of American Politics* (New York, 1952); J. Joseph Huthmacher, *Massachusetts People and Politics* (Cambridge, Mass., 1959); Allswang, "The Political Behavior of Chicago's Ethnic Groups, 1918–1932."

45. Gosnell, *Negro Politicians*, 32.

46. *Chicago Defender*, Nov. 3, 1928, Sec. II, p. 2.

47. *Chicago Tribune*, Oct. 8, 1928, p. 1.

48. *Chicago Defender*, Oct. 20, 1928, p. 8; *Chicago Eagle*, Oct. 13, 1928, p. 1. Other notices of apparent bigotry on the part of Hoover's associates were seen: *Defender*, Aug. 4, p. 4, Oct. 20, p. 1, 1928.

49. *Chicago Defender*, Nov. 3, 1928, Sec. II, p. 2.

50. *Chicago Eagle*, Nov. 3, 1928, p. 1. See also June 9, p. 1, July 7, p. 1, Sept. 8, p. 1, issues of Sept. and Oct., *passim*, 1928.

51. *Chicago Defender*, Oct. 27, 1928, p. 6.

52. *Chicago Tribune*, Aug. 21, 1928, p. 8; *Chicago Defender*, Oct. 27, 1928, p. 9.

53. *Chicago Defender*, Nov. 3, 1928, p. 3.

54. *Chicago Tribune*, Oct. 31, 1928, p. 3.

55. See *Chicago Tribune*, April 8, 1931, p. 1; Gosnell, *Machine Politics*, 13; Wendt and Kogan, *Big Bill of Chicago*, 329–331; Alex Gottfried, *Boss Cermak of Chicago: A Study of Political Leadership* (Seattle, 1962), 205–206; Merriam, "Recollections," Chap. 6, p. 14.

56. *Chicago Tribune*, March 27, 1931, pp. 1, 2; Gosnell, *Machine Politics*, 11–12; Gottfried, *Boss Cermak of Chicago*, 235.

57. Cermak played a central role, as secretary, in the United Societies for Local Self Government, an inter-ethnic organization founded in 1906 to fight Prohibition. He had made anti-Prohibition and ethnic activities central foci in his political career.

58. A copy can be found in the H. F. Gosnell materials, filed in the Merriam Papers, University of Chicago. See also Gottfried, *Boss Cermak of Chicago*, 205–206.

59. A copy can be found in the H. F. Gosnell materials, filed in the Merriam Papers, University of Chicago.

60. *Chicago Defender*, April 4, 1931, p. 2.

61. *Ibid.*, March 14–April 6, 1931, *passim*.

62. It was at this late date that William Dawson and other Negro politicians formally switched parties.

63. *Chicago Defender*, April 11, 1931, p. 1.

64. William H. Stuart, *The Twenty Incredible Years* (Chicago, 1935), 412, 437–439; McLemore, "The Role of the Negroes in Chicago in the Senatorial Election, 1930," pp. 17–18, 24.

65. *Chicago Tribune*, Oct. 22, p. 9, Oct. 27, p. 8, 1930. Wendt and Kogan, *Big Bill of Chicago*, 318–319; McLemore, "The Role of the Negroes in Chicago in the Senatorial Election, 1930," pp. 42–47, 62–71. The Gosnell materials in the Merriam Papers, University of Chicago, include copies of various materials used.

66. *Chicago Tribune*, Nov. 2, 1930, p. 11. See also *Chicago Bee*, Nov. 1, 1930 (quoted in McLemore, p. 12).

67. *Chicago Defender*, Sept. 24, 1932, Sec. II, p. 1.

68. *Ibid.*, Nov. 5, 1932, p. 3.

69. *Ibid.*, Oct. 15, p. 1, Oct. 22, Sec. II, p. 14, 1932.

70. *Ibid.*, Nov. 4, 1932, p. 3.

71. See Paul F. Lazarsfeld, *et al.*, *The People's Choice: How the Voter Makes Up His Mind in a Presidential Campaign* (New York, 1948); Bernard R. Berelson, *et al.*, *Voting: A Study of Opinion Formation in a Presidential Campaign* (Chicago, 1954); Angus Campbell, *et al.*, *The Voter Decides* (Evanston, Ill., 1954); Morris Rosenberg, "Some Determinants of Political Apathy," in Heinz Eulau, *et al.*, eds., *Political Behavior: A Reader in Theory and Research* (Glencoe, Ill., 1956); A. J. Brodbeck, "The Problem of Irrationality and Neuroticism Underlying Political Choice," in Eugene Burdick and Arthur J. Brodbeck, eds., *American Voting Behavior* (Glencoe, Ill., 1959).

72. *Chicago Defender*, Nov. 3, 1934, p. 4.

73. After 1921, aldermanic (city council) elections were nonpartisan, and party tags were absent from ballots. But aldermanic candidates seldom failed to make clear the party of which they were members, and this was often shown on campaign materials. Thus aldermanic contests in the 1920's, as later, were never really nonpartisan.

74. *Chicago Defender*, March 16, p. 3, March 23, p. 3, 1935.

75. *Ibid.*, March 2, 1935, pp. 1, 2, 4.

76. *Ibid.*, March 23, pp. 1, 14, March 30, pp. 1, 14, 1935.

77. *Ibid.*, Oct. 10, p. 1, Oct. 31, pp. 1, 18, 1936.

78. *Ibid.*

79. By 1940, for example, the *Defender* would be Democratic to stay, bemoaning its earlier "blind, child-like faith" in a Republican Party which had "failed to redeem its pledges," and finding in the New Deal the Negroes' real salvation, and in Roosevelt "the greatest champion of the cause of the common people." Nov. 2, pp. 1, 2, Oct. 12, p. 1, Oct. 19, p. 1, 1940.

80. *Ibid.*, Nov. 2, 1940, pp. 1, 2.

Negro Democratic Vote in Chicago Presidential and Mayoral Elections, 1919–1936

(Superior Figures, Democratic Percent; Parenthetical Figures, Total Vote, which consists of total vote cast for Democratic and Republican candidates only, except in the 1924 presidential election in which the Progressive vote is included.)

Election	Total: 5 Areas	Area Ia	Area Ib	Area IIa	Area IIb	Area III
Presidential:						
1920	11 (55,978)	7 (25,835)	6 (325)	19 (29,084)	3 (454)	21 (280)
1924	10 (50,702)	8 (21,653)	5 (350)	9 (27,907)	12 (425)	14 (367)
1928	23 (46,426)	30 (18,247)	27 (378)	27 (26,348)	16 (1,158)	17 (295)
1932	21 (64,245)	25 (35,894)	29 (450)	20 (25,804)	15 (1,428)	15 (669)
1936	45 (79,615)	48 (41,089)	47 (331)	50.1 (35,792)	44 (1,456)	36 (947)
Mayoral:						
1919	22 (37,136)	17 (18,892)	15 (269)	40 (17,525)	5 (249)	33 (201)
1923	53 (28,837)	69 (11,993)	52 (210)	56 (16,121)	25 (254)	65 (259)
1927	7 (59,090)	6 (25,960)	8 (355)	11 (31,199)	2 (1,051)	10 (525)
1931	16 (48,115)	17 (20,387)	25 (363)	18 (25,724)	9 (1,295)	11 (346)
1935	72 (43,361)	80 (25,093)	71 (253)	70 (16,584)	79 (987)	52 (644)

CINCINNATI NEGROES
AND PRESIDENTIAL POLITICS

ERNEST M. COLLINS

*This selection by Ernest M. Collins complements the preceding
article by John M. Allswang, carrying the story of urban Negro
voting behavior forward to 1952. Collins stresses the importance
of the black vote, particularly when Negroes vote "in bloc," in
areas where the black vote is sizable and competition between the
two parties is keen. (Henry Lee Moon,* Balance of Power: The
Negro Vote *[Garden City, N.Y.: Doubleday, 1948], develops this
point.) Collins also notes that the Negro population of Ohio increased 65 per cent from 1920 to 1950, compared with a 19 per
cent increase in the state's total population for the same period.
Concentrating on voter behavior in the heavily black Ward 16 of
Cincinnati, he compares the percentages of the two-party vote received by Democratic and Republican presidential candidates in
Ward 16 and in the city as a whole. The Democratic candidate's
percentage in Ward 16 rose from 28.8 per cent in 1932, to 65.1
per cent in 1936, to 81.2 per cent in 1952, while in the entire city
it rose from 51.2 per cent in 1932 to 59.2 per cent in 1936, but
declined to 43.4 per cent in 1952. The pattern of predominantly
Democratic black voting in Cincinnati from 1936 on holds for
many other cities and has persisted down to the present. (See the
analyses of Negro voter behavior in various cities listed in the
Suggested Reading, and, for example, Robert S. Sigel, "Race
and Religion as Factors in the Kennedy Victory in Detroit, 1960,"*
Journal of Negro Education *[Fall 1962].) Collins judges the election of 1948 the most interesting of the six he considers because
the Negro emphasis on New Deal economic benefits gave way to
a primary concern with the civil rights planks of the Truman
program.*

*

The migration of the Negroes from the South to the cities of the border states and the North has greatly increased their political significance. In many of the areas to which they have migrated, competition between the two major political parties is so keen that the Negroes when "voting in bloc" hold the balance of power.

Most of the early studies of the political activity of Negroes were confined to the South. Recently, professional politicians have been devoting more attention to the Negro voters in Northern cities. This has been particularly true in Chicago, Detroit, and New York. At present there is little or no organized information relative to political behavior of Negroes in Ohio cities. A study of some of the senatorial and presidential elections in Ohio will reveal that party competition is so close that the Negro voters are in a position to hold the balance of power. In view of this fact, an analysis of the voting behavior of Cincinnati Negroes in presidential elections from 1932 to 1952 should be of value to both scholars and professional politicians.

From the time of their political emancipation to 1932, there seemed to be little difference of opinion among the great majority of Negroes in Cincinnati as to which political party merited their support. Year after year the Republican Party relied successfully upon the memory of the Great Emancipator to keep the Negro voters safely in the fold.

Information relative to the political affiliation of Negroes in Cincinnati from 1880 to 1900 revealed a scarcity of Democrats. In the words of a Negro writer, "To be a Negro Democrat required courage of a high order, because a great mass of the Negroes regarded white democrats as the Devil's chosen children, and a Negro Democrat was a creature of such depravity that hell was far too good for him."[1]

From the evidence available in newspaper accounts, the Negroes in Cincinnati continued to support the Republican Party until 1932. However, there were signs on the political horizon as early as 1921 which indicated that the Republicans would have to do more than mention the name of Abraham Lincoln to hold the Negro voters. The Republicans were accused by some of the Negro leaders of being ungrateful for their support and threatened to leave the party.[2]

From 1921 to 1932 the Negroes continued to support the Republican Party in Cincinnati, but with less zeal than previously

Reprinted by permission of *Journal of Negro History*, XLI (April 1956), 131–137.

shown. During this period some of the Negroes indicated a willingness to "take a walk," but they had no place to go, since the Democrats did not show a willingness to solicit the favor of those Negroes who indicated a desire to leave the Republican Party.

It was a foregone conclusion in the presidential election of 1932 that the Republicans would lose votes as a result of the depression. It seemed reasonable to assume that the Negro voters, because of their economic status, would desert the Republican Party to a greater extent than other voters who were in a better position economically to withstand the effects of the depression.

However, this assumption proved to be fallacious for the returns in the 1932 presidential election showed that the Negro voters were not ready to desert the Republican Party. The vote in Ward 16, which was approximately 80% Negro, increased from 59.5% in 1928 to 71.2% in 1932.

As the Democratic Party manifested more interest in the Negro voters, the Negroes became more aggressive in expressing their dissatisfaction with the Republicans. In the presidential election of 1936 the Negro voters made a definite swing to the Democratic Party. In Ward 16, which was predominantly Negro, Roosevelt received 65.1% of the vote compared to 28.8% in 1932. The same trend was noticeable in the other Negro wards and precincts. From Table I, it may be noted that Roosevelt received a greater percent of votes in Ward 16 than in the city at large. In commenting on this election, The Cincinnati *Times Star* on November 4, 1936, noted that "a very important factor that was costly to the Republican ticket was the desertion of Negro voters in Ward 16 to the Democrats."

By 1936, the economic aspects of the New Deal program were apparent to the Negroes, and they, like other groups in similar economic circumstances who had shared in this program, voted for its continuance. In a period of economic depression, concrete things such as jobs, unemployment compensation, and old age pensions were far more attractive to the majority of Negro voters than abstract promises of Civil Rights.

In the presidential elections of 1940 and 1944 the vote for the Democratic presidential candidate continued to increase in Ward 16 from 65.1% in 1936, to 66.9% in 1940, and 67.7% in 1944. The vote for Roosevelt in the city at-large during these elections was 59.2%, 49.9%, and 49.8% respectively. While a larger percentage of Negroes voted for Roosevelt, a smaller percentage of the voters in the rest of the city voted for the Democrats.

TABLE I

Vote in Presidential Election in Ward 16
in Cincinnati, 1932–1952

	WARD 16				CINCINNATI			
Year	Dem. Vote	Rep. Vote	% Dem.	% Rep.	Dem. Vote	Rep. Vote	% Dem.	% Rep.
1932	2,404	5,957	28.8	71.2	90,280	85,965	51.2	48.8
1936	6,957	3,727	65.1	34.9	113,754	78,439	59.2	40.8
1940	6,882	3,399	66.9	33.1	107,681	108,256	49.9	50.1
1944	5,425	2,578	67.7	32.3	103,367	104,512	49.8	50.2
1948	5,403	1,732	75.0	24.0	97,406	102,663	48.3	50.9
1952	6,248	1,444	81.2	18.2	99,783	130,933	43.4	56.6

TABLE II

Negro Population of Ohio, Cincinnati,
and Ward 16 in Cincinnati

Year	Ohio	% Negro	Cincinnati	% Negro	Ward 16	% Negro
1930	309,304	4.5	47,818	10.6	9,641	78.1
1940	339,461	4.9	55,593	12.2	18,805	92.1
1950	513,072	6.5	78,196	15.5	18,547	94.5

It may also be interesting to note that Roosevelt received a larger proportion of the vote in Negro wards in Cincinnati than the Democratic gubernatorial candidate, Frank Lausche. The vote for Lausche in 1944 in Ward 16 was only 55% compared to 67.7% for Roosevelt. In commenting upon the political behavior of Negro voters in Cincinnati, Jesse D. Locker, Negro city councilman, observed that many of his constituents were "Roosevelt Republicans" in that they voted for a Democrat for President and a Republican for the city council.[3]

Judged by the volume of newspaper comments, the presidential election of 1948 was the most interesting one to the Negro voters since 1870. This special interest is understandable in the light of President Truman's Civil Rights program and Henry Wallace's special plea for support from Negro voters.

In the three previous presidential campaigns the Negro press in Cincinnati emphasized the economic benefits derived by the Negroes from the New Deal program. In this campaign the primary interest centered around the Civil Rights planks of the Truman program. In commenting on President Truman's executive order to end segregation in the army, *The Cincinnati Inde-*

pendent, a Negro paper, stated, "Mr. Truman in making an order to accord equal treatment and opportunities in the armed services has nothing to lose. Negroes and all other minorities will back him to the limit."[4]

The Republican leaders in Cincinnati in 1948 were well aware of the fact that they had lost most of the Negro vote and that they would have to do more than talk about the Emancipation Proclamation, Thirteenth, Fourteenth, and Fifteenth Amendments to win back the Negro votes. A vigorous campaign was waged among the Negro voters in Ward 16. Joseph Fulton, Negro Republican ward chairman, conducted a series of political rallies in which he ardently extolled the virtues of Thomas E. Dewey and the Republican Party.

The results of the 1948 election in the Negro wards in Cincinnati further convinced the Republican leaders that winning back the Negro vote would indeed be a prodigious task. In Ward 16, in which the Negroes constitute approximately 94% of the population, Truman received 75% of the vote, Dewey 24%, and Wallace 1%.

Prior to the presidential election in 1948 the impression was gained from interviews with several Negro leaders in Cincinnati that in spite of Wallace's promises of economic prosperity and equality for all men, the Negro vote for the Progressive Party would be small. Typical of the comments made about Wallace was that of Madison C. Perkins, Negro Democratic candidate for the House of Representatives of Ohio, who said, "There is much in the domestic program of Wallace that appeals to the Negroes, but they know that Wallace can't win, and they have no desire to support a lost cause."

The pattern of Negro voting previously established continued in the presidential election of 1952. The election returns showed that neither the platform nor the personalities of the Republican Party had much appeal for the Negro voters. Stevenson received 81.2% of the vote in Ward 16 and Eisenhower only 18.2%. However, in the city of Cincinnati 56% of the total vote was cast for Eisenhower.

The Negro political leaders in Cincinnati are well aware of the fact that the closeness of some of the senatorial and presidential elections in Ohio places the Negro voters in a bargaining position. These leaders have not been timid in requesting from their respective parties rewards for their services commensurate with their contributions to political victories. While the white political leaders have found it politically expedient to comply with some of these requests, the Negroes have not been satisfied with the measure of recognition accorded them. They have requested appointment to more of the important public positions; positions other than those in the "keeper of the cuspidors" category.

The Republican political leaders in Cincinnati are seriously concerned about the voting trend in presidential elections in Negro wards in Cincinnati during the last twenty years. They have not yet discovered a political elixir which will persuade the Negro voters to recant for their political conversion and return to their "first love."

From the evidence contained in the Negro press in Cincinnati and from interviews with white and Negro political leaders, there seems to be little reason to doubt that the economic aspects of the New Deal program were the primary factor responsible for Negro voters deserting the Republican Party. They looked upon Franklin D. Roosevelt as a political Moses who would deliver them from economic hardships. They continued to support the Democratic Party in the belief that the New Deal program would be continued, with an added attraction of Civil Rights.

It may be recalled that the margin of victory of Republican George H. Bender was only 6,041 votes over his Democratic opponent, Thomas A. Burke, in the 1954 senatorial contest in Ohio. In view of the keen competition between the two major parties in Ohio the political behavior of the Negroes takes on added significance.

The total population of Ohio increased only 19% from 1920 to 1950 compared to a 65% increase in Negro population. Negroes of voting age in Ohio in 1950 numbered 337,635. If the Negro population of Ohio continues to increase at the 1930–1950 rate, and the voting behavior of Negroes in Cincinnati is duplicated in other cities of the state, the Republican Party will be forced to reappraise its political strategy.

NOTES

1. Dabney, Wendel Philips, *Cincinnati's Colored Citizens,* Cincinnati, 1926, page 113.
2. *The Cincinnati Post,* November 8, 1921.
3. Letter of Jesse D. Locker, March 12, 1948.
4. *The Cincinnati Independent,* August 7, 1948.

IV

Black and White Activists

The motives and behavior of dissenters and reformers have attracted vast attention from scholars in various disciplines. In probing into these phenomena, historians have since World War II increasingly used the concepts and methods of the behavioral sciences. An outstanding example of this development in historiography is the use of the concept of "status anxiety" to interpret the activities of Jacksonian "venturous conservatives," abolitionists, civil-service reformers, mugwumps, populists, and progressives.[1] The anxiety-theorists' methodology and conclusions have naturally provoked a critical response.[2] Henry F. May illustrates the complexity of dissenters' motives. He summarizes nine theories that have been advanced as answers to the question, "Why did so many gifted Americans of the early twentieth century reject their own civilization and its dominant values with eloquence and fervor?," and he finds none of the nine explanations—including the one that stresses status anxiety—very satisfying or profound.[3]

The motives and behavior of American reformers and dis-

1. Robert W. Doherty, "Status Anxiety and American Reform: Some Alternatives," *American Quarterly* (Summer 1967), Part 2, p. 331, summarizes the anxiety theorists' argument: "1) persons of certain statuses 2) engaged in a specified type of activity because 3) those persons were anxious about status as a result of 4) shifts in power and prestige in the overall community." Doherty (p. 329n) cites studies by Richard Hofstadter, David Donald, Marvin Meyers, Ari Hoogenboom, Rowland Berthoff, and George E. Mowry that have applied the concept of status anxiety to various groups.
2. Doherty, *ibid.*, pp. 330–337, summarizes the methodological criticism of the anxiety-theorists' work.
3. Henry F. May, ed., *The Discontent of the Intellectuals: A Problem of the Twenties* (Chicago: Rand McNally, 1963), pp. 56–59.

senters take on an obvious added dimension when their skin is black or when, as in the case of the Communists, the dissenters rule out reform in favor of revolution, rejecting the assumption that "one could wring a higher standard of living out of the Industrial Revolution for all the people within the framework of constitutional government and capitalism."[4] The article by Hugh T. Murray, Jr., examines the behavior of activists in a predominantly black organization (NAACP) and a predominantly white one (CPUSA) in connection with the Scottsboro cases, which rank with the Sacco-Vanzetti affair as a *cause célèbre* in recent American history. In the next selection Wilson Record, a sociologist, compares black and white intellectuals in reform movements.

4. Arthur Mann, "The Progressive Tradition," in John Higham, ed., *The Reconstruction of American History* (New York: Harper Torchbook, 1962), p. 164.

THE NAACP VERSUS
THE COMMUNIST PARTY:
THE SCOTTSBORO RAPE CASES,
1931–1932

HUGH T. MURRAY, JR.

*The lawyers of the International Labor Defense, a close affiliate
of the Communist party, and the NAACP battled for control of the
defense of the "Scottsboro boys." (The most extensive and intensive study of the Scottsboro cases by a historian is Dan T. Carter,*
Scottsboro: A Tragedy of the American South [*Baton Rouge:
Louisiana State University Press, 1969*].) *The performance in the
Scottsboro cases of the victors in this struggle, the ILD, was decidedly more commendable than that of the NAACP in the
opinion of Hugh T. Murray, Jr., the author of this selection. The
only part of a defense appeal on which the Supreme Court ruled
in favor of the Scottsboro boys in November 1932 was the contention that the youths had been denied effective counsel. "It is
doubtful," Murray asserts, "if the NAACP had supervised the
cases, that the reform organization would have offered such an
argument. For months the NAACP had claimed responsibility
for the defense cited as inadequate by the Court." Meanwhile, the
ILD attorneys, despite the status of the CPUSA as an instrument
of an international movement, and despite evidence of the insin-
cerity of the Communist party's efforts to recruit Negroes (see
Nathan Glazer,* The Social Basis of American Communism [*New
York: Harcourt, Brace, 1961*], *Chap. 5, pp. 169–192), refrained
from using revolutionary rhetoric and "did not attempt to make
martyrs of the Scottsboro boys" in order to discredit a capitalist
society.*

*

In the South, conservatives are certain that communists are the instigators of the civil rights movement. American liberals hold that communists merely pose as advocates of civil rights in order that they may sabotage the aspirations of Negroes, thereby blackening the image of American democracy throughout the world. Diverse authorities can be cited in support of the liberal view. For example, both J. Edgar Hoover and W. E. B. Du Bois could agree (at least, at one time) on communist perfidy in the Scottsboro rape cases.[1] More recently, Langston Hughes wrote concerning the same cases in which nine young Negroes were accused of rape in Alabama:

> . . . the NAACP's initial efforts in behalf of the boys were nullified by the intervention of the Communists. The latter, seeking to exploit the matter for their own ideological purposes, misrepresented the NAACP . . . and persuaded the boys to abandon the NAACP-provided counsel, which included Clarence Darrow and Arthur Garfield Hays.[2]

Walter White judged that communist strategy in the Scottsboro cases was calculated to create "martyrs" of innocent Negro boys.[3]

Criticism of communist activities in the Scottsboro cases is numerous and varied. Some works of scholarship record that communists stole millions of dollars intended for the defense of the boys; others dwell on the incompetence of the communist attorneys, while a Jesuit scholar damns the Reds for betraying one of the Scottsboro boys, who had escaped, to the Federal Bureau of Investigation. This paper will be limited to a discussion of the most serious charge against the Communist Party—that it sought to sacrifice the young Negroes to martyrdom for the cause of communist propaganda.

In March, 1931, two white prostitutes were allegedly raped by nine blacks on a freight train near Scottsboro, Alabama. Feelings in the community were inflamed, and over a thousand National Guardsmen were needed to protect the boys (the eldest of whom was twenty years old) from lynching. For the trial, Judge A. E. Hawkins appointed the entire local bar to defend the youths, but before proceedings could begin a Chattanooga lawyer, Stephen Roddy, arrived. He informed the judge, "I am here . . . not as employed counsel for the defense, [but] people who are interested in them have spoken to me about it. . . ."[4] After some discussion Roddy agreed to defend the lads with the aid of a Scottsboro barrister, Milo Moody. Eight of the boys were quickly found guilty,

Reprinted by permission from *Phylon*, XXVIII (Third Quarter 1967), 276–287.

and all but the youngest were sentenced to die in the electric chair. It appeared as if most of the cases had ended on April 9, 1931.

Even before this date the International Labor Defense, a communist front organization, had shown interest in the cases. Its avowed purpose was to defend radicals and workers in the courts through two methods used in conjunction: first, the ILD endeavored to defend persons by the use of regular legal channels, *e.g.*, by providing lawyers and appeals to higher courts; second, it sought to influence the courts with mass pressure by such means as demonstrations, petitions, and telegrams. Prior to these cases, ILD had been inactive in defense of Negroes.[5]

On April 2, the *New York Daily Worker* declared that "Alabama bosses" planned to lynch nine Negro "workers" in Scottsboro, and as the first trial opened in Alabama, communists had distributed anti-lynching leaflets. When the first verdicts were announced, the Party press decried them as frameups. The ILD telegraphed Judge Hawkins and other Alabama officials denouncing the trials and demanding the immediate release of the Negro boys. Should these ultimatums be ignored, the ILD warned, the recipients would be held personally responsible for the "legal lynching."[6]

Judge Hawkins replied that such accusations were absurd. The Scottsboro boys "were given every opportunity to provide themselves with counsel," he noted, "and I have appointed able members of the Jackson County bar to represent them. I personally will welcome any investigation of the trial." Although Governor Miller of Alabama deigned not to recognize the telegrams, the attorney for the defense was less reticent. Stephen Roddy remarked, "I do not see how any one can say that we were not striving to see that the defendants were getting the fairest trial." On April 9, Roddy moved that the defendant Patterson receive a new trial, a motion that invoked an automatic stay of execution for the Negro. Roddy also contemplated similar actions for the other defendants.[7]

The ILD apparently attempted to lure Roddy and, with him, the defense of the Scottsboro boys to the Red banner, but Roddy rejected its appeal. Nor did he display any inclination of abandoning the cases to the communists. The ILD then tried to retain Clarence Darrow; he, too, declined the offer.[8] Failing to secure either the attorney already managing the cases or the leading trial lawyer in the nation, the ILD employed George W. Chamlee of Chattanooga, a former Attorney General for the State of Tennessee.[9]

In addition to the legal defense, the ILD organized "mass action." On April 12, some 1,300 workers demonstrated in Cleveland to protest the Scottsboro verdicts. The following day 20,000 persons attending a rally in New York adopted a resolution calling for the immediate release of the boys. Under ILD auspices other mass meetings were held in Philadelphia, Milwaukee, Omaha, Sioux City, Kansas City, Boston, Buffalo, Niagara Falls, New Haven, and Elizabeth, New Jersey. All echoed the same message —free the Scottsboro boys.[10] Negro groups swamped the ILD and the League of Struggle for Negro Rights, another communist front, with requests for speakers on the Scottsboro cases. These speakers informed them that the boys were innocent, the girls were prostitutes, the courts were biased, and the defense had been inadequate.[11] The organizations of Negro reform, the National Association for the Advancement of Colored People, the National Urban League, and the Universal Negro Improvement Association, were chided on their silence by the communists.[12] However, on April 24, a letter from William Pickens, field secretary of the NAACP, was reprinted on page one of the *Daily Worker*. Writing on the stationery of his organization, Pickens praised the efforts of the ILD in the Scottsboro affair. "This is one occasion for every Negro who has intelligence enough to read, to send aid to you [the *Daily Worker*] and to I.L.D."[13] Finally, it appeared as if a united movement was gathering in support of the ILD and the Scottsboro defendants.

The same day that Pickens' letter appeared in the *Worker*, the *New York Times* reported that the Scottsboro boys did not want communist help. The eight who were sentenced to die issued a statement to Stephen Roddy, two Negro ministers, and a former truant officer, all of Chattanooga. The youngsters, some of whom were illiterate, condemned the ILD and urged the communists "to lay off."[14] But the following day Mamie Williams, Ada Wright, and Claude Patterson, parents of three of the boys, solicited support for the ILD. They declared they had rejected the plea of some ministers that they repudiate the communists. Further, the parents reported that they had never been consulted about having Roddy represent their boys as defense counsel, and they denounced the ministers for sending Roddy to the Birmingham jail to entice their children into an attack upon the ILD. Some of the parents rushed to Birmingham to consult with their children, and one day after their first statement, all of the Scottsboro boys reversed themselves and paid tribute to the ILD.[15]

Communist hopes to monopolize the Scottsboro cases shattered, however, when on May 1, 1931, the NAACP announced that it had entered the cases and planned to manage the defense of the boys.[16] Mutual denunciations by the ILD and the NAACP were precipitated by this unexpected statement of interest in the defense by the less radical Negro body. Both the NAACP and the ILD hoped to banish the other group from the cases as each organization coveted exclusive control of the defense. The NAACP had many advantages over its communist rival. While the ILD was a novice in the field of Negro rights, the NAACP had twenty years experience. While the ILD was dominated by communists, the NAACP leadership was liberal and reformist. While the ILD demonstrated concern for the Scottsboro boys with telegrams and ultimatums, the NAACP had demonstrated greater concern earlier. This, at least, was the claim of the NAACP, and it was not to be dismissed lightly. The NAACP, since its inception in 1909, had fought many court battles under the banner of Negro rights. One pertinent instance was the Arkansas riot case (1926), which culminated in a United States Supreme Court ruling that a trial dominated by mob atmosphere is not a trial at all and is, therefore, a violation of due process of law. No Negro organization in America had the power, ability, and respectability of the NAACP. It was the accepted watchtower of Negro rights.

The NAACP maintained that it was the initial defender in the Scottsboro cases. According to Walter White, secretary of the organization, upon news of the arrests near Scottsboro, a number of Negro ministers in Chattanooga, along with the local chapter of the NAACP, stirred to action. Aware of the hostile feelings in Scottsboro, they feared that a Negro lawyer sent to defend the black youths would be ineffective, at best, in saving the lives of the defendants; at worst, ineffective in saving his own life. These Negro leaders asked a white attorney, Stephen Roddy, to represent them in Scottsboro. From this perspective, it was the ILD and not the NAACP that was interloping in the Scottsboro cases.[17]

There followed a scramble for signatures; both the ILD and the NAACP attempted to persuade the parents and sons that their respective organizations alone should govern the defense. Liberals supporting the NAACP soon charged that the ILD had hidden the parents of the Scottsboro youths to prevent the NAACP from presenting its views to them.[18] Yet, *The Crisis*, organ of the Negro reform group, recorded in May, 1931, that one of its secretaries simply failed to convince the parents that they should engage the

NAACP.[19] Others of the "hidden" parents, Ada Wright, Josephine Powell, and Janie Patterson, were appearing at mass rallies in the East to gain support for their sons and the ILD. Some even attended NAACP convocations where the reform leaders denied them the privilege of speaking.[20] The ILD asserted that the NAACP, failing to ensnare the parents, had attempted to influence the accused—minors, ignorant of many issues in the cases.[21] The communists blamed the NAACP for the earlier visit of Roddy to the prison to "trap" the boys into signing a statement that they could not read and was not read to them.[22]

Fighting within the defense ranks continued. The City Interdenominational Ministers' Alliance of Negro Divines of Chattanooga devoted its weekly broadcast to an assault upon the ILD "for its activities on behalf of eight Negro youths. . . ." The Alliance warned that communists posed a threat to the "peace and harmony" existing in the South. In addition, cautioned the ministers, the ILD's objective was to win Negroes to the Red cause.[23] Similar was the official NAACP analysis. According to its view, the aim of the ILD was to use the Scottsboro cases to spread revolutionary propaganda and to weaken and destroy the NAACP.[24] It chastised the communists for being too narrow to see the superiority of the NAACP.

If the Communistic leadership in the United States had been broadminded and far-sighted, it would have acknowledged frankly that the honesty, earnestness and intelligence of the NAACP during twenty years of desperate struggle proved this organization under present circumstances to be the only one, and its methods the only methods available, to defend these boys.[25]

Although much of the energy of the communists was absorbed in portraying the innocence of the Scottsboro boys to the public, they could not ignore the charges directed against them by the NAACP and its allies. In rebuttal, the communists first reviewed the past. Either Stephen Roddy was or was not employed by the Chattanooga Ministers' Alliance and the NAACP. The *New Republic* claimed that Roddy received $50.80 for his services, while Arthur Hays placed the figure at "about $100."[26] But in discourse with Judge Hawkins, Roddy denied that he was employed as counsel. The communists also questioned the quality of the services rendered by Roddy. Carol Weiss King, a civil rights attorney who assisted the ILD, described the defense as "half-hearted, or at least thoroughly incompetent."[27] At no time before the trials did Roddy interview his clients. He finally talked to them in the courtroom, immediately before the trials began. Although Roddy admitted he was unprepared for the task, he at no time asked for a postponement so that he might prepare. At none of the trials did he bother to summarize the case of the defendants.[28] Finally, there was an attempt at compromise between Roddy and the prosecution that would have meant life imprisonment for the boys.[29] In the eyes of the ILD, Roddy's was no defense at all.

Thus, to the NAACP contention that it was the first and most effective defender of the Scottsboro boys, the ILD retorted that if the NAACP were first, it was horribly ineffective; and if it were not first, why was it intruding upon the ILD? If the Roddy defense were the best the NAACP could provide, it should surrender the cases to those who might do better. If the NAACP were not responsible for the Roddy defense, why did it claim to be? Could the communists, once they had entered the cases, withdraw in favor of an organization that claimed responsibility, rightly or wrongly, for a completely inadequate defense?[30]

Although only ILD counsel was present for hearings on May 6 and May 20, on June 5, 1931, Scottsboro became a mecca for various attorneys.[31] Joseph R. Brodsky, ILD lawyer, obtained signed statements from the nine youths authorizing him and George Chamlee to act as their counsel.[32] Roddy, who also appeared, announced he was happy "he did not represent any New York organization."[33] To this the NAACP made no comment. On June 23, the Jackson County Circuit Court denied the defense motion for a new trial and the attorneys for the boys filed notice of appeal to the Alabama Supreme Court.[34]

By early summer, 1931, the ILD, with the approval of the defendants, seemed to be in charge of the Scottsboro cases. But the NAACP was unwilling to capitulate, and it prepared a new offensive to gain control of the defense. In accord with changed NAACP policy, Walter White and William Pickens, organization secretaries, revealed that the Scottsboro youths had indeed been "railroaded" at their trials.[35] This completely contradicted Roddy. Therefore, in appraising the past trials of the lads, the outlooks of the ILD and the NAACP converged. Notwithstanding the acceptance by the NAACP of the communist interpretation of the first trials, the NAACP was not planning to accept communist leadership in the Scottsboro cases.

The principal issue separating the two organizations was no longer the Roddy defense, but the role ascribed to mounting extralegal activities. The ILD, like the NAACP, believed in providing a good defense in the courtroom; but the ILD believed more should be done. Rallies, demonstrations, and telegrams, or as the polemicists phrased it, "mass pressure," were equally essential if the courts were to free the Scottsboro boys. Committees in the United States and abroad emerged devoted to the liberation of the Scottsboro youngsters. Albert Einstein, Thomas Mann, Theodore Dreiser, Lion Feuchtwanger, Lincoln Steffens, John Dos Passos, and Suzanne LaFollette were all prominent in this effort.[36] By July 7, 1931, Montgomery, Alabama, had received nearly 1,700 protests.[37] Rallies and riots on behalf of the Scottsboro boys spread to Leipzig, Havana, the South, the world.[38]

The NAACP chose to do battle next with the ILD over the issue of mass action. "If the Communists want these lads murdered, then their antics of threatening judges and yelling for mass action . . . is calculated to insure this," editorialized Du Bois.[39] The NAACP singled out a particular Red protest rally for special criticism. On July 17 at Camp Hill, Alabama, Negro sharecroppers met at a church to discuss the Scottsboro affair, but sheriffs' guns closed the meeting. Some were killed, others wounded, and the church was burned. The NAACP viewed the incident as proof of the failure of communist tactics:

. . . black sharecroppers, half-starved and desperate, were organized . . . and then induced to meet and protest against Scottsboro. . . . If this was instigated by Communists, it is too despicable for words; not because the plight of the black peons does not shriek for remedy but because this is no time to bedevil a delicate situation by dragging a red herring across the trail of eight innocent children.[40]

However, while the NAACP aligned itself with the upholders of the law of Alabama in condemning communists (the Reds acknowledged instigating the rally) for causing the disturbance, the journal of the National Urban League and Roger Baldwin of the American Civil Liberties Union placed blame on the Alabama officials who smashed the protest meeting.[41]

Despite the NAACP slurs on the communists and the ILD, it was George Chamlee of the ILD who, on August 7, filed a bill of exceptions in the Scottsboro cases; and it was he who asked for a change in venue to Birmingham in the case of the youngest defendant, who had to be retried because of a hung jury.[42]

The NAACP hoped next to stage a coup that would bring the prisoners back to their standard. On September 14, it announced that Clarence Darrow had been retained by the NAACP to defend the boys.[43] Arthur Hays, attorney for the Civil Liberties

Union, volunteered to serve the NAACP with Darrow.[44] The day following their arrival in Birmingham, they were greeted with a telegram from the Scottsboro lads pleading with the famed counselors not "to fight the ILD and make trouble for Mr. Chamlee just to help the NAACP."[45] Instead, the boys begged them to join with Chamlee and the communists. A conference was arranged at which Darrow and Hays confronted Chamlee and ILD representatives. The latter offered to allow the entrance of Hays and Darrow on two conditions. "First, you must repudiate the National Association for the Advancement of Colored People. Secondly, the tactics in the case must be left to the International Labor Defense." Darrow, opposed to ILD tactics, retorted with a counter proposal. All lawyers involved would repudiate their respective organizations and work as an independent force for the release of the Scottsboro youths.[46] There could be little doubt as to which of these lawyers would dominate the independent coalition. To the ILD, mass pressure was essential to victory, while Darrow reasoned "it is idle to suppose that the State of Alabama can be awed by threats or that such demonstrations can have any effect, unless it is to injure the defendants."[47] Darrow had previously spurned the ILD's offer to defend the Scottsboro youths; it now rejected him.[48]

Darrow then dropped the Scottsboro struggle, as did Hays.[49] The NAACP, without support from parents, defendants, or lawyers, officially withdrew from the cases on January 4, 1932.[50] The NAACP then characterized the ILD as opportunist, completely disinterested in the fate of the Scottsboro boys. The Reds rebuffed America's leading lawyer merely for the sake of spreading propaganda through "mass action." The ILD replied that Darrow was just the latest tool whereby the NAACP hoped quietly to sacrifice the defendants to "lynch courts."[51]

The effects of the mass protest movement were indicated in Montgomery, when on January 21, 1932, Negroes and whites jammed the chamber of the highest court in Alabama and heard Chief Justice John C. Anderson announce that the jurists would not be "bulldozed." He deemed the resolutions and letters that flooded the mails of the court highly improper.[52] Not until March 24 did the State Supreme Court render its verdict, and in each of the cases Anderson alone dissented.[53] The majority found nothing incorrect in the speedy trials and they viewed the National Guard as a bulwark against mob spirit.[54] Anderson presented many reasons for his minority opinion: the trial occurred during the height of hostility against the boys a few days after the alleged crime; the presence of the military, which guarded the boys from the first night in Scottsboro and escorted them back and forth to Gadsden, was bound to have an effect upon the jury's thinking; and the efforts of the defense were "rather *pro forma* than zealous and active."[55] Not for any one of these reasons alone would Anderson order a new trial, but when considered conjointly, he discovered he could not uphold the verdicts of the Scottsboro juries.[56]

Nevertheless, the sentences were affirmed by a six to one vote. Only in the case of Eugene Williams did the outcome differ. Acknowledging that affidavits submitted by the defense to prove the youth yet a juvenile might be false, the court opined, "there is nothing in this case to prove their falsity." Williams was remanded for a new trial, and the others were set to die on May 13, 1932.[57]

Although the ILD had succeeded in winning a new trial for one of the boys, the future for the other seven looked bleak. The *New Republic* lamented that without a violation of the federal Constitution, a murder case could not be appealed from the state to the federal courts. Because the cases concerned no question of constitutional law, the United States Supreme Court had refused to review the rulings on Sacco, Vanzetti, and Tom Mooney. Unless the ILD could demonstrate a violation of the Constitution, the Supreme Court woud remain indifferent to the Scottsboro boys, also. Because of the similarity between the Scottsboro and the Arkansas riot cases, however, the *New Republic* held a faint hope of an appeal to the highest court.[58]

As the date of execution approached, public agitation intensified. The Berlin Committee for Saving the Scottsboro Victims wired President Hoover and Governor Miller of Alabama urging pardon for the Negroes. On April 7, a mob in Havana stoned the windows of an Amercian bank, denounced Yankee imperialism, and demanded the freedom of the Scottsboro defendants. In response to foreign protests, the State Department in Washington asked Governor Miller for a statement of facts in the cases. American consulates abroad had requested the information in order to dispel the "misconception of the circumstances" in the cases.[59]

When the United States Supreme Court agreed to hear the Scottsboro cases, the executions were suspended. On election eve, 1932, the tribunal's decision on the cases was announced. Writing for the majority, Justice Sutherland chose to consider all of the cases as one. He observed that there were three contentions of the defense in support of its proposition that the defendants had been denied due process of law:

> (1) they were not given a fair, impartial and deliberate trial; (2) they were denied the right of counsel, with the accustomed incidents of consultation and opportunity of preparation for trial; and (3) they were tried before juries from which qualified members of their own race were systematically excluded. . . .
>
> The only one of the assignments which we shall consider is the second, in respect of the denial of counsel; . . .[60]

The Justice continued that at no time were the boys asked if they wanted counsel appointed. No one asked them if their parents or friends might hire attorneys. "That it would not have been an idle ceremony to give the defendants reasonable opportunity to obtain counsel is demonstrated by the fact that, very soon after conviction, able counsel appeared in their behalf."[61] Sutherland quoted from the court record where Roddy admitted that he was unprepared for the trial, unknown to the defendants, and unfamiliar with the procedure in Alabama. The appointment of the whole Scottsboro bar to defend the boys prior to the entrance of Roddy was designated as an "expansive gesture" on the part of Judge Hawkins; the appointment of the entire bar gave responsibility to so many that it gave it to none. Furthermore, Sutherland disclosed that one of the leading members of the bar had accepted employment on the side of the prosecution. Therefore, concluded the majority opinion, because the prisoners had been deprived of counsel in the significant pre-trial period, the period in which preparations for trial are made, the Scottsboro boys, even with lawyers at the moment of trial, were effectively deprived of counsel.[62]

In dissent Justice Butler proclaimed that the defendants had been adequately represented by counsel. He noted that if defense counsel had lacked time to prepare for the cases, it would have requested postponement. But this was not done.

> There was no suggestion, at the trial or in the motion for a new trial which they made, that Mr. Roddy or Mr. Moody was denied such opportunity or that they were not in fact fully prepared. The amended motion for new trial, by counsel who succeeded them contains the first suggestion that defendants were denied counsel or opportunity to prepare for trial. But neither Mr. Roddy nor Mr. Moody has given any support to this claim. Their silence requires a finding that the claim is ground for, if it had any merit, they would be found to support it.[63]

Butler complimented the original attorneys for their defense and remarked that no mob hysteria existed at Scottsboro. For these reasons Justices Butler and McReynolds upheld the convictions of the Scottsboro boys.

The majority ruling was, in the words of Felix Frankfurter, "the first application of the limitations of the [fourteenth] amendment to a state criminal trial."[64]

The Scottsboro ruling, whatever its significance to the legal profession, was momentous to the ILD-NAACP dispute. The ILD appealed the cases on three grounds—mob atmosphere, denial of counsel, and exclusion of Negroes from the jury. Although one cannot state with certainty what the NAACP would have done had it governed the defense, one may speculate with a certain probability. The NAACP would have stressed the first point, attempting to demonstrate similarity between the Scottsboro and the Arkansas riot cases. This was the path suggested by Roddy, the *New Republic*, and, the day after the decision of the Supreme Court, by Walter White:

The National Association for the Advancement of Colored People is elated at the Supreme Court's decision granting a new trial in the Scottsboro cases. We are specially gratified that the decision reaffirms the principle and precedent established in a previous case, the Arkansas riot cases . . . , carried to the Supreme Court by this association, in which it was ruled that a court dominated by a mob is not due process of law.[65]

The high court did no such thing. Not only did Justices Butler and McReynolds deny that mob domination of the trials existed, but the majority also observed, "It does not sufficiently appear that the defendants were seriously threatened with, or that they were actually in danger of mob violence. . . ."[66] An appeal based merely upon the town's hostility to the defendants, then, probably would have failed in persuading the Supreme Court to overturn the convictions of the youngsters.

The third ground of appeal, regarding exclusion of Negroes from the juries, evoked no comment from the high tribunal. Therefore, if the NAACP had managed the defense and if it had appealed the cases employing this contention, it would be impossible to state the outcome in the Court. However, it is not impossible to ask if the NAACP would have made such a contention in appealing the cases. In its twenty-year history it had not done so. When the issue finally came before the Supreme Court, the ILD, not the NAACP, presented the arguments that ended, in theory, Negro exclusion from juries.

Only on the second point did the Supreme Court rule in favor of the Scottsboro boys, the claim that the youths had been denied effective counsel. It is doubtful, if the NAACP had supervised the cases, that the reform organization would have offered such an argument. For months the NAACP had claimed responsibility for the defense cited as inadequate by the Court—the NAACP had employed Roddy. Hardly could the Association have informed the Supreme Court that the counsel it had provided was the equivalent of denial of effective counsel. In fact, the position of the Court's minority in upholding the Scottsboro verdicts was simply a paraphrase of earlier NAACP claims. The Communist Party stated, with justification, that not only had the ILD won a new trial, but that an NAACP defense would have resulted in the execution of the Scottsboro defendants.[67]

There were many more trials of the Scottsboro boys before an inconclusive denouement was to be achieved. Mass action in favor of the defendants continued, with songs, plays, poems, sports events, parades and a march on Washington devoted to their cause. It was the first time such widespread mass efforts had been staged on behalf of Negro rights, and the NAACP opposed them. Authorities criticize the communists for their mass campaign of the 1930's, but the times and the Negroes are changing.

This paper began by noting the caricature of communists as held by many liberals and as reinforced by American scholarship. On closer inspection, allegations by Du Bois, White, Hughes, Hoover, Nolan, Record, *et al.*, that the Scottsboro case was an example of Red perfidy proves inaccurate—false. The communists did not attempt to make martyrs of the Scottsboro boys. Instead, through the ILD, the Communist Party saved the lads from a bungling defense and initiated a mass movement on behalf of the Negroes. Of course, there are other charges against the communists originating from their efforts in the Scottsboro cases—the ILD attorneys were incompetent, the Party stole millions intended for the defense of the boys, it betrayed one of the boys to the FBI after he had escaped from Alabama. Though these charges are as untenable as the one related in this article, lack of space precludes a detailed refutation.[68]

The Communist Party may or may not be villainous, but there is no evidence of its villainy in the Scottsboro cases. On the contrary, it saved the lives of nine young boys and opened new avenues of protest to Negroes.

NOTES

1. J. Edgar Hoover, *Masters of Deceit: A Study of Communism in America and How to Fight It* (New York, 1958), p. 252; W. E. B. Du Bois, *Dusk at Dawn: An Essay Toward an Autobiography of a Race Concept* (New York, 1940), pp. 297–298. Du Bois wrote this before his conversion to communism.

2. Langston Hughes, *Fight for Freedom: The Story of the NAACP* (New York, 1962), p. 87. Hughes wrote this after he had praised the communists for their efforts on behalf of the Scottsboro boys many times in poems and plays.

3. Walter White, *How Far the Promised Land?* (New York, 1955), p. 215.

4. Arthur Garfield Hays, *Trial by Prejudice* (2nd ed., New York, 1935), p. 43.

5. James W. Ford and Anna Damon, "Scottsboro in the Light of Building the Negro People's Front," *The Communist*, X (September, 1937), 841; Wilson Record, *The Negro and the Communist Party* (Chapel Hill, 1951), p. 34; William A. Nolan, *Communism Versus the Negro* (Chicago, 1951), p. 75.

6. *New York Daily Worker*, April 2, 7, 1931; *New York Times*, April 9, 1931.

7. *New York Times*, April 9, 10, 1931.

8. Edmund Wilson, "The Freight-Car Case," *New Republic*, LXVIII (August 26, 1931), 41; Walter White, "The Negro and the Communists," *Harper's Magazine*, CLXIV (December, 1931), 66; Hays, *op. cit.*, p. 85; "A Statement by the N.A.A.C.P. on the Scottsboro Cases," *The Crisis*, XXXIX (March, 1932), 82.

9. Wilson, *op. cit.*, p. 41.

10. *New York Daily Worker*, April 13, 14, 15, 1931.

11. *Ibid.*, April 21, 1931.

12. *Ibid.*, April 22, 1931.

13. *Ibid.*, April 24, 1931.

14. *New York Times*, April 24, 1931.

15. *New York Daily Worker*, April 25, 1931.

16. *Ibid.*, May 5, 1931.

17. White, *op. cit.*, 64; "A Statement by the N.A.A.C.P. . . . ," *op. cit.*, 82; "Correspondence: The Scottsboro Rape Case," *New Republic*, XLVII (June 24, 1931), 864. The latter contains a letter from Herbert J. Seligman, then Director of Publicity for the NAACP.

18. Wilson, *op. cit.*, 42.

19. "A Statement by the N.A.A.C.P. . . . ," *op. cit.*, p. 82.

20. Files Crenshaw, Jr., and Kenneth A. Miller, *Scottsboro: The Firebrand of Communism* (Montgomery, Alabama: Press of the Brown Printing Company, 1936), p. 56. For a description of an ILD rally at which Mrs. Patterson appeared, see *New York Times*, April 26, 1931.

21. *New York Daily Worker*, June 29, July 6, 1931.

22. Wilson, *op. cit.*, p. 42.

23. *New York Times*, May 24, 1931.

24. "A Statement by the N.A.A.C.P. . . . ," *op. cit.*, p. 82.

25. W. E. B. Du Bois, "Postscript," *The Crisis*, XXXVIII (September, 1931), 313.

26. Wilson, *op. cit.*, p. 40; Hays, *op. cit.*, p. 85.

27. Carol Weiss King, "Correspondence: The Scottsboro Case," *New Republic*, LXVII (June 24, 1931), 155.

28. *Ibid.*, pp. 155–156; King, "Correspondence: The Scottsboro Case," *The Nation*, CXXXIII (July 1, 1931), 16.
29. Crenshaw and Miller, *op. cit.*, p. 17; *New York Daily Worker*, November 16, 1931.
30. *New York Daily Worker*, May 5, 1931.
31. *Ibid.*, May 23, 1931.
32. *New York Times*, June 6, 1931.
33. King, "Correspondence," *New Republic*, *op. cit.*, 155; King, "Correspondence," *The Nation*, *op. cit.*, 16.
34. Crenshaw and Miller, *op. cit.*, p. 57.
35. *New York Times*, June 29, 1931.
36. *Ibid.*, July 5, 1931; *New York Daily Worker*, May 20, 1931.
37. Crenshaw and Miller, *op. cit.*, p. 57.
38. *New York Times*, July 1, 8, 12, 1931; *New York Daily Worker*, June 2, 1931. A German youth was killed in Chemnitz while protesting on behalf of the Scottsboro boys; see *New York Daily Worker*, December 14, 1932.
39. Du Bois, "Postscript," *op. cit.*, p. 313.
40. *Ibid.*, p. 314.
41. "Communism and the Negro Tenant Farmer," *Opportunity*, IX (August, 1931), 36; *New York Times*, July 19, 1931.
42. *New York Times*, August 8, 1931.
43. *Ibid.*, September 15, 1931.
44. "A Statement by the N.A.A.C.P. . . . ," *op. cit.*, p. 82.
45. As quoted in Hays, *op. cit.*, p. 87.
46. *Ibid.*, p. 88; Clarence Darrow, "Scottsboro," *The Crisis*, XXXIX (March, 1932), 81; "A Statement by the N.A.A.C.P. . . . ," *op. cit.*, p. 83.
47. Darrow, *op. cit.*, p. 81.
48. *New York Times*, December 30, 1931.
49. *Ibid.*
50. *Ibid.*, January 5, 1932.
51. Melvin P. Levy, "Correspondence: Scottsboro and the I.L.D.," *New Republic*, LXIX (January 20, 1932), 273; Robert Minor, "The Negro and His Judases," *The Communist*, X (July, 1931), 632 ff; James W. Ford and James S. Allen, *The Negroes in a Soviet America* (New York, 1935), p. 13.
52. Crenshaw and Miller, *op. cit.*, p. 64.
53. Hays, *op. cit.*, p. 92; *New York Times*, March 25, 1932.
54. Hays, *op. cit.*, p. 92; *New York Times*, March 25, 1932.
55. Hays, *op. cit.*, p. 98.
56. *New York Times*, March 25, 1932.
57. *Ibid.*
58. "Legal Murder in Alabama," *New Republic*, LXX (April 6, 1932), 194.
59. *New York Times*, March 27, 31, April 9, 16, 1932.
60. *Powell v. State of Alabama*, 287 U.S. 50 (1932).
61. *Ibid.*, p. 52.
62. *Ibid.*, pp. 53–58.
63. *Ibid.*, p. 76.
64. *New York Times*, November 13, 1932.
65. *Ibid.*, November 8, 1932.
66. *Powell v. State of Alabama*, 287 U.S. 51 (1932).
67. *New York Daily Worker*, August 9, 1933.
68. Hugh Murray, Jr., "The Scottsboro Rape Case and the Communist Party" (Unpublished Master's Thesis, Tulane University, 1963), p. 220 ff.

INTELLECTUALS IN
SOCIAL AND RACIAL MOVEMENTS

WILSON RECORD

In this selection, resting on a study of white intellectuals in the labor movement of the 1930's and in the feminist movement, Negro intellectuals in racial movements, and Negro and white intellectuals in interracial movements, Wilson Record considers the difference between black intellectuals, who "have a grievance that is specific, obvious, and constant," and white intellectuals, whose grievance "is only occasionally defined in a concrete way."

❋

Negro intellectuals in America can be distinguished from their white counterparts by the fact that the former have a grievance that is specific, obvious and constant while that of the latter is only occasionally defined in a concrete way. The character of this difference and its implications for involvement in social movements can be understood by an examination of concrete instances in which Negro and white intellectuals have engaged in organized efforts to redress the balance between constituent social groupings.

Our procedure will be as follows: First, we will examine in a brief and general way the motivations of white and Negro intellectuals in their identification with social and racial movements. Second, we will examine the involvement of white intellectuals in the labor movement as a means of demonstrating the fluctuating character of their grievances, and their divorcement from the mass in whose interest they propose to act. Third, we will examine

Reprinted by permission from *Phylon*, XV (Third Quarter 1954), 231–242.

the role of white intellectuals in the feminist movement, and contrast their involvement with that of Negro intellectuals in racial movements, at the same time calling attention to certain parallels in Negro and women's movements. Fourth, we will explore in some detail the participation of white and Negro intellectuals in interracial movements, since this provides us a most appropriate opportunity to examine the differences which we will have outlined.

The grievances of white intellectuals are complex and varied, and they are not constant in their thinking and motivations. While members of this group may find it difficult at times to conform with the demands of an order whose highest rewards are reserved for the businessmen and industrialists, there are numerous compensating factors in the picture. White intellectuals obtain substantially higher than average shares of the community's material goods and services and the social prestige which it has to confer. This enables them to live at middle-class and in some cases at upper-class levels. And among certain segments of the population, primarily among the better educated group who constitute an increasingly larger proportion of the public, they secure a rewarding amount of recognition and prestige. The segmentation of American society includes meaningful sub-groups, and it is these that the intellectual can respond to or identify with on some selective basis. The white intellectuals are usually engaged in occupations having a relatively high place on the job prestige scale. While the performance of such work may involve compromise with certain intellectual impulses and principles, there are significant compensations in the high valuations placed on these activities, even when their scope and character may not be very well understood by the persons making judgments. Finally, the white intellectuals are generally free to make choices concerning their participation in social movements. They can decide first of all whether or not they will engage in any kind of organized social action consciously aimed at introducing social changes.[1] In addition they can exercise a wide amount of discretion in selecting the areas and organizations in which they will undertake action. This choice is a consequence of the fact that there is not either a specific personal grievance or constant group pressures propelling the white intellectual in the direction of discontent and protest.

The Negro intellectual by contrast has a grievance that is specific and constant, his identification with an oppressed racial minority. The white intellectual at times feels alienated by a business-industrial society which displays little sympathy for the values with which he is concerned. The Negro feels alienated continuously by a white-dominated social order which denies his individuality. His income may be above the average of the Negro community. However, it will be much lower than the average of his white counterparts of similar training and occupation. This is a consequence of the fact that he is a Negro, or at least it is so defined in his own thinking. Although a member of the upper stratum of Negroes, his level of living will be substantially below that of white intellectuals. The number of groups in the Negro community from which he may obtain recognition at the intellectual level and with which he may identify is indeed small, while numerous restrictions are imposed on his prestige changes among groups in the larger white society. This again is the result of the fact of race. His job may have relatively high social value in the Negro community, and it will not permit him the recognition attached to similar work and accomplishments in the white world. In the latter he will be regarded as a "Negro writer," a "Negro artist," a "Negro professor," rather than as an accomplished individual in these or other highly valued occupations. Finally, the Negro intellectual has a much narrower range of choices concerning participation in social movements. Community pressures are such that, whether he wills it or not, he is likely to be caught up in demands to "give the white folks hell," and to participate in movements dedicated to Negro betterment.[2] Not only does he have little choice in whether or not to act, but a similar situation confronts him with reference to the types of action in which he will engage and the specific movements and organizations with which he will become identified.

During the 1930s many white intellectuals became involved in the labor movement in this country. They made important contributions to the development of the industrial union program, although there was no close identity between their intellectual and occupational interests and the political and economic needs of working peoples in whose behalf they presumed to speak and act. Since that time labor organizations have achieved a high degree of institutional stability and the welfare of members has been greatly improved. It is no mere coincidence that white intellectuals have departed the labor movement, or have remained behind only in the roles of administrators and techicians. And it should come as no surprise that many labor organizations themselves have developed attitudes and policies which, if implemented, would be destructive of the values and functions of intellectuals, even in areas outside their own immediate spheres.[3] Labor movements in America may find the intellectuals indispensable during the earlier stages of protest and organization, but they are just as likely to find them either disruptive or dangerous during a period when the principal concern is organizational stability and immediate membership welfare.

In going to the labor movement, white intellectuals have been seeking two things. First, they have been attempting to find some specific focus for their more general discontent and identification with a group that has the possibility of large-scale action. Second, they have been searching for leadership roles which are likely to be open to them as new movements get under way and as new organizational structures are developed. In going to the labor movement, intellectuals perform certain functions. First, they articulate the vague dissatisfactions of the workers, both for the workers themselves and for the other constituent groups in the society. Second, they pose goals which it is thought should be the aim of the movement and suggest the strategies and techniques which should be employed in their realization. Finally, they function as publicists and propagandists, using their skills of communication—writing and speaking—in stirring the rank and file to action, and as legal and administrative technicians in handling matters of law and organization. Having no specific grievances of their own, they attempt to identify with the labor movement and make its cause focal in their actions.[4]

However, when workers cease to have grievances, or where they devise institutional patterns for handling them, but the white intellectuals find that there is no longer any need for their services. Earlier goals which they posed have been achieved. Earlier discontents which they articulated are no longer meaningful and are not the precipitates of concerted action. Organizational stability becomes one of the chief determinants of the behavior of labor leaders. In such situations the intellectuals have no function as intellectuals, although they may in some cases perform technical jobs as attorneys, editors, researchers and social workers. Even the labor educators become instruments for institutional stability and for the perpetuation of existing leadership.[5]

The grievances of Negro intellectuals, however, are much more concrete and continuous. Racial identification persists in their own minds, and in the attitudes of the larger society.[6] While certain immediate problems may be solved, new ones emerge at both the personal and group levels. The goals of Negro intellectuals are much too large to be solved by the realization of a few immediate gains. The significance of Negro-ness is not thereby removed. These goals involve full and equal citizenship, and until they are realized, complaints will persist. The grievance of the Negro intellectuals, of course, is defined in immediately different ways. Ultimately, however, it is seen as a consequence of race and of race prejudice. In this respect it is the same as that of non-intellectual Negroes.[7]

The differences between Negro and white intellectuals in social movements are reflected further in the feminist and racial movements. Although there are significant parallels among these two movements, comparisons can be undertaken only if certain careful qualifications are introduced. It is suggested here that white intellectual participation in non-proletarian and non-labor social movements is also a manifestation of the lack of specific and concrete grievances. Even the intellectual participants in the feminist movement, which most clearly parallels the more characteristic Negro movements in this country, frequently lack well-defined complaints of their own of which action was a consequence. The feminist movement was essentially an organized effort among certain women to eliminate various forms of discrimination based on the biological fact of sex while Negro movements have aimed at the removal of discrimination based on the biological fact of race. Neither sex nor race *per se* makes for mechanical differential treatment and the subordination of women and Negroes. It is the social meanings that are attached to these features which determine the type and amount of discrimination which will occur.[8]

Significant parallels in the economic, political and educational status of women and Negroes in this country can be discerned. Furthermore the ideologies of feminist and Negro movements are highly similar in that they are reactions against the denial of full participation in social, political and economic life, and in that they emphasize equalitarian values and goals. In addition, the methods and techniques which these movements employ have numerous common characteristics. The feminist movement at the present time is only a shadow of the militant effort to redress the sexual balance which reached its zenith in the period between 1890 and 1920. The reasons for its decline are suggestive for any inquiry into contemporary Negro movements and the role of intellectuals in them.[9]

Leadership of the feminist movement was in the hands of well-educated women who usually came from middle and upper-class families. In this respect they were similar to the intellectual leaders of both historical and contemporary racial movements. The fact of basically high native intelligence coupled with the acquisition of above average education equipped these women to perform jobs and engage in mental endeavors that were ordinarily reserved for the able and not-so-able white men. One result was that the educated woman tended to become a marginal individual in that she could not fit into the traditional and prescribed role of mother and housewife, while at the same time she could not enter the male world of politics, business, industry and the professions on any basis approaching an equal footing.[10] In this respect intellectual women were placed in a position highly similar to that of the contemporary Negro intellectual who finds it difficult to belong either to the Negro world or to the white.[11]

Intellectual women in the feminist movement, however, did not have grievances as concrete or persistent as do Negro intellectuals in racial movements, in spite of numerous other similarities. These women were not subjected to the multiple pressures from other women to engage in activities designed to better the condition of the female sex as a group. Participation to a large extent was a voluntary matter, although personal psychological compulsives were operative in the behavior of individuals. On the contrary, some of the most severe critics of the feminist leaders were themselves women who were content with their status as traditionally defined, something that can be said of few Negroes at any level. Discontent in the individual is dependent to a considerable extent on its being shared by members of the group with which he is identified, and on its being reinforced by pressures from the group. The absence of a mutual sharing of discontent among women and the lack of continuing pressures to articulate such unrest made for relaxation on the part of feminist intellectuals in their effort to redress the sexual balance.[12]

Another aspect of the feminist movement which had significant implications for the intellectual participants was the general lack of agreement concerning goals which should be sought. Since women were distributed through all the various strata of society, they tended to define the woman problem in various ways. Many upper-strata women who had profited most from the existing patterns of men-women relations were reluctant to demand any drastic changes.[13] Lower-strata women, lacking in education and social literacy, recognized few problems as exclusively relevant to women, and could not visualize alternatives to the traditional forms of sex relationships. Not only was the formulation of goals difficult as a consequence of varied "definitions of the situation" at the ideological level, but at the organizational one as well. Class, educational, racial and social-psychological differences came to the fore when the specific task of organization was confronted. The intellectual feminists therefore found it difficult to articulate the goals of the movement, although they were highly effective in calling to public attention the more general plight of the female sector of the population.[14]

While Negro movements have frequently reflected strata differences in the Negro community, they have not been nearly as significant as for the feminist movement. In the first place, Negroes constituted only about ten percent of the population, thus reducing the number of persons whose views and aims had to be reconciled. Second, the Negroes did not have as many conflicting component elements within the group; and it was possible, particularly at an earlier period, for a few Negroes to assume the role of recognized race spokesmen and race leaders, whereas the feminist leaders could never be sure that they voiced the aspirations of more than a few women. Third, the grievances of Negroes and of Negro intellectuals were similar and relatively constant. Although there were differences concerning methods and techniques, there was little disagreement concerning ultimate goals. Even Booker T. Washington, particularly in his later years, had to take a more forthright position with reference to equal citizenship for the Negro. Finally, it might be emphasized that the external pressures exerted by the white community were continuous so far as Negroes were concerned, while the feminist movement did not confront equal hostility, and as a consequence was able to make gains here and there which satisfied some of the more immediate needs. The choices were more meaningful for women in that although they failed to realize all the equalitarian aims espoused by the feminist movement, they had socially approved and psychologically rewarding alternatives in becoming housewives and mothers. Failure to realize feminist goals could not be defined as an oppressive continuance of group and individual inferiority as in the case of Negro movements. The lack of specific and constant grievances most clearly distinguishes the feminist from Negro movements.[15]

Our contention may be tested further by references to movements in which both Negro and white intellectuals participate. Specifically, we have in mind those movements which are non-proletarian and non-political, and which are usually referred to as "interracial cooperation" endeavors. It has been our contention that white intellectuals in America find it difficult to realize a sense of usefulness and belonging in a business civilization, but that they lack a real grievance of their own. In participating in social movements they fill two needs. First, they obtain a specific focus for their discontent, and, secondly, they find opportunities for leadership. The participation of white intellectuals in inter-racial movements is one means whereby such needs are filled.[16]

One of the most notable characteristics of interracial coopera-tion movements is that they are composed primarily of intellec-tuals from both racial groups. Negro and white educators, social workers, teachers, journalists, writers and other professional people make up the membership of such organizations and are occupants of crucial leadership positions. It is they who define the problems with which such movements will be concerned, and determine the techniques and strategies which will be followed. The preponderance of intellectual participants gives a number of distinctive emphases to these interracial cooperation en-deavors.[17]

Such movements are not organized, mass efforts. On the con-trary, they are relatively small in membership numbers, and have usually neither the inclination nor the resources with which to undertake large-scale mobilization of Negroes or of whites around the specific issues at which they direct attention. Furthermore, they exhibit a dependence on education and persuasion rather than the exertion of political or social power as a means of achiev-ing their aims. While they do not avoid political action, their em-phasis in most cases is on non-political means. For example, the Congress of Racial Equality stresses the use of non-violent direct action. The Council of Social Action of the Congregational Chris-tian Churches relies primarily on community organization, lead-ership training and field services. The Southern Regional Council emphasizes research, education, and community welfare organi-zation. Numerous local groups of which there are several hun-dred in the United States in general rely on education and nego-tiation as a means for realizing better interracial and intergroup relations.[18]

White intellectuals who participate in such endeavors do so for a variety of reasons. However, both in terms of social characteristics and motivations they appear to have much in common. They are substantially above average in educational attainments. The bulk of them will have completed high school and a majority will have obtained college degrees. Their occupations tend to fall within a rather narrow range; they are usually professional people such as teachers, social workers, educators, journalists, writers and lawyers. For the most part they are members of the white middle-class, and usually come from middle-class backgrounds.

Involvement in such activities requires at times a considerable amount of sacrifice on their part. Their concern with race relations is likely to be viewed with some suspicion by the general white community which may exert pressures to curtail their activities or to prohibit them altogether. The professed ethical motivations of such persons are likely to be regarded as a cloak for more devious patterns. Since these individuals are largely divorced from the sources of economic and political power in the community, they tend to be highly vulnerable to the criticism of opposition groups. Continued involvement is contingent upon a high degree of personal motivation, exceptional social skills, and the realization of compensating values in the activity itself. The short duration of white participation in interracial movements is largely a consequence of the absence of one or all of these factors.[19]

Religious beliefs are the underpinnings of the participation of many of the white intellectuals. Ethical conviction enables them to withstand a considerable amount of white community disapproval. Since they are associating with an immediate group frequently having similar motivations, they obtain a continuous reinforcement of moral values through direct personal contact. Social disapproval is more nebulous and only occasionally does it result in direct personal antagonisms and conflicts. The religious-like dedication of white southerners who are concerned actively with race relations has been noted before. Even among those who have no formal religious ties there is a pronounced tendency to define race relations issues in terms of religiously derived moral values.

However, other motives are involved in white participation in such movements. White intellectuals have no racial grievances of their own since they do not experience isolation and segregation as a consequence of any distinctive physical features. Nor do they experience deprivation in the economic area, having incomes substantially above the average of the labor force, and engaging in occupations that have relatively high prestige rank. While they experience some feeling of political impotence, they are not barred from participation in the making of public policy decisions. Their involvement in interracial movements is not an effort to compensate for specific restrictions in these areas. Rather it is a result of a sense of frustration in intellectual endeavors and of a failure to establish meaningful identification with groups that wield power.[20] The motivations of white intellectuals who become active in interracial movements are much the same as those of white intellectuals who enter labor movements. They are seeking some immediate and specific focus for their discontent and opportunities to engage in leadership functions. In addition, they are searching for chances for the wider exercise of their intellectual as opposed to their strictly technical capabilities. In making the Negro's grievance their own, the white intellectuals become identified with a group that places high value on their functions, even though there may be little comprehension of the nature of intellectual life and processes. At the same time, the white intellectual is elevated to a position of leadership and provided with a sense of identification with a group that at least potentially has the possibility of exercising a considerable amount of power.[21] There is also the fact that participation in such movements in itself brings a degree of recognition in the white community. That such recognition is for the most part negative may not be important. What is crucial in the case of the impotent intellectuals is that it calls attention to persons who would otherwise remain obscure and unknown.

The Negro intellectual participants in interracial cooperation movements are activated by a different set of motives. Unlike the white intellectuals who risk their social prestige in the white community by interracial involvements, the Negro intellectuals enhance their standing by such activity. The participation of the latter tends to be viewed as a step in racial advancement, and the intellectuals become spokesmen for Negroes as a group at a level which can be attained by few members of the race. The Negro intellectuals may be subjected to certain criticism by their fellow Negroes who feel that interracial cooperation movements are too compromising in their programs and too mild in the use of certain techniques. There will also be a certain suspicion that these intellectuals will bargain racial advantage for personal gains. However, for the most part their roles are approved, and they are encouraged and sometimes pressured to play them.[22]

Furthermore the Negro intellectuals in these organizational situations have an individual concern with the success or failure of
the joint undertakings. At stake are issues which affect them as
Negroes and as intellectuals. The consequences of success or
failure for the white colleagues are much less involved. The latter
are likely to continue very much as they are whether or not the
goals of the movement are realized. For example, a successful
campaign to remove racial restrictions in housing may well mean
that the Negro intellectuals will be able to move from slum areas
into decent neighborhoods. The residential and housing status of
the white participants, however, will probably be affected not at
all. The same is true with a host of other issues which are the
concern of interracial movements.[23]

If Negro intellectuals welcome the initiative of their white
colleagues in interracial movements, they also view it with a certain amount of suspicion. This is a consequence in part of the
psychological conditioning produced by the isolation of Negroes
generally from the people and institutions of the larger community, a matter which even the most insightful colored intellectual finds it difficult to overcome. But other more specific considerations are involved. The motives of white intellectuals are frequently far from clear. Their colored colleagues may well wonder
why, in view of the numerous opportunities open to persons with
the proper skin coloration, the latter bother to concern themselves
with the Negro at all. The colored intellectuals may well suspect
that concerns deeper than racial betterment inform the activities
of the whites.[24] Whereas the Negro's grievance is clear in his own
mind and is apparent also to his white colleagues, the complaint
of the latter is obscure. The Negro intellectuals know what they
want from interracial movements; the whites can hardly be as
specific.[25]

The tensions which result are further aggravated by the fact
that the Negro intellectuals are much more dependent on the
whites than the whites are on them in such movements. The limits
of activity are determined by how far the whites are willing to go,
and the methods which will be used tend to be a result of what
the whites consider right and proper. Ostensibly the Negro intellectual participates as an equal, but all too frequently in practice
he occupies a subordinate role. Coupled with this is the fact that
the Negro intellectual participants have a higher standing in the
Negro community than their white colleagues have in the white
world. The result usually produces an association of upper-strata

Negroes with middle-class whites.[26] There is also the feeling among the Negro intellectuals that the interest of the whites is not genuine, or if genuine, it is not durable. The former suspect that they may be deserted when the going gets rough, or when the white intellectuals find some new area or group around which their discontent may be focused.[27] Negro intellectuals who participate in racial movements are ever under the watchful eye of other Negroes. Deviations from what may be regarded as a Negro "Party Line" are quickly noted and just as quickly criticized. Any public expressions of Negro intellectuals in such movements must follow the route of insistence on equality, while privately they may condone organizational action that compromises this principle. For example, few Negro intellectuals today can take a position in opposition to fair employment practice legislation although they may be convinced that such measures are not the solution to the job problems of their race. The same may be said with reference to numerous other issues bearing on Negro-white relations.

In the foregoing pages an attempt has been made to isolate and explain crucial differences between white and Negro intellectuals by reference to the involvement of members of the two groups in contemporary social movements. It has been suggested that these differences can be understood in terms of the impact of social meanings attached to racial characteristics which in turn produce varied self-images among intellectuals and engender differential functional roles. Any discussion of American intellectuals which ignores these determinants and fails to measure their implications runs serious risks of imprecision and incompleteness.

NOTES

1. Granville Hicks, *Small Town* (New York, 1947), p. 269.
2. Interview, San Francisco, 1952.
3. The current preoccupation of labor leaders with the influence of communists in the trade unions is substantially more involved than would be supposed at first glance. For while anti-communism is presumably motivated by a desire to eliminate an alien-oriented and disruptive faction in the labor organizations, the means employed can be and are used to stifle other forms of opposition, including that of non-communists who may be intellectuals.
4. Eric Hoffer, Interview, February 23, 1953.
5. Irving Howe and B. J. Widick, *The UAW and Walter Reuther* (New York, 1949), p. 251. "In recent years," say the authors, "the UAW has hired a considerable number of specialists—economists, lawyers, newspapermen,

lobbyists—whose work is valuable and indispensable. There are good reasons to welcome this development. It brings into the union men with a broader social vision than that enjoyed by most union leaders: it makes possible some contact between intellectuals and workers, with benefits to both. Yet the presence of these specialists has certain dangers. An unsatisfactory relationship can very easily be established between the union official and the intellectual employee of the union . . . [This] means that one man [labor leader] has the power and the other man [intellectual] does the thinking for him. At the same time the intellectual employee of the union, even though he is supposed to articulate its ideas and defend it in public controversy, may find himself in a subsidiary position. Since he does not 'rest on' the ranks, he lacks the power of the local union leaders. He finds that if, for any reason, he does not toe the line set by the union leadership, he may be dismissed and have no possibility of appealing his dismissal to the ranks. Too often he is wanted for the use to which his skills may be put rather than for the ideas his mind may produce." See also Soule, *The Intellectuals and the Labor Movement* (New York, 1923), pp. 9–10 and Wilson Record, "Labor Unions and Intellectuals as Educators," *New Leader*, 34 (November 26, 1951), 28.

6. Oliver C. Cox, "Leadership Among Negroes in the United States," in Alvin W. Gouldner, ed., *Studies in Leadership* (New York, 1950) p. 228.

7. *Ibid.*, p. 229.

8. Robert E. Park, *Race and Culture* (Glencoe, Illinois, 1950), pp. 230–231.

9. Arnold W. Green and Elanor Melnick, "What Has Happened to the Feminist Movement?" in Gouldner, *op. cit.*, p. 295.

10. Helen Matthews Lewis, *The Woman Movement and the Negro Movement*, Publications of the University of Virginia Phelps-Stokes Fellowship Papers, No. 19. (Charlottesville, Virginia, 1949), p. 9.

11. Park, *op. cit.*, p. 373.

12. Green and Melnick, *op. cit.*, p. 288.

13. *Ibid.*, p. 285.

14. Ida M. Tarbell, *All in the Day's Work* (New York, 1939), p. 32.

15. Green and Melnick, *op. cit.*, pp. 284, 296.

16. It should be emphasized here that Negro and white intellectuals are frequently involved in movements which do not have race relations as their focal concern. The labor movement is one example. Radical political movements constitute another.

17. Louis C. Kesselman, *The Social Politics of FEPC* (Chapel Hill, 1948), pp. 26–27. Gunnar Myrdal, *An American Dilemma* (New York, 1944), p. 830.

18. See *Directory of Agencies in Intergroup Relations* (Chicago, 1949), *passim.*

19. The present inquiry cannot explore in any detail the characteristics of white participants in interracial movements, although certain general observations will be offered at a later point.

20. Eric Hoffer, *The True Believer* (New York, 1951), p. 131. "Whatever the type," says Hoffer, "there is a deep-seated craving common to almost all men of words which determines their attitude toward the prevailing order. It is a craving for recognition; a craving for clearly marked status above the common run of humanity. . . . There is apparently an irremediable insecurity at the core of every intellectual be he noncreative or creative. Even the most gifted and prolific seem to live a life of eternal self-doubting and have to prove their worth anew each day."

21. As far as can be determined by the writer, sociologists have undertaken no systematic studies of white intellectual participants in interracial cooperation movements. Such inquiries could shed light on the types of white intellectuals and their motives for such identification. Moreover, and

perhaps more important, they could reveal the consequences of the crucial roles of these types for structures and specific functions of such movements.

22. This suspicion has a real basis in the experience of members of the Negro community. Interracial cooperation organizations frequently come into being as a result of mounting tensions between minority groups and certain sectors of the "white" population. Their immediate aims under these circumstances are to avert violence and bloodshed, and this is frequently done by exhortations to Negro leaders and their followers to stay within the bounds of the existing framework while appeals are addressed to whites to be less intolerant of Negroes in their midst. In other words these aims are frequently seen by Negroes as efforts to keep the racial pot from boiling over without any effort to douse the fire beneath the vessel.

23. Oliver C. Cox, "The Problems of Negro Civil Rights Organizations," *The Journal of Negro Education*, 20 (Summer Issue, 1951), 363.

24. Wilson Record, *The Negro and the Communist Party* (Chapel Hill, 1951), p. 294. "Many Negroes resent—and understandably so—those whites who pose as their friends, and who attempt in their formal programs and in their personal relations to break through the traditional race barriers. This is the case for several reasons. For one thing, there is the suspicion that such whites want to use Negroes for some ulterior purpose. Also Negroes tend to accept the values of the dominant white majority; the idea of success or getting ahead. And they are likely to view with skepticism and distaste those individuals who do not succeed in these terms." See also Henry Lee Moon, *Balance of Power: The Negro Vote* (Garden City, New York, 1948).

25. This lack of specificity of white objectives in interracial cooperation movements is overcome in a few instances where the whites adhere to some overall political philosophy whereby their specific associations with an organization have some definite place in a totality of actions.

26. A Former Faculty Wife (anonymous), "A Note on Intergroup Conditioning Among an Interracial Faculty at a Negro College," *Journal of Social Forces*, 27, No. 4 (May, 1949); Robert Lucas, "How Negroes Look at Whites," *Tomorrow*, 9, No. 5 (May, 1950), 7.

27. In the war period numerous white intellectuals in the South joined with conservative elements to demand that Negroes forego their insistence on a recognition of their rights during the conflict. Such appeals were frequently offered in terms of "unity" against a common foe. However, most Negroes recognize that such cohesion is usually on the white man's terms, and that this means the continuing subordination of Negroes.

V

World War II and the Negro

The significance of the war years for American Negro history did not lie in government action—notwithstanding Executive Order 8802, which banned discrimination in defense industries, and the appointment of a President's Fair Employment Practices Committee. Nor did a new day in race relations dawn. True, the depression had produced and the New Deal had symbolized and demonstrated increased concern for the oppressed and the poor, white and black; important religious groups and private organizations such as the American Civil Liberties Union and the Southern Conference for Human Welfare had been showing such concern; racist views had for two decades been losing their intellectual respectability; and the CIO had demanded equal treatment for white and black workers and had been admitting many Negroes into its membership. On the other hand, there were major interracial riots in 1943 in Mobile, Beaumont, and Detroit. The significant development in race relations during the war, "overlooked by many recent writers on civil rights" comments Richard M. Dalfiume, was that "a mass militancy became characteristic of the American Negro . . ."

THE "FORGOTTEN YEARS"
OF THE NEGRO REVOLUTION

RICHARD M. DALFIUME

The starting point for gaining an understanding of the Negro's reaction to World War II, according to Richard M. Dalfiume, is knowledge of the discrimination the Negro faced: "Added to the rebuffs from industry and the armed services were a hundred others." The result was paradoxical: "While the morale of the Negro, as an American, was low in regard to the war effort, the Negro, as a member of a minority group, had high morale in his heightened race consciousness and determination to fight for a better position in American society." Exploiting the opportunity provided by the discrepancy between the call for the defense of democracy overseas and the failure to practice it at home, Negroes determined to fight for democracy on two fronts. Cynicism was accompanied by hope and increased militancy as Negroes mounted a growing protest against the racial status quo. Dalfiume traces these developments and white America's limited response to them—a combination of black action and white reaction which set the stage for the civil rights revolution of the 1950's and 1960's.

✱

A recent president of the American Sociological Society addressed himself to a puzzling question about what we know as the Civil Rights Revolution: "Why did social scientists—and sociologists in particular—not foresee the explosion of collective action of Negro Americans toward full integration into American society?"

Reprinted by permission from *Journal of American History*, LV (June 1968), 90–106.

He pointed out that "it is the vigor and urgency of the Negro demand that is new, not its direction or supporting ideas."[1] Without arguing the point further, the lack of knowledge can be attributed to two groups—the ahistorical social scientists, and the historians who, until recently, have neglected modern Negro history.

The search for a "watershed" in recent Negro history ends at the years that comprised World War II, 1939–1945. James Baldwin has written of this period: "The treatment accorded the Negro during the Second World War marks, for me, a turning point in the Negro's relation to America. To put it briefly, and somewhat too simply, a certain hope died, a certain respect for white Americans faded."[2] Writing during World War II, Gunnar Myrdal predicted that the war would act as a "stimulant" to Negro protest, and he felt that "There is bound to be a redefinition of the Negro's status in America as a result of this War."[3] The Negro sociologist E. Franklin Frazier states that World War II marked the point where "The Negro was no longer willing to accept discrimination in employment and in housing without protest."[4] Charles E. Silberman writes that the war was a "turning point" in American race relations, in which "the seeds of the protest movements of the 1950s and 1960s were sown."[5] While a few writers have indicated the importance of these years in the recent Negro protest movement, the majority have failed to do so. Overlooking what went before, most recent books on the subject claim that a Negro "revolution" or "revolt" occurred in 1954, 1955, 1960, or 1963.[6] Because of the neglect of the war period, these years of transition in American race relations comprise the "forgotten years" of the Negro revolution.

To understand how the American Negro reacted to World War II, it is necessary to have some idea of the discrimination he faced. The defense build-up begun by the United States in 1940 was welcomed by Negroes who were disproportionately represented among the unemployed. Employment discrimination in the revived industries, however, was rampant. When Negroes sought jobs at aircraft factories where employers begged for workers, they were informed that "the Negro will be considered only as janitors and in other similar capacities. . . ."[7] Government financed training programs to overcome the shortages of skilled workers discriminated against Negro trainees. When government agencies issued orders against such discrimination, they were ignored.[8]

Increasing defense preparations also meant an expansion of the armed forces. Here, as in industry, however, Negroes faced restrictions. Black Americans were assigned a minimal role and rigidly segregated. In the navy, Negroes could enlist only in the all-Negro messman's branch. The marines and the air corps excluded Negroes entirely. In the army, black Americans were prevented from enlisting, except for a few vacancies in the four regular army Negro units that had been created shortly after the Civil War; and the strength of these had been reduced drastically in the 1920s and 1930s.[9]

Although the most important bread-and-butter issue for Negroes in this period was employment discrimination, their position in the armed forces was an important symbol. If one could not participate fully in the defense of his country, he could not lay claim to the rights of a full-fledged citizen. The NAACP organ, the *Crisis*, expressed this idea in its demand for unrestricted participation in the armed forces: "this is no fight merely to wear a uniform. This is a struggle for status, a struggle to take democracy off of parchment and give it life."[10] Herbert Garfinkel, a student of Negro protest during this period, points out that "in many respects, the discriminatory practices against Negroes which characterized the military programs . . . cut deeper into Negro feelings than did employment discrimination."[11]

Added to the rebuffs from industry and the armed services were a hundred others. Negroes, anxious to contribute to the Red Cross blood program, were turned away. Despite the fact that white and Negro blood is the same biologically, it was deemed inadvisable "to collect and mix caucasian and Negro blood indiscriminately."[12] When Negro citizens called upon the governor of Tennessee to appoint some black members to the state's draft boards, he told them: "This is a white man's country. . . . The Negro had nothing to do with the settling of America."[13] At a time when the United States claimed to be the last bulwark of democracy in a war-torn world, the legislature of Mississippi passed a law requiring different textbooks for Negro schools: all references to voting, elections, and democracy were to be excluded from the black student's books.[14]

The Negro's morale at the beginning of World War II is also partly explained by his experience in World War I. Black America had gone into that war with high morale, generated by the belief that the democratic slogans literally meant what they said. Most Negroes succumbed to the "close ranks" strategy announced by the crusading NAACP editor, W. E. B. Du Bois, who advocated subduing racial grievances in order to give full support to winning the war. But the image of a new democratic order was smashed by the race riots, lynchings, and continued rigid discrimination. The result was a mass trauma and a series of movements among Negroes in the 1920s which were characterized by a desire to withdraw from a white society which wanted little to do with them. When the war crisis of the 1940s came along, the bitter memories of World War I were recalled with the result that there was a built-in cynicism among Negroes toward the democratic slogans of the new war.[15]

Nevertheless, Negroes were part of the general population being stimulated to come to the defense of democracy in the world. When they responded and attempted to do their share, they were turned away. The result was a widespread feeling of frustration and a general decline of the Negro's morale toward the war effort, as compared with the rest of American society. But paradoxically, the Negro's general morale was both low and high.

While the morale of the Negro, as an American, was low in regard to the war effort, the Negro, as a member of a minority group, had high morale in its heightened race consciousness and determination to fight for a better position in American society. The same slogans which caused the Negro to react cynically also served to emphasize the disparity between the creed and the practice of democracy as far as the Negro in America was concerned. Because of his position in society, the Negro reacted to the war both as an American and as a Negro. Discrimination against him had given rise to "a sickly, negative attitude toward national goals, but at the same time a vibrantly positive attitude toward racial aims and aspirations."[16]

When war broke out in Europe in 1939, many black Americans tended to adopt an isolationist attitude. Those taking this position viewed the war as a "white man's war." George Schuyler, the iconoclastic columnist, was a typical spokesman for this view: "So far as the colored peoples of the earth are concerned," Schuyler wrote, "it is a toss-up between the 'democracies' and the dictatorships. . . . [W]hat is there to choose between the rule of the British in Africa and the rule of the Germans in Austria?"[17] Another Negro columnist claimed that it was a blessing to have war so that whites could "mow one another down" rather than "have them quietly murder hundreds of thousands of Africans, East Indians and Chinese. . . ."[18] This kind of isolationism took the form of anticolonialism, particularly against the British. There was some sympathy for France, however, because of its more liberal treatment of black citizens.[19]

Another spur to isolationist sentiment was the obvious hypocrisy of calling for the defense of democracy abroad while it was not a reality at home. The NAACP bitterly expressed this point:

> THE CRISIS is sorry for brutality, blood, and death among the peoples of Europe, just as we were sorry for China and Ethiopia. But the hysterical cries of the preachers of democracy for Europe leave us cold. We want democracy in Alabama and Arkansas, in Mississippi and Michigan, in the District of Columbia—*in the Senate of the United States.*[20]

The editor of the Pittsburgh *Courier* proclaimed that Negroes had their "own war" at home "against oppression and exploitation from without and against disorganization and lack of confidence within"; and the Chicago *Defender* thought that "peace at home" should be the main concern of black Americans.[21]

Many Negroes agreed with columnist Schuyler that "Our war is not against Hitler in Europe, but against the Hitlers in America."[22] The isolationist view of the war in Europe and the antagonism toward Great Britain led to an attitude that was rather neutral toward the Nazis and the Japanese, or, in some extreme cases, pro-Axis. Appealing to this latent feeling, isolationist periodicals tried to gain Negro support in their struggle against American entrance into the war.[23] By 1940 there were also Negro cults such as the Ethiopian Pacific Movement, the World Wide Friends of Africa, the Brotherhood of Liberty for the Black People of America, and many others, which preached unity among the world's darker people, including Japanese. Many of these groups exploited the latent anti-semitism common among Negroes in the urban ghettos by claiming that the racial policies of Germany were correct.[24]

Reports reached the public that some black Americans were expressing a vicarious pleasure over successes by the "yellow" Japanese and by Germany. In a quarrel with her employer in North Carolina, a Negro woman retorted: "I hope Hitler does come, because if he does he will get you first!" A Negro truck driver in Philadelphia was held on charges of treason after he was accused of telling a Negro soldier that he should not be in uniform and that "This is a white man's government and war and it's no damned good." After Pearl Harbor, a Negro share cropper told his landlord: "By the way, Captain, I hear the Japs done declared war on you white folks." Another Negro declared that he was going to get his eyes slanted so that the next time a white man shoved him around he could fight back.[25]

It is impossible to determine the extent of this kind of pro-Axis sentiment among Negroes, but it was widespread enough for the Negro press to make rather frequent mention of it.[26] In 1942 and 1943 the federal government did arrest the members of several pro-Japanese Negro cults in Chicago, New York, Newark, New Jersey, and East St. Louis, Illinois. Although the numbers involved were small, the evidence indicated that Japanese agents had been at work among these groups and had capitalized on Negro grievances.[27]

By the time of the Pearl Harbor attack, certain fundamental changes were taking place among American Negroes. Nowhere is this more evident than in a comparison of Negroes' reactions to World Wars I and II. The dominant opinion among them toward World War I was expressed by Du Bois. In World War II, most Negroes looked upon the earlier stand as a great mistake. The dominant attitude during World War II was that the Negro must fight for democracy on two fronts—at home as well as abroad. This opinion had first appeared in reaction to the discriminatory treatment of Negro soldiers;[28] but with the attack on Pearl Harbor, this idea, stated in many different ways, became the slogan of black America.[29]

American Negroes took advantage of the war to tie their racial demands to the ideology for which the war was being fought. Before Pearl Harbor, the Negro press frequently pointed out the similarity of American treatment of Negroes and Nazi Germany's treatment of minorities. In 1940, the Chicago *Defender* featured a mock invasion of the United States by Germany in which the Nazis were victorious because a fifth column of southern senators and other racists aided them.[30] Later the *Crisis* printed an editorial which compared the white supremacy doctrine in America to the Nazi plan for Negroes, a comparison which indicated a marked similarity.[31] Even the periodical of the conservative Urban League made such comparisons.[32]

Many Negroes adopted a paradoxical stand on the meaning of the war. At the same time that it was labeled a "white man's war," Negroes often stated that they were bound to benefit from it. For example, Schuyler could argue that the war was not for democracy, but "Peace means . . . a continuation of the status quo . . . which must be ended if the Negro is to get free." And accordingly, the longer the war the better: "Perhaps in the shuffle we who have been on the bottom of the deck for so long will find ourselves at the top."[33]

Cynicism and hope existed side by side in the Negro mind. Cynicism was often the attitude expressed after some outrageous example of discrimination. After Pearl Harbor, however, a mixture of hope and certainty—great changes favorable to the Negro would result from the war and things would never be the same again—became the dominant attitude. Hope was evident in the growing realization that the war provided the Negro with an excellent opportunity to prick the conscience of white America. "What an opportunity the crisis has been . . . for one to persuade, embarrass, compel and shame our government and our nation . . . into a more enlightened attitude toward a tenth of its people!" the Pittsburgh *Courier* proclaimed.[34] Certainty that a better life would result from the war was based on the belief that revolutionary forces had been released throughout the world. It was no longer a "white man's world," and the "myth of white invincibility" had been shattered for good.[35]

There was a growing protest against the racial status quo of black Americans; this was evidenced by the reevaluation of segregation in all sections of the country. In the North there was self-criticism of past acceptance of certain forms of segregation.[36] Southern Negroes became bolder in openly questioning the sacredness of segregation. In October 1942, a group of southern Negro leaders met in Durham, North Carolina, and issued a statement on race relations. In addition to endorsing the idea that the Negro should fight for democracy at home as well as abroad, these leaders called for complete equality for the Negro in American life. While recognizing the "strength and age" of the South's racial customs, the Durham meeting was "fundamentally opposed to the principle and practice of compulsory segregation in our American society." In addition, there were reports of deep discontent among southern Negro college students and evidence that political activity among the blacks of the South, particularly on the local level, was increasing.[37]

The American Negro, stimulated by the democratic ideology of the war, was reexamining his position in American society. "It cannot be doubted that the spirit of American Negroes in all classes is different today from what it was a generation ago," Myrdal observed.[38] Part of this new spirit was an increased militancy, a readiness to protest loud and strong against grievances.

The crisis gave Negroes more reason and opportunity to protest. Representative of all the trends of black thought and action—the cynicism, the hope, the heightened race consciousness, the militancy—was the March on Washington Movement (MOWM).

The general idea of exerting mass pressure upon the government to end defense discrimination did not originate with A. Philip Randolph's call for a march on Washington, D.C., in early 1941.[39] Agitation for mass pressure had grown since the failure of a group of Negro leaders to gain any major concessions from President Franklin D. Roosevelt in September 1940.[40] Various organizations, such as the NAACP, the Committee for Participation of Negroes in the National Defense, and the Allied Committees on National Defense, held mass protest meetings around the country in late 1940 and early 1941.[41] The weeks passed and these efforts did not seem to have any appreciable impact on the government; Walter White, Randolph, and other Negro leaders could not even secure an appointment to see the President. "Bitterness grew at an alarming pace throughout the country," White recalled.[42]

It remained, however, for Randolph to consolidate this protest. In January 1941, he wrote an article for the Negro press which pointed out the failure of committees and individuals to achieve action against defense discrimination. "Only power can effect the enforcement and adoption of a given policy," Randolph noted; and "Power is the active principle of only the organized masses, the masses united for a definite purpose." To focus the weight of the black masses, he suggested that 10,000 Negroes march on Washington, D.C., with the slogan: "We loyal Negro-American citizens demand the right to work and fight for our country."[43]

This march appeal led to the formation of one of the most significant—though today almost forgotten—Negro protest movements. The MOWM pioneered what has become the common denominator of today's Negro revolt—"the spontaneous involvement of large masses of Negroes in a political protest."[44] Furthermore, as August Meier and Elliott Rudwick have recently pointed out, the MOWM clearly foreshadowed "the goals, tactics, and strategy of the mid-twentieth-century civil rights movement." Whites were excluded purposely to make it an all-Negro movement; its main weapon was direct action on the part of the black masses. Furthermore, the MOWM took as its major concern the economic problems of urban slum-dwellers.[45]

Randolph's tactic of mass pressure through a demonstration of black power struck a response among the Negro masses. The number to march on Washington on July 1, 1941, was increased to 50,000, and only Roosevelt's agreement to issue an executive order establishing a President's Committee on Fair Employment Practices led to a cancellation of the march. Negroes then, and scholars later, generally interpreted this as a great victory. But the magnitude of the victory is diminished when one examines the original MOWM demands: an executive order forbidding government contracts to be awarded to a firm which practiced discrimination in hiring, an executive order abolishing discrimination in government defense training courses, an executive order requiring the United States Employment Service to supply workers without regard to race, an executive order abolishing segregation in the armed forces, an executive order abolishing discrimination and segregation on account of race in all departments of the federal government, and a request from the President to Congress to pass a law forbidding benefits of the National Labor Relations Act to unions denying Negroes membership. Regardless of the extent of the success of the MOWM, however, it represented something different in black protest. Unlike the older Negro movements, the MOWM had captured the imagination of the masses.[46]

Although overlooked by most recent writers on civil rights, a mass militancy became characteristic of the American Negro in World War II. This was symbolized by the MOWM and was the reason for its wide appeal. Furthermore, older Negro organizations found themselves pushed into militant stands. For example, the NAACP underwent a tremendous growth in its membership and became representative of the Negro masses for the first time in its history. From 355 branches and a membership of 50,556 in 1940, the NAACP grew to 1,073 branches with a membership of slightly less than 450,000 in 1946.[47] The editors of the Pittsburgh *Courier* recognized that a new spirit was present in black America. In the past, Negroes

made the mistake of relying entirely upon the gratitude and sense of fair play of the American people. Now we are disillusioned. We have neither faith in promises, nor a high opinion of the integrity of the American people, where race is involved. Experience has taught us that we must rely primarily upon our own efforts. . . . That is why we protest, agitate, and demand that all forms of color prejudice be blotted out. . . .[48]

By the time of the Japanese attack on Pearl Harbor, many in America, both inside and outside of the government, were worried over the state of Negro morale. There was fear that the Negro would be disloyal.[49] The depth of white ignorance about the causes for the Negro's cynicism and low morale is obvious from the fact that the black press was blamed for the widespread discontent. The double victory attitude constantly displayed in Negro newspapers throughout the war, and supported by most black Americans, was considered as verging on disloyalty by most whites. White America, ignorant of the American Negroes' reaction to World War I, thought that black citizens should subdue their grievances for the duration.

During World War II, there was pressure upon the White House and the justice department from within the federal government to indict some Negro editors for sedition and interference with the war effort. President Roosevelt refused to sanction this, however. There was also an attempt to deny newsprint to the more militant Negro newspapers, but the President put an end to this when the matter was brought to his attention.[50] The restriction of Negro newspapers from military installations became so widespread that the war department had to call a halt to this practice in 1943.[51] These critics failed to realize that, although serving to unify black opinion, the Negro press simply reflected the Negro mind.

One of the most widely publicized attacks on the Negro press was made by the southern white liberal, Virginius Dabney, editor of the Richmond *Times Dispatch*. He charged that "extremist" Negro newspapers and Negro leaders were "demanding an overnight revolution in race relations," and as a consequence they were "stirring up interracial hate." Dabney concluded his indictment by warning that "it is a foregone conclusion that if an attempt is made forcibly to abolish segregation throughout the South, violence and bloodshed will result."[52] The Negro press reacted vigorously to such charges. Admitting that there were "all-or-nothing" Negro leaders, the Norfolk *Journal and Guide* claimed they were created by the "nothing-at-all" attitude of whites.[53] The Chicago *Defender* and Baltimore *Afro-American* took the position that they were only pointing out the shortcomings of American democracy, and this was certainly not disloyal.[54] The NAACP and the Urban League claimed that it was patriotic for Negroes to protest against undemocratic practices, and those who sought to stifle this protest were the unpatriotic ones.[55]

The Negro masses simply did not support a strategy of moderating their grievances for the duration of the war. After attending an Office of Facts and Figures conference for Negro leaders in March 1942, Roy Wilkins of the NAACP wrote:

> . . . it is a plain fact that no Negro leader with a constituency can face his members today and ask full support for the war in the light of the atmosphere the government has created. Some Negro educators who are responsible only to their boards or trustees might do so, but the heads of no organized groups would dare do so.[56]

By 1942, the federal government began investigating Negro morale in order to find out what could be done to improve it. This project was undertaken by the Office of Facts and Figures and its successor, the Office of War Information.[57] Surveys by these agencies indicated that the great amount of national publicity given the defense program only served to increase the Negro's awareness that he was not participating fully in that program. Black Americans found it increasingly difficult to reconcile their treatment with the announced war aims. Urban Negroes were the most resentful over defense discrimination, particularly against the treatment accorded black members of the armed forces. Never before had Negroes been so united behind a cause: the war had served to focus their attention on their unequal status in American society. Black Americans were almost unanimous in wanting a show of good intention from the federal government that changes would be made in the racial status quo.[58]

The government's inclination to take steps to improve Negro morale, and the Negro's desire for change, were frustrated by the general attitude of white Americans. In 1942, after two years of militant agitation by Negroes, six out of ten white Americans felt that black Americans were satisfied with things the way they were and that Negroes were receiving all of the opportunities they deserved. More than half of all whites interviewed in the Northwest and West believed that there should be separate schools, separate restaurants, and separate neighborhoods for the races. A majority of whites in all parts of the country believed that the Negro would not be treated any better after the war than in 1942 and that the Negro's lesser role in society was due to his own shortcomings rather than anything the whites had done.[59] The white opposition to racial change may have provided the rationale for governmental inactivity. Furthermore, the white obstinance must have added to the bitterness of black Americans.

Although few people recognized it, the war was working a revolution in American race relations. Sociologist Robert E. Park felt that the racial structure of society was "cracking," and the equilibrium reached after the Civil War seemed "to be under attack at a time and under conditions when it is particularly difficult to defend it."[60] Sociologist Howard W. Odum wrote from the South that there was "an unmeasurable and unbridgeable distance between the white South and the reasonable expectation of the Negro."[61] White southerners opposed to change in the racial mores sensed changes occurring among "their" Negroes. "Outsiders" from the North, Mrs. Franklin Roosevelt, and the Roosevelt Administration were all accused of attempting to undermine segregation under the pretense of wartime necessity.[62]

Racial tensions were common in all sections of the country during the war.[63] There were riots in 1943. Tensions were high because Negro Americans were challenging the status quo. When fourteen prominent Negroes, conservatives and liberals, southerners and northerners, were asked in 1944 what they thought the black American wanted, their responses were almost unanimous. Twelve of the fourteen said they thought that Negroes wanted full political equality, economic equality, equality of opportunity, and full social equality with the abolition of legal segregation.[64] The war had stimulated the race consciousness and the desire for change among Negroes.

Most American Negroes and their leaders wanted the government to institute a revolutionary change in its race policy. Whereas the policy had been acquiescence in segregation since the end of Reconstruction, the government was now asked to set the example for the rest of the nation by supporting integration. This was the demand voiced by the great majority of the Negro leaders called together in March 1942 by the Office of Facts and Figures.[65] *Crisis* magazine summarized the feelings of many black Americans: Negroes have "waited thus far in vain for some sharp and dramatic notice that this war is not to maintain the status quo here."[66]

The White House, and it was not alone, failed to respond to the revolutionary changes occurring among the nation's largest minority. When the Fraternal Council of Negro Churches called upon President Roosevelt to end discrimination in the defense industries and armed forces, the position taken was that "it would be very bad to give encouragement beyond the point where actual results can be accomplished."[67] Roosevelt did bestir himself over particularly outrageous incidents. When Roland Hayes, a noted Negro singer, was beaten and jailed in a Georgia town, the Presi-

dent dashed off a note to his attorney general: "Will you have
someone go down and check up . . . and see if any law was vio-
lated. I suggest you send a northerner."[68]

Roosevelt was not enthusiastic about major steps in the race
relations field proposed by interested individuals within and without the government.[69] In February 1942 Edwin R. Embree of the
Julius Rosenwald Fund, acutely aware of the growing crisis in
American race relations, urged Roosevelt to create a commission
of experts on race relations to advise him on what steps the government should take to improve matters. FDR's answer to this proposal indicates that he felt race relations was one of the reform
areas that had to be sacrificed for the present in order to prosecute
the war. He thought such a commission was "premature" and that
"we must start winning the war . . . before we do much general
planning for the future." The President believed that "there is a
danger of such long-range planning becoming projects of wide
influence in escape from the realities of war. I am not convinced
that we can be realists about the war and planners for the future
at this critical time."[70]

After the race riots of 1943, numerous proposals for a national
committee on race relations were put forward; but FDR refused
to change his position. Instead, the President simply appointed
Jonathan Daniels to gather information from all government departments on current race tensions and what they were doing to
combat them.[71] This suggestion for what would eventually become a President's Committee on Civil Rights would have to wait
until a President recognized that a revolution in race relations was
occurring and that action by the government could no longer be
put off. In the interim, many would share the shallow reasoning
of Secretary of War Stimson that the cause of racial tension was
"the deliberate effort . . . on the part of certain radical leaders of
the colored race to use the war for obtaining . . . race equality and
interracial marriages. . . ."[72]

The hypocrisy and paradox involved in fighting a world war for
the four freedoms and against aggression by an enemy preaching
a master race ideology, while at the same time upholding racial
segregation and white supremacy, were too obvious. The war
crisis provided American Negroes with a unique opportunity to
point out, for all to see, the difference between the American
creed and practice. The democratic ideology and rhetoric with
which the war was fought stimulated a sense of hope and certainty in black Americans that the old race structure was de-

stroyed forever. In part, this confidence was also the result of the mass militancy and race consciousness that developed in these years. When the expected white acquiescence in a new racial order did not occur, the ground was prepared for the civil rights revolution of the 1950s and 1960s; the seeds were indeed sown in the World War II years.

NOTES

1. Everett C. Hughes, "Race Relations and the Sociological Imagination," *American Sociological Review*, XXVIII (Dec. 1963), 879.

2. Quoted in J. Milton Yinger, *A Minority Group in American Society* (New York, 1965), 52. Many Negroes agreed with James Baldwin in recalling the bitterness they experienced. William Brink and Louis Harris, *The Negro Revolution in America* (New York, 1964), 50.

3. Gunnar Myrdal, *An American Dilemma: The Negro Problem and Modern Democracy* (New York, 1944), 756, 997.

4. E. Franklin Frazier, *The Negro in the United States* (rev. ed., New York, 1957), 682.

5. Charles E. Silberman, *Crisis in Black and White* (New York, 1964), 60, 65.

6. See, for example, Lewis M. Killian and Charles Grigg, *Racial Crisis in America* (Englewood Cliffs, 1964); Louis E. Lomax, *The Negro Revolt* (New York, 1962); Leonard Broom and Norval D. Glenn, *Transformation of the Negro American* (New York, 1965); Brink and Harris, *Negro Revolution in America*.

7. Quoted in Louis Coleridge Kesselman, *The Social Politics of FEPC: A Study in Reform Pressure Movements* (Chapel Hill, 1948), 7.

8. Charles H. Thompson, "The American Negro and the National Defense," *Journal of Negro Education*, IX (Oct. 1940), 547–552; Frazier, *Negro in the United States*, 559–606; Robert C. Weaver, "Racial Employment Trends in National Defense," *Phylon*, II (4th Quarter, 1941), 337–358.

9. See Richard M. Dalfiume, "Desegregation of the United States Armed Forces, 1939–1953" (doctoral dissertation, University of Missouri, 1966), 30–57; Ulysses Lee, *United States Army in World War II: Special Studies: The Employment of Negro Troops* (Washington, 1966), 32–87.

10. "For Manhood in National Defense," *Crisis*, 47 (Dec. 1940), 375.

11. Herbert Garfinkel, *When Negroes March: The March on Washington Movement in the Organizational Politics for FEPC* (Glencoe, Ill., 1959), 20.

12. General James C. Magee, Surgeon General, to Assistant Secretary of War John J. McCloy, Sept. 3, 1941, ASW 291.2, Record Group 335 (National Archives); Pittsburgh *Courier*, Jan. 3, 1942.

13. Pittsburgh *Courier*, Nov. 2, 1940.

14. "Text Books in Mississippi," *Opportunity*, XVIII (April 1940), 99.

15. Kenneth B. Clark, "Morale of the Negro on the Home Front: World Wars I and II," *Journal of Negro Education*, XII (Summer 1943), 417–428; Walter White, " 'It's Our Country, Too': The Negro Demands the Right to be Allowed to Fight for It," *Saturday Evening Post*, 213 (Dec. 14, 1940), 27, 61, 63, 66, 68; Metz T. P. Lochard, "Negroes and Defense," *Nation*, 152 (Jan. 4, 1941), 14–16.

16. Cornelius L. Golightly, "Negro Higher Education and Democratic Negro Morale," *Journal of Negro Education*, XI (July 1942), 324. See also Horace R. Cayton, "Negro Morale," *Opportunity*, XIX (Dec. 1941), 371–375; Louis Wirth, "Morale and Minority Groups," *American Journal of Sociology*, XLVII (Nov. 1941), 415–433; Kenneth B. Clark, "Morale Among Negroes," Goodwin Watson, ed., *Civilian Morale* (Boston, 1942), 228–248; Arnold M. Rose, *The Negro's Morale: Group Identification and Protest* (Minneapolis, 1949), 5–7, 54–55, 122–124, 141–144.

17. Pittsburgh *Courier*, Sept. 9, 1939.

18. P. L. Prattis in *ibid.*, Sept. 2, 1939. Similar sentiments were expressed by Chicago *Defender* editorials, May 25, June 15, 1940.

19. Pittsburgh *Courier*, Sept. 9, 16, 1939.

20. "Lynching and Liberty," *Crisis*, 47 (July 1940), 209.

21. Pittsburgh *Courier*, Sept. 9, 1939; Chicago *Defender*, May 25, 1940.

22. Pittsburgh *Courier*, Dec. 21, 1940.

23. Lee, *The Employment of Negro Troops*, 65–67; Horace Mann Bond, "Should the Negro Care Who Wins the War?" *Annals*, CCXXIII (Sept. 1942), 81–84; Adam Clayton Powell, Jr., "Is This a 'White Man's War'?" *Common Sense*, XI (April 1942), 111–113.

24. Roi Ottley, "A White Folk's War?" *Common Ground*, II (Spring 1942), 28–31, and *'New World A-Coming'* (Boston, 1943), 322–342; Lunnabelle Wedlock, *The Reaction of Negro Publications and Organizations to German Anti-Semitism* (Washington, 1942), 116–193; Alfred M. Lee, "Subversive Individuals of Minority Status," *Annals*, CCXXIII (Sept. 1942), 167–168.

25. St. Clair Drake and Horace R. Cayton, *Black Metropolis* (New York, 1945), 744–745; Ottley, *'New World A-Coming,'* 306–310; Horace R. Cayton, "Fighting for White Folks?" *Nation*, 155 (Sept. 26, 1942), 267–270.

26. "The Negro and Nazism," *Opportunity*, XVIII (July 1940), 194–195; Horace R. Cayton in Pittsburgh *Courier*, Dec. 20, 1941; J. A. Rodgers in *ibid.*, Dec. 27, 1941; Chandler Owen in Norfolk *Journal and Guide*, Dec. 13, 1941; report in Baltimore *Afro-American*, Nov. 21, 1942.

27. New York *Times*, Sept. 15, 22, 1942, Jan. 14, 28, 1943.

28. "Conference Resolutions," *Crisis*, 47 (Sept. 1940), 296; "Where the Negro Stands," *Opportunity*, XIX (April 1941), 98; Lester M. Jones, "The Editorial Policy of Negro Newspapers of 1917–1918 as Compared with That of 1941–1942," *Journal of Negro History*, XXIX (Jan. 1944), 24–31.

29. Baltimore *Afro-American*, Dec. 20, 1941, Feb. 7, 1942; Norfolk *Journal and Guide*, March 21, 1942; "Now Is the Time Not to Be Silent," *Crisis*, 49 (Jan. 1942), 7; "The Fate of Democracy," *Opportunity*, XX (Jan. 1942), 2. Two Negro newspapers adopted this theme for their war slogans. The Pittsburgh *Courier*, Feb. 14, 1942, initiated a "Double V" campaign—"victory over our enemies at home and victory over our enemies on the battlefields abroad." When a Negro was brutally lynched in Sikeston, Missouri, a few weeks after Pearl Harbor, the Chicago *Defender*, March 14, 1942, adopted as its war slogan: "Remember Pearl Harbor and Sikeston Too." See also Ralph N. Davis, "The Negro Newspapers and the War," *Sociology and Social Research*, XXVII (May-June 1943), 373–380.

30. Chicago *Defender*, Sept. 25, 1940.

31. "Nazi Plan for Negroes Copies Southern U. S. A.," *Crisis*, 48 (March 1941), 71.

32. "American Nazism," *Opportunity*, XIX (Feb. 1941), 35. See also editorials in Pittsburgh *Courier*, March 15, April 19, 26, 1941, May 30, 1942; Chicago *Defender*, Sept. 7, 1940; Norfolk *Journal and Guide*, April 19, 1941; Baltimore *Afro-American*, Feb. 17, 1940, Sept. 6, 1941.

33. Pittsburgh *Courier*, Oct. 5, 1940; George S. Schuyler, "A Long War Will Aid the Negro," *Crisis*, 50 (Nev. 1943), 328–329, 344. See also J. A.

Rodgers in Pittsburgh *Courier*, June 28, 1941; Horace R. Cayton in *ibid.*, March 22, 1941; Baltimore *Afro-American*, Sept. 12, 16, 1939; Guion Griffis Johnson, "The Impact of War Upon the Negro," *Journal of Negro Education*, X (July 1941), 596–611.

34. Pittsburgh *Courier*, Jan. 10, Aug. 8, 1942. Charles S. Johnson, "The Negro and the Present Crisis," *Journal of Negro Education*, X (July 1941), 585–595. Opinion surveys indicated that most Negro soldiers expressed support for this kind of opportunism. Samuel A. Stouffer and others, *The American Soldier* (2 vols., Princeton, 1949), I, 516–517.

35. Baltimore *Afro-American*, June 12, Oct. 31, 1942; Walter White in Pittsburgh *Courier*, May 23, 1942. The impact of world affairs on the American Negro is detailed in Harold R. Isaacs, *The New World of Negro Americans* (New York, 1963).

36. See editorials in Pittsburgh *Courier*, Dec. 28, 1940; Feb. 1, June 28, 1941; May 30, 1942; Baltimore *Afro-American*, May 23, 1942.

37. Charles S. Johnson, *To Stem This Tide* (Boston, 1943), 131–139; Malcolm S. MacLean, president of Hampton Institute, to Marvin H. McIntyre, Nov. 20, 1942, OF 93, Roosevelt Papers (Franklin D. Roosevelt Library, Hyde Park); George B. Tindall, "The Significance of Howard W. Odum to Southern History: A Preliminary Estimate," *Journal of Southern History*, XXIV (Aug. 1958), 302. Anthropologist Hortense Powdermaker, *After Freedom: A Cultural Study of the Deep South* (New York, 1939), 331–333, 353, supports the observations of a tendency to rebel among the younger Negroes of the South. See also Ralph J. Bunche, "The Negro in the Political Life of the United States," *Journal of Negro Education*, X (July 1941), 567–584; Myrdal, *American Dilemma*, 499; Henry Lee Moon, *Balance of Power: The Negro Vote* (Garden City, 1948), 178–179.

38. Myrdal, *American Dilemma*, 744.

39. Garfinkel, *When Negroes March*, fails to emphasize this point.

40. Walter White, *A Man Called White* (New York, 1948), 186–187; "White House Blesses Jim Crow," *Crisis*, 47 (Nov. 1940), 350–351, 357; Dalfiume, "Desegregation of the United States Armed Forces, 1939–1953," 46–51.

41. Pittsburgh *Courier*, Dec. 7, 14, 21, 1940; Jan. 4, 25, Feb. 8, 1941.

42. White, *A Man Called White*, 189–190.

43. Pittsburgh *Courier*, Jan. 25, 1941.

44. Garfinkel, *When Negroes March*, 8.

45. August Meier and Elliott M. Rudwick, *From Plantation to Ghetto: An Interpretative History of American Negroes* (New York, 1966), 222.

46. "Proposals of the Negro March-On-Washington Committee to President Roosevelt for Urgent Consideration," June 21, 1941, OF 391, Roosevelt Papers. The standard versions of a Negro "victory" are Garfinkel, *When Negroes March*; Kesselman, *The Social Politics of FEPC*; and Louis Ruchames, *Race, Jobs, & Politics: The Story of FEPC* (New York, 1953). For a different interpretation, see Dalfiume, "Desegregation of the United States Armed Forces, 1939–1953," 172–177. The Negro press generally recognized that the MOWM represented something new. The Pittsburgh *Courier*, July 5, 1941, claimed: "We begin to feel at last that the day when we shall gain full rights . . . of American citizenship is now not far distant." The Chicago *Defender*, June 28, July 12, 1941, felt that the white man will be convinced that "the American black man has decided henceforth and forever to abandon the timid role of Uncle-Tomism in his struggle. . . ." The tactics of the MOWM had "demonstrated to the doubting Thomases among us that only mass action can pry open the iron doors that have been erected against America's black minority."

47. Frazier, *The Negro in the United States*, 537; Charles Radford Lawrence, "Negro Organizations in Crisis: Depression, New Deal, World War II"

(doctoral dissertation, Columbia University, 1953), 103; Myrdal, *American Dilemma*, 851–852. Such close observers of American race relations as Will Alexander, Edwin Embree, and Charles S. Johnson recognized the changing character of Negro protest. They believed that "the characteristic movements among Negroes are now for the first time becoming proletarian, as contrasted to upper class or intellectual influence that was typical of previous movements. The present proletarian direction grows out of the increasing general feelings of protest against discrimination, especially in the armed forces and in our war activities generally. The present movements are led in part by such established leaders as A. Philip Randolph, Walter White, etc. There is likelihood (and danger) that the movement may be seized upon by some more picturesque figure who may be less responsible and less interested in actual improvement of conditions. One of the most likely of the potential leaders is A. Clayton Powell, Jr." Memorandum of Conferences of Alexander, Johnson, and Embree on the Rosenwald Fund's Program in Race Relations, June 27, 1942, Race Relations folder, Rosenwald Fund Papers (Fisk University).

48. Pittsburgh *Courier*, Sept. 12, 1942. See also Roscoe E. Lewis, "The Role of Pressure Groups in Maintaining Morale Among Negroes," *Journal of Negro Education*, XII (Summer 1943), 464–473; Earl Brown, "American Negroes and the War," *Harper's Magazine*, 184 (April 1942), 545–552; Roi Ottley, "Negro Morale," *New Republic*, 105 (Nov. 10, 1941), 613–615; Thomas Sancton, "Something's Happened to the Negro," *New Republic*, 108 (Feb. 8, 1943), 175–179; Stanley High, "How the Negro Fights for Freedom," *Reader's Digest*, 41 (July 1942), 113–118; H. C. Brearley, "The Negro's New Belligerency," *Phylon*, V (4th Quarter 1944), 339–345.

49. Memorandum to Assistant Secretary of War McCloy from G-2, June 27, 1942, ASW 291.2, Record Group 335.

50. White, *A Man Called White*, 207–208; R. Keith Kane to Ulric Bell, May 14, 1942, OFF 992.11, Record Group 208; Memorandum to Robert A. Lovett from McCloy, March 6, 1942, ASW 291.2, Record Group 335.

51. Baltimore *Afro-American*, Sept. 30, 1941; Pittsburgh *Courier*, March 8, 1941, Nov. 13, 1943. Assistant Secretary of War McCloy, who was also head of the war department's Advisory Committee on Negro Troop Policies, held a critical view of the Negro press that was common in the army. McCloy to Herbert Elliston, editor of the Washington *Post*, Aug. 5, 1943, ASW 292.2, Record Group 335.

52. Virginius Dabney, "Nearer and Nearer the Precipice," *Atlantic Monthly*, 171 (Jan. 1943), 94–100; Virginius Dabney, "Press and Morale," *Saturday Review of Literature*, XXV (July 4, 1942), 5–6; 24–25.

53. Norfolk *Journal and Guide*, Aug. 15, 1942. See also *Journal and Guide* editorials of Oct. 17, April 25, 1942; and March 6, 1943, for a defense of Negro militancy.

54. Chicago *Defender*, Dec. 20, 1941; Baltimore *Afro-American*, Jan. 9, 1943.

55. Pittsburgh *Courier*, May 8, June 19, 1943. A few conservative Negroes joined whites in criticizing the growing militancy. James E. Shepard, Negro president of North Carolina College for Negroes, asked the administration to do something to undercut the growing support of the militants among young Negroes: "Those who seek to stir them up about rights and not duties are their enemies." Shepard to Secretary of the Navy Frank Knox, Sept. 28, 1940, OF 93, Roosevelt Papers. Frederick D. Patterson, president of Tuskegee Institute, made it clear in his newspaper column and in talks with administration officials that he believed in all-out support for the war effort by Negroes regardless of segregation and discrimination. "Stimson Diary," Jan. 29, 1943 (Yale University Library), and columns by Patterson in the Pittsburgh *Courier*, Jan. 16, July 3, 1943. Such conservatives were bitterly attacked in

the Negro press. The black leader who urged his people to relax their determination to win full participation in American life was a "misleader and a false prophet," the Norfolk *Journal and Guide*, May 2, 1942, proclaimed. Such people "endangered" the interests of Negroes by "compromising with the forces that promote and uphold segregation and discrimination," wrote the editor of the Chicago *Defender*, April 5, 1941. The *Crisis* charged that those Negroes who succumbed to segregation as "realism" provided a rationale for those whites who sought to perpetuate segregation. "Government Blesses Separatism," *Crisis*, 50 (April 1943), 105.

56. Memorandum to White from Roy Wilkins, March 24, 1942, Stephen J. Spingarn Papers (Harry S. Truman Library, Independence).

57. Memorandum to Archibald MacLeish from Kane, Feb. 14, 1942; Bell to Embree, Feb. 23, 1942, OFF 002.11, Record Group 208. Some government agencies displayed timidity when it came to a subject as controversial as the race question. Jonathan Daniels, Assistant Director in Charge of Civilian Mobilization, Office of Civilian Defense, urged the creation of a Division of American Unity within the OCD, but his superiors decided Negro morale was "too hot a potato." Memoranda to James Landis, April 1, 7, 1942; Daniels to Howard W. Odum, Aug. 24, 1942, Jonathan Daniels Papers (University of North Carolina).

58. "Reports from the Special Services Division Submitted April 23, 1942; Negro Organizations and the War Effort"; Cornelius Golightly, "Negro Morale in Boston," Special Services Division Report No. 7, May 19, 1942; Special Services Division Report No. 5, May 15, 1942: "Negro Conference at Lincoln University"; Special Services Division Memorandum, "Report on Recent Factors Increasing Negro-White Tension," Nov. 2, 1942. All are in OFF and OWI files in Record Group 44.

59. "Intelligence Report: White Attitudes Toward Negroes," OWI, Bureau of Intelligence, Aug. 5, 1942; same title dated July 28, 1942, Record Group 44. Hazel Gaudet Erskine, "The Polls: Race Relations," *Public Opinion Quarterly*, XXVI (Spring 1962), 137–148.

60. Robert E. Park, "Racial Ideologies," William Fielding Ogburn, ed., *American Society in Wartime* (Chicago, 1943), 174.

61. Howard W. Odum, *Race and Rumors of Race: Challenge to American Crisis* (Chapel Hill, 1943), 7; for a similar view, see Johnson, *To Stem This Tide*, 67–68, 73, 89–107, 113, 117.

62. John Temple Graves, "The Southern Negro and the War Crisis," *Virginia Quarterly Review*, 18 (Autumn 1942), 500–517; Clark Foreman, "Race Tension in the South," *New Republic*, 107 (Sept. 21, 1942), 340–342.

63. Alfred McClung Lee and Norman Daymond Humphrey, *Race Riot* (New York, 1943); Carey McWilliams, "Race Tensions: Second Phase," *Common Ground*, IV (Autumn 1943), 7–12.

64. Rayford W. Logan, ed., *What the Negro Wants* (Chapel Hill, 1944).

65. Memorandum to White from Wilkins, March 23, 1942, Spingarn Papers; Pittsburgh *Courier*, March 28, 1942; Norfolk *Journal and Guide*, March 28, 1942.

66. "U. S. A. Needs Sharp Break With the Past," *Crisis*, 49 (May 1942), 151.

67. "A Statement to the President of the United States Concerning the Present World Crisis by Negro Church Leaders Called by the Executive Committee of the Fraternal Council of Negro Churches of America," Feb. 17, 1942; McIntyre to MacLean, Chairman of the President's Committee on Fair Employment Practice, Feb. 19, 1942, OF 93, Roosevelt Papers.

68. Memorandum to the Attorney General from the President, Aug. 26, 1942, OF 93, *ibid*.

69. Franklin Roosevelt's conservative and "leave well enough alone" attitude toward Negro rights is discussed in Arthur M. Schlesinger, Jr., *The*

Age of Roosevelt: The Politics of Upheaval (Boston, 1960), 431; Frank Freidel, *F. D. R. and the South* (Baton Rouge, 1965), 73, 81, 97; Mary McLeod
Bethune, "My Secret Talks with F. D. R.," *Ebony*, IV (April 1949), 42–51. Perhaps Roosevelt's conservative attitude is responsible for his privately expressed dislike of the NAACP. In 1943 Arthur B. Spingarn, president of the
NAACP, asked him to write a letter praising the twenty-five years of service
by White to that organization. On one version of the proposed letter there is
an attached note which reads: "Miss Tully brought this in. Says the President doesn't think too much of this organization—not to be to[o] fullsome—
tone it down a bit." Roosevelt to Spingarn, Oct. 1, 1943; PPF 1226, Roosevelt
Papers.

70. Roosevelt to Embree, March 16, 1942, in answer to Embree to Roosevelt, Feb. 3, 1942, OF 93, Roosevelt Papers. In his covering letter to the President's secretary, Embree emphasized that his proposed commission should
address itself to the problem of race around the world as well as at home: "A
serious weakness both in America and among the united nations is the low
morale of the 'colored peoples' to whom this war is being pictured as simply
another struggle of the white man for domination of the world. This condition is becoming acute among the Negro group at home and among important allies abroad, especially the Chinese and the residents of Malaya, the
East Indies, and the Philippines." Embree to McIntyre, Feb. 3, 1942, Commission on Race and Color folder, Rosenwald Fund Papers.

71. In June 1943, Embree and John Collier, Commissioner of Indian
Affairs, developed an idea for a committee established by the President "to
assume special responsibility in implementing the Bill of Rights of the Con-
stitution, particularly in defending racial minorities at a time of crisis."
Memorandum to Johnson and Alexander from Embree, June 16, 1943, Race
Relations folder, Rosenwald Fund Papers. See also John Collier and Saul K.
Padover, "An Institute for Ethnic Democracy," *Common Ground*, IV (Au-
tumn 1943), 3–7, for a more elaborate proposal.

Embree probably passed along his idea to Odum of the University of
North Carolina so that he could discuss it with a fellow North Carolinian in
the White House, Daniels, administrative assistant to the President. Odum
and Daniels had a conference in August 1943 from which emerged a recommendation for a "President's Committee on Race and Minority Groups."
Odum to Daniels, Aug. 23, 1943; Memorandum to Daniels from Odum, Aug.
30, 1943, Howard W. Odum Papers (University of North Carolina).

Although Daniels apparently gave Odum the impression that he was interested in a national committee, this was not the case. "It has been suggested that a committee of prominent men be named to study this situation,"
he wrote the President. "I am sure the naming of such a committee would
not now halt the procession of angry outbreaks which are occurring. I doubt
that any report could be made which would be so effective as a statement
now from you would be. I am very much afraid, indeed, that any committee
report would only serve as a new ground for controversy." Memorandum to
the President from Daniels, Aug. 2, 1943, Daniels Papers. Roosevelt apparently agreed with Daniels, and Odum was informed that "My boss does not
think well of the idea that we discussed." Daniels to Odum, Sept. 1, 1943,
Odum Papers.

Daniels' appointment as White House coordinator of information on race
relations was actually suggested by him to the President in June 1943.
Memorandum to the President from Daniels, June 29, 1943, Daniels Papers.
By July 1943, Roosevelt had approved of the new role for his administrative
assistant, and Daniels was hard at work gathering information. Daniels to
Secretary of War Stimson, July 28, 1943, ASW 291.2, Record Group 335.

72. "Stimson Diary," June 24, 1943.

SUGGESTED READING

This bibliography is intended to be a relatively complete list of historical books and articles and contemporary books. Contemporary articles are selected. Historical publications antedating the period 1930–1945 or dealing with developments of previous years have been included in the section on "The Migration," while selected sources treating the postwar period have been cited in some of the other sections. I have included more writings on the recent period when publication has been less (as in the case of "The Courts and the Negro") and been more selective when publication has been greater (as in the case of "Politics and the Negro"). Books marked with an asterisk (*) are available in a paperback edition.

I. The Depression and the Negro

Newell D. Eason, "Attitudes of Negro Families on Relief," *Opportunity* (December 1935).

Thyra J. Edwards, "Attitudes of Negro Families on Relief—Another View," *Opportunity* (July 1936).

E. Franklin Frazier, *The Negro in the United States* (New York: Macmillan, 2nd ed., 1957).

———, "The Status of the Negro in the American Social Order," *Journal of Negro Education* (July 1935).

Albert B. George, "The Negro and the Public Mind Today," *Journal of Negro History* (October 1935).

Abram L. Harris, *The Negro as Capitalist: A Study of Banking and Business among American Negroes* (Philadelphia: American Academy of Political and Social Science, 1936).

Albion Hartwell, "The Need of Social and Unemployment Insurance for Negroes," *Journal of Negro Education* (January 1936).

George Edmund Hayes, "The American Negro in the Changing Economic Order," *Journal of Negro Education* (January 1936).

T. Arnold Hill, *The Negro and Economic Reconstruction* (Washington, D.C.: Associates in Negro Folk Education, 1937).

Charles S. Johnson, *The Economic Status of the Negro* (Nashville: Fisk University Press, 1933).

Journal of Negro Education, January 1936, is devoted to the economic crisis and the Negro. Other articles from this issue, in addition to those by Hartwell and Hayes cited above, are listed below under appropriate topics.

Gunnar Myrdal, assisted by Richard Sterner and Arnold Rose, *An American Dilemma: The Negro Problem and Modern Democracy* (New York: Harper, 2 vols., 1944).* Louis Harlan calls *An American Dilemma* the "greatest monument of modern scholarship on the Negro" but cautions that much of it is "now anachronistic and irrelevant."

Arnold Rose, *The Negro in America* (New York: Harper, 1944);* a condensation of *An American Dilemma.*

Richard Sterner, *The Negro's Share: A Study of Income, Consumption, Housing and Public Assistance* (New York: Harper, 1943).

John G. Van Deusen, *Black Man in White America* (Washington, D.C.: Associated Publishers, rev. ed., 1944).

Black novels that illuminate Negro life in the years 1930–1945 are:
Ralph Ellison, *Invisible Man* (New York: Random House, 1947).*
Richard Wright, *Black Boy: A Record of Childhood and Youth* (New York: Harper, 1945).*
———, *Native Son* (New York: Harper, 1940).*

Periodicals providing contemporary materials are:
The Crisis (National Association for the Advancement of Colored People; see the article by Michael A. Malec listed below under "Negro Intellectuals")
Ebony (see Paul M. Hirsh, "An Analysis of *Ebony:* The Magazine and Its Readers," *Journalism Quarterly* [Summer 1968])
Journal of Negro Education (occasional publisher of historical articles)
The Negro Digest
Opportunity: Journal of Negro Life (National Urban League)
Phylon: The Atlanta University Review of Race and Culture (occasional publisher of historical articles)

The *Journal of Negro History* occasionally publishes articles on contemporary subjects.

Important Negro newspapers are:
Amsterdam News
Atlanta Daily World
Baltimore Afro-American
Chicago Defender
Kansas City Call
Norfolk Journal and Guide
Philadelphia Independent
Pittsburgh Courier
St. Louis Argus

II. The New Deal and the Negro

A. A RADICAL CRITIQUE
Ernest Kaiser, "The Federal Government and the Negro," *Science and Society* (Winter 1956).

B. NEGROES IN THE NEW DEAL
Lawrence J. W. Hayes, *The Negro Federal Government Worker: A Study of His Classification Status in the District of Columbia, 1883–1938* (Washington, D.C.: Howard University Graduate School, 1941).
Rackham Holt, *Mary McLeod Bethune: A Biography* (Garden City: Doubleday, 1964).
Roi Ottley, *New World A-Coming* (Boston: Houghton Mifflin, 1943).
Catherine Owens Peare, *Mary McLeod Bethune* (New York: Vanguard, 1961).

C. NEGROES ON THE NEW DEAL
Ralph J. Bunche, "A Critique of New Deal Planning as It Affects Negroes," *Journal of Negro Education* (January 1936).
"The Campaign," *Crisis* (November 1936).
John P. Davis, "A Black Inventory of the New Deal," *Crisis* (May 1935).
———, "A Survey of the Problems of the Negro Under the New Deal," *Journal of Negro Education* (January 1936).
———, "What Price National Recovery?," *Crisis* (December 1933).
W. E. B. Du Bois, "Federal Action Programs and Community Action in the South," *Social Forces* (March 1941).
Guy B. Johnson, "Does the South Owe the Negro a New Deal?," *Social Forces* (October 1934).

"The Roosevelt Record," *Crisis* (November 1940).

Robert C. Weaver, "The Negro in a Program of Public Housing," *Opportunity* (July 1938).

———, "The New Deal and the Negro: A Look at the Facts," *Opportunity* (July 1935).

Walter White, "The United States Department of (White) Justice," *Crisis* (October 1935).

D. NEW DEALERS ON THE NEGRO

Harold L. Ickes, "The Negro as Citizen," *Crisis* (August 1936).

Eleanor Roosevelt, "The Negro and Social Changes," *Opportunity* (January 1936).

E. SOUTHERNERS ON A NEW DEALER

Howard Odum, *Race and Rumors of Race: Challenge to American Crisis* (Chapel Hill: University of North Carolina Press, 1943), "The Eleanor Clubs," pp. 73–80.

F. NEW DEAL AGENCIES AND THE NEGRO

1. HISTORICAL STUDIES TOUCHING ON THE NEGRO

Hubert Humphreys, "In a Sense Experimental: The Civilian Conservation Corps in Louisiana," *Louisiana History* (Fall 1964, Winter 1965). Humphreys notes (Part II, p. 47) the inferiority of educational and on-the-job training programs for Negroes compared to those for whites.

John A. Salmond, *The Civilian Conservation Corps, 1933–1942: A New Deal Case Study* (Durham, N.C.: Duke University Press, 1967).

Larry Whatley, "The Works Progress Administration in Mississippi," *Journal of Mississippi History* (February 1968). Whatley mentions the expenditure of $400,000 in the period 1935–1937 for Negro education (p. 49) but provides no basis for comparing outlays for education of blacks and whites on a per capita basis.

2. CONTEMPORARY COMMENTARIES AND STUDIES

J. Max Bond, "The Training Program of the Tennessee Valley Authority for Negroes," *Journal of Negro Education* (July 1938).

Cranston Clayton, "The TVA and the Race Problem," *Opportunity* (April 1934).

Walter G. Daniel and Carroll L. Miller, "The Participation of Negroes in the National Youth Administration Program," *Journal of Negro Education* (July 1938).

John P. Davis, "Blue Eagles and Black Workers," *New Republic* (November 14, 1934).

————, "The Plight of the Negro in the Tennessee Valley," *Crisis* (October 1935).

Charles L. Franklin, *The Negro Labor Unionist in New York: Problems and Conditions among Negroes in Manhattan, with Special Reference to the N.R.A. and Post-N.R.A. Situations* (New York: Columbia University Press, 1936).

Bonita Golda Harrison, "Social Security—What Does It Mean for the Negro?," *Opportunity* (June 1936).

Charles H. Houston and John P. Davis, "TVA: Lily-White Construction," *Crisis* (October 1934).

E. E. Lewis, "Black Cotton Farmers and the AAA," *Crisis* (March 1935).

A. Howard Myers, "The Negro Workers Under the NRA," *Journal of Negro Education* (January 1936).

Howard W. Oxley, "The Civilian Conservation Corps and the Education of the Negro," *Journal of Negro Education* (July 1938).

Gustav Peck, "The Negro Worker and the NRA," *Crisis* (September 1934).

Luther C. Wandall, "A Negro in the CCC," *Crisis* (August 1935).

Robert C. Weaver, "The PWA School Building Program and Separate Negro Schools," *Journal of Negro Education* (July 1938).

Marian T. Wright, "Negro Youth and the Federal Emergency Programs: CCC and NYA," *Journal of Negro Education* (July 1940).

Also see the books by T. Arnold Hill and Richard Sterner listed above, and the items, contemporary and historical, on New Deal agricultural agencies and policies listed below under "Negro Rural Life."

G. SOUTHERN POLITICS

1. SOUTHERN POLITICAL INFLUENCE

Leonard Dinnerstein, "The Senate's Rejection of Aubrey Williams as Rural Electrification Administrator," *Alabama Review* (April 1968).

Frank Freidel, *F.D.R. and the South* (Baton Rouge: Louisiana State University Press, 1965).

Dewey W. Grantham, Jr., "The South in the Reconstruction of American Politics," *Journal of American History* (September 1966).

Fletcher M Green, "Resurgent Southern Sectionalism, 1933–1935," *North Carolina Historical Review* (April 1956).

Alexander Heard, *A Two-Party South* (Chapel Hill: University of North Carolina Press, 1952).

V. O. Key, Jr., *Southern Politics in State and Nation* (New York: Knopf, 1949).

John Robert Moore, "The Conservative Coalition in the United States Senate, 1942–1945," *Journal of Southern History* (August 1967).

James T. Patterson, *Congressional Conservatism and the New Deal* (Lexington: University of Kentucky Press, 1967).

————, "A Conservative Coalition Forms in Congress, 1933–1939," *Journal of American History* (March 1966).

————, "The Failure of Party Realignment in the South, 1937–1939," *Journal of Politics* (August 1965).

Elmer L. Puryear, *Democratic Party Dissension in North Carolina, 1918–1936* (Chapel Hill: University of North Carolina Press, 1962).

2. SOUTHERN POLITICIANS

A fuller understanding of the collective influence in Washington of Southern politicians, as well as an awareness that they did not show unanimity on either the New Deal or race relations, can be gleaned from the growing body of literature on individual political figures:

Ellis Arnall, *The Shore Dimly Seen* (Philadelphia: Lippincott, 1946).

Merlin G. Cox, "David Scholtz: New Deal Governor of Florida," *Florida Historical Quarterly* (October 1964).

E. David Cronon, "A Southern Progressive [Jonathan Daniels] Looks at the New Deal," *Journal of Southern History* (May 1958).

Jeanne Graham, "Kenneth McKellar's 1934 Campaign: Issues and Events," *West Tennessee Historical Society Papers*, No. 18 (1964).

A. Wigfall Green, *The Man Bilbo* (Baton Rouge: Louisiana State University Press, 1963).

Walter J. Heacock, "William Bankhead and the New Deal," *Journal of Southern History* (August 1955).

Jack Brien Key, "Henry B. Steagall: The Conservative as Reformer," *Alabama Review* (July 1964).

Sarah M. Lemmon, "The Ideology of Eugene Talmadge," *Georgia Historical Quarterly* (June 1954).

Reinhard Luthin, "Flowering of the Southern Demagogue [Bilbo, Long, Smith, Talmadge]," *American Scholar* (Spring 1961).

John Robert Moore, "Senator Josiah W. Bailey and the 'Conservative Manifesto' of 1937," *Journal of Southern History* (February 1965).

————, *Senator Josiah William Bailey of North Carolina: A Political Biography* (Durham, N.C.: Duke University Press, 1968).

Daniel C. Roper, with Frank H. Lovette, *Fifty Years of Public Life* (Durham, N.C.: Duke University Press, 1941).

Frank Smith, *Congressman from Mississippi* (New York: Pantheon Books, 1964).

Virginia Van Der Veer, "Hugo Black and the KKK," *American Heritage* (April 1968).

Luther H. Zeigler, Jr., "Senator Walter George's 1938 Campaign" *Georgia Historical Quarterly* (December 1959).

Among politicians, Huey P. Long is *sui generis*. For a bibliography of the writings on this figure, see Henry C. Dethloff, editor, *Huey P. Long: Southern Demagogue or American Democrat?* (Boston: D. C. Heath, 1967), pp. 113–115. Roy Wilkins, "An Interview with Louisiana's Kingfish," *Crisis* (February 1935), is revealing on Long's position toward the Negro.

III. The Courts and the Negro

Charles Aikin, *The Negro Votes* [12 Supreme Court decisions] (San Francisco: Chandler, 1962).*

Raymond Pace Alexander, "The Upgrading of the Negro's Status by Supreme Court Decisions [1872–1945]," *Journal of Negro History* (April 1945).

C. A. Chick, "Some Recent United States Supreme Court Decisions Affecting the Rights of Negro Workers," *Journal of Negro Education* (Spring 1947).

Norman Dorsen, *Discrimination and Civil Rights* (Boston: Little, Brown, 1969).

Harry Kalven, Jr., *The Negro and the First Amendment* (Columbus: Ohio State University Press, 1965).*

Sarah M. Lemmon, "Transportation Segregation in the Federal Courts Since 1865," *Journal of Negro History* (April 1963).

Loren E. Miller, *The Petitioners. The Story of the United States Supreme Court and the Negro* (New York: Pantheon Books, 1966).*

Bernard Nelson, *The Fourteenth Amendment and the Negro Since 1920* (Washington: Catholic University Press, 1946).

———, "The Negro Before the Supreme Court," *Phylon* (First Quarter 1947).

Donald B. Strong, *Negroes, Ballots, and Judges: National Voting Rights Legislation in the Federal Courts* [Civil Rights Acts of 1957, 1960, 1964] (University: University of Alabama Press, 1968).

Joseph Tussman, ed., *The Supreme Court on Racial Discrimination* (New York: Oxford University Press, 1963).*

Clement E. Vose, *Caucasians Only: The Supreme Court, the NAACP, and the Restrictive Covenant Cases* (Berkeley: University of California Press, 1959).

Hugh Williamson, "The Role of the Courts in the Status of the Negro,"
Journal of Negro History (January 1955).

Benjamin Munn Ziegler, ed., *Desegregation and the Supreme Court*
(Boston: D. C. Heath, 1958).*

Also see the relevant items listed below under "The NAACP."

IV. Protestantism and the Negro

Trevor Bowen, *Divine White Right: A Study of Racial Segregation and
Interracial Cooperation in Religious Organizations and Institutions
in the United States* (New York: Harper, 1934).

Harrison Daniel, "Southern Protestantism and the Negro," *North
Carolina Historical Review* (Summer 1964).

Joseph C. Hough, Jr., *Black Power and White Protestantism: A Christian Response to the New Negro Pluralism* (New York: Oxford University Press, 1968).*

Robert Lee, "The Church in a Case of Neighborhood Exclusion," *Phylon*
(Fourth Quarter 1952).

Frank S. Loescher, *The Protestant Church and the Negro* (New York:
Association Press, 1948).

Robert Moats Miller, "The Protestant Churches and Lynching, 1919–
1939," *Journal of Negro History* (April 1957).

———, "Southern White Protestantism and the Negro, 1865–1965,"
in Charles E. Wynes, ed., *The Negro in the South Since 1865: Selected Essays in American Negro History* (University: University of
Alabama Press, 1965).*

David Reimers, *White Protestantism and the Negro* (New York: Oxford University Press, 1965).

V. Negro Workers

Mary Anderson, "The Plight of Negro Domestic Labor," *Journal of Negro Education* (January 1936).

Lloyd H. Bailer, "The Negro Automobile Worker," *Journal of Political
Economy* (August 1943).

Herman D. Bloch, "Craft Unions a Link in the Circle of Negro Discrimination [New York City, 1886–1945]," *Phylon* (Fourth Quarter
1958).

———, "Craft Unions and the Negro in History," *Journal of Negro
History* (January 1958).

———, "The Employment Status of the New York Negro in Retrospect," *Phylon* (Fourth Quarter 1959).

Brailsford R. Brazeal, *The Brotherhood of Sleeping Car Porters: Its Origin and Development* (New York: Harper, 1946).

George O. Butler, "The Black Worker in Industry, Agriculture, Domestic and Personal Service," *Journal of Negro Education* (July 1939).

Horace R. Cayton and George S. Mitchell, *Black Workers and the New Unions* (Chapel Hill: University of North Carolina Press, 1939).

C. A. Chick, see above, "The Courts and the Negro."

Lester B. Granger, "The Negro—Friend or Foe of Organized Labor?," *Opportunity* (May 1935).

Lorenzo J. Greene and Carter G. Woodson, *The Negro Wage Earner* (Washington, D.C.: Association for the Study of Negro Life and History, 1930).

Herbert Hill, "Labor Unions and the Negro: The Record of Discrimination," *Commentary* (December 1959).

T. Arnold Hill, "The Plight of the Negro Industrial Worker," *Journal of Negro Education* (January 1936).

Irving Howe and B. J. Widick, "The U.A.W. Fights Race Prejudice: Case History on the Industrial Front," *Commentary* (September 1949).

Julius Jacobson, ed., *The Negro and the American Labor Movement* (New York: Anchor Books, 1968)*, especially pp. 155–208.

Lucy Randolph Mason, "The CIO and the Negro in the South," *Journal of Negro Education* (Fall 1945).

Allan Morrison, "A. Philip Randolph: Dean of Negro Leaders," *Ebony* (November 1958).

Paul Mundy, "The Young Negro Worker in Washington, D.C.," *Journal of Negro Education* (Spring 1949).

Herbert R. Northrup, *Organized Labor and the Negro* (New York: Harper, 1944).

———, "The Negro and the Railway Unions," *Phylon* (Second Quarter 1956).

———, "The Negro and the United Mine Workers of America," *Southern Economic Journal* (April 1943).

A. Philip Randolph, "The Trade Union Movement and the Negro," *Journal of Negro Education* (January 1936).

Walter P. Reuther, "The Negro Worker's Future," *Opportunity* (Fall 1945).

Sterling D. Spero and Abram L. Harris, *The Black Worker: The Negro and the Labor Movement* (New York: Columbia University Press, 1931).*

Willard S. Townsend, "Full Employment and the Negro Worker," *Journal of Negro Education* (Winter 1945).

Robert C. Weaver, *Negro Labor: A National Problem* (New York: Harcourt, Brace, 1946).

———, "Negro Labor Since 1929," *Journal of Negro History* (January 1950).

Charles H. Wesley, "Organized Labor and the Negro," *Journal of Negro Education* (July 1939).

Also see the items on the NRA and the Negro worker listed above under "New Deal Agencies and the Negro," and the relevant items listed below under "World War II and the Negro."

VI. Communism and the Negro

James S. Allen, *The Negro Question in the United States* (New York: International Publishers, 1936).

Vaughn D. Bornet, "Historical Scholarship, Communism, and the Negro," *Journal of Negro History* (July 1952), a review of Nolan's *Communism versus the Negro* and Record's *The Negro and the Communist Party* (see below).

George Charney, *A Long Journey* (Chicago: Quadrangle Books, 1968), Chapter 5, "Harlem, 1937–42," pp. 83–121.

"Communism and the Negro Tenant Farmer," *Opportunity* (August 1931).

"The Communist International Resolution on the Negro Question," *Communist* (January 1930).

Harold Cruse, see below, "Negro Intellectuals."

Benjamin J. Davis, "Why I Am a Communist," *Phylon* (Second Quarter 1947).

W. E. B. Du Bois, "The Negro and Communism," *Crisis* (September 1931).

James W. Ford, *The Negro and the Democratic Front* (New York: International Publishers, 1938).

——— and James E. Allen, *The Negroes in a Soviet America* (New York: Workers' Library Publishers, 1935).

Nathan Glazer, *The Social Basis of American Communism* (New York: Harcourt, Brace, 1961), Chapter 5, pp. 169–192.

T. H. Kennedy and T. F. Leary, "Communist Thought and the Negro," *Phylon* (Second Quarter 1947).

John Kosa and Clyde Z. Nunn, "Race, Deprivation, and Attitude Toward Communism," *Phylon* (Fourth Quarter 1964).

Joseph C. Mouledous, "From Browderism to Peaceful Co-Existence: An Analysis of Developments in the Communist Position on the American Negro," *Phylon* (Fourth Quarter 1964).

"New Steps in the United Front," *Communist* (November 1935).

William A. Nolan, *Communism versus the Negro* (Chicago: Regnery, 1951).

A. Philip Randolph, "A. Philip Randolph Tells Why I Would Not Stand for Re-election as President of the National Negro Congress," *American Federationist* (July 1940).

Wilson Record, "The Development of the Communist Position on the Negro Question in the United States," *Phylon* (Third Quarter 1958).

———, *The Negro and the Communist Party* (Chapel Hill: University of North Carolina Press, 1951).*

———, *Race and Radicalism: The NAACP and the Communist Party in Conflict* (Ithaca, N.Y.: Cornell University Press, 1964).*

George S. Schuyler, "Have Communists Stopped Fighting for Negro Rights?," *Negro Digest* (December 1944).

Walter White, "The Negro and Communism," *Harper's Magazine* (December 1931).

Richard Wright, chapter in *The God That Failed* (New York: Harper, 1950).*

Also see the relevant items listed below under "The Scottsboro Cases."

VII. The NAACP

Francis L. Broderick, *W. E. B. Du Bois: Negro Leader in a Time of Crisis* (Stanford: Stanford University Press, 1959).

Ralph J. Bunche, "A Critical Analysis of the Tactics and Programs of Minority Groups," *Journal of Negro Education* (July 1935).

———, "The Programs of Organizations Devoted to the Improvement of the Status of the American Negro," *Journal of Negro Education* (July 1939).

Jack Greenberg, *Race Relations and American Law* (New York: Columbia University Press, 1959).

Langston Hughes, *Fight for Freedom: The Story of the NAACP* (New York: W. W. Norton, 1962).

Robert L. Jack, *History of the National Association for the Advancement of Colored People* (Boston: Meador, 1943).

Michael A. Malec, see below, "Negro Intellectuals."

Charles S. Mangum, *The Legal Status of the Negro* (Chapel Hill: University of North Carolina Press, 1940).

Thurgood Marshall, "An Evaluation of Recent Efforts to Achieve Racial Integration Through Resort to the Courts," *Journal of Negro Education* (Summer 1952).

Wilson Record, see above, "Communism and the Negro"; see below, "Negro Intellectuals."

Elliott M. Rudwick, *W. E. B. Du Bois: A Study in Minority Group Leadership* (Philadelphia: University of Pennsylvania Press, 1960).*

Warren D. St. James, *The National Association for the Advancement of Colored People: A Case Study in Pressure Groups* (New York: Exposition Press, 1968).

Clement E. Vose, "NAACP Strategy in the Covenant Cases," *Western Reserve Law Review* (1955).

————, see above, "The Courts and the Negro."

Gilbert Ware, "Lobbying as a Means of Protest: The NAACP as an Agent of Equality," *Journal of Negro Education* (Spring 1964).

Walter F. White, *A Man Called White* (New York: Viking, 1948).

VIII. Politics and the Negro

Charles Aikin, see above, "The Courts and the Negro."

C. A. Bacote, "The Negro in Atlanta Politics [1869–1955]," *Phylon* (Fourth Quarter 1955).

William M. Brewer, "The Poll Tax and the Poll Taxers," *Journal of Negro History* (July 1944).

Andrew Buni, *The Negro in Virginia Politics, 1902–1965* (Charlottesville: University of Virginia Press, 1967).

Joseph M. Brittain, "Some Reflections on Negro Suffrage and Politics in Alabama—Past and Present," *Journal of Negro History* (April 1962).

Ralph J. Bunche, "The Negro in the Political Life of the United States," *Journal of Negro Education* (July 1941).

Carl N. Degler, *Out of Our Past: The Forces That Shaped Modern America* (New York: Harper, 1959)*, pp. 394–399.

Brainerd Dyer, "One Hundred Years of Negro Suffrage," *Pacific Historical Review* (February 1968).

"The Fortune Quarterly Survey: XIII," *Fortune* (July 1938).

Herbert J. Gans, "Political Participation and Apathy," *Phylon* (Third Quarter 1952).

Harold F. Gosnell, *Negro Politicians: The Rise of Negro Politics in Chicago* (Chicago: University of Chicago Press, 1935).*

————, "The Negro Vote in Northern Cities," *National Municipal Review* (May 1941).

James A. Harrell, "Negro Leadership in the Election Year 1936," *Journal of Southern History* (November 1968).

Elmer Henderson, "Political Changes Among Negroes in Chicago During the Depression," *Social Forces* (May 1941).

Harry Holloway, *The Politics of the Southern Negro: From Exclusion to Big City Organization* (New York: Random House, 1969).

Paul Lewinson, *Race, Class, and Party: A History of Negro Suffrage and White Politics in the South* (New York: Oxford University Press, 1932).*

Pierce F. Lewis, "Impact of Negro Migration on the Electoral Geography of Flint, Michigan, 1932–1962: A Cartographic Analysis," *Annals of the Association of American Geographers* (March 1965).

Edward Litchfield, "A Case Study of Negro Political Behavior in Detroit," *Public Opinion Quarterly* (June 1941).

Samuel Lubell, *The Future of American Politics* (New York: Harper Colophon Books, 3rd ed. rev., 1965)*, pp. 89–105.

Thurgood Marshall, "The Rise and Collapse of the 'White Democratic Primary,'" *Journal of Negro Education* (Summer 1957).

William J. McKenna, "The Negro Vote in Philadelphia Elections," *Pennsylvania History* (October 1965).

Henry Lee Moon, *Balance of Power: The Negro Vote* (Garden City, N.Y.: Doubleday, 1948).

William F. Nowlin, *The Negro in American National Politics* (Boston: Stratford, 1931).

Arthur M. Schlesinger, Jr., *The Politics of Upheaval* (Boston: Houghton Mifflin, 1960)*, pp. 598–600.

Donald B. Strong, see above, "The Courts and the Negro."

Elbert L. Tatum, *The Changed Political Thought of the Negro, 1915–1940* (New York: Exposition Press, 1951).

———, "The Changed Political Thought of the Negroes in the United States, 1915–1940," *Journal of Negro Education* (Fall 1947).

John G. Van Deusen, "The Negro in Politics," *Journal of Negro History* (July 1936).

IX. *The Scottsboro Cases*

Dan T. Carter, "A Reasonable Doubt," *American Heritage* (October 1968).

———, *Scottsboro: A Tragedy of the American South* (Baton Rouge: Louisiana State University Press, 1969).

Allan K. Chalmers, *They Shall Be Free* (Garden City, N.Y.: Doubleday, 1951).

Files Crenshaw, Jr. and Kenneth A. Miller, *Scottsboro: The Firebrand of Communism* (Montgomery, Ala.: Brown Printing Company, 1936).

Clarence Darrow, "Scottsboro," *Crisis* (March 1932).

James W. Ford and Anna Damon, "Scottsboro in the Light of the Building of the Negro People's Front," *Communist* (September 1937).

Harry Haywood, "The Scottsboro Decision," *Communist* (December 1932).

Haywood Patterson and Earl Conrad, *Scottsboro Boy* (Garden City, N.Y.: Doubleday, 1950).

"A Statement by the N.A.A.C.P. on the Scottsboro Cases," *Crisis* (March 1932).

X. *The Negro Elite*

A. NEGRO INTELLECTUALS

Harold Cruse, *The Crisis of the Negro Intellectual* (New York: William Morrow, 1967).* This book has had a substantial sale (*New York Times Book Review*, February 16, 1969, p. 30), and its thesis—that Jewish Marxists were responsible for the Negro's failure to develop a cultural consciousness—is controversial. Michael Harrington, in a review of Christopher Lasch, *The Agony of the American Left*, in the *New Republic* (April 12, 1969), states that at times Cruse's "ethnocentric history becomes anti-Semitic. The Communist Party did not take up the anti-Hitler crusade because of Jewish pressure, as Cruse thinks, but because Stalin, on the basis of Russian considerations, ordered the united front in 1935."

Michael A. Malec, "Some Observations on the Content of *Crisis*, 1932–1962," *Phylon* (Second Quarter 1967). Dividing articles into two categories—civil rights and non–civil rights—Malec finds the increase in the number of civil rights articles a function of editorship, not the result of the passage of time. Dividing civil rights articles into two categories—legalistic and moralistic—he discovers two periods of noticeable increase in legalistic articles: one began in 1940, the other, more pronounced, in 1958. Malec maintains that the "shift of the intellectuals," under way five years before 1963, fits into Crane Brinton's thesis on the role of intellectuals in revolutions.

Wilson Record, "Negro Intellectual Leadership in the National Association for the Advancement of Colored People, 1910–1940," *Phylon* (Second Quarter 1956).

———, "Negro Intellectuals and Negro Movements in Historical Perspective," *American Quarterly* (Spring 1956).

———, "Negro Intellectuals and Negro Movements: Some Methodological Notes," *Journal of Negro Education* (Spring 1955).

———, "Negro Intellectuals and Negro Nationalism," *Social Forces* (October 1954).

———, "Social Stratification and Intellectual Roles in the Negro Community," *British Journal of Sociology* (September 1957).

Daniel C. Thompson, *The Negro Leadership Class* [New Orleans, 1940–1960] (Englewood Cliffs, N.J.: Prentice-Hall, 1963).*

Relevant to this topic is William B. Hixson, Jr., "The Negro Revolution and [White] Intellectuals," *American Scholar* (Autumn 1964).

B. PROMINENT NEGROES

Richard Bardolph, "The Distinguished Negro in America, 1770–1936," *American Historical Review* (April 1955).

———, "The Negro in *Who's Who in America*, 1936–1955," *Journal of Negro History* (October 1957).

———, *The Vanguard* (New York: Holt, Rinehart and Winston, 1959).* Also see August Meier's commentary on *The Vanguard* in the *Journal of Negro Education* (Winter 1960).

XI. World War II and the Negro

A. FEPC

Brailsford R. Brazeal, "The Present Status and Programs of Fair Employment Practices Commissions—Federal, State, and Municipal," *Journal of Negro Education* (Summer 1951).

Charles W. Cobb, Jr., "The Outlook Regarding State FEPC Legislation," *Journal of Negro History* (July 1946).

G. James Fleming, "Educational Aspects of FEPC Laws," *Journal of Negro Education* (Winter 1950).

Herbert Garfinkel, *When Negroes March: The March on Washington Movement in the Organizational Politics for FEPC* (Glencoe, Ill.: Free Press, 1959).*

Louis Coleridge Kesselman, "The Fair Employment Practices Commission Movement in Perspective," *Journal of Negro History* (January 1946).

———, *The Social Politics of FEPC: A Study in Reform Pressure Movements* (Chapel Hill: University of North Carolina Press, 1948).

Elwood S. McKenney, "Fair Employment in Massachusetts," *Phylon* (First and Second Quarters 1952).

———, "National Politics of Fair Employment," *Phylon* (Third Quarter 1952).

A. Philip Randolph, "Why Should We March?," *Survey Graphic* (November 1942).

Louis Ruchames, *Race, Jobs and Politics: The Story of FEPC* (New York: Columbia University Press, 1953).

B. ARMED FORCES

W. Y. Bell, Jr., "The Negro Warrior's Home Front," *Phylon* (Third Quarter 1944).

Richard M. Dalfiume, *Fighting on Two Fronts: Desegregation of the Armed Forces, 1939–1953* (Columbia: University of Missouri Press, 1969).

Paul C. Davis, "The Negro in the Armed Services," *Virginia Quarterly Review* (October 1948).

L. D. Reddick, "The Negro in the Navy in World War II," *Journal of Negro History* (April 1947).

———, "The Negro Policy of the United States Army, 1775–1945," *Journal of Negro History* (January 1949).

Joseph Schiffman, "The Education of Negro Soldiers in World War II," *Journal of Negro Education* (Winter 1949).

Seymour J. Schoenfeld, *The Negro in the Armed Forces: His Value and Status—Past, Present and Potential* (Washington, D.C.: Associated Publishers, 1945).

John D. Silvera, *The Negro in World War II* (New York: Arno Press, 1969); reprint.

Richard J. Stillman, *Integration of the Negro in the Armed Forces* (New York: Praeger, 1968).

C. GENERAL

Herbert Aptheker, "Literacy, the Negro and World War II," *Journal of Negro Education* (Fall 1946).

James A. Bayton, "The Psychology of Racial Morale," *Journal of Negro Education* (April 1942).

Earl Brown and George R. Layton, *The Negro and the War* (New York: Public Affairs, 1942).

———, "The Negro's War," *Fortune* (June 1942).

Council for Democracy, *The Negro and Defense* (New York: American Council on Public Affairs, 1941).

John A. Davis and Cornelius L. Golightly, "Negro Employment in the Federal Government [1941]," *Phylon* (Fourth Quarter 1945).

Lester B. Granger, "Barriers to Negro War Employment," *Annals of the American Academy of Political and Social Science* (September 1942).

Frank Horne, "Niggers Ought to Quit [poem]," *Phylon* (Second Quarter 1941).

Carey McWilliams, "How the Negro Fared in the War," *Negro Digest* (May 1946).

J. Saunders Redding, "A Negro Looks at This War," *American Mercury* (November 1942).

Grant Reynolds, "What the Negro Thinks of This War," *Crisis* (September 1944).

Anson Phelps Stokes, "American Race Relations in Wartime," *Journal of Negro Education* (Fall 1945).

Walter F. White, *A Rising Wind* (New York: Doubleday, 1945).

Several journals devoted entire issues to ethnic and race relations during the war:

"Color, Unfinished Business of Democracy," *Survey Graphic* (November 1942).

"Minority Peoples in a Nation at War," *Annals of the American Academy of Political and Social Science* (September 1942).

"Negro Higher Education and the War," *Journal of Negro Education* (July 1942).

"The Negro in the North During Wartime," *Journal of Educational Sociology* (January 1944).

"The Negro in World War I and World War II," *Journal of Negro Education* (Summer 1943).

"Race Relations on the Pacific Coast," *Journal of Negro Education* (November 1945).

XII. The South and the Negro

A. NEGRO RURAL LIFE

Jerold S. Auerbach, "Southern Tenant Farmers: Socialist Critics of the New Deal," *Labor History* (Winter 1966).

Sidney Baldwin, *The Rise and Decline of the Farm Security Administration* (Chapel Hill: University of North Carolina Press, 1968).

J. Phil Campbell, "The Government's Farm Policies and the Negro Farmer," *Journal of Negro Education* (January 1936).

Louis Cantor, "A Prologue to the Protest Movement: The Missouri Sharecropper Roadside Demonstration of 1939," *Journal of American History* (March 1969). According to official estimates, over 90 per cent of the sharecroppers participating in this demonstration were blacks. The incident, however, was not "primarily a Negro protest," Cantor notes, "but a protest against the economic deprivation and injustice of the sharecropping system." In any event, this "vivid example of an early use of the non-violent demonstration to dramatize human want and suffering" commands attention because of its "remarkable similarity to the contemporary protest movement."

William H. Cobb and Donald H. Grubbs, "Arkansas' Commonwealth College and the Southern Tenant Farmers Union," *Arkansas Historical Quarterly* (Winter 1966).

"Communism and the Negro Tenant Farmer," see above, "Communism and the Negro."

David Eugene Conrad, *The Forgotten Farmers: The Story of the Sharecroppers in the New Deal* (Urbana: University of Illinois Press, 1965).

Donald H. Grubbs, "Gardner Jackson, That 'Socialist' Tenant Farmers Union, and the New Deal," *Agricultural History* (April 1968).

Charles S. Johnson, *Growing Up in the Black Belt: Negro Youth in the Rural South* (Washington, D.C.: American Council on Education, 1941).

———, *Shadow of the Plantation* (Chicago: University of Chicago Press, 1933).*

Howard Kester, *Revolt Among the Sharecroppers* (New York: Covici, Friede, 1936).

Sarah M. Lemmon, "The Agricultural Policies of Eugene Talmadge," *Agricultural History* (January 1954).

Arthur F. Raper, *Preface to Peasantry* (Chapel Hill: University of North Carolina Press, 1933).*

——— and Ira DeA. Reid, *Sharecroppers All* (Chapel Hill: University of North Carolina Press, 1941).

Olive M. Stone, "The Present Position of the Negro Farm Population," *Journal of Negro Education* (January 1936).

M. S. Venkataramani, "Norman Thomas, Arkansas Sharecroppers, and the Roosevelt Agricultural Policies," *Mississippi Valley Historical Review* (September 1960).

Carter G. Woodson, *The Rural Negro* (Washington, D.C.: Association for the Study of Negro Life and History, 1930).

Works Projects Administration Study, *The Negro in Virginia* (New York: Arno Press, 1969); reprint.

Although it describes the life of three white tenant families, special mention should be made of James Agee and Walker Evans, *Let Us Now Praise Famous Men* (Boston: Houghton Mifflin, 1941)*; also see Alan Holder, "Encounter in Alabama: Agee and the Tenant Farmer," *Virginia Quarterly Review* (Spring 1966).

B. SOUTHERN LIFE

Horace Mann Bond, *Negro Education in Alabama* (Washington, D.C.: Associated Publishers, 1939).*

Tom P. Brady, *Black Monday* (Winona, Miss.: Association of Citizens' Councils, 1955).

Henry Allen Bullock, *A History of Negro Education in the South* (Cambridge, Mass.: Harvard University Press, 1967).

Hodding Carter, *Southern Legacy* (Baton Rouge: Louisiana State University Press, 1950).

Wilbur J. Cash, *The Mind of the South* (New York: Knopf, 1941).*

Thomas D. Clark, *The Southern Country Editor* (Indianapolis: Bobbs-Merrill, 1948).

———, *The Emerging South* (New York: Oxford University Press, 2nd ed., 1968).*

David L. Cohn, *Where I Was Born and Raised* (Boston: Houghton Mifflin, 1948).

W. T. Couch, ed., *Culture in the South* (Chapel Hill: University of North Carolina Press, 1934).

Jonathan Daniels, *A Southerner Discovers the South* (New York: Macmillan, 1938).

John Dollard, *Caste and Class in a Southern Town* (New York: Doubleday, 1937).

Robert W. Dubay, "Mississippi and the Proposed Federal Anti-Lynching Bills of 1937–1938," *Southern Quarterly* (October 1968).

Wilma Dykeman and James Stokely, *Seeds of Southern Change: The Life of Will Alexander* (Chicago: University of Chicago Press, 1962).

John S. Ezell, *The South Since 1865* (New York: Macmillan, 1963).

Sheldon Hackney, "Southern Violence," *American Historical Review* (February 1969).

William B. Hesseltine and David L. Smiley, *The South in American History* (Englewood Cliffs, N.J.: Prentice-Hall, 2nd ed., 1960).

Charles S. Johnson, *et al.*, *Into the Main Stream: A Survey of the Best Practices in Race Relations in the South* (Chapel Hill: University of North Carolina Press, 1947).

Stetson Kennedy, *Southern Exposure* (New York: Doubleday, 1946).

Thomas A. Kreuger, *And Promises to Keep: The Southern Conference for Human Welfare, 1938–1948* (Nashville: Vanderbilt University Press, 1968).

Katherine DuPre Lumpkin, *The Making of a Southerner* (New York: Knopf, 1947).

Joseph L. Morrison, *W. J. Cash: Southern Prophet* (New York: Knopf, 1967).

Claude H. Nolen, *The Negro's Image in the South: The Anatomy of White Supremacy* (Lexington: University of Kentucky Press, 1967).*

Howard Odum, *Southern Regions of the United States* (Chapel Hill: University of North Carolina Press, 1936).

Hortense Powdermarker, *After Freedom: A Cultural Study of the Deep South* (New York: Viking, 1939).*

Willard Range, *The Rise and Progress of Negro Colleges in Georgia, 1865–1949* (Athens: University of Georgia Press, 1957).

John Shelton Reed, "An Evaluation of an Anti-Lynching Organization [Southern Women for the Prevention of Lynching, 1930—]," *Social Problems* (Fall 1968).

Carl Rowan, *South of Freedom* (New York: Knopf, 1952).

Henry Savage, Jr., *Seeds of Time: The Background of Southern Thinking* (New York: Holt, 1959).

Charles G. Sellers, Jr., ed., *The Southerner as American* (Chapel Hill: University of North Carolina Press, 1960).

Francis B. Simkins, *A History of the South* (New York: Knopf, 3rd ed. rev., 1963).

John Ray Skates, "From Enchantment to Disillusionment: A Southern Editor Views the New Deal," *Southern Quarterly* (April 1967).

Lillian E. Smith, *Killers of the Dream* (New York: W. W. Norton, 1949).

Wendell H. Stephenson, *The South Lives in History: Southern Historians and Their Legacy* (Baton Rouge: Louisiana State University Press, 1968).*

George B. Tindall, *The Emergence of the New South, 1913–1945* (Baton Rouge: Louisiana State University Press, 1967).

Thomas J. Woofter, *Southern Race Progress: The Wavering Color Line* (Washington, D.C.: Public Affairs Press, 1957).

Charles E. Wynes, ed., *The Negro in the South Since 1865: Selected Essays in American Negro History* (University: University of Alabama Press, 1965).*

XIII. The City and the Negro

A. THE MIGRATION

Arna Bontemps and Jack Conroy, *They Seek a City* (Garden City, N.Y.: Doubleday, Doran, 1945)*; paperback reprint entitled *Anyplace but Here.*

Louise V. Kennedy, *The Negro Peasant Turns Cityward: Effects of Re-*

cent Migrations to Northern Centers (New York: Columbia University Press, 1930).

Pierce F. Lewis, see above, "Politics and the Negro."

Dewey H. Palmer, "Moving North: Negro Migration During World War I," *Phylon* (First Quarter 1967).

Ira DeA. Reid, *The Negro Immigrant: His Background, Characteristics and Social Adjustment, 1899–1937* (New York: Columbia University Press, 1939).

Frank A. Ross and Louise V. Kennedy, *A Bibliography of Negro Migrations* (New York: Columbia University Press, 1934).

Seth M. Scheiner, *Negro Mecca: A History of the Negro in New York City, 1865–1920* (New York: New York University Press, 1965).

T. Lynn Smith, "The Redistribution of the Negro Population of the United States, 1910–1960," *Journal of Negro History* (July 1966).

Allan H. Spear, *Black Chicago: The Making of a Negro Ghetto, 1890–1920* (Chicago: University of Chicago Press, 1967), Part II: The Migration Years, 1915–1920.*

Robert C. Weaver, "Non-White Population Movements and Urban Ghettos," *Phylon* (Third Quarter 1959).

Carter G. Woodson, *A Century of Negro Migration* (Washington, D.C.: Association for the Study of Negro Life and History, 1918).

B. NEGRO URBAN LIFE

Joseph Boskin, ed., *Urban Racial Violence in the Twentieth Century* (Beverly Hills: Glencoe Press, 1969).*

Kenneth Clark, *Dark Ghetto: Dilemmas of Social Power* (New York: Harper and Row, 1965).

St. Clair Drake and Horace Cayton, *Black Metropolis: A Study of Negro Life in a Northern City* (New York: Harcourt, Brace, 1945).*

Arthur Huff Fausett, *Black Gods of the Metropolis: Negro Religious Cults of the Urban North* (Philadelphia: University of Pennsylvania Press, 1944).

J. S. Himes, "Forty Years of Negro Life in Columbus, Ohio [1900–1940]," *Journal of Negro History* (April 1942).

James Weldon Johnson, *Black Manhattan* (New York: Knopf, 1930).*

Claude McKay, *Harlem: Negro Metropolis* (New York: E. P. Dutton, 1940).

August Meier and David Lewis, "History of the Negro Upper Class in Atlanta, Georgia, 1890–1958," *Journal of Negro Education* (Spring 1959).

——— and Elliott M. Rudwick, eds., *The Making of Black America* (New York: Antheneum, 1969)*, Volume II, Sections 6 and 7.

Gilbert Osofsky, *Harlem: The Making of a Ghetto—Negro New York, 1890–1930* (New York: Harper and Row, 1966).*

———, "The Enduring Ghetto," *Journal of American History* (September 1968).

Robert A. Parker, *The Incredible Messiah: The Deification of Father Divine* (Boston: Little, Brown, 1937).

Robert C. Weaver, *The Negro Ghetto* (New York: Harcourt, Brace, 1948).

A NOTE
ON THE EDITOR

Bernard Sternsher was born in Fall River, Massachusetts, and studied at the University of Alabama and Boston University. His book *Rexford Tugwell and the New Deal* has been highly praised, and he has edited *The New Deal: Doctrines and Democracy*. Mr. Sternsher is now Professor of History at Bowling Green State University.

QUADRANGLE PAPERBACKS

American History

Frederick Lewis Allen. *The Lords of Creation*. (QP35)
Lewis Atherton. *Main Street on the Middle Border*. (QP36)
Thomas A. Bailey. *Woodrow Wilson and the Lost Peace*. (QP1)
Thomas A. Bailey. *Woodrow Wilson and the Great Betrayal*. (QP2)
Charles A. Beard. *The Idea of National Interest*. (QP27)
Carl L. Becker. *Everyman His Own Historian*. (QP33)
Barton J. Bernstein. *Politics and Policies of the Truman Administration*. (QP72)
Ray A. Billington. *The Protestant Crusade*. (QP12)
Allan G. Bogue. *From Prairie to Corn Belt*. (QP50)
Kenneth E. Boulding. *The Organizational Revolution*. (QP43)
Robert V. Bruce. *1877: Year of Violence*. (QP73)
Roger Burlingame. *Henry Ford*. (QP76)
Gerald M. Capers. *John C. Calhoun, Opportunist*. (QP70)
David M. Chalmers. *Hooded Americanism*. (QP51)
John Chamberlain. *Farewell to Reform*. (QP19)
Alice Hamilton Cromie. *A Tour Guide to the Civil War*.
Robert D. Cross. *The Emergence of Liberal Catholicism in America*. (QP44)
Richard M. Dalfiume. *American Politics Since 1945*. (NYTimes Book, QP57)
Carl N. Degler. *The New Deal*. (NYTimes Book, QP74)
Chester McArthur Destler. *American Radicalism, 1865-1901*. (QP30)
Robert A. Divine. *American Foreign Policy Since 1945*. (NYTimes Book, QP58)
Robert A. Divine. *Causes and Consequences of World War II*. (QP63)
Robert A. Divine. *The Illusion of Neutrality*. (QP45)
Elisha P. Douglass. *Rebels and Democrats*. (QP26)
Felix Frankfurter. *The Commerce Clause*. (QP16)
Lloyd C. Gardner. *A Different Frontier*. (QP32)
Edwin Scott Gaustad. *The Great Awakening in New England*. (QP46)
Ray Ginger. *Altgeld's America*. (QP21)
Ray Ginger. *Modern American Cities*. (NYTimes Book, QP67)
Ray Ginger. *Six Days or Forever?* (QP68)
Gerald N. Grob. *Workers and Utopia*. (QP61)
Louis Hartz. *Economic Policy and Democratic Thought*. (QP52)
William B. Hesseltine. *Lincoln's Plan of Reconstruction*. (QP41)
Granville Hicks. *The Great Tradition*. (QP62)
Dwight W. Hoover. *Understanding Negro History*. (QP49)
Stanley P. Hirshson. *Farewell to the Bloody Shirt*. (QP53)
Frederic C. Howe. *The Confessions of a Reformer*. (QP39)
Harold L. Ickes. *The Autobiography of a Curmudgeon*. (QP69)
William Loren Katz. *Teachers' Guide to American Negro History*. (QP210)
Burton Ira Kaufman. *Washington's Farewell Address*. (QP64)
Edward Chase Kirkland. *Dream and Thought in the Business Community, 1860-1900*. (QP11)
Edward Chase Kirkland. *Industry Comes of Age*. (QP42)
Adrienne Koch. *The Philosophy of Thomas Jefferson*. (QP17)
Gabriel Kolko. *The Triumph of Conservatism*. (QP40)
Aileen S. Kraditor. *Up from the Pedestal*. (QP77)
Walter LaFeber. *John Quincy Adams and American Continental Empire*. (QP23)
Lawrence H. Leder. *The Meaning of the American Revolution*. (NYTimes Book, QP66)
David E. Lilienthal. *TVA: Democracy on the March*. (QP28)
Arthur S. Link. *Wilson the Diplomatist*. (QP18)
Huey P. Long. *Every Man a King*. (QP8)
Gene M. Lyons. *America: Purpose and Power*. (QP24)
Jackson Turner Main. *The Antifederalists*. (QP14)
Ernest R. May. *The World War and American Isolation, 1914-1917*. (QP29)
Henry F. May. *The End of American Innocence*. (QP9)
Thomas J. McCormick. *China Market*. (QP75)
August Meier and Elliott Rudwick. *Black Protest in the Sixties*. (NYTimes Book, QP78)
George E. Mowry. *The California Progressives*. (QP6)
William L. O'Neill. *American Society Since 1945*. (NYTimes Book, QP59)
Frank L. Owsley. *Plain Folk of the Old South*. (QP22)
David Graham Phillips. *The Treason of the Senate*. (QP20)
Julius W. Pratt. *Expansionists of 1898*. (QP15)
C. Herman Pritchett. *The Roosevelt Court*. (QP71)
Moses Rischin. *The American Gospel of Success*. (QP54)
John P. Roche. *The Quest for the Dream*. (QP47)
David A. Shannon. *The Socialist Party of America*. (QP38)
Andrew Sinclair. *The Available Man*. (QP60)

American History (continued)

John Spargo. *The Bitter Cry of the Children.* (QP55)
Bernard Sternsher. *Hitting Home.* (QP79)
Bernard Sternsher. *The Negro in Depression and War.* (QP65)
Richard W. Van Alstyne. *The Rising American Empire.* (QP25)
Willard M. Wallace. *Appeal to Arms.* (QP10)
Norman Ware. *The Industrial Worker, 1840-1860.* (QP13)
Albert K. Weinberg. *Manifest Destiny.* (QP3)
Bernard A. Weisberger. *They Gathered at the River.* (QP37)
Robert H. Wiebe. *Businessmen and Reform.* (QP56)
William Appleman Williams. *The Contours of American History.* (QP34)
William Appleman Williams. *The Great Evasion.* (QP48)
Esmond Wright. *Causes and Consequences of the American Revolution.* (QP31)

European History

William Sheridan Allen. *The Nazi Seizure of Power.* (QP302)
W. O. Henderson. *The Industrial Revolution in Europe.* (QP303)
Raul Hilberg. *The Destruction of the European Jews.* (QP301)
Richard N. Hunt. *German Social Democracy.* (QP306)
Telford Taylor. *Sword and Swastika.* (QP304)
John Weiss. *Nazis and Fascists in Europe, 1918-1945.* (NYTimes Book, QP305)

Philosophy

F. H. Bradley. *The Presuppositions of Critical History.* (QP108)
E. M. Cioran. *The Temptation to Exist.* (QP119)
William Earle. *Objectivity.* (QP109)
James M. Edie, James P. Scanlan, Mary-Barbara Zeldin, George L. Kline. *Russian Philosophy.*
   (3 vols, QP111, 112, 113)
James M. Edie. *An Invitation to Phenomenology.* (QP103)
James M. Edie. *New Essays in Phenomenology.* (QP114)
James M. Edie. *Phenomenology in America.* (QP105)
R. O. Elveton. *The Phenomenology of Husserl.* (QP116)
Manfred S. Frings. *Heidegger and the Quest for Truth.* (QP107)
Moltke S. Gram. *Kant: Disputed Questions.* (QP104)
James F. Harris, Jr., and Richard Severens. *Analyticity.* (QP117)
E. D. Klemke. *Studies in the Philosophy of G. E. Moore.* (QP115)
Lionel Rubinoff. *Faith and Reason.* (QP106)
Stuart F. Spicker. *The Philosophy of the Body.* (QP118)
Paul Tibbetts. *Perception.* (QP110)
Pierre Thévenaz. *What Is Phenomenology?* (QP101)
Robert E. Wood. *The Future of Metaphysics.* (QP120)

Social Science

Abraham S. Blumberg. *Criminal Justice.* (QP227)
Shalom Endleman. *Violence in the Streets.* (QP215)
Nathan Glazer. *Cities in Trouble.* (NYTimes Book, QP212)
William J. Goode. *The Contemporary American Family.* (NYTimes Book, QP223)
George and Eunice Grier. *Equality and Beyond.* (QP204)
Morris Janowitz. *Political Conflict.* (QP226)
Kurt Lang and Gladys Engel Lang. *Politics and Television.* (QP216)
Charles O. Lerche, Jr. *Last Chance in Europe.* (QP207)
Raymond W. Mack. *Prejudice and Race Relations.* (NYTimes Book, QP217)
David Mitrany. *A Working Peace System.* (QP205)
Earl Finbar Murphy. *Governing Nature.* (QP228)
H. L. Nieburg. *In the Name of Science.* (QP218)
Martin Oppenheimer. *The Urban Guerrilla.* (QP219)
Martin Oppenheimer and George Lakey. *A Manual for Direct Action.* (QP202)
James Parkes. *Antisemitism.* (QP213)
Fred Powledge. *To Change a Child.* (QP209)
Lee Rainwater. *And the Poor Get Children.* (QP208)
The Rockefeller Report on the Americas. (QP214)
Ben B. Seligman. *Molders of Modern Thought.* (NYTimes Book, QP224)
Ben B. Seligman. *Permanent Poverty.* (QP229)
Clarence Senior. *The Puerto Ricans.* (QP201)
Harold L. Sheppard. *Poverty and Wealth in America.* (NYTimes Book, QP220)
Arthur L. Stinchcombe. *Rebellion in a High School.* (QP211)
Edward G. Stockwell. *Population and People.* (QP230)
Harry M. Trebing. *The Corporation in the American Economy.* (NYTimes Book, QP221)
David Manning White. *Pop Culture in America.* (NYTimes Book, QP222)
Harold Wolozin. *American Fiscal and Monetary Policy.* (NYTimes Book, QP225)